SHAKESPEARE

STAGING THE WORLD

SHAKESPEARE

STAGING THE WORLD

JONATHAN BATE & DORA THORNTON

OXFORD
UNIVERSITY PRESS

FOR OUR PARTNERS, PAULA AND JEREMY

OXFORD
UNIVERSITY PRESS

Oxford University Press, Inc., publishes works that further
Oxford University's objective of excellence
in research, scholarship, and education.

Oxford   New York

Auckland   Cape Town   Dar es Salaam   Hong Kong   Karachi
Kuala Lumpur   Madrid   Melbourne   Mexico City   Nairobi
New Delhi   Shanghai   Taipei   Toronto

With offices in

Argentina   Austria   Brazil   Chile   Czech Republic   France   Greece
Guatemala   Hungary   Italy   Japan   Poland   Portugal   Singapore
South Korea   Switzerland   Thailand   Turkey   Ukraine   Vietnam

Library of Congress Cataloging in Publication Data
Data available

ISBN 978-0-19-991501-9

1 3 5 7 9 8 6 4 2

Designed by Will Webb Design
Printed by Printer Trento S.r.l., in Italy

Papers used by The British Museum Press are recyclable products
made from wood grown in well-managed forests and other controlled
sources. The manufacturing processes conform to the environmental
regulations of the country of origin.

Many of the images illustrated in this book are from the collection
of the British Museum. Their museum registration numbers can be
found on pages 286–297. Further information about the Museum
and its collection can be found at britishmuseum.org.

Frontispiece: detail of a portrait of the Moroccan ambassador,
see chapter 1, fig. 26, p. 36

This book is published to accompany the exhibition at the British Museum
from 19 July to 25 November 2012.

Contents

SPONSOR'S FOREWORD

BP is delighted to support *Shakespeare: staging the world* at the British Museum, a unique collaboration with the Royal Shakespeare Company. This exhibition, inspired by London 2012, forms part of the World Shakespeare Festival.

Four hundred years ago the playhouse dominated society and Shakespeare used it to showcase his own particular take on history and contemporary cultures from across the world. Shakespeare's influence was huge in his own time and his tales echo down through the ages. This BP exhibition provides an exceptional insight into the emerging role of London as a world city, seen through the innovative perspective of Shakespeare's plays. It also explores the pivotal role of the playhouse as a window to the world outside London and the playwright's importance in shaping a new sense of national identity.

BP has a very long-standing relationship with the British Museum. Our support for *Shakespeare: staging the world* is part of the company's wider contribution to society, connecting communities with excellence in arts and culture worldwide.

Bob Dudley
Group Chief Executive BP

DIRECTOR'S FOREWORD

William Shakespeare is the most famous writer in the history of the world. His name is synonymous with theatre, with poetry and with Britain's cultural contribution to the world. His characters – Hamlet, Romeo and Juliet, Macbeth, Falstaff, Cleopatra – are known to millions who have never even seen his plays. And his works have been studied and adapted, translated into more languages and more media, than those of anyone else.

For all these reasons, the London 2012 Festival has at its centre the World Shakespeare Festival, produced by the Royal Shakespeare Company (with contributions from the National Theatre, the Globe and many international theatre companies). This exhibition, *Shakespeare: staging the world*, is the British Museum's special contribution to the Cultural Olympiad, a series of events to showcase the nation's art and culture to the rest of the world. As the world comes to London in 2012, it is timely to explore how the world came to London, and was viewed from London, four hundred years ago, in the era when so many aspects of global modernity had their origins.

In both the exhibition and the book, we look at the early modern period through the eyes of Shakespeare, his players and audiences. The things they saw mattered at least as much as what they read in shaping their vision of the world. This exhibition brings together an astonishingly diverse array of objects, working across the British Museum collection, with the addition of generous loans from private and public collections elsewhere. We examine these things through the lens of Shakespeare's plays, and in doing so we have drawn on the expertise and knowledge of specialist curators, collectors and scholars across the world in sourcing objects and interpreting their intellectual context. Our exhibition and its accompanying book allow us to see a selection of things which survive from Shakespeare's world, and to build an understanding as to how our predecessors – whether London residents or visitors – interpreted their world four centuries ago.

Shakespeare's friend, rival and fellow dramatist Ben Jonson described him as the 'soul of the age': his plays are brilliantly animated embodiments of the preoccupations of the culture into which he was born and in which he lived and worked. To look at a woodcut of a Jewish household in Venice and a sixteenth-century Caribbean wood carving of a spirit imprisoned in a tree and a pack of playing cards in which Cleopatra and Queen Elizabeth appear side-by-side is to be given a new historical and intellectual perspective on the characters of Shylock, Ariel and Cleopatra. The journey through our exhibition opens up the diverse cultures of the early modern world as it stood on the threshold of globalization. The juxtaposition of particular objects and particular Shakespearean characters, images or ideas proves mutually illuminating in extraordinary ways: Othello takes us to the perception of Moor and Turk, Shylock to early modern Jewish culture, Caliban to the New World, Brutus to the formative influence of the ancient world, Macbeth to the representation of Scotland, Owain Glyndŵr to the Welsh, MacMorris to the Irish, Cymbeline and Lear to the debates about the unity or division of 'Britain' in the early years of the seventeenth century.

The professional theatre was a new phenomenon in Shakespeare's time, the first mass medium for the presentation of the cultures of the world to a wide public. Where people in the late twentieth century viewed the globe through their television screens and we in the early twenty-first century do so through the internet, in Shakespeare's time the globe was brought to life on the bare platform of the Globe Theatre in Southwark.

The exhibition offers us the chance to develop new collaborations in the world of the arts. We are grateful to Professor Jonathan Bate, Provost of Worcester College, Oxford, and a world-renowned Shakespearean scholar, for his essential contribution as Shakespearean consultant working with the exhibition's curator, Dr Dora Thornton. We would also like to thank the Royal Shakespeare Company: this is the first time that the Museum and a theatre company have worked together. The RSC has brought to the relationship not just creativity and friendship, but a transforming insight into the life of Shakespeare's stage. We are very grateful.

This BP exhibition is part of an ongoing partnership with the British Museum. We are most grateful to them for making possible this enthralling glimpse into Shakespeare's imagined worlds.

Neil MacGregor
Director, British Museum

Authors' Preface

This book serves as both catalogue to the exhibition, *Shakespeare: staging the world*, and the product of a substantial body of research in its own right. Our approach in both the exhibition and the book is new and distinctive: through a series of case studies, focused on a wide range of locations, cultures and themes, we create a dialogue between Shakespeare's imaginary worlds and the material objects of the real world of the late sixteenth and early seventeenth centuries.

'I have another weapon in this chamber, / It is a sword of Spain, the ice-brook's temper.' So says Othello shortly before his suicide at the climax of one of Shakespeare's greatest tragedies. Scholars have noted that Spain was famous for its fine swords (notably Toledo blades) and have puzzled over the tempering process (even suggesting that 'ice-brook' might be a misprint for 'Innsbruck', also known for fine metal). But a series of questions present themselves: what did a sword of Spain look like? What more specific associations did it have? In what context could Shakespeare and his original audience have seen one? Our exhibition answers these questions in a fresh way by bringing together a sword of Spain and a series of powerful images of Moors. Both Shakespeare and his world are seen anew when we use objects to illuminate dramatic texts and dramatic texts to illuminate objects.

In the book we explore the status and significance of particular artefacts and their role in the making of early modern collective memory. Some of these objects are previously unpublished, others are known only to specialist curators or have never been displayed before, and many of them have not been linked to Shakespeare, his work or his world, until now. Taken together, exhibition and book create an innovative cultural anthropology of Shakespeare's key characters, suggesting the range of associations – the knowledge and the misconceptions, the prejudices, fears and fascination – upon which they drew and to which they contributed in his culture.

As Shakespeare's creative life was made possible by collaboration – between him and his actors, co-writers, sources and audiences – so this exhibition and book has been a richly rewarding collaboration. Dora Thornton served as curator of the exhibition at the British Museum, Jonathan Bate as consultant Shakespearean. We could not have written the book or conceived the exhibition without each other. We have also had the help of a wonderful team of further collaborators. The concept and shape of the exhibition was explored in the course of a series of in-house curatorial debates, hosted by Neil MacGregor and Jonathan Bate. It was fascinating to see curators who specialize in such a diverse range of world cultures coming together to debate how to approach Shakespeare and his world, and in so doing discovering a wealth of hitherto unseen connections. In the course of these discussions, we refined

Jonathan Bate's idea that the exhibition should be structured around Shakespeare's real and imaginary locations. Particular thanks at the British Museum are due to the following curators at those seminars: Silke Ackermann, Sheila Canby, Frances Carey, Barrie Cook, Jill Cook, Jessica Harrison-Hall, Ian Jenkins, Jonathan King, James Robinson, Chris Spring and Jonathan Williams.

We also had the benefit of a team of highly distinguished academic readers who served as our advisory board and read our chapter drafts with both speed and authority, and made many valuable suggestions for improvement. We thank Professor Anthony Grafton of Princeton University; Professor Kate Lowe of Queen Mary College, University of London; and Professor William Sherman of the University of York.

We are grateful to specialist curators who commented on objects and sections of text: John Cherry, Barrie Cook, George Dalgleish, Anne-Marie Ezé, José Oliver, Angus Patterson, Kim Sloan and Jeremy Warren.

We received invaluable assistance from librarians and archivists at the following institutions: the British Library, the Bodleian Library, the Middle Temple Library, the University of Edinburgh Library, the National Library of Scotland, the College of Arms, Lambeth Palace Library, the Warburg Institute, Westminster Abbey, the Archives of the British Province of the Society of Jesus, Stonyhurst College Library and the London Library.

For work specifically on the book we would like to thank: Becky Allen, exhibition project curator and a key member of the core team for the exhibition as well as co-author with us of the giftbook; Dr Peter Kirwan of the University of Nottingham, who checked the Shakespeare references with great efficiency; Teresa Francis, who worked indefatigably as a volunteer on the catalogue section, and a succession of interns: Lucy Spearman, Roisìn Watson and Roland Walters – who gave Dora invaluable assistance. We are grateful to our editor, Claudia Bloch, and to Rosemary Bradley, Coralie Hepburn and Melanie Morris at The British Museum Press, as well as our copy-editor, Laura Lappin. John Williams and Axelle Russo organized and oversaw the programme of photography of British Museum objects, assisted by expert photographers Ivor Kerslake and Saul Peckham, and Will Webb designed the two exhibition books.

We would like especially to thank the exhibition's core team in addition to Becky and Claudia: our successive project managers, Claire Everitt and Jane Bennett, the exhibition's designer, Alan Farlie, and RSC design consultant, Tom Piper, our interpretation officers, Iona Keen and Jane Batty, 2D designer Paul Goodhead, and Pippa Cruickshank, Sarah Jameson, James Baker and Matt Weaver. We are also indebted to Carolyn Marsden-Smith, Caroline Ingham, David Saunders, Stuart Frost, Charlotte Kewell, David McNeff, James Peters and his team of curatorial assistants, Rosanna Kwok, Susan Raikes, Hannah Boulton, Olivia Rickman and Jennifer Suggitt. Further acknowledgements are given on page 298.

Jonathan Bate and Dora Thornton

Wiliam Shakespeare of Stratford vpon Avon in the Countye of Warwicke gent of the age of xlviij yeres or thereabouts sworne and examined the daye and yere abovesaid deposeth & sayeth

1. To the first Interr this deponent sayeth he knoweth the partyes plt and deft and hath know[ne] them bothe as he now remembrethe for the space of tenne yeres or thereabouts

2. To the second Interr this deponent sayeth he did know the deft at the tyme of the makinge of the said assurance of the ... and ... and how longe he hath ... he can not depose ... as to this deponent knoweth did make ... because this deponent camenot then to ... but the deponent sayth he ... that the said wytnes doe ... and was good and industrious servant ... the said ... and that he coulde depose to the said Interr

3. To the third Interr this deponent sayeth that it did evidentlye appeare that the said deft did all the tyme of the said wytnes being with him beare ... good and great ... and affection towardes the said wytnes, and that he hath heard the deft and his wyfe ... devyse that he would that the said wytnes ... that he the said wytnes ... a very good ... and that the said defendant did make a mocion vnto the wytnes of marriage with the said ... in the ... married howse the said deponents ... daughter And accordinglye affirmed to ... the said ... the said ... that ... to be vnto ... And further the deponent sayeth that the said wyfe ... did sollicite and intreat this deponent to move and perswade the said wytnes to effect the said marriage And accordinglye the deponent did move and perswade the wytnes thereunto: and more he can not depose

4. To the fourthe Interr this deponent sayeth that the defendant promised to geve the said complt A porcion in marriadge with Marye his daughter but what porcion he remembreth not, nor when to be payed ... nor ... that the deft promised the plt twoe hundred poundes with his daughter Marye at the tyme of his decease But sayth that the plt was dwellinge with the deft in his howse And they had amongest them selves many Conferences about there marriadg w[hich] was Consumated and Solempnized. And more he cannot

5. To the vth Interr this deponent sayeth he can saye nothinge touchinge any parte or parcell of the same Interr for he knoweth not what Implements and necessaries of houshold stuffe the deft gave the plt in marriadge of his daughter Marye.

Wilm Shakp

1 LONDON, CIRCA 1612: WORLD CITY

T HE YEAR OF OUR LORD 1612. It was the year when Galileo Galilei became the first astronomer to observe the planet Neptune (though he mistakenly assumed it was a fixed star), the year when John Rolfe exported his first crop of improved tobacco from Jamestown (the seeds had been imported from Trinidad) and the year when the greatest novel of the age, Miguel de Cervantes' *Don Quixote*, was published in English translation.

The following year the playwright William Shakespeare and his younger collaborator John Fletcher (1579–1625) seem to have set to work on a dramatization of the narrative of the love-crazed Cardenio that was woven within the adventures of Cervantes' errant knight. They also worked jointly on a play about the reign of King Henry VIII (r. 1509–1547), whose bulky and charismatic presence towered over the previous century and whose break from the Church of Rome had been the most momentous political decision of the age.

In that year of 1612 William Shakespeare himself, having made a sizeable fortune from his writing and his shareholding in the acting company of the King's Men, was in semi-retirement in his large house in Stratford-upon-Avon. His day-to-day duties as house dramatist for his theatre company were in the process of being handed over to Fletcher. But on 11 May there was a sighting of him in the city of London.

A case had come before the Court of Requests at Westminster. Among the witnesses was 'William Shakespeare of Stratford upon Aven in the Countye of Warwicke, gentleman of the Age of xlviii [48 years] or thereabouts'. He was sworn and examined. A clerk recorded the contents of his deposition and he signed the document (fig. 1). The deposition is the only surviving document that we can say with absolute certainty provides a record of words actually spoken by William Shakespeare. There is hearsay elsewhere – reports by rival dramatist Ben Jonson (1572–1637), theatrical anecdotes,

1. Shakespeare in his own words: his witness statement (deposition) in the Belott v. Mountjoy case, Court of Requests, Westminster, 11 May 1612.
40.6 x 30.5 cm. National Archives, Kew

13

2. Map showing Bishopsgate, 1559 (detail). Shakespeare was listed as a tax defaulter here in November 1597 and October 1598.
Copper plate, 37.7 x 50.5 cm.
Museum of London, London

business notes in the journals and letters of Stratford neighbours – but this witness statement is the thing itself, unaccommodated Shakespeare.

Although the action only came to court in 1612, it concerned events of 1604. Belott v. Mountjoy: a family dispute, 'trivial, pecuniary, faintly sordid' – standard fare at the Court of Requests, whose function was broadly equivalent to the Small Claims Court of today.[1] Christopher and Marie Mountjoy were Huguenot (French Protestant) tiremakers, 'tire' meaning head-tire or attire. Stephen Belott, of French extraction, was their apprentice. As was common at that time, a marriage was arranged between the daughter and the apprentice, with a view to sustaining the business into the next generation. A dowry of £60 seems to have been agreed, but was never paid, so Belott eventually took his father-in-law to court.

Shakespeare had been lodging in the Mountjoy's house on Silver Street for a couple of years. In his deposition he spoke up for Belott's good character. But he also revealed that Mrs Mountjoy had enlisted his services 'to move and persuade' Belott to go through with the marriage, somewhat against the young man's will. Such a situation was the very subject of Shakespeare's bestselling poem *Venus and Adonis*, of the first group of his sonnets, and of two plays that he wrote in the Silver Street years, *Measure for Measure* and *All's Well that Ends Well*. Mrs Mountjoy had approached the right man for the job, and Shakespeare duly fulfilled his side of the bargain. We learn from another witness that he actually presided over the handfasting ceremony that sealed the union.

The world opened up by the court case was full of interconnections. Mrs Mountjoy was commissioned to make tires for the queen, as Shakespeare was commissioned to write plays for the court. Mrs Mountjoy was a regular visitor to Simon Forman the astrologer, who was also a Shakespearean playgoer: his diary

'This is the straingers case And this your montanish inhumanity'

(The Booke of Sir Thomas More pp. 135–6)

3. A manuscript of *c.* 1601–4 with revisions in several hands: this page contains the riot scene, written in Shakespeare's hand. *The Booke of Sir Thomas More*, Anthony Munday (?) and Henry Chettle. Manuscript, ink on paper, approx. 37 x 27 cm. British Library, London

contains the only detailed eyewitness accounts we have of the original stage productions of Shakespeare's plays (see below p. 47). Another witness in the case was George Wilkins, a hack writer and brothel-keeper, who co-wrote with Shakespeare the sweeping romance of voyage and exile, *Pericles* – though rather surprisingly it was Shakespeare, not Wilkins, who contributed the vividly realized brothel scene.

The Silver Street neighbourhood teemed with immigrants. Indeed each parish had its own distinctive flavour. Resident aliens of different ethnic identities tended to stick together. In Bishopsgate (fig. 2) there were many Dutch and French Protestants, who had fled from the religious wars across the English Channel. Immigrants often gathered on the margins, in the parishes 'without' the city gates. Shakespeare's extraordinarily sympathetic evocation of Huguenot asylum seekers in his contribution to the multi-authored play *Sir Thomas More* seems to have been written some time between 1601 and 1604. The scene – the only one that survives in his handwriting (fig. 3) – may well have been written in the very room in which he lodged on Silver Street with his Huguenot landlady at work with her needle below (see below pp.43–4).

The year of grace 1612. Elsewhere in the world the Ottoman Turks and Safavid Persians made peace by way of the Treaty of Nasuh Pasha, while further east, off the coast of Suvali (known to the English as Swally), the galleons of the British East India Company defeated a Portuguese fleet, marking the beginning of the end of Portugal's commercial monopoly over India and a first step towards the dominance of the English East India Company.

January was clouded by the death of Rudolf II (b. 1552), Holy Roman Emperor, King of Bohemia, King of Hungary, King of Croatia, Archduke of Austria and inveterate enemy of the Ottomans. He was the keeper of a menagerie of exotic animals, of botanical gardens and of Europe's richest cabinet of curiosities. He was also a patron of the arts, practitioner of the occult sciences, and employer of the English magician John Dee (1527–1608/9) and of the most admired English-born poet in Europe, Elizabeth Jane Weston (1581–1612).

In April a radical Anabaptist called Edward Wightman was burned at the stake in Lichfield. Having proclaimed himself saviour of the world, he earned the distinction of becoming the last person in English history to be executed for heresy. A more common form of execution was carried out in Norhamptonshire a few months later: one man and four women were hanged as witches.

On 6 November 1612 the eighteen-year-old Henry, Prince of Wales, the cultured and adored son of King James VI and I of Scotland and England (r. 1603–1625) and his wife, Anne of Denmark (1574–1619), the bright hope for the future of the monarchy, died of typhoid fever. The heirship to the English and Scottish thrones passed to his less charismatic and diplomatic younger brother Charles (r. 1625–1649), whose life would end on the executioner's block in Whitehall thirty-seven years later. Prince Henry's body lay in state at St James's Palace for a month, after which on 7 December over a thousand people walked in a mile-long cortège to Westminster Abbey. After the Archbishop of Canterbury had delivered a two-hour sermon, Henry's body was lowered into the earth with his entourage breaking their staves of office at the graveside. An insane man ran naked through the mourning crowd, proclaiming that he was the boy's ghost.

Henry's sister, the Princess Elizabeth (1596–1662), was due to marry Frederick V (1596–1632), Elector of the Palatinate in Germany, but as a result of the royal death the wedding was postponed until the following February. When it did take place, the celebrations included command performances of more than twenty plays at court. John Hemminges, business manager of Shakespeare's acting company the King's Men, duly received payment for the presentation of, among other titles, *Much Ado about Nothing*, *The Tempest*, *The Winter's Tale*, *Sir John Falstaff*, *The Moor of Venice* and *Caesar's Tragedy*. Comedies, tragedies and histories. Plays set in Sicily, Bohemia, Venice, Rome, as well as England and an imaginary 'uninhabited island' (*The Tempest*, 'The Scene'). In those court festivities we witness something of the range of Shakespeare's imaginative achievement. A decade later thirty-six of his plays would be collected in magnificent folio format and the full extent of that theatrical world would become apparent (fig. 4).

From rural England to Padua, the battlefields of Bosworth and Agincourt, Verona to Milan, frequent visits to ancient Rome, Ephesus, Navarre, an ancient Athens that is also the English countryside, Venice, Messina, the Forest of Arden in Warwickshire merged with that of Ardennes in France, Elsinore, Windsor, Illyria (roughly speaking, Croatia), the battlefield of Troy, Venice again and Cyprus, Vienna, the province of Roussillon in the Pyrenees, Paris, Florence, ancient Britain, Scotland, Wales, sundry outposts of the Roman Empire, Egypt, Antioch, Tyre, Tarsus, Pentapolis, a ship on the Mediterranean sea, Mytilene, Sicily and Bohemia (now the Czech Republic), an imaginary island that appears to be simultaneously in the Mediterranean and

'He was not of an age, but for all time!'

4. Ben Jonson's tribute in the preliminary pages of the 'First Folio' celebrates Shakespeare's imaginative achievement. The famous engraved 'portrait' of Shakespeare by Martin Droeshout is one of only two verified likenesses of Shakespeare (the other is his tomb monument). Neither is a life portrait: Jonson called the engraving a good likeness but exhorted the reader to 'look / Not on his picture, but his book'. Title page from a copy of the 'First Folio', 1623, which later belonged to Thomas, 2nd Lord Arundell of Wardour.

Printed book, 32 x 21.8 cm. Stonyhurst College, Lancashire

Mr. WILIAM
SHAKESPEARES
COMEDIES
HISTORIES, &
TRAGEDIES,

Publiſhed according to the True Originall Copies.

LONDON
Printed by Iſaac Iaggard, and Ed. Blount. 1623.

the Caribbean: the settings of Shakespeare's plays constitute a panoramic theatre of the world.

The list of locations is undoubtedly Eurocentric, but into the plays wander 'strangers' from what Coriolanus memorably calls 'a world elsewhere' (3.3.159). Othello comes from Mauritania in North Africa, Caliban has an Algerian mother, Shylock and Tubal are born of the Jewish diaspora. In *Love's Labour's Lost* we see courtly gentlemen disguised as Muscovites. In *Timon of Athens* there are dancing masquers cross-dressed as Amazonian warrior women. In *Henry VIII* the king and his courtiers play at being 'A noble troop of strangers … great ambassadors / From foreign princes' (1.4.69–72) (incongruously 'habited like shepherds', 1.4.80.1). In *The Tempest* we glimpse an airy spirit fetching dewdrops from the Bermudas and a young girl witnessing a 'brave new world' (5.1.205). Shakespeare's culture was European and his own travels were, as far as we know, confined to England, yet his imaginary universe extends across the known planet and tunes into a global conversation in which

'I hope to see London once ere I die'

(Henry IV Part 2 5.3.45)

5. *London* ('The Long View'),
Wenceslaus Hollar, 1647.
Etching comprising four sheets, overall 47.1 x 158.7 cm.
British Museum, London

we hear of dishes from China and the Patagonian god Setebos, even a whisper of the Antipodes.

What was it like to visit London at this historical moment? Let's begin by following in the footsteps of Philip Hentzner, a German lawyer. He found a job as tutor to a nobleman from Silesia, an area of Central Europe in the west of modern-day Poland. Hentzner accompanied his master on a European tour in the closing years of the sixteenth century, visiting London in 1599, the year of the Globe's opening. In 1612, back at Nuremberg, he published an account in Latin of the buildings, the people and the customs they encountered.[2]

Border controls were not a problem, despite the fact that England was at war with Spain. The party arrived at the little port of Rye on the south-east coast and gave their names to the local notary. He enquired after their business and once they had explained that they only wanted to see the sights, they were conducted to an inn and entertained with good English hospitality.

Swift post-horses took them to London (fig. 5). 'London, the head and metropolis of England: called by Tacitus, Londinium; by Ptolemy, Logidinium … by foreigners, Londra, and Londres; it is the seat of the British Empire and the chamber of the English kings.' Hentzner's reference to the ancient names of the city reveals how educated people across Europe were taught to think in Shakespeare's time: the present was understood through reference to the past. It was a polyglot culture, held together by Latin, the shared language of the educated. The theatre of the world was at once geographical and historical. Distant places and distant times were brought into lively dialogue with the present.

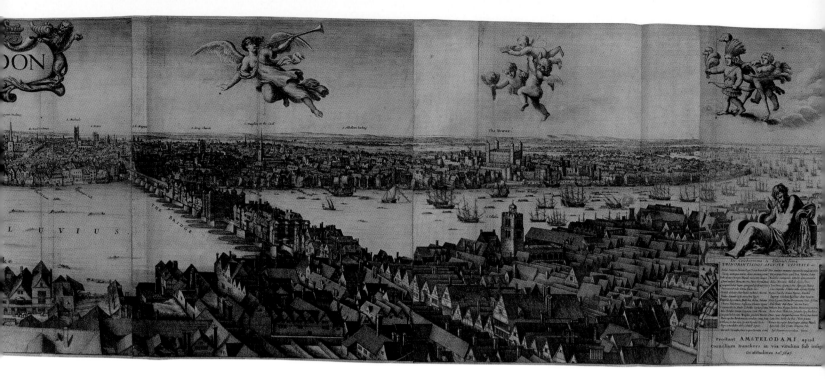

People were fascinated by questions of origin. A sense of cultural identity had been shaped by legends and myths. So what was the origin of London? The city was founded, Hentzner reports, 'as all historians agree',

> by Brutus … [who] chose this situation for the convenience of the river, calling it Troja Nova, which name was afterwards corrupted into Trinovant. But when Lud, the brother of Cassibilan, or Cassivelan, who warred against Julius Caesar, as he himself mentions (lib. v. *de Bell. Gall.*), came to the crown, he encompassed it with very strong walls, and towers very artfully constructed, and from his own name called it Caier Lud, i.e., Lud's City. This name was corrupted … by change of language, into Londres. Lud, when he died, was buried in this town, near that gate which is yet called in Welsh, Por Lud – in Saxon, Ludesgate.

Britain's hybrid ethnic identity is here summed up in a nutshell. The Britons are allegedly named from their founder, Brutus, a descendant of Aeneas, the prince who escaped from burning Troy and founded the city of Rome (see further Chapter 8, p. 217). Although once colonized by Julius Caesar and his successors, England now had hopes of being a legitimate descendant of Rome, and of becoming a second great empire – though, despite Hentzner's description of London as the 'seat of the British Empire' (*Britannici imperii sedes*), that empire was still very much in its infancy. If it existed at all in the time of Queen Elizabeth I (r. 1558–1603), it did so only internally within the 'British Isles', where for centuries Celts had mingled and fought first with Romans and then with later colonizing powers, Saxons, Danes and Norman French.

'Dwell I but in the suburbs Of your good pleasure?'

(Julius Caesar 2.1.297-8)

6. *Going to Bankside*, from Michael van Meer's friendship album, *c.* 1619. The suburbs were notorious for licentious entertainment, from brothels and alehouses to playhouses and bear-baiting. In these lines from *Julius Caesar*, Portia berates her troubled husband, who is preoccupied in the run-up to the assassination of Julius Caesar, by wondering if she has become merely 'Brutus' harlot, not his wife' (2.1.299). The association of suburbs and brothels was a strong feature of contemporary London culture. Pen and ink with watercolour and gold highlighting on paper, 8 x 16.7 cm. Edinburgh University Library, Edinburgh

The main thoroughfare of the city was the famous River Thames, spanned by a single stone bridge. London Bridge was 800 feet in length, 'of wonderful work', supported by twenty sturdy piers of square stone, joined by great arches. Hentzner marvelled at how 'the whole is covered on each side with houses so disposed as to have the appearance of a continued street, not at all of a bridge'. And at the southern end there was a tower, 'on whose top the heads of such as have been executed for high treason are placed on iron spikes: we counted above thirty'.

Although London was far smaller than it is today, it had, by the standards of the time, extensive suburbs. The south bank of the river – the district of Southwark – was all suburb. That was where you went for entertainment. In 1599, the year of Hentzner's visit, a brand new theatre called the Globe opened its doors. The first play staged there is likely to have been Shakespeare's *Julius Caesar* (see Chapter 4, p. 119).[3] Some of the audience would have arrived by water taxi, others would have walked over the bridge. The tragedy of Caesar's death was played out within sight of the Tower of London, across the river, that he was supposed (incorrectly) to have erected. The drama of ancient conspiracy and treason would have been given edge by the very modern sight of those heads on spikes witnessed on the way to and from the theatre.

A lovely visitor's image of the crossing of the Thames is to be found in Michael van Meer's friendship album (fig. 6). Friendship albums, which were popular among German university students, included names, signatures, coats of arms, and views of people and places encountered on their travels. Michael van Meer, from Hamburg, was in London in about 1614 or 1615. His album records miniatures from London life, including this one showing well-dressed people in a skiff being rowed over the Thames for an afternoon's entertainment on Bankside. London Bridge is seen

'Within this wooden O'

(*Henry V* Prologue.13)

7. Detail of Sheet 2 from Wenceslaus Hollar's print *London* (see fig. 5), showing Southwark with the second Globe, built in 1614 after the first Globe burned down, mistakenly labelled as the 'Beere bayting house'. The building labelled the Globe was the Hope, built in 1613 as a dual-purpose venue for animal-baiting and as a theatre.

Etching, 46.6 x 39 cm. British Museum, London

'A marble monument'

(*Measure for Measure* 5.1.253)

8. Tomb monument of John Donne by Nicholas Stone, showing Donne in his shroud. Commissioned by Donne shortly before his death in 1631 and one of the few monuments in St Paul's Cathedral to survive the Great Fire in 1666.

St Paul's Cathedral, London

in the background.[4] If you worked in the theatre, you had to make this trip almost daily: the diary of Edward Alleyn (1566–1626), the most celebrated actor of the 1590s, documents frequent payments to ferrymen among his day-to-day expenses.[5]

This was an era when the world was being brought together by trade. 'The wealth of the world', wrote Hentzner, was 'wafted to London' by the Thames, which was swelled by the tide and navigable to merchant ships through a safe and deep channel for sixty miles, from its mouth to the city. Its banks, he observed,

> are everywhere beautified with fine country seats, woods, and farms; below is the royal palace of Greenwich; above, that of Richmond … At the distance of twenty miles from London is the castle of Windsor, a most delightful retreat of the Kings of England, as well as famous for several of their tombs, and for the ceremonial of the Order of the Garter.

The country was cheek by jowl with the city. Gardens and open fields lay a stone's throw from the narrow streets around the theatres (fig. 7). The houses of the great stood in privileged waterfront settings. The court, meanwhile, was mobile: there was no Buckingham Palace, but rather a series of residences – Greenwich, Whitehall, Richmond, then Nonsuch and Windsor further afield – between which Queen Elizabeth moved by carriage or barge with great ceremony and display.

As you looked across the river from the suburbs on the South Bank, the most prominent building of all was the old cathedral of St Paul's. It was already a tourist attraction as well as a place for divine service. In the churchyard outside booksellers manned their stalls. It was here that Shakespeare browsed for raw materials and where purchasers with a spare shilling could buy reading texts of his scripts. And it was also in the yard that John Donne (1572–1631), poet and Dean of St Paul's, preached sermons that drew crowds as large and attentive as those for a play (fig. 8).

The cathedral itself was in a state of some disrepair. John Gipkyn's *Dipytch of Old St Paul's* (fig. 9) was a plea for its restoration, which belongs beside a poem by one Henry Farley called 'The Complaint of Paules to all Christian Soules, or, An humble Supplication, to our good King and Nation, for her new Reparation' (1616). James I had appointed a commission to consider repair of the cathedral in 1608, when Inigo Jones (1573–1652) made a plan for a new spire which oddly resembles that in Gipkyn's painting (fig. 10). The Gipkyn Diptych, which once belonged to John Donne, offers a rare and special topographical view of London, showing open-air

9. *Dipytch of Old St Paul's*, John Gipkyn, 1616. Henry Farley's vision of St Paul's Cathedral restored, with rejoicing angels.
Oil on panel, each 110.5 x 87.6 cm.
Society of Antiquaries, London

preaching and a procession of James I over London Bridge to the cathedral. It is perhaps the first painting of a historic monument in British art.[6]

Inside the cathedral Hentzner noted memorials to the great, among them the marble monument of William Herbert, Earl of Pembroke, whose descendant, of the same name and title, was patron of Shakespeare's acting company and perhaps also the 'fair youth' addressed in his sonnets. Nearby lay 'Old John of Gaunt, time-honoured Lancaster', whose deathbed scene dominates the early part of *Richard II*. Hentzner noted the inscription on the tomb, which bore witness to the inextricable entwining of history and geography: Old John of Gaunt (1340–1399) was the quintessence of England and yet he took his name from Ghent, in Flanders, where he was born. His wives and children summon up a lineage that sweeps across the monarchies of Europe and embodies a turbulent century of conflict with France and the internecine strife of the Wars of the Roses at home. The inscription on the tomb of Gaunt gave any literate visitor to St Paul's an epitome – a precis – of the arc of history during the century from

10. *Below right* Design for the new spire for St Paul's Cathedral, Inigo Jones, 1608. Pen and wash, 75 x 51 cm. Worcester College, Oxford

'How art thou a king / But by fair sequence and succession?'

(Richard II 2.1.200–1)

11. *The Family of Henry VIII: An Allegory of the Tudor Succession*, attributed to Lucas De Heere, *c.* 1572. Lucas de Heere was one of many Protestant immigrant artists who played a part in shaping the Elizabethan representation of English national history.
Oil on panel, 131.2 x 184 cm.
National Museum of Wales, Cardiff

the reign of Richard II (r. 1377–1399) to the victory over Richard III (r. 1483–1485) at Bosworth Field of Gaunt's great-great-grandson, Henry Richmond, who in 1485 became King Henry VII (until his death in 1509), first of the Tudors, father of Henry VIII and grandfather of Queen Elizabeth. For anyone who could not read, that same national story was dramatized on the London stage in the course of the 1590s in Shakespeare's two mighty tetralogies of English historical drama.

Lucas de Heere was one of many Dutch immigrant artists who played a part in shaping the Elizabethan representation of English national history. His *Allegory of the Tudor Succession* (fig. 11) evokes the great fissure between Roman Catholic and Protestant that sundered the nation in the middle of the sixteenth century. Henry VIII and his successors are shown in two clearly demarcated camps. Catholic Mary Tudor (r. 1553–1558) and her husband King Philip II of Spain are accompanied by Mars, the god of war, while Elizabeth is served by Peace and Plenty, who trample on weapons. She is in the foreground, while Catholic Mary is pushed further back to show that her brief and bloody reign was an aberration from the divinely ordained

'proofs of holy writ'

(*Othello* 3.3.360)

12. Hand-coloured title page of the Bishops' Bible, showing Elizabeth I seated in majesty as Supreme Governor of the English church, accompanied by the inscription 'God Save the Queene'. Quarto edition of 1569, approved for parish use.
Printed book, 21.5 x 16 cm. British Library, London

13. Silver Communion cup made in the prescribed form for the parish of Wiggenhall St Germans in Norfolk. Marked for Norwich 1567–8 and the maker Thomas Buttell. Shown here with a medieval paten (the small plate used to hold the bread for consecration) retained by the parish after the Reformation.
Silver, H. (of chalice) 16 cm. British Museum, London

Protestant succession. The painting's dedicatory inscription, addressed to the ultra-Protestant Sir Francis Walsingham (*c.* 1532–1590), emphasizes Elizabeth's virginity as a political virtue which will keep England Protestant and out of foreign wars, independent of Catholic powers.[7]

Each of the 120 London parish churches noted by Hentzner would have contained a large Bishops' Bible (fig. 12) on the lectern, its frontispiece in this printing of 1569 showing Queen Elizabeth as supreme governor of the English Church. This was an English translation of the Bible, authorized by church and state.[8] The book embodied the middle way of the Anglican religious settlement that Elizabeth had so skilfully guided into place in 1559. It was not a Latin book, like that of the Catholics. But nor was it a book annotated with radically Protestant doctrinal marginalia, like the Geneva Bible (1557) favoured by more extreme Puritans.

So too with the sacraments. The Anglican settlement had purified many Catholic doctrines – the seven sacraments were reduced to two (Baptism and Communion), the doctrine of Purgatory and the veneration of saints were abolished – but the

25

'Bare ruined choirs, where late the sweet birds sang'

(*Sonnet 73, 4*)

14. The Stonyhurst Salt, made from fragments of old reliquaries or church plate destroyed at the Reformation. Marked for London 1577–8 and the probable maker John Robinson.
Silver-gilt, decorated with rock crystals, rubies and garnets, H. 26.2 cm. British Museum, London

ceremony of the Eucharist remained the central enactment of faith. The Communion cup of the parish of Wiggenhall St Germans in Norfolk (fig. 13) was made in prescribed form by melting down the old parish chalice, but used with a pre-Reformation paten (the small plate used to hold the bread for consecration) which belonged to the church: continuity was retained alongside change, old customs and traditions held in delicate balance with a new dispensation.[9] Shakespeare kept his own beliefs closely guarded, but his plays are indelibly marked with the religious controversies of the age. The ghost of Old Hamlet says that he is in Purgatory, a Catholic concept, while young Hamlet goes to university at Wittenberg, home of Martin Luther and birthplace of the Reformation.

The injunctions of 1559 demanded the destruction of the outward forms of Catholic worship, 'so that there remain no memory of the same'.[10] An object which embodies the impact of that unprecedented attack on custom, and the sense of Catholicism as a lost faith, is a secular salt cellar made from the rescued fragments of Catholic reliquaries or elaborate ecclesiastical plate destroyed during the Reformation (fig. 14). Marked for London 1577–8, it incorporates garnets and rubies, which were specifically associated in the medieval mind with the blood of Christ or the Catholic martyrs. It also displays carved rock-crystal elements, symbolic of Christ's purity, and often used to protect and display a relic in medieval reliquaries.[11] It is rare for a piece of secular silver to incorporate jewels in this way – let alone ones that look like drops of blood – which suggests that the viewer is supposed to recognize the provenance of the fragments. This is perhaps why the salt was later acquired by the Jesuit foundation, Stonyhurst College in Lancashire, for liturgical use as a pyx, to hold the consecrated host. It was not recognized as a secular salt until much more recently.[12] Whether at the time it was made or later, could an object like this be regarded as a touchstone of Catholic allegiance?

Out in the shires, particularly in Lancashire, the old faith was harder to put down than in London.[13] Several important Catholic families were concentrated in Shakespeare's Warwickshire. As he toured the country with his acting company, he would have seen the most conspicuous relics of this lost world: the deserted, crumbling monasteries, dissolved by Henry VIII, that pockmarked the countryside and that are vividly evoked in the image 'Bare ruined choirs, where late the sweet birds sang' (*Sonnet 73*, 4) and in the passing observation of the Goth soldier in *Titus Andronicus*: 'From our troops I strayed / To gaze upon a ruinous monastery' (5.1.20–1). When Shakespeare takes his characters into the countryside, they sometimes express nostalgia for the old Catholic ways. 'True is it that we have seen better days' says the exiled Duke in the forest of Arden, 'And have with holy bell been knolled to church' (*As You Like It* 2.7.121–2).

The Bishopton Cup (fig. 15) takes us close to Shakespeare in several senses. It was made for use in a small chapel close to Shakespeare's family church of Holy Trinity during a second push at religious conformity in Stratford-upon-Avon, when the playwright's father was Head Alderman, responsible for carrying through the required

15. The Bishopton Cup, marked for London
1571–2 and the maker Robert Durrant.
The lid can also be used as a paten.
Silver, H. (cup) 12.7 cm; H. (lid) 3.3 cm.
Holy Trinity Church, Stratford-upon-Avon

16. The Clifford Chambers chalice and paten,
marked for London 1494–5. A rare survival of
pre-Reformation, Catholic church plate.
Silver-gilt, H. (cup) 15.4 cm; diam. (of paten) 14.6 cm.
Clifford Chambers, Stratford-upon-Avon

measures.[14] The cup is hallmarked 1571–2, revealing that it was made soon after
the appointment of Nicholas Bullingham, a known reformer, as the local Bishop of
Worcester, and of Henry Heycroft as the new vicar in Stratford. He replaced a vicar
who had been ousted for supposed sympathy with the pro-Catholic Northern
Rebellion of 1569.[15] The cup, from which Shakespeare himself may have taken
Communion, is a textbook example of the religious changes enforced by the state at
the parish level. Even then the neighbouring parish of Clifford Chambers managed
to keep a medieval chalice and paten, hallmarked for London 1494–5, which is still
in use to this day (fig. 16).[16] Reverence for tradition was not shared by everyone:
some wit incised the words 'A pox on you' on the bosses around the stem of the
Clifford Chambers Chalice.

Among the wealthiest of the monasteries had been the abbey dedicated to St Peter
in Westminster. In 1539 Henry VIII took direct royal control over it, sparing it from
dissolution. In Mary's reign it was restored to the Benedictine order, but they were
again ejected by Elizabeth in 1559. Twenty years later she re-established Westminster
Abbey as a 'Royal Peculiar' – a church responsible directly to the sovereign rather than
to a diocesan bishop, a status it retains to this day. Westminster lay to the west of
London itself. Hentzner describes how it was 'joined to the city by a continual row
of palaces belonging to the chief nobility, of a mile in length' (that row is now called
The Strand). The Collegiate Church of St Peter, as it was known, was the place where
England's kings and queens were crowned and buried. Here Hentzner saw the tomb
of Richard II and his wife, fashioned of brass and gilt, and with verses written around
it that begin 'Perfect and prudent, Richard, by right the Second, / Vanquished by
Fortune, lies here now graven in stone'. Henry V (r. 1413–1422) was nearby. Again,

Hentzner noted down the inscription: 'Henry, the scourge of France, lies in this tomb. Virtue subdues all things. A.D. 1422.' Next to his tomb lay the coffin of his queen Catherine (r. 1420–1422), the young French princess whom his stage double wooed so memorably at the climax of Shakespeare's *The Life of Henry V*. She was unburied and her coffin could be opened by anyone that pleased. In 1669 Samuel Pepys (1633–1703) allowed himself as a birthday treat to hold the upper part of her body and kiss her on the lips. History was close to the touch.

Adjacent to the church was Westminster Hall, where Parliament held its sessions and the Courts of Justice heard their trials. The Queen's Bench, which administered the Common Law, met at one end and the Court of Chancery at the other. Not far away was the royal Palace of Whitehall, formerly the house of Cardinal Wolsey (1473–1530), whose fall from royal favour was dramatized by Shakespeare and John Fletcher in *All is True: The Famous History of King Henry VIII*. It was during a performance of this play, in the summer of 1613, that the Globe Theatre burned to the ground as a result of an accident involving a special effect with a cannon.

Whitehall Palace was also a prime tourist attraction. Hentzner carefully recorded the objects that he saw there, the things that he found 'worthy of observation', ranging from 'The Royal Library, well stored with Greek, Latin, Italian and French books' to 'The Queen's bed, ingeniously composed of woods of different colours, with quilts of silk, velvet, gold, silver, and embroidery'. Also noted was an array of portraits, among them, gloriously mingling history and mythology, English and Continental, Protestant and Catholic,

> Queen Elizabeth, at sixteen years old; Henry, Richard, Edward, Kings of England; Rosamond; Lucrece, a Grecian bride, in her nuptial habit; the genealogy of the Kings of England; a picture of King Edward VI, representing at first sight something quite deformed, till by looking through a small hole in the cover which is put over it, you see it in its true proportions [fig. 17]; Charles V, Emperor; Charles Emanuel, Duke of Savoy, and Catherine of Spain, his wife; Ferdinand, Duke of Florence, with his daughters; one of Philip, King of Spain, when he came into England and married Mary; Henry VII, Henry VIII, and his mother; besides many more of illustrious men and women; and a picture of the Siege of Malta.

As well as books and paintings, jewels and household items, he was impressed by an assortment of curiosities, such as 'a piece of clock-work' in the shape of 'an Ethiop riding upon a rhinoceros, with four attendants, who all make their obeisance when it strikes the hour', and a variety of 'emblems on paper, cut in the shape of shields, with mottoes, used by the nobility at tilts and tournaments, hung up here for a memorial'.[17] Hentzner's list of memorable objects tells us a great deal about the way in which the early modern imagination worked, the watchword being curiosity – regarding the new, the strange, the unfamiliar. The variety of the world was understood by means of close attention to objects. Even small things, such as a little carved wooden hermitage, were worthy of

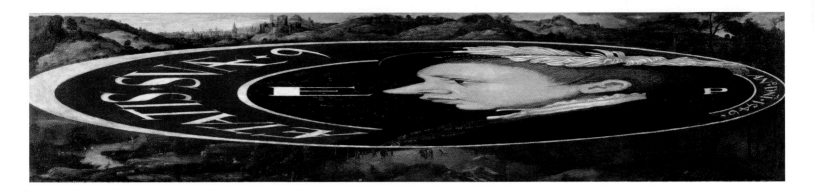

'Like perspectives, which rightly gazed upon / Show nothing but confusion: eyed awry / Distinguish form'

(*Richard II* 2.2.18–20)

17. Anamorphic portrait of Edward VI aged nine, by William Scrots, 1546, recorded by visitors who saw it in Whitehall Palace between 1584 and 1613. It is seen in correct perspective when viewed from the right.
Oil on panel, 42.5 x 160 cm.
National Portrait Gallery, London

observation. Hentzner, Shakespeare and their contemporaries would have had no difficulty comprehending our modern habit of visiting museums and art galleries, in which a wondrous variety of objects and pictures are juxtaposed in ways that seek to develop a narrative about the world, the past and the interplay of different cultures.

Shakespeare and his acting company frequently visited the palace at Whitehall when they were called upon to perform their plays in front of the monarch and the court, at festival occasions and when special events were arranged for visiting dignitaries. Thoughtful writers, actors, and indeed playgoers, would have perceived consonances between the objects in the palace and the plots and props of the drama. Books, letters, beds, chests, jewels (albeit probably fake) and musical instruments were all important items in the property cupboard at the Globe, while the paintings at Whitehall conjure up the contours of Shakespeare's imaginative world as it ranged from English monarchs past and present to stories from Greek and Roman antiquity, and to Mediterranean encounters between Christian and Muslim. The events shown in the 'picture of the Siege of Malta', for example, mentioned by Hentzner, inspired *The Jew of Malta* (1592) by Christopher Marlowe (1564–1593), which in turn influenced both *Othello* and *The Merchant of Venice*. The little carved hermitage, meanwhile, was a reminder of the great theme of pastoral, of retreat from the active world of court preferment and intrigue to the contemplative life in a natural setting – a play of two worlds to which Shakespeare returns again and again in his comedies.

Those 'emblems on paper, cut in the shape of shields, with mottoes, used by the nobility at tilts and tournaments' evoke the importance of spectacle, of ritualized battle and of honour – again, all great themes of the Shakespearean drama. Tournament devices of this kind feature prominently in one of Shakespeare's co-authored plays, *Pericles, Prince of Tyre*. And, indeed, one of the lattermost references we have to Shakespeare's work is a record of him and his fellow actor and close friend, Richard Burbage (1568–1619), being paid 44 shillings in March 1613 for designing an *impresa* for the shield of the 6th Earl of Rutland. Shakespeare's own social aspirations were nowhere more conspicuous than in his attempt to obtain a coat of arms for his own family in the late 1590s, in order to assert their respectability and pedigree (see Chapter 2, pp. 85–6).

Francis Manners, Earl of Rutland, was, as far as we know, the last aristocratic

'... and in woman out-paramoured the Turk'

(*King Lear* 3.4.78)

18. A leaf from Peter Mundy's album of 1618, made up for him in Istanbul as a tourist souvenir, with his annotations discussing steam baths as meeting places for Ottoman Turkish women. European commentators were fascinated by the erotic allure of the harem.

Opaque watercolour on paper and paper cut-outs, 19.9 x 13 cm. British Museum, London

'Basins and ewers to lave her dainty hands'

(*The Taming of the Shrew* 2.1.350)

19. Iznik Turkish ceramic ewer with silver-gilt mounts, marked for London 1597–8.

H. 33.2 cm. British Museum, London

patron to give money to Shakespeare. The first was Henry Wriothesley, 3rd Earl of Southampton (1573–1624), to whom the young Shakespeare dedicated 'the first heirs of his invention', his exquisitely crafted narrative poems *Venus and Adonis* and *The Rape of Lucrece*. The cult of chivalry and honour is superbly evoked by Southampton's ceremonial armour – here we bring together the armour itself and the portrait of Southampton wearing it (see Chapter 4, figs 11–13).

The Ethiopian on the rhinoceros at the climax of Hentzner's list of Whitehall curiosities conjures up an image of distant worlds, chiming with theatre's interest in representing outsiders, strangers and aliens. As travellers from many countries were bringing new customs and strange objects to London, so Englishmen were venturing ever further abroad. Consider the case of Peter Mundy. He was the son of a Cornish pilchard merchant – an extremely lucrative business in the sixteenth century, to the extent that Thomas Bodley refounded the Library of the University of Oxford as the Bodleian on the basis of his wife's pilchards fortune in 1602.[18] Mundy eventually became a leading figure in the East India Company. He started out as a cabin boy in 1611, sailing the Mediterranean, then spent eight years in Spain and Istanbul, where a souvenir album was made up for him by local artists (fig. 18).[19] He jotted down his own thoughts and observations to the Turkish woodcuts and stencils on the pages. He took a particular interest in Turkish baths and the phenomenon of the harem, as he scribbles around the images on the page illustrated here.[20] As in Shakespeare's *Antony and Cleopatra*, the Orient is a place of both fascination and fear, associated especially with alluring female sexuality.

The East was also a source of alluring objects for Western consumers. Many of these items were transformed after their sea voyage 'into something rich and strange' on their arrival in London, to be enjoyed as curiosities as well as luxury imports. Around the time of Hentzner's London visit, an exquisite ewer was crafted in London out of an Iznik ceramic vessel imported from Ottoman Turkey through the Levant trade (fig. 19). Iznik pottery was outstanding for its bold floral designs and brilliant pigments, and it was extremely rare in contemporary London: Walter Cope, 'a citizen of London who spent much time in the Indies', owned 'a Turkish pitcher and dishes' among his curiosities listed by Thomas Platter in 1599. Cope's pitcher may have resembled this piece.[21] The rarity and value of the ceramic body is indicated by the elaborate silver-gilt mounts marked for London 1597–8, which transform a straightforward jug into a ewer with an eagle-headed spout. It could have been made for a powerful merchant alderman such as Paul Baning, one of four London merchants who handled 94 per cent of imports from the Levant in 1589. He was to be one of the founder directors of the reorganized Levant Company, which was granted a charter in 1592.[22]

Chinese porcelain, which was even rarer than Iznik pottery, may have reached England via Portugal, or through the Levant trade via Ottoman Turkey. Figure 20 shows the earliest known blue-and-white Chinese porcelain with a dated European silver mount. It is a simple Ming porcelain bowl, not at all special by Chinese standards, painted with a hare in underglaze blue on the inside. It belonged to a Devonshire man, Samuel Lennard, who had it mounted by a London goldsmith: the hallmarks are for 1569–70. The goldsmith copied the motif of the hare at the centre of the bowl on to the silver rim, either at his own whim or that of his client: the synergy suggests a sympathetic response to the design of the original object. Chinese porcelain also appears among Cope's curiosities.[23]

'China dishes'

(*Measure for Measure* 2.1.82)

20. The earliest known blue-and-white Chinese porcelain with a dated silver mount, which is marked for London 1569–70. This rare treasure belonged to an Englishman, Samuel Lennard (1553–1618).
H. 16 cm; diam. 12 cm. British Museum, London

It was the lure of trade with China that took English merchants from the East India Company as far as Japan. The company, set up in 1600, was encouraged in its activities by an Englishman, William Adams, who was already in Japan. Adams was a Dutch agent, later employed by the Dutch East India Company, who had been shipwrecked from the *Leifde* (*Charity*) in Japan in 1600 (fig. 21).[24] He encouraged the English to come out in 1613: 'I boldly say our countrymen shalbe so welcome and free in comparison as in the river of London'. His letter to England crossed paths with the English East India Company ship, the *Clove*, which was already on its way. As head of the company's expedition, John Saris delivered James I's presentation letter to the shogun in 1613 with the gift of a Turkish carpet and a telescope; in return he received two suits of Japanese armour that went straight into the Royal Armouries in the Tower of London on arrival there in 1615 (fig. 22).[25]

It was the East India Company that also sent Sir Thomas Roe (*c.* 1581–1644) as the first English ambassador to Mughal India in 1615, following on William Finch's expedition of 1607.[26] Roe sought to win trade privileges for the British and to muscle in on the Portuguese and Dutch trade networks that were also represented among the *farangis* or 'Franks', i.e. Europeans, at the court of Emperor Jahangir (r. 1605–1627).

21. Poop ornament showing the figure of Erasmus, dated 1598 and supposedly from the *Charity*, the first Dutch ship to arrive in Japan in 1600, piloted by an Englishman, William Adams. The carving was enshrined in a Zen temple in Tochigi.
H. 104.5 cm. Tokyo National Museum

22. Japanese armour (*do maru*), *c.* 1610. Made by Iwai Yozaemon of Nambu and presented to King James I by Tokugawa Hidetada in 1613, via Captain Saris of the East India Company.
Copper, iron, gold, leather, silk and leather,
H. (of helmet) 22 cm, H. (of curirass, waist to shoulder) 44 cm. Royal Armouries, Leeds

'they / Made Britain India: every man that stood / Showed like a mine'

(*Henry VIII 1.1.25–7*)

23. This sixteenth-century gold and ruby bangle is from Sri Lanka, famous for its goldsmiths' work. It is traditionally said to have been given by Queen Elizabeth to Lord Hunsdon, Shakespeare's patron, and regarded as an exotic family heirloom.
Gold, rock crystal, rubies and sapphires, diam. 9 cm.
Private collection

24. *A European*, unknown Mughal artist, *c.* 1610–15. The head is perhaps based on a European portrait miniature of the kind known and admired at Jahangir's court.
Opaque watercolour on paper, 32.9 x 18.8 cm (excluding borders). Victoria and Albert Museum, London

India was the source for diamonds and rubies used in European jewellery, as seen in the gold and ruby bangle illustrated here (fig. 23).[27] Adventurers intermingled with craftsmen, missionaries, traders and soldiers. One such foreigner, painted by an anonymous Mughal artist, is shown in figure 24. He wears the kind of dress adopted by Europeans after residence in India: loose trousers gathered at the ankle worn with a lace-edged shirt and open doublet, a velvet cap and the all-important status symbol, a rapier.[28] The particularity of the face, its three-quarter presentation and the European touches, suggest that the painter may have based his image on a European portrait miniature.[29] Miniatures by English artists were known and valued at Jahangir's court, and were copied by his artists: Roe commented that five Mughal copies of a particular Isaac Oliver miniature which he had presented succeeded 'beyond all expectation'.[30] This delicate miniature suggests a complex set of social and artistic exchanges within the one image.[31]

'I speak of Africa and golden joys'

(*Henry IV Part 2* 5.3.76)

25. African horn from the Calabar region (modern Nigeria), 1500s. Recarved, inscribed and dated 1599 in England and then later altered into an oil lamp.

Ivory and brass, L. 83 cm. British Museum, London

People as well as objects came to London from across the Ottoman Empire, which extended far beyond what is now Turkey. There were Ottoman client states all along the Mediterranean coast of North Africa. The names of many 'blackamoors' – servants and labourers, not slaves – are to be found in the registers of the city's outer parishes.[32] Trade and cultural interchange with Africa is represented by a fascinating artefact from the collection of Sir Hans Sloane (1660–1753), which presents a whole cultural history in one object (fig. 25). It was originally made as a horn in the Calabar region of modern Nigeria, probably in the sixteenth century, then adapted as a drinking horn in Europe by the end of the century, and then further adapted as an oil lamp. It is identified as Nigerian on account of the characteristic relief carving with a crocodile and transverse zigzag decoration on the body. The reason it looks so odd – and was long thought to be a fake – is that it was apparently recarved, either in Africa or in Europe, to look more like a well-known type of Afro-Portuguese horn from Sierra Leone. Thus a rare object was 'improved' in line with fashionable European taste in the sixteenth century so as to look more recognizably 'African'.[33] A bawdy English inscription, not unlike the language of Elizabethan comic drama, is carved on the horn: 'Drinke you this and thinke no scorne although the cup be much like a horn 1599 Fines'. This wonderful object shows not only the nature of contacts between England and Africa in Shakespeare's lifetime, but also the cultural interaction between exotic imports and English consumers, craftsmen and collectors. Shakespeare's own works very early became part of this process of cultural exchange.

In the summer of 1600 a high-profile group of exotic strangers appeared on the streets of London. Muley Hamet was king of Barbary, a vast domain in northern Africa, covering modern-day Morocco and beyond. He dreamed of reoccupying Spain, from where, following the fall of Granada in 1492, his Moorish people had been expelled after centuries of coexistence with the Christians. He sent an ambassador, with a party of sixteen men, to Queen Elizabeth for exploratory talks on the possibility of forming an alliance whereby Spain would be conquered by the combined forces of the English navy and African troops.[34] The diplomatic party landed at Dover early in August 1600 and was escorted by water to Gravesend.

A few days later they had their first audience with the queen at Nonsuch Palace. The interview was conducted in Spanish, with a learned courtier called Lewis

Lewkenor serving as interpreter. At the end of the meeting, the Barbary interpreter had some additional private words with Queen Elizabeth in Italian. Further meetings followed in September. There was talk of an encounter in Aleppo and of an alliance to seize both the East and West Indies from the Spaniards, dividing the spoils. But nothing definite was concluded and the delegation planned to depart at the end of October. There then followed a delay as a result of the sudden death (from natural causes) of 'the eldest of them, which was a kind of priest or prophet'.[35] So the strangers were still in London to witness the triumphal festivities on the anniversary of the queen's coronation on 17 November. A special viewing enclosure was built for them in Whitehall. It is not known when they finally departed, but Muley Hamet wrote to tell Elizabeth of their safe return at the end of February 1601. Since the sea voyage would have taken six or seven weeks, they probably left in mid-January, which means that they are likely to have been present during the Christmas festivities at court when Shakespeare's acting company, the Lord Chamberlain's Men, played before the queen.

Whether or not the Barbary delegation witnessed a Shakespeare play, they formed such a spectacle in London that Shakespeare must have known of their presence and, in all probability, seen them in the flesh. The antiquary John Stow wrote of the interest – and hostility – that they aroused during the 'six months' space' of their stay in London. The ambassador himself, Abd el-Ouahed ben Messaoud ben Mohammed Anoun, sat – or rather stood – for his portrait (fig. 26). The very image of a noble Moor, berobed and wearing a magnificent sword, the figure of ben Messaoud must have been in the hinterland of Shakespeare's imagining of Othello a few years later (see Chapter 6, pp. 176). A Moroccan ambassador in London transformed into a blacked-up white stage player representing a Venetian General. Politics and imagination, distant places and immediate histories, all thrown together: that was Shakespeare's theatre of the world.

Othello is a drama rich in allusion to the southern shoreline of the Mediterranean: a maid called Barbary, the Arabian tree, an encounter in Aleppo. And yet the play's source, Giovanni Battista Giraldi Cinthio's story in his Italian collection of tales *Gli Hecatommithi*, concerning a Venetian lady, a Moorish captain and his ensign, is very unspecific in its atmosphere. The narrative is confined entirely to plotting and dialogue and there is no realization of historical setting. It was Shakespeare who gave the story local texture – Venetian, Cypriot and Moorish – perhaps courtesy of such recently published books as Lewis Lewkenor's 1599 translation of Contarini's *The Commonwealth and Government of Venice*, John Pory's 1600 translation of *A Geographical History of Africa* by 'Leo Africanus' and Richard Knolles's 1603 *General History of the Turks*. We have already met Lewkenor in his capacity as interpreter in the negotiations with the Moorish ambassador. Pory's book – a tale of slavery, travel and military prowess, of 'moving accidents by flood and field, / Of hair-breadth scapes i'th'imminent deadly breach' – was published during Abd el-Ouahed ben Messaoud's time in London: its preface alludes to his presence and was dated to the very day of that coronation anniversary triumph watched by the Moors from their 'special place' in Whitehall.

1600

ABDVLGVAHID·

ÆTATIS:42·

LEGATVS REGIS BARBARIÆ
IN ANGLIAM·

The focal point of the Whitehall gallery of curiosities, in a sense the focal point of all London, was the queen herself. She was a perpetual source of wonder and of gossip, the subject of poems and paintings, ballads and bids for patronage. Protestant immigrant painters played an especially important role in shaping her quasi-mythical image. Elizabeth I as the Vestal Virgin Tuccia (fig. 27) was painted soon after the failure of the attempt to marry her to the Duke of Anjou. The representation of her as the Roman Vestal Virgin makes a virtue of her virginity. The sieve is symbolic of her chastity, while the imperial column with roundels depicts the story of Aeneas and Dido, thus suggesting an association with the mythical Trojan line that founded London and Britain. The globe with ships plying west suggests the foundation of a new western empire: the badge on the central figure is that of Sir Christopher Hatton (1540–1591), who was against the Anjou marriage and was a financier of that foundational gesture of British empire-building, the circumnavigation of the globe by Sir Francis Drake.[36] This kind of mythologizing of the Virgin Queen was a feature of drama as well as of portraiture (see further Chapter 4, p. 141). In *A Midsummer Night's Dream*, Shakespeare imagines Elizabeth as a figure closely analogous to a Vestal Virgin, namely an 'imperial votress', who is also associated with the rising of empire in the West:

> That very time I saw, but thou couldst not,
> Flying between the cold moon and the earth,
> Cupid all armed; a certain aim he took
> At a fair vestal thronèd by the west,
> And loosed his love-shaft smartly from his bow,
> As it should pierce a hundred thousand hearts.
> But I might see young Cupid's fiery shaft
> Quenched in the chaste beams of the wat'ry moon;
> And the imperial votress passèd on,
> In maiden meditation, fancy-free.
> (2.1.158–67)

Another of Elizabeth's iconic personae was Diana, classical goddess of chastity. At the Whitehall entrance into the royal deer park, Hentzner noted an inscription:

> The fisherman who has been wounded, learns, though late, to beware;
> But the unfortunate Actaeon always presses on.
> The chaste virgin naturally pitied:
> But the powerful goddess revenged the wrong.
> Let Actaeon fall a prey to his dogs,
> An example to youth,
> A disgrace to those that belong to him!
> May Diana live the care of Heaven;

'the valiant Moor'

(*Othello 1.3.52*)

26. Portrait of the Moroccan ambassador Abd el-Ouahed ben Messaoud, unknown artist, painted during his embassy to London, *c.* 1600. Oil on panel, 114.5 x 79 cm. University of Birmingham Research and Cultural Collections, Birmingham

The delight of mortals;
The security of those that belong to her!

Again, an inscription provides a clue as to the way in which Shakespeare's contemporaries read the world. A deer park is adorned with a text that carries a moral message – about purity of mind and behaviour. And yet the 'example' is conveyed through a story that is anything but puritanical. In Ovid's *Metamorphoses*, the Elizabethans' prime source for the tales of classical mythology, Actaeon is a hunter who chances upon the goddess Diana and her nymphs while they are bathing naked. She turns him into a stag and he is torn to pieces by his own dogs – symbolically destroyed by the hounds of his own desire. Shakespeare frequently alluded to the tale, expecting his audience to know both the story and its symbolic meaning. Thus Orsino, early in *Twelfth Night*: 'That instant was I turned into a hart, / And my desires, like fell and cruel hounds, / E'er since pursue me' (1.1.22–4). When Falstaff appears wearing a pair of antlers in *The Merry Wives of Windsor*, he is at once the classical Actaeon and the English folk figure of Herne the Hunter (see p. 84).

Among the other tourist attractions ticked off by Hentzner and his master was the Tower of London, where they were shown not only the royal menagerie, which included a variety of exotic beasts mentioned by Shakespeare (lions, a tiger, a porcupine, an eagle and a mangy old wolf), but also the armoury, stuffed with spears, shields, halberds, lances, cannon, handguns and crossbows. This was a militarized society, in which Shakespeare was a war poet: there was war in the Netherlands in the 1580s, war with Spain through the 1590s and rebellion in Ireland during Hentzner's trip to London. It was also a society in which street violence was common. *Romeo and Juliet* is Shakespeare's tragedy of Elizabethan knife crime. The dagger in figure 28 was found in the Thames; it would have been worn together with a rapier, at court and in the city and suburbs. They were both weapon and luxury accessory, a mark of status and a means of self-defence.[37] Actors and playwrights were notorious for getting into street fights, and real brawls were as common around the playhouses as choreographed fighting was on stage. Ben Jonson once killed a man; Marlowe was stabbed with a twelvepenny dagger. In the theatrical world Shakespeare was unusual in keeping himself out of trouble.

A militarized society, but also a mercantile one. New commercial opportunities were bringing change: the Tower also housed the Royal Mint, where money was coined. Thus for Hentzner the next thing worthy of note was the Royal Exchange:

so named by Queen Elizabeth, built by Sir Thomas Gresham, citizen, for public ornament and the convenience of merchants. It has a great effect, whether you consider the stateliness of the building, the assemblage of different nations, or the quantities of merchandise [fig. 29].

'Imperial votress... In maiden meditation, fancy-free'

(*Midsummer Night's Dream* 2.1.166–7)

27. Elizabeth I ('The Sieve Portrait'), attributed to Quentin Metsys the Younger, signed and dated 1583. The queen is shown in the guise of the Vestal Virgin Tuccia (the sieve is a symbol of chastity).
Oil on canvas, 124.5 x 91.5 cm.
Pinacoteca Nazionale, Siena

The Exchange was the place above all others where different peoples, languages, customs and faiths, forms of dress and address, came together for the exchange of goods, of stories, of cash and of credit. The increase in maritime confidence during Elizabeth's reign is demonstrated by the founding of joint stock companies (fig. 30), which managed new trading opportunities and made the English global competitors with the Dutch, Portuguese and Spanish.

Where there is business, there is also litigation. Not far from the Exchange Hentzner wandered around the legal quarter, where he discovered fifteen colleges 'nobly built, with beautiful gardens adjoining'. These were the Inns of Court and of Chancery, most famous among them being Gray's Inn, Lincoln's Inn and the Temple. The latter carried another historical memory, since it was once inhabited by the Knights Templar and 'seems to have taken its name from the old temple, or church, which has a round tower added to it, under which lay buried those Kings of Denmark that reigned in England'. Hentzner was not at all sure how seriously the young nobility, gentry and others who crowded these colleges applied themselves to the study of the law, despite the fact that the Inns represented London's intellectual centre.[38] The Inns were also a kind of finishing school for young gentry after university and before taking up their place in public life,[39] but to Hentzner they seemed notable more for very good dinners, 'silver cups to drink out of', and after-dinner entertainment in the form of plays – the earliest recorded performances of both *The Comedy of Errors* and *Twelfth Night* took place at the Inns of Court.[40]

At Middle Temple on 2 February 1602 a play was performed as part of the festivities for Candlemas. Law student John Manningham noted in his diary:

> At our feast we had a play called *Twelve Night, or What You Will*, much like *The Comedy of Errors* or *Menaechmi* in Plautus but most like and near to that in Italian called *Inganni*. A good practice in it to make the steward believe his lady widow was in love with him, by counterfeiting a letter as from his lady, in general terms telling him what she liked best in him, and prescribing his gesture in smiling, his apparel, etc., and then when he came to practise, making believe they took him to be mad.[41]

'My naked weapon is out. Quarrel, I will back thee'

(*Romeo and Juliet* 1.1.27)

28. Rapier and dagger from the Thames. The opening fight in *Romeo and Juliet* between rival noble houses in the street evokes the duelling culture of Shakespeare's London. Rapier and dagger sets were worn as both defensive and offensive weapons. They were also status symbols. Steel with iron guard and pommel, and original wooden grips bound with wire, rapier, L. 128 cm; dagger, L. 46.3 cm. Royal Armouries, Leeds

It is not known precisely how Middle Temple Hall was transformed from dining room to theatre auditorium, but it is highly probable that among the paintings which remained on the walls for the duration of the show was *The Judgement of Solomon*, executed by an unknown Anglo-Flemish painter (fig. 31).[42] Lawyers were supposed to show good judgement, as Solomon did in the Bible when two women came to him with a maternity dispute (1 Kings 3:16–28).[43] The painting's Latin inscription highlights the applicability of the subject to the legal profession: 'And now whoever holds the reins of justice let him learn this mighty lesson of just decision, and at a distance let him adore the footsteps of the King fully taught by God.'

Although plays were a form of entertainment, they likewise presented spectators

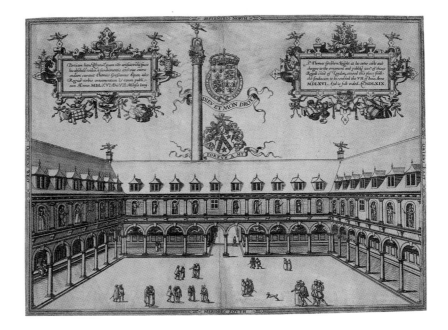

29. The site of an increasingly global conversation: London's Royal Exchange, in a print by Frans Hogenburg, c. 1569.
Engraving, 39 x 53 cm. British Museum, London

'Sea-sick, I think, coming from Muscovy!'

(*Love's Labour's Lost* 5.2.415)

30. Seal-die of the Muscovy Merchants Company, 1555. The increase in maritime confidence during Elizabeth's reign is demonstrated by the founding of joint stock companies, which managed new trading opportunities and made the English global competitors with the Dutch, Portuguese and Spanish. (Shown in reverse.)
Silver, diam. 5.1 cm. British Museum, London

with representations of human dilemmas and moral choices. Different characters gave voice, often in elaborate rhetorical speeches, to different points of view. Like a jury in a law court, audience members were asked to pass judgement, to make up their own minds about the force of the conflicting arguments presented before them. There were exceptionally close connections between the theatres and the Inns of Court: many of Shakespeare's fellow dramatists had legal training, while he himself had close friends and kinsmen at Middle Temple. The Shakespeare family lawyer, John Harborne, was prominent in the affairs of the Inn. Shakespeare stages trials of one sort or another within the action of plays as varied as *Richard II*, *The Merchant of Venice*, *Measure for Measure*, *King Lear* and *The Winter's Tale*. In each case, spectators onstage and off are invited to show the judgement of Solomon.[44]

Shakespeare and his fellow actors had to adapt their work for several different stages. They needed a repertoire of new plays constantly available for the summons – which could come at very short notice – to perform at court. From 1594 his acting company was under the direct patronage of Lord Hunsdon (1526–1596), the Lord Chamberlain, Queen Elizabeth's cousin and one of her most loyal and intimate servants, who was in charge of all festivities at court (fig. 32). In 1603 the Lord Chamberlain's Men became the King's Men. They played at court more frequently than any other acting company. There is a real sense in which public performances of plays were trial runs, open rehearsals, for the occasions that really mattered: command performances in front of the monarch.[45] It was precisely because of the need to have the acting companies in constant readiness for such occasions that the Lord Chamberlain and his officials, such as the Master of the Revels, gave protection to the actors in the face of hostility from the city authorities, who were

'You are right, Justice, and you weigh this well'

(*Henry IV Part 2* 5.2.103)

31. *The Judgement of Solomon*, unknown Anglo-Flemish artist, *c.* 1586–1602. Shakespeare often staged trials in his plays, and audiences were required to consider conflicting arguments and explore moral judgements.
Oil on panel, approx. 188.5 x 165 cm.
Middle Temple, London

in the vanguard of the Protestant revolution. With their strongly Puritan leanings, they regarded the theatres as a source of public disorder and plague infection due to overcrowding, prostitution, afternoon absenteeism on the part of apprentices, undue freedom and sexual opportunity for citizen's wives – not to mention the immoral conduct of the actors themselves (since female parts were played by the actors' teenage male apprentices, who were frequently kissed and fondled on stage, it was generally assumed that the boys also served the actors sexually backstage). In *Measure for Measure*, set in a Vienna that is also contemporary London, the puritanical Angelo takes pleasure in ordering the razing of buildings in the suburbs, replicating a proclamation for slum clearance that was issued in September 1603, early in King James's reign. The brothels in the vicinity of the South Bank theatres were one of the targets.

An important tranche of a theatre company's income stream came from private hire, whether by the royal court, the Inns or as after-dinner entertainment in the houses of the great. Courts and elites had employed actors for this purpose for many generations. What was new in late Elizabethan England was the commercial theatre. Six afternoons per week, for most of the year, except when closed due to plague or censorship, the actors played in open-air theatres for the paying public (fig. 33).[46] 'Without [i.e. outside] the city are some theatres', Hentzner recorded, 'where English actors represent almost every day tragedies and comedies to a very numerous audiences; these are concluded with excellent music, variety of dances, and the excessive applause of those that are present.'

Purpose-built theatres, professional writers, plays written for the general public as opposed to an aristocratic patron: all these were new phenomena in the dying years of Queen Elizabeth's reign. Theatre is a collaborative art and in Shakespeare's time this was as true of the scriptwriting as it was of the performance. Shakespeare seems to have begun as a fixer-up of old plays. Some of his earliest original works were collaborative – perhaps a scene or more for the domestic tragedy of *Arden of Faversham*, almost certainly the Countess of Salisbury scenes in the history play of *Edward III*. There are signs of George Peele's hand in *Titus Andronicus* and Thomas Nashe's in *Henry VI Part 1*, though in neither case is it entirely clear whether Shakespeare was revising their earlier work independently or actively co-writing with them. Young Shakespeare was in considerable measure a collaborative author.

Ironically, the only literary composition to survive in Shakespeare's handwriting is a scene for a play which was never performed and with which he had very limited involvement (see fig. 3). It seems to have been some time around the turn of the century that his acting company the Lord Chamberlain's Men obtained the script of a play about Sir Thomas More (1478–1535). It had not been staged due to political objections from the Master of the Revels, the official in the Lord Chamberlain's office whose licence was required before any play could be taged. The subject matter of immigration and civil disobedience was too hot to handle. Shakespeare contributed a skilful scene in which More quelled a rioting crowd through the force of his rhetoric. In a characteristic balancing act, he managed both to animate the ordinary people in the crowd with colourful detail (a woman called Doll says that More's care for the people is witnessed by his having 'made my brother, Arthur Watchins, Sergeant Safe's yeoman' [55–6]) and to argue in More's voice on behalf of both empathy with the dispossessed (in this case immigrants) and respect for the order of the state ('For to the

32. Portrait of Henry Carey, 1st Baron Hunsdon, unknown Anglo-Netherlandish artist, 1591. Carey was patron of the Lord Chamberlain's Men, Shakespeare's company of players, from 1594 until his death in 1596.
Oil on panel, 90 x 75 cm. Berkeley Castle, Berkeley

king God hath his office lent / Of dread, of justice, power and command, / Hath bid him rule, and willed you to obey' [116–18]). This was not enough to make the play acceptable: 'Leave out the insurrection wholly, with the cause thereof', demanded the Master of the Revels. As a result it languished in manuscript until the nineteenth century, when a scholar realized for the first time that here were a few precious pages in Shakespeare's fluent, barely punctuated hand. His fellow actors John Hemings and Philip Condell observed in the preface to the First Folio of Shakespeare's collected plays that when he handed his manuscripts over to his acting company there was barely a crossing out. But the scene from *Sir Thomas More* suggests that their statement was an exaggeration, no doubt intended to heighten admiration for their friend's literary fluency: these precious pages reveal him in the process of having second thoughts even as he composes.

The particular context of the speech in *Sir Thomas More* concerning persecuted immigrants was the 'Ill May Day' riot of 1517, when apprentices had taken to the streets to complain about foreigners taking their jobs. The incident was given contemporary resonance by the arrival in London during the 1590s of a fresh wave of asylum seekers, Huguenots fleeing from the French civil wars. The encounter between the domestic and the alien, civil society and the outsider, became one of the great themes of the drama because it was a live, controversial, politically charged issue in Shakespeare's London. Given the censorship regime to which plays were submitted, such issues were often approached indirectly. By locating a play in modern Venice or ancient Rome, Shakespeare could tackle the problems of his own time without taking too many risks. In one of his earliest hit plays, *Titus Andronicus*, he offered a critique of Roman culture by inventing a story that involved invading Goths and a scheming Moor. A gentleman called Henry Peacham copied out some of the text and accompanied it with a sketch that offers a fascinating insight into the ease with which the Elizabethans imagined the past in conjunction with the present and the familiar with the exotic: the principal Roman characters are dressed in togas, while the soldiers have a contemporary look (see Chapter 4, fig. 2). The queen of the Goths looks distinctly medieval, while the Moor is defined by his blackness. Whether or not Peacham saw *Titus Andronicus* on stage himself, his way of imagining the play accords with the eclecticism of costumes, make-up and props in the Shakespearean theatre.

Unfortunately, Hentzner does not have anything to say about the particulars of the plays performed in those theatres. He goes straight on to note that 'Not far from one of these theatres, which are all built of wood, lies the royal barge, close to the river. It has two splendid cabins, beautifully ornamented with glass windows, painting, and gilding; it is kept upon dry ground, and sheltered from the weather'. When Shakespeare wrote about Mark Antony's first sight of Cleopatra, he was working from a textbook of ancient history (Plutarch's *Lives*), but the idea of a splendid royal barge on which the queen showed herself to her public was entirely familiar from contemporary London.

33. Turned oak baluster excavated from the site of the Rose Playhouse, perhaps from the safety rail around the upper galleries or stage.
Oak, L. 43.5 cm. Museum of London, London

Hentzner actually writes in more detail about the other form of public spectacle that was popular on the South Bank:

There is still another place, built in the form of a theatre, which serves for the baiting of bulls and bears; they are fastened behind, and then worried by great English bull-dogs, but not without great risk to the dogs, from the horns of the one and the teeth of the other; and it sometimes happens that they are killed upon the spot; fresh ones are immediately supplied in the places of those that are wounded or tired. To this entertainment there often follows that of whipping a blinded bear, which is performed by five or six men, standing circularly with whips, which they exercise upon him without any mercy, as he cannot escape from them because of his chain; he defends himself with all his force and skill, throwing down all who come within his reach and are not active enough to get out of it, and tearing the whips out of their hands and breaking them. At these spectacles, and everywhere else, the English are constantly smoking tobacco; and in this manner – they have pipes on purpose made of clay, into the farther end of which they put the herb, so dry that it may be rubbed into powder, and putting fire to it, they draw the smoke into their mouths, which they puff out again through their nostrils like funnels, along with it plenty of phlegm and defluxion from the head. In these theatres, fruits, such as apples, pears, and nuts, according to the season, are carried about to be sold, as well as ale and wine.

34. Clay pipe, *c.* 1580–*c.* 1610, excavated from the site of the Rose Playhouse. L. 6.2 cm. Museum of London, London

The excavation of the Rose Theatre has indeed turned up clay pipes and the archaeological evidence suggests a strong association between smoking and the playhouse. Smoking was well established as a fashionable habit and had been promoted at court by Sir Walter Ralegh (*c.* 1554–1618) by the time the pipe in figure 34 was made in London, somewhere between 1580 and 1610. James I's hectoring *Counterblaste to Tobacco* of 1604 completely failed to put a stop to it.[47] Other small finds from the Rose and the Globe testify to the private lives and public activities of the audiences in the playhouses in early modern London. They include dice, a manicure implement that combines a toothpick with an ear scoop, a ring with an amorous inscription and a sucket fork for sweetmeats with the owner's initials engraved on top of the finial (figs 35–6). Eating and drinking during performances was part of the playgoing experience as well as being a crucial element in the playhouse economy: adjoining tap houses supplied beer for the audience on their way in, while pedlars, or players who had not quite made it yet on to the stage, pressed through the yard selling food and drink, or squeezed in front of people's knees in the galleries.[48]

The symbiosis of theatre and bear-baiting is readily apparent: in Wenceslaus Hollar's famous 'Long View' of the city of London, the captions on the Globe Theatre and the bear-baiting arena (also known as the Hope) are reversed, serendipitously suggesting the interchangability of the two forms of entertainment (see fig. 7). Philip

35. Ring excavated from the site of the Rose
Playhouse, inscribed 'PENCES POVR MOYE
DV' ('Think of me God willing'), 1587–1606.
Gold, H. 0.6 cm, diam. 2 cm.
Museum of London, London

36. Bone dice, brass-topped iron fork and
bone manicure implement excavated from
the site of the Rose Playhouse, c. 1587–1606.
Dice 0.7 x 0.7 cm and 0.4 x 0.4 cm, fork L. 22.1 cm,
manicure implement L. 8.8 cm.
Museum of London, London

Henslowe, manager of the Rose, was both a theatre producer and the owner of a string
of bears, not to mention a chain of brothels. Plays and baitings were advertised in
similar ways, with posters stuck up in public places: the only one to survive features
a bear, not a Shakespeare play (figs 37–8).[49] The best bears, like the best actors,
achieved celebrity status. Most famous of all was Sackerson, kept at the Paris Garden
on Bankside, who gets a namecheck in Shakespeare's *Merry Wives of Windsor*:

SLENDER	I had rather walk here, I thank you. I bruised my shin th'other day with playing at sword and dagger with a master of fence – three veneys for a dish of stewed prunes – and, by my troth, I cannot abide the smell of hot meat since. Why do your dogs bark so? Be there bears i'th'town?
ANNE	I think there are, sir. I heard them talked of.
SLENDER	I love the sport well, but I shall as soon quarrel at it, as any man in England. You are afraid if you see the bear loose, are you not?
ANNE	Ay, indeed, sir.
SLENDER	That's meat and drink to me, now. I have seen Sackerson loose twenty times, and have taken him by the chain: but, I warrant you, the women have so cried and shrieked at it that it passed. But women, indeed, cannot abide 'em: they are very ill-favoured rough things.

(1.1.197–208)

Hentzner was not the only tourist to write about blood sports. Thomas Platter,
a native of Basel in Switzerland, kept a journal of his visit to England, also in 1599.
He too wrote at length about bear-baiting as well as cockfighting. He was also
intrigued and surprised by London's pub culture, in which women drank in
public as much as, perhaps more than, men (fig. 39):

There are a great many inns, taverns, and beer-gardens scattered about the
city, where much amusement may be had with eating, drinking, fiddling, and
the rest, as for instance in our hostelry, which was visited by players almost
daily. And what is particularly curious is that the women as well as the men,
in fact more often than they, will frequent the taverns or ale-houses for
enjoyment. They count it a great honour to be taken there and given wine
with sugar to drink; and if one woman only is invited, then she will bring
three or four other women along and they gaily toast each other; the husband
afterwards thanks him who has given his wife such pleasure, for they deem
it a real kindness.[50]

'Bear-like I must fight the course'

(*Macbeth 5.7.2*)

37. Skull of a Brown Bear, probably a female, excavated from the site of the Globe in 1989. This bear's teeth have been ground down to make her less ferocious when baited by mastiffs.
H. 13.5 cm, W. 20 cm, L. 32 cm.
Dulwich College, London

'I have seen Sackerson loose twenty times, and have taken him by the chain'

(*The Merry Wives of Windsor 1.1.205–6*)

38. Advertisement for bear-baiting at the Bear Garden in Southwark, *c.* 1603–25. Bears were celebrities, and bear-baiting was advertised in a similar way and in similar places to plays.
Manuscript, ink on paper, 25 x 19 cm.
Dulwich College, London

Platter made some particular observations about women and crime:

> And since the city is very large, open, and populous, watch is kept every night in all the streets, so that misdemeanor shall be punished. Good order is also kept in the city in the matter of prostitution, for which special commissions are set up, and when they meet with a case, they punish the man with imprisonment and fine. The woman is taken to Bridewell, the King's palace, situated near the river, where the executioner scourges her naked before the populace. And although close watch is kept on them, great swarms of these women haunt the town in the taverns and playhouses.

Like all crowded public places, the playhouses were a magnet for petty criminals. Simon Forman (1552–1611) was a celebrity astrologer and sought-after physician. He kept a diary in which he recorded intimate consultations with a wide range of London society, from prostitutes to fine ladies, who came to him with their problems and concerns (he had a tendency to take advantage of the doctor–patient relationship). In 1611 he went to see Shakespeare's *Winter's Tale* at the Globe (fig. 40). He drew a moral from the performance in noting how the trickster Autolycus 'feyned him sicke & to have bin Robbed of all that he had and hoe he cozened the por man of all his money' and reminded himself to 'beware of trusting feined beggars or fawning fellouse'.[51] The

success of Shakespeare's representation of a feigned beggar and pickpocket on stage came in no small measure from the presence around the theatres of numerous real-life figures of just such a kind. In popular literature there was a vigorous market in pamphlets describing the tricks and jargon of the petty criminals who duped their victims, known as 'conies' or rabbits, in the streets of London (fig. 41).[52]

The most valuable sequence for our purposes in Thomas Platter's diary is his account of theatregoing, including a visit to Shakespeare's Globe:

39. *An Allegorical Scene*, Isaac Oliver, *c.* 1590–5. Perhaps an allegory of conjugal love. Thomas Platter noted the London pub culture, in which husbands and wives drank together openly in mixed company, as something distinctive and different.
Watercolour and gouache on vellum on card, 11.3 x 17 cm. Statens Museum for Kunst, Copenhagen

On September 21st [September 11th in the English calendar] after lunch, about two o'clock, I and my party crossed the water, and there in the house with the thatched roof witnessed an excellent performance of the tragedy of the first Emperor Julius Caesar with a cast of some fifteen people; when the play was over, they danced very marvellously and gracefully together as is their wont, two dressed as men and two as women.

On another occasion not far from our inn, in the suburb at Bishopsgate, if I remember, also after lunch, I beheld a play in which they presented diverse nations … Thus daily at two in the afternoon, London has two, sometimes three plays running in different places, competing with each other, and those which play best obtain most spectators. The playhouses are so constructed that they play on a raised platform, so that everyone has a good view. There are different galleries and places, however, where the seating is better and more comfortable and therefore more expensive. For whoever cares to stand below only pays one English penny, but if he wishes to sit he enters by another door and pays another penny, while if he desires to sit in the most comfortable seats, which are cushioned, where he not only sees everything well, but can also be seen, then he pays yet another English penny at another door. And during the performance food and drink are carried round the audience, so that for what one cares to pay one may also have refreshment. The actors are most expensively and elaborately costumed; for it is the English usage for eminent lords or knights at their decease to bequeath and leave almost the best of their clothes to their serving men, which it is unseemly for the latter to wear, so that they offer them then for sale for a small sum to the actors.

How much time then they may merrily spend daily at the play everyone knows who has ever seen them play or act.

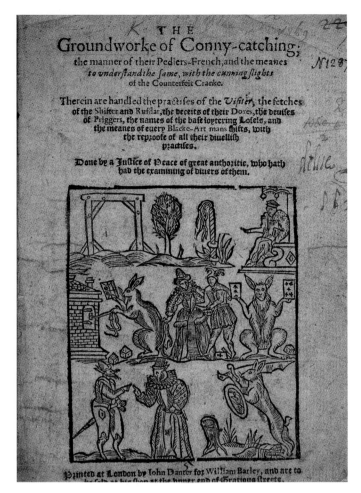

40. Simon Forman's diary, open at his description of seeing *The Winter's Tale* at the Globe in 1611. Manuscript, ink on paper, approx. 30 x 20 cm. Bodleian Library, Oxford

'A snapper-up of unconsidered trifles'

(*The Winter's Tale* 4.3.24–5)

41. Pickpockets on stage drew upon street life around the playhouses and from pamphlet literature on criminal lowlife. A good example of the latter is this pamphlet, by an anonymous author after Thomas Harman, *The Groundworke of Conny-catching*, London, 1592. Title page, 18.5 x 14.5 cm. British Library, London

The value of this account goes far beyond the information it gives about such details as entrance prices (fig. 42), starting time, costumes, dance routines at the end of the show, the competition between different venues, and so forth. Platter also reveals how plays helped to shape cultural identity. The 'play in which they presented diverse nations' shows how the theatre was an arena in which national stereotypes were forged (or overturned). The centrality of theatre to London life is suggested by the idea that merely to witness how the English 'play or act' in their social encounters is to see how much time they have clearly spent at the playhouse: the English go to the theatre, Platter implies, in order to learn how to behave like English men and women. What is more, he continues, it is from the theatre that they learn about the world elsewhere: 'With these and many more amusements the English pass their time, learning at the play what is happening abroad; indeed men and womenfolk visit such places without scruple, since the English for the most part do not travel much, but prefer to learn foreign matters and take their pleasures at home.'

'to split the ears of the groundlings'

(*Hamlet* 3.2.7)

42. Pottery money-box, *c.* 1550–1650.
A groundling is a kind of fish that lies on the
bottom of rivers and gazes up towards the surface
with its mouth open – just like the standing
playgoers, who paid a penny to stand in the
yard in front of the stage.
Lead-glazed earthenware, H. 9 cm.
British Museum, London

43. Sir Henry Unton, unknown artist, *c.* 1596.
A pictorial biography to parallel Jaques's
'seven ages of man'.
Oil on panel, 74 x 16.3 cm.
National Portrait Gallery, London

This is not strictly true. Some of the English did, on the contrary, 'travel much'.
The Unton memorial picture of about 1596 (fig. 43) follows the travels of the soldier
and diplomat Sir Henry Unton (1557?–1596). This unique pictorial biography was
commissioned by Unton's widow Dorothy Wroughton and is recorded in her will of
1634. It presumably illustrates Dorothy's narrative of her husband's life from birth to
death, radiating from Sir Henry's portrait in the middle, accompanied by Fame and
Death. He appears as an infant in arms at the bottom right with his mother, Anne
Seymour, formerly Countess of Warwick, at the Unton residence of Ascott-under-
Wychwood. He is shown studying at Oriel College, Oxford, travelling to Venice and
Padua, and serving with the Earl of Leicester in the Netherlands (1585–6). He is
then portrayed as emissary to Henry IV of France (r. 1589–1610), and finally on his
deathbed in France. The most detailed scenes of all are those showing how his body
was brought back to Wadley House, Faringdon, near Oxford, then scenes from his
funeral on 8 July 1596 and his magnificent monument in Faringdon Church (bottom
left).[53] Perhaps most interesting of all, though, is the evocation of Unton's life at
Wadley House, with him sitting in his study and making music, and finally, seated
after dinner at home, watching a masque of Mercury and Diana. From infant to
student to tourist to soldier to diplomat to the oblivion of the grave: the ten ages of
Henry Unton are as evocative to the eye as Jaques' 'seven ages of man' are to the ear.

The ultimate English traveller was Sir Francis Drake (1540–1596), who became a
national hero when he successfully matched Magellan's historic achievement and led
the second expedition to sail around the world, a feat which took him two years and
ten months (between December 1577 and September 1580).[54] The silver medal in

figure 44 is the earliest map of the voyage, made in 1589, possibly at the command of Drake himself. It is one of several surviving examples, of which the prototype is signed by its maker, Michael Mercator.[55] He appears to have been especially well informed about Drake's route, marked with a dotted line.

Drake specialized in the kind of privatized state warfare that was regarded with nationalistic and Protestant pride by the English and their allies, but with fear and loathing by the Spanish.[56] He raided many Spanish ports on the western coast of South America during his voyage, including Lima and Panama (named on the medal map), looting large quantities of Spanish gold and silver. It was therefore appropriate that Mercator chose to make his map from silver which may indeed have been stolen from the Spanish, and certainly had great symbolic significance in England's fight against Spain as a global power. Drake is also celebrated as circumnavigator of the globe and hero in the fight against the enemies of 'true Christianity' – Spain – in the run-up to the Armada in a rare German broadside in figure 45.[57] A Spanish poem of 1586–7 gives the opposite opinion of Drake in this propaganda war as a bloodthirsty and infamous Lutheran, but even so it built him into a legendary figure:

O fiera crueldad, furor insano
nefando crimen, inferno motivo
(O fierce cruelty, insane frenzy, infamous crime, infernal motive).[58]

It was as a national celebrity that Drake made a special visit to the Middle Temple in 1586 following his return from plundering the Caribbean.[59] The Inns of Court had a particular financial interest in geography and exploration, and in the plantations in the Caribbean and in America that followed. This interest was well represented in the Middle Temple, of which many West Country adventurers were members, including Walter Ralegh, John Hawkins and Martin Frobisher.[60] The globes in figure 46 have a special significance in documenting the unique intellectual culture of the Inns of

'They shall be my East and West Indies, and I will trade to them both'

(*The Merry Wives of Windsor* 1.3.50)

44. Falstaff's concept of plunder and possession is akin to the thinking behind this silver medal, designed by Michael Mercator and made in 1589, commemorating Francis Drake's circumnavigation of the globe.
Obverse and reverse. Silver, diam. 6.7 cm.
British Museum, London

45. German broadside celebrating Sir Francis Drake as a Protestant hero, freedom-fighter and scourge of the Catholic Spanish, late 1580s.
Hand-coloured etching and engraving, 29 x 54 cm.
British Library, London

Court in Shakespeare's London. Maps, then globes, were part of the mental furniture of educated men, and these special globes became the actual furniture of courts, libraries, grammar schools and colleges by the late 1590s.[61] Using globes became part of a gentleman's education, as Shakespeare amusingly portrays it in *The Comedy of Errors*, in which one character compares a serving girl to a globe: 'She is spherical, like a globe. I could find out countries in her', going on to say that he could locate Ireland by the bogs, England by the chalky cliffs, Spain by her hot breath and 'America, the Indies' upon her nose, 'all o'er embellished with rubies, carbuncles, sapphires' (3.2.104–21).

The Molyneux Globes were the first English printed globes. They were made by the Englishman, Emery Molyneux, and the Netherlandish engraver, Jocodus Hondius, in London in 1592.[62] The terrestrial globe was based on Edward Wright's world map in Mercator's projection, the 'new map with the augmentation of the Indies' that Shakespeare mentions in *Twelfth Night* (3.2.52–3). It shows the most recent voyages made by English adventurers such as Frobisher in 1576–7 and Drake, as well as English settlements made by Ralegh at Roanoke, Virginia; the royal arms are blazoned over America.

The significance of this globe was not lost on the Italian ambassador, Petruccio Ubaldini, who commented that Elizabeth I could now 'see at a glance how much of the world she could control by means of her naval forces'.[63] The globes, which were closely linked with adventuring and also with the plantation of new colonies in Virginia, may have been given to the Middle Temple by one such adventurer who wanted to push the queen beyond the point of no return against the Spanish. They exemplify a growing global awareness.

Drake and his crew were the first Englishmen to travel all the way around the world. No one thereafter could doubt that we live upon a globe. But for the vast majority of Londoners who did not travel abroad – those who, as Thomas Platter put it, learned foreign matters at home – the strangeness and variety of the world and of humankind were encountered in an artificial globe: in a cluster of polygonal theatre buildings on the southern and eastern fringes of their city. And the experience of the London playhouse was one which Englishmen carried with them on their travels. The English ambassador to Mughal India, Sir Thomas Roe, was no stranger to the London theatre. When he visited the court of Jahangir he compared an audience there

'She is spherical, like a globe. I could find out countries in her'

(*The Comedy of Errors* 3.2.104–5)

46. The Molyneux Globes, made by Emery Molyneux and engraved by Jocodus Hondius, London 1592 and 1592 (updated 1603), and possibly given to the Middle Temple by a member and adventurer who wished to profit from a global push against the Spanish.
Papier mâché, plaster and printed paper, with wooden stands and brass surrounds, diam. of each 63.5 cm.
Middle Temple Library, London

to attending a performance back in London, in terms which his readers could easily envisage:

> The palace is a great court, whither resort all sorts of people. The king sits in a little Gallery over head; Ambassadors, the great men and strangers of qualety within the inmost rayle under him, raysed from the ground, Covered with Canopyes of velvet and silk, under foote layed with good carpets; the meaner men representing gentry within the first rayle, the people without in a base court, but soe that all may see the king. This sitting out hath soe much affinitye with a Theatre, the manner of the king in his gallery; the great men lifted on a stage as actors; the vulgar below, gazing on them [fig. 47].[64]

From about 1590 to 1612 William Shakespeare wrote plays for the London theatre. These dramas of love and death, of youth and age, of political intrigue and cross-cultural conflict, were witnessed by travellers from many nations. But they also represented many peoples and places, past and present. Shakespeare's audiences learned at the play what was happening abroad – or what they imagined to be happening abroad. In London in 1612, almost a world city, all the world was a stage and the stage was all the world.

47. *The Darbar of Jahangir*, attributed to Manohar or Abul Hasan, *c*. 1625. This contemporary Mughal miniature shows the ranking and partitioning of visitors at a court audience, which Sir Thomas Roe compared to a London playhouse stage and audience.
Opaque watercolour and gold on paper, 35 x 20 cm.
Museum of Fine Arts, Boston

2 'Now am I in Arden': Country, County and Custom

WILLIAM SHAKESPEARE was born in 1564, on or about 23 April, St George's Day. He was baptized in Holy Trinity Church in the market town of Stratford-upon-Avon in the Midland county of Warwickshire, on 26 April. His father was John Shakespeare (*c.* 1531–1601), a glove-maker. His mother, Mary Shakespeare (*c.* 1537–1608), was born Mary Arden, daughter of a yeoman farmer from the nearby village of Wilmcote.

Stratford was a crossroads between very different worlds. The ancient forest of Arden lay to the north, while there was rich farming land to the south. Within a hard day's walk was the university city of Oxford. To the east, and closer, were Kenilworth, home of Queen Elizabeth's favourite, Robert Dudley, Earl of Leicester (1532–1588), and Warwick, where stood (in considerable disrepair) the castle of the Earls of Warwick. Just beyond that lay Coventry, the fourth largest city in the land. At the time of Shakespeare's birth, the old biblical plays from medieval times – Creation and Flood, Crucifixion and Judgement – were still performed there annually on pageant carts stationed around town. The country and the city, the old rural ways and the new learning, the traditions of play-acting and the powerful presence of the aristocracy: some of the key resources for the creation of Shakespeare's imaginary worlds were present in his very childhood environment.

For centuries the administration of government and of the law in England had depended on the king or queen, or their representatives, notably the judges, travelling the country on 'circuits'. Shakespeare was born on the margin between the Midland circuit, which consisted of Northamptonshire, Warwickshire, Leicestershire, Derbyshire, Nottinghamshire, Rutland and Lincolnshire, and the Oxford circuit, which covered Oxfordshire, Berkshire, Worcestershire, Staffordshire, Shropshire, Herefordshire and Gloucestershire. Among the many hundreds of stage plays that

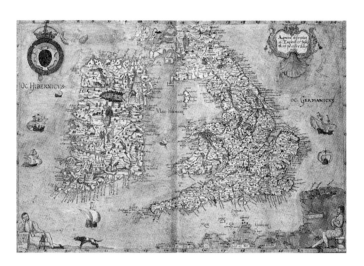

'Give me the map there'

(*King Lear* 1.1.28)

1. 'A general description of England and Ireland with the costes adioyning', Laurence Nowell, *c.* 1564, the year of Shakespeare's birth. Stratford-upon-Avon is marked.

Ink and coloured wash on vellum, 21.2 x 30.9 cm.
British Library, London

survive from his lifetime, the only ones that include scenes located in Warwickshire and Gloucestershire are his. His territory, then, was the Midlands. In the national imagination, 'Shakespeare country' would eventually become synonymous with 'Middle England'.[1]

In the year that he was born it became possible to visualize the shape and disposition of the counties or shires for the first time. Laurence Nowell's 'A general description of England and Ireland' (fig. 1) was made for Sir William Cecil, later Lord Burghley (1521–1598). Stratford-upon-Avon is marked near its centre. Six years into the reign of Elizabeth I, it shows a view of Englishness and nationhood as Shakespeare's generation experienced it. It demonstrates a new degree of accuracy in mapmaking and incorporates Nowell's research into local surveys, drafts of other maps and, perhaps, books and papers in Cecil's possession. The map provided a visual record of a wealth of information that was valuable for the government of the nation. The relationship between Cecil and Nowell as patron and client is amusingly shown in the lower corners. Cecil is shown sitting on an hourglass with arms folded and a stern expression, as if to indicate he has waited long enough for the map. At lower left, Nowell is shown leaning wearily on one arm, propped up against a stone tablet with his initials, LN, carved into it. His pose is that of a contemporary tomb monument, and his weary expression is partly due to the fact that he is being vigorously barked at by a dog. The map, a small version of which Cecil

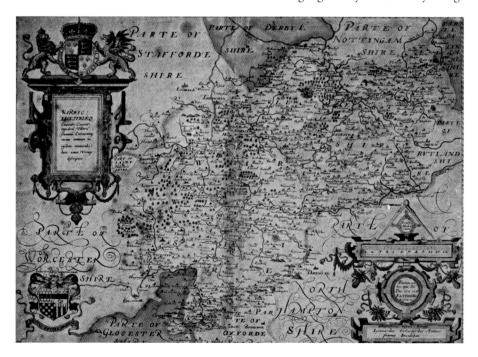

allegedly carried with him at all times, improves on earlier cartographic ventures in several respects. But its accuracy was less important than its purpose: maps were instruments of power, not objects for helping people find their way when travelling. On the two occasions when maps are used as props in Shakespeare's play, the context is not route-finding but the division of the kingdom, in one case between the rebels in *Henry IV Part 1* ('Come, here's the map: shall we divide our right / According to our threefold order ta'en?' 3.1.69–70) and in the other between the three daughters of King Lear ('Give me the map there' *King Lear* 1.1.28).

In Nowell's map the separate kingdom of Scotland is present for the first time – only sketched in, but with Edinburgh in a reasonably correct location. The map gestures towards Queen Elizabeth I's pride, inherited from her father, Henry VIII, in the unification of England and Wales into a single nation: it shows 'Wales beyond the Severn shore' (*Henry IV Part 1* 3.1.75) in some detail, defining the Caernarvon peninsula of north Wales. Ireland is clearly a problem from the English viewpoint presented here in that there is a particular interest in noting the Gaelic landholding patterns and the names of harbours in the ungovernable southwest of Munster. The fact that this map was made for Cecil indicates the importance of maps as political tools; of bureaucracy and surveying the land as a means of control; and of Cecil as the man, under Elizabeth I, who held the country together.[2]

'In Warwickshire I have true-hearted friends' says the Earl of Warwick in *Henry VI Part 3* (4.8.9). Christopher Saxton's map of Warwickshire and Leicestershire (fig. 2) is the earliest accurate map of Shakespeare's home county. Engraved and hand-coloured, it was reissued in 1579 as part of Saxton's survey of thirty-four maps of counties to

3. Elizabeth I ('The Ditchley Portrait'), Marcus Gheeraerts the Younger, *c.* 1592. Elizabeth I is presented as a divinity, standing on the globe with her feet on Saxton's map of Oxfordshire.
Oil on canvas, 241.3 x 152.4 cm.
National Portrait Gallery, London

'In Warwickshire I have true-hearted friends'

(*Henry VI Part 3* 4.8.9)

2. Map of Warwickshire and Leicestershire, Christopher Saxton, 1576. Hand-coloured engraving showing Shakespeare's native county, first published in 1576 and then reissued by Saxton in 1579 as part of the first national atlas to appear for any country.
49.7 x 37 cm. Shakespeare Birthplace Trust, Stratford-upon-Avon

NORTHAMPTŌS the 8 of y East hath Miles
In Quantitie superficiall 539 In Circuite 123
In Length from Lincolnshire to Oxfordshire 48
In Bredth from Warwickshire to Bedford 22

NORTHAMPTŌS much Inhabited with nobilit
Very plesaunt & fertile, ritch in corne, and sheepe
Hauinge Huntingtō & Bedford East Warwick West
Rutland & Lincoln North Oxford & Buck South

THIS mayden queene, like Debora doth raign
She by hir wisdom, and hir constant zeale
In peace, and plentie, doth gods worde maintaine,
Would god J coulde hir vertues all reveale

TWISE sixteene yeares y scepter in hir had,
No traitors could, nor forraie foes wrest out:
Great warres abrode, yet god defends hir land,
Lord let thy Angells, compasse hir aboute

EDWARD the 3 did add this armes of Fraūc
And Henry 5 made Fraunce to Brittaine yeelde
But civill warres, did breede vs this mischaunce
Smale gaynes remaynes of that well foughte fedd

KINGE Henrie 7, from strife the state restorde
To Henrie right, he left it in great welth
He wise and boulde, good happ his fates afford
But in his doughter most Lord bleß hir helth

WARWICKS the 9 of the East hath Miles
In Quantitie superficiall 555 In Circuite 122
In Length from Staffordshire to Oxford 37
In Bredth from Lecestershire to Worcester 28

WARWICKS one pte champion, thother wooddland
Aboundinge with corne & graße, well Inhabited
Hauinge Lecester & Northāp East Worcest West
Lecester & Stafford North Glo & Oxo South

FROM East to West Londō is most in Lengthe,
The Bredth therof is from the North to South:
What place so fit for pleasure store & strength,
And for all trades, and trayninge vp of youth

FOR fruitfull ground, for riuer, and good ayre,
For store of welth, of people, and of powre,
Did Troye att any tyme, seeme halfe so faire,
As doth hir doughter Londō att this hour

THVS much in Miles whole Englād it cōtaines 34863
Thus much in Miles will reatch aboute it rounde 1800
Hir Length from Lizard point to Barwick is 334
Twixt Douer Holyhead the breedth is founde 250

AMOGST good neigbors thus doth Englād stand
Each shire presents first letter of hir name
For other worthie places in this land
My fiftie two pticulers haue the same

4. Playing cards with maps of English and Welsh counties. Stratford is marked with an S on the map of Warwickshire. Designed by William Bowes and engraved by Augustine Ryther in 1590, this is the earliest known set of cards with English county maps.
Hand-coloured engravings, 9.5 x 5.7 cm.
British Museum, London

form a national atlas, the first anywhere. His maps were the model for all English maps for almost two centuries. No roads are shown, but rather a network of rivers. Stratford's importance here is as a ford across the Avon. Kenilworth can also be seen, as Leicester's seat, and Arden, the forest with its Celtic name. The availability of Saxton's maps meant that for the first time educated English people could get a sense of how their county or region related to others, a sense of its distinct geography and character.[3]

The coloured counties of Saxton's maps are clearly visible beneath the feet of Queen Elizabeth in the famous 'Ditchley Portrait' of her by Marcus Gheeraerts II (or 'the Younger') (fig. 3), executed around 1592, just at the time when Shakespeare's acting and writing career was beginning to bring him into the view of the royal court. One of the few full-length portraits of Elizabeth, it was probably commissioned by Sir Henry Lee of Ditchley Park, Oxfordshire (1533–1611), who entertained the queen in 1592. As the Queen's Champion he knew the chivalric conventions beloved of the queen and enacted annually in ceremonial jousts on the anniversary of her accession to the throne. He could accordingly turn his hand to the right kind of allegorical poetic tribute. Here Elizabeth is depicted standing on the curved surface of the earth, represented as a globe, with Ditchley at the toe of her left foot and Oxford beneath it. The representation of Oxfordshire is from Saxton's coloured map. The sonnet to the right compares the queen's divinely ordained powers to those of Nature herself. She is an icon of majesty, standing on the map to show how she commands the loyalties of her subjects – in this case Lee and his Ditchley powerbase – but also how she embodies the nation itself.[4]

It is notable that this key image in the national self-imagining and mythologizing owes so much to the immigrant contribution to English culture. Gheeraerts was at the heart of the London community of immigrants from the Low Countries. His father, Marcus Gheeraerts the Elder, was born in Bruges, but fled from religious persecution to England in 1568 with his young son. In London he married his second wife, Sussanah de Critz, herself a member of an exiled family from Antwerp. She was a close relative of Queen Elizabeth I's serjeant-painter, John de Critz, and one of her daughters by Gheeraerts the Elder would marry the French-born English miniaturist Isaac Oliver. Gheeraerts the Younger, meanwhile, married de Critz's sister. His immigrant status was no obstacle to his pursuit of patronage: having been taken up by Lee in the 1590s, he was much admired by King James I's wife, Queen Anne of Denmark, in the early years of the new century.

As Shakespeare's plays reached both the court and the ordinary people of London, so Saxton's maps were diffused into popular culture as well as high art. An astonishing and rare set of playing cards with English county maps appeared in London around the time that Shakespeare began his theatrical career. The complete pack of fifty-two cards was assembled in sheets to be cut out and pasted on to the cards by the owner (fig. 4). Each card is printed with an engraved map of one of the counties of England or Wales. Suits are distinguished by the inner frame around the maps, and cards within

'Wast born i' th' forest here?'

(As You Like It 5.1.17)

5. 'The Sheldon tapestry map of Warwickshire'. Perhaps made in the Sheldon tapestry workshop at Barcheston, Warwickshire or in London, *c.* 1588. This is the only complete map of a series showing four Midland counties, woven for Ralph Sheldon to decorate his house at Weston, Warwickshire. North is on the left.
Tapestry-woven in wool and silk, approx. 390 x 510 cm.
Warwickshire Museums Service, Warwick

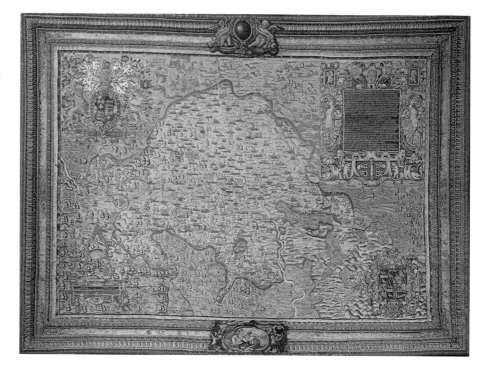

6. Portrait of Ralph Sheldon, commissioner of the 'Sheldon tapestry' map series, by Hieronimo Custodis, *c.* 1590.
Oil on canvas, 92 x 77.5 cm.
Warwickshire Museums Service, Warwick

each suit are numbered one to thirteen. The set would have been confusing to use for many card games, but not perhaps for lotto-type games, when the name of the card, the county, would have been called out. A modern analogy might be the game of Top Trumps: card games in Shakespeare's plays seem to involve winning with a high number. Thus Tranio in *The Taming of the Shrew*: 'I have faced it with a card of ten' (2.1.407); and Aaron describing the bad boys and their wicked mother Tamora in *Titus Andronicus*: 'That codding spirit had they from their mother, / As sure a card as ever won the set' (5.1.100–1). As with the famous chess scene in *The Tempest*, cheating at games was a favoured metaphor for larger-scale deceit: 'She, Eros, has / Packed cards with Caesar, and false-played my glory / Unto an enemy's triumph' (*Antony and Cleopatra* 4.14.21–3).

The maps on the cards are schematic miniatures, showing river courses, hills and woodland. Principal towns are indicated by their initial – Stratford is marked on the Warwickshire card – and information is given as to the area of each county, distances and the commodities produced there. In addition to the playing cards there are a further eight introductory cards, one with a portrait of the queen modelled on that in Saxton's 1579 survey, one with a map of England and Wales, one with a bird's-eye view of London, inscribed: 'Lo London now with Paris maye compare / For learned men, for valient men, with Rome: / With Ormus eke, for every kind of ware / O Lord grant London, long in blisse to blome.' Another card with the royal arms and cipher is inscribed 'W.B. inuen. 1590', indicating that the designer of the cards was William Bowes. The sheets of cards were engraved by Augustine Ryther, who had engraved four

7. Fragment from 'The Sheldon tapestry map of Oxfordshire' showing Ralph Sheldon's arms, *c.* 1588.
Wool and silk, 122 x 61.5 cm.
Victoria and Albert Museum, London

of the county maps for Saxton's survey of 1579.[5]

The remarkable set of tapestry maps known as the 'Sheldon tapestries' was another spin-off from Saxton's survey, showing the excitement generated by the maps that were published as a set in 1579. The Warwickshire map (fig. 5) that gives prominence to the Forest of Arden, which loomed over Shakespeare's imaginative world, was one of a set of four tapestries showing the Midland counties of England commissioned by Ralph Sheldon (1537–1613) for his house at Weston, near Long Compton in Warwickshire, around 1588, probably as a unique decorative scheme for a particular room in the house.[6] This would explain the odd orientation of the maps: it would have made it possible to fit the counties on to the walls of the room. Two of the surviving maps have north at the top, as we would now expect, but the other two – this one and Gloucestershire – have east at the top. These were the counties in which Sheldon lived, owned land, and had friends and family connections. The total length of the set would have been 21 metres, showing England from London in the east to the Bristol Channel in the west in a single Midlands sweep. The artistic conception is remarkable, but the fact that these maps are made of tapestry – woven pictures made on a loom, the vertical threads (warp) made of wool and the horizontal threads (weft) of silk – makes them even more extraordinary. Tapestry maps are very unusual. The inspiration for this set may have been the painted cloth showing Oxfordshire and Berkshire at Leicester's seat in Kenilworth, but this is much richer and more ambitious.[7] This rare survival in tapestry is a representation of unusual warmth and character, evoking the weathered landscape of the county that Shakespeare knew so intimately.

The origin of the Sheldon tapestries is debated. The traditional view is that they were commissioned in the tapestry workshops of William Sheldon, Ralph's father, at Barcheston; the weaving was probably carried out by local men.[8] It is possible, however, that the tapestries were woven by Flemish weavers in a London workshop, given the kind of skills shortage which demanded English patrons to 'abandone our owne countraymen and resort unto straungers' if they should wish to have 'anything well paynted, kerved or embrawdred', as Sir Thomas Elyot noted, rather acidly, in *The Book Named the Governour* (1531).[9]

Given the times and place in which he lived, an important element in Ralph Sheldon the Elder's makeup was his Catholicism. His portrait by Hieronimo Custodis in figure 6 perhaps suggests the tension that this caused him. It was painted in around 1590, showing Sheldon dressed in sober and expensive black at the age of fifty-three, after he had been regularly under house arrest in the 1580s, a difficult decade for Catholics in England.[10] He managed later to keep out of the Gunpowder Plot despite its local roots (see Chapter 7, p. 189).[11] His wish to display his loyalty to the queen as well as proclaim his own standing in the Midland counties is shown on each of the tapestry maps by the presence of the royal arms as well as his own. The detail from a border fragment of the Oxfordshire map in figure 7 shows his arms with the mythical Erymanthian boar, showing how the heroic classical past was intermingled with the present.[12]

WARWIKSHEAR:SONAMIDASWELBY:THE:SAXONS:AS:OF:VS:AT:THIS
DAYE:IT:IS:DEVIDED:IN:TWO:PARTS:BY:THE:RIVER:AVON:RONNINGE
THROVCH:THE:MIDEST:THE:ON:IS:CALLED:FELDON:THE:OTHER:WOOD
LAND:THE:MOST:MEMORABLE:TOWNES:IN:THE:FELDON:ARE:LEMINGTON
TAKING:THE:NAME:OF:THE:RIVER:LEAM:WHERE:A:SALT:WELL:SPRINGETH
ICHINGTON:AND:HARBVRY:BETWENE:WHICH:TWO:TOWNES:FREMVDVS
THE:SONN:OF:KINGE:OFFA:WAS:SLAYN:A:MAN:OF:SINGVLER:VERTVE
AND:WAS:BVRIED:IN:HIS:FATHERS:PALACE:CALLED:OF:CHVRCH
THE:WOODLAND:BEINGE:THE:NORTH:PART:AND:THE:GREATER:WAS
BY:AN:AVNCIENT:NAME:CALLED:ARDEN:WHICH:SIGNIFIETH:A:WOOD
IN:THE:MIDLE:OF:THIS:REGION:STANDETH:COVENTRE:SO:CALLED:OF
THE:COVENT:OR:MONKES:A:CITIE:IN:TIMES:PASTE:POPVLVS:AND
RICHE:BY:THE:TRADE:OF:CLOTHING:AND:MAKING:OF:CAPPES
NEAR:COVENTRE:ON:THE:EAST:PART:IS:CALEDOM:THE:AVNGLENTS
SEAT:OF:THE:LORDE:SECRAVE:FROM:WHOM:IT:IS:DESCENDED
TO:THE:BARONS:OF:BARKLEY:BYTH:MOWBRAIES:DVKES:OF:NORTHFOLK
WESTWARD:FROM:COVENTRE:STANDETH:THE:CASTLE:OF:KENELWO
RTH:COMPASSED:ABOVT:WITH:A:GREAT:POOL:FIRSTE:BIVLDED:BY
IEFFREY:CLINTON:CHAMBERLAYNE:TO:KINGE:HENRE:THE:FIRST
ABOVT:V:MILES:FROM:THENCE:STANDETH:WARWICKE:CALLED:BY
THE:BRITAYNES:CAER:GVARVIC:WHICH:SIGNIFIETH:A:PLACE:OF
DEFENCE:WHEAR:IS:A:CASTLE:OF:GREAT:FORCE:BIVLDED:BY:THE
ROMANES:WILLIAM:THE:CONQVEROR:ORDEYNED:XII:BVRGESSES:IN
WARWICKE:TO:ATTENDE:ON:HIM:IN:HIS:WARRES
NEAR:VNTO:WARWICK:IS:GVYES:CLIFFE:A:PLACE:OF:WONDERFVL
PLEASVRE:WHEAR:GVYE:OF:WARWICKE:BVILDED:A:CHAPPEL
AND:WAS:THERE:BVRIED::READ:W:CAMDEN:HIS:DISCRIPCION:OF:BRI

8. Detail from 'The Sheldon tapestry map of Warwickshire' (fig. 5), showing text describing the county, derived from William Camden's *Britannia*.

Each of the Sheldon maps has a cartouche with a long English text based on material in William Camden's vast antiquarian survey of the nation, *Britannia*, first printed in Latin in 1586 but not translated into English until 1610. The fusion of information derived from Camden and from Saxton, woven in tapestry, make the maps unique records of English regional sensibility in Shakespeare's day.[13] Perhaps as a result of the influence of Camden, who was fascinated by ancient British history, ancient sites appear on the Warwickshire map, among them the Rollright Stones near Long Compton, the Brailes burial mound and the Stretton Roman road. The Warwickshire text (fig. 8) also mentions Guy of Warwick, a legendary local hero whose fight with Colbrand the Giant is mentioned in both *King John* (1.1.226) and *Henry VIII* (5.3.19). As testimony to their true Warwickshire pedigree, the Arden family claimed descent from Guy.

Shakespeare's sense of his own locality would have been dominated by the houses and estates of the great. When he was a young man, his family became involved in a dispute over a mortgage with some kinsmen, the Lamberts, who lived in Barton-on-the-Heath, some miles south of Stratford. It was the next village to Long Compton, so he would have come within the purview of the Sheldons' land and of the Rollright Stones. The tapestries reveal a vivid sense of the significance of the seats of the gentry and the aristocracy by giving individual character to Weston and other Sheldon family houses. Some of the houses selected are those of fellow Catholics, and all are associated with friends, if not kin. The map represents a local, educated gentleman's-eye view of the Midlands, with more than a tinge of Catholicism. It is as if the kinship networks of recusant families are woven into the very landscape.[14] We are given a vivid reminder of the prevalence of the old Catholic ways in the communities of Shakespeare's early years.

The Warwickshire map offers bird's-eye views of towns such as Lichfield and Coventry, and Stratford-upon-Avon itself (fig. 9), but also shows small villages, including Wilmcote (home of the Ardens, Shakespeare's mother's family), Snitterfield (where his father's family farmed before John Shakespeare moved into Stratford and entered the glover's trade), Temple Grafton and Shottery (the places associated with his wife, Anne Hathaway). Clifford Chambers, the first village Shakespeare would have passed through whenever he set off for London, is shown, as is Bishopton, where the chapel is one of the candidates for the location of Shakespeare's marriage (see Chapter 1, pp. 26–7).

The map depicts several great deer parks, such as the Queen's Park at Kenilworth. According to a well-attested early tradition Shakespeare poached from the park at Charlecote of the local grandee, Sir Thomas Lucy (1532–1600). Regardless of the

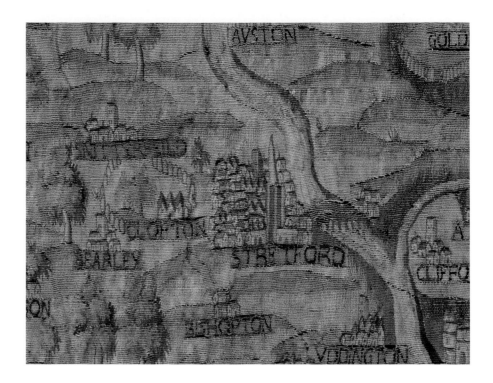

9. Detail from 'The Sheldon tapestry map of Warwickshire' (fig. 5) showing Stratford.

veracity of the story that he went to London and became a player in order to escape punishment for this crime, there can be no doubt that the country pursuits of hunting, poaching and falconry provided a rich seam of imagery throughout his work. His name became well known in 1593 when, the theatres being closed to prevent the spread of plague infection, he published his long poem, *Venus and Adonis* (see further Chapter 4, pp. 126–30). This became the bestselling poem of the age not only because of its verbal dexterity, its skilful imitation of the great Roman poet Ovid and its witty eroticism, but also because of its fresh and 'lively' (lifelike) animations of the wild wood and the hunting of boar and hare.

The tapestry bed valance with hunting scenes illustrated here (fig. 10) also seems to have come from the Sheldon workshops in Warwickshire during Shakespeare's lifetime. Brightly coloured and almost unused, it was designed to be hung, above heavy curtains, around the top of a posted bed, which would have been a household's most valuable piece of furniture.[15] On this Elizabethan valance men and women are shown hunting, hawking and conversing in an idealized landscape. We see couples who look as if they have stepped straight from the Forest of Arden in *As You Like It*, gathered under a tree and accompanied by a fool and the music of bagpipes. Different vignettes – scenes in the theatrical sense – are separated by vases of fruit and flowers. Borders worked with flowers and plants add to the abundance, creating a pastoral idyll that was inspired as much by real landscapes as by classical literary precedents.

The pastoral convention idealizes the past and the country in order to criticise the values of the present and the court. But in *As You Like It* Shakespeare refuses to view

'I remember when I was in love'

(*As You Like It* 2.4.38)

10. Valance to be hung around the top of a posted bed together with curtains, with a design of lovers and hunting scenes. Perhaps woven in the Sheldon tapestry workshops at Barcheston in Warwickshire or London, *c.* 1600–10.

Tapestry in silk and wool, with some silver thread, 25 x 534 cm. Victoria and Albert Museum, London

the Arden of his youth through rose-tinted spectacles. The forest order, based on hunting and old customs of hospitality, is contrasted sharply with the intrigue, flattery and ambition of the court, but at the same time the harsh realities of country life are exposed. The hunt is viewed from the point of view of the deer as well as the fired-up hunters, and the plight of the tenant farmer, at the mercy of his landlord, is revealed in the figure of Corin. Nevertheless, Shakespeare shared with many of his contemporaries a strong degree of nostalgia for an older way of life, a lost 'golden age' (which never really existed) of harmonious relations within society as well as between humans and their natural environment. The forest, ruled over by its own royal law, was often the locus for that nostalgia. Dr Johnson noted in his 1755 dictionary under 'modern' that Shakespeare used the word nine times in the plays, after its Latin derivation *modernus*, to mean 'vulgar, mean and common'.[16] If that was the meaning of modernity, then what the duke in *As You Like It* calls 'old custom' (2.1.2) would have seemed all the more attractive. As in many of Shakespeare's *Sonnets*, there is a sense of 'Devouring Time' (*Sonnet* 19.1) and the world simply getting older. The Jesuit John Gerard, in his

preface to his autobiography of around 1609, states that it was written 'in this last era of a declining and gasping world'.[17]

There is no avoiding the fact that a sporting, as opposed to a subsistence, relationship with the natural world was the preserve of the social elite. Another tapestry fragment (fig. 11) shows a young well-dressed gentleman, set in a green landscape. He wears hat, doublet and trunk hose, and stands with his hawk on his wrist while his dog looks up expectantly. He holds a dead bird, possibly a duck, in his other hand. This is from a tapestry border woven in silk on a wool warp, the kind of domestic furnishing that brought idealized hunting and country scenes indoors for the middling sort: to hang such a thing in one's house was to display one's aspiration to gentility. Such decoration would have befitted John Shakespeare's status as High Bailiff, effectively mayor, of Stratford-upon-Avon.

But fortune was fickle. Having risen to the top in local government, John Shakespeare ran into financial difficulties and stopped attending council meetings. For the rest of his life he was overshadowed by debt and disgrace. The Elizabethans, living

in an age of disease, infection and financial turbulence, had a strong sense of the precariousness of well-being. The figure in the tapestry bears an uncanny resemblance to a very similar figure from a print, labelled as an emblem of earthly vanity (fig. 12). Entitled 'The misery of mans life' [*sic*], it is annotated: 'Behold and see, thy stat and dignitie / Is wormes meate, dust and ashes, / Live to dye'.[18]

It was in the context of John Shakespeare's social disgrace and financial decline that his son William sought to restore the family fortune and name. No one could have predicted, however, that he would do so through going to London and making money from the disreputable trade of play-acting. The circumstances under which he left his home town remain unknown, with many different theories as to how he spent the 'lost years' between the baptism of his children in the early 1580s and the first records of him in the London theatre world of the early 1590s. But nothing could better sum up the transformation in his status than two stories, one of which may be apocryphal and the other of which is exceptionally well documented: the poaching story and the acquisition of a coat of arms for the family (the latter is discussed at the end of this chapter). Both involve country sports.

The Charlecote hawking vervel (fig. 13) is a flat silver ring inscribed with the name 'Sir Thomas Luci ... of Charlecote'. The vervel was used to connect the leather

12. A man hawking, from Thomas Trevelyon's *Miscellany*, 1608.
Pen and ink with hand-colouring, 42 x 26.5 cm.
Folger Shakespeare Library, Washington DC

13. Silver hawking vervel inscribed with the name of Sir Thomas Lucy at Charlecote, Warwickshire, one of three squires of that name between 1551 and 1640, found locally in 2005.
Diam. 1 cm. Warwickshire Museums Service, Warwick

thongs or jesses on a hawk's legs to the leash which ties the bird to the block. Vervels are inscribed with the name, crest or arms of the bird's owner and the place of origin, in this case Sir Thomas Lucy's seat at Charlecote. This example was recently found less than a mile away on what is now Wellesbourne airfield.[19] It belonged to one of three Lucys of that name between 1551 and 1640. The first of them was the Sir Thomas from whose park Shakespeare allegedly poached game: several versions of this story circulated in the seventeenth century, making it more likely to have some truth than some of the later stories about why Shakespeare left Stratford. Whether the story is true or apocryphal, once he began writing plays he displayed his detailed technical knowledge of genteel country pursuits. To revel in such language was to become, as it were, poacher turned sportsman.

There is another old tradition linking Shakespeare to the art of falconry. When he married the pregnant Anne Hathaway it is said that the ceremony was performed not at Stratford or Bishopton, but at Temple Grafton, by the old priest John Frith, a relic from the reign of Queen Mary. He was described in a biased Puritan survey of Warwickshire clergy as 'Unsound in religion, he can neither preach nor read well, his chiefest trade is to cure hawks that are hurt or diseased, for which purpose many do usually repair to him'.[20] It is somehow fitting that Shakespeare may well have been married by a man who was renowned less for his adherence to the old Catholic ways than for his role as a vet for local falconers.

Shakespeare writes about hawking and falconry as part of the traditional medieval language of erotic love, but with a real immediacy derived from his country origins. Romeo refers to Juliet as his 'nyas' or young hawk which has yet to fly, while she refers to him as a young male falcon or 'tassel-gentle' (*Romeo and Juliet* 2.1.211–20). Romeo compares the sound of a man and woman's voices to that of the silver bells, a semitone apart, which are tied on to a hawk's legs with leather thongs (jesses) sounding on the night air: 'How silver-sweet sound lovers' tongues by night / Like softest music to attending ears!' (2.1.217–8).[21] The sound was as instantly recognizable as the emotion. Petruchio in *The Taming of the Shrew* talks about how to 'man my haggard' (3.3.156) and Othello, doubting Desdemona's chastity, vows: 'If I do prove her haggard, / Though that her jesses were my dear heartstrings, / I'd whistle her off and let her down the wind / To prey at fortune' (*Othello* 3.3.290–3). A haggard was a wild female hawk caught when in her adult plumage, thus suggesting a wild and intractable woman.

Command of such technical language was a mark of insider status. On his arrival in England as a hidden priest, John Gerard SJ gives a fascinating account of pretending to be a falconer who has lost his falcon, and the usefulness of hawking terms in contemporary English society:

> When I got the opportunity I spoke about hunting and falconry, a thing no one could do in correct technical language unless he was familiar with the sports. It is an easy thing to trip up in one's terms, as Father Southwell used to complain. Frequently, as he was travelling about with me later, he would ask me to tell him the correct terms and worried because he could not remember and use them when need arose: for instance, when he fell in with Protestant gentlemen who had practically no other conversation except, perhaps, obscene subjects or rant against the saints and the Catholic faith. On occasions like this there is often a chance of bringing the talk round to some other topic simply by throwing out a remark about horses or hounds or the like.[22]

The copy of *Venus and Adonis* seen here (fig. 14), the poem that established Shakespeare's name as a writer, is open at the much-admired description of the 'dew-bedabbled wretch', Wat the hare (703). Warwickshire and neighbouring Gloucestershire were especially known for hare coursing. In *The Merry Wives of Windsor*, Slender, the Gloucestershire Justice of the Peace, refers to Page's greyhound being 'outrun on Cotsall' (1.1.59–60). This is a reference to the annual Cotswold games, where the hunting of hares with greyhounds was among the most popular events. Annual country sports days were well established in the region, though it was only in 1612, near the end of Shakespeare's life, that the Cotswold Olympics were set up by Robert Dover.[23]

As so often, Shakespeare has it both ways in *Venus and Adonis*. The poem displays

'the deaw-bedabelled wretch'

(Venus and Adonis 703)

14. *Venus and Adonis*, first printed by Richard Field, London, 1593, this copy (the only one to survive) is open at the passage concerning the hunting of Wat the hare.
Printed book, approx. 18 x 13 cm.
Bodleian Library, Oxford

VENVS AND ADONIS.

For there his fmell with others being mingled,
The hot fent-fnuffing hounds are driuen to doubt,
Ceafing their clamorous crie, till they haue fingled
VVith much ado the cold fault cleanlie out,
  Then do they fpend their mouth's, eccho replies,
    As if an other chafe were in the skies.

By this poore wat farre off vpon a hill,
Stands on his hinder-legs with liftning eare,
To hearken if his foes purfue him ftill,
Anon their loud alarums he doth heare,
  And now his griefe may be compared well,
    To one fore ficke, that heares the paffing bell.

Then fhalt thou fee the deaw-bedabbled wretch,
Turne, and returne, indenting with the way,
Ech enuious brier, his wearie legs do fcratch,
Ech fhadow makes him ftop, ech murmour ftay,
  For miferie is troden on by manie,
    And being low, neuer releeu'd by anie.

Lye quietly, and heare a litle more,
Nay do not ftruggle, for thou fhalt not rife,
To make thee hate the hunting of the bore,
Vnlike my felfe thou hear'ft me moralize,
  Applying this to that, and fo to fo,
    For loue can comment vpon euerie wo,

                 VVhere

his classical learning (it is based on Ovid's *Metamorphoses*) and it relishes in the customs, language and dress of the elite. Yet at the same time, by entering into the sensibility of the hunted hare, he shows his characteristic sympathy for the victim and the outsider. We can assume that at some point in the 1580s he left Stratford on foot, in search of a fortune and an opportunity to restore the family name. With the publication in 1593 of *Venus and Adonis*, dedicated to a great lord and read by the brightest students of Cambridge and most well-connected young gentlemen of the Inns of Court in London, he would have been in a position to hire a horse for his occasional return trips to Stratford. Whether or not we believe another old story, that his first break into the theatre world came when he held the horses of the gentlemen who had ridden to the playhouse, he certainly showed as

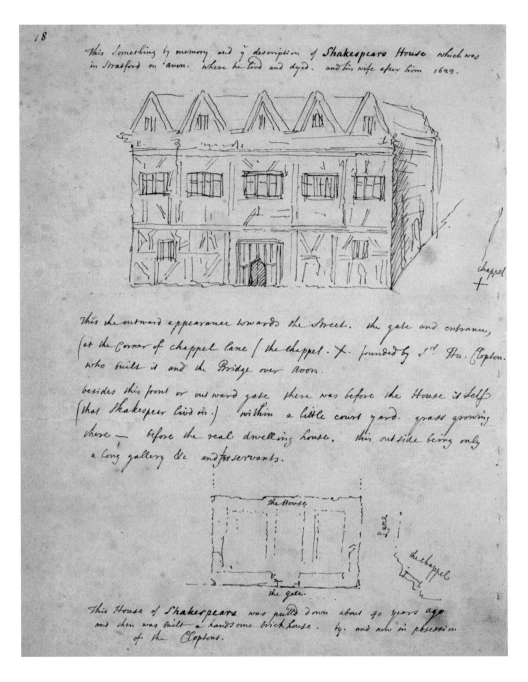

15. Shakespeare's house in Stratford, New Place, acquired in 1597, as drawn by George Vertue in 1737.
Pen and ink, 8.5 x 14 cm. British Library, London

much technical knowledge of horse matters as he did of hunting:

… his horse hipped, with an old mothy saddle and stirrups of no kindred: besides, possessed with the glanders and like to mose in the chine, troubled with the lampass, infected with the fashions, full of windgalls, sped with spavins, rayed with yellows, past cure of the fives, stark spoiled with the

staggers, begnawn with the bots, swayed in the back and shoulder-shotten, near-legged before and with a half-checked bit and a head-stall of sheep's leather which, being restrained to keep him from stumbling, hath been often burst and now repaired with knots, one girth six times pieced, and a woman's crupper of velure, which hath two letters for her name fairly set down in studs, and here and there pieced with packthread.
(*The Taming of the Shrew* 3.2.43–52)

In 1597 Shakespeare had accumulated enough money, from his writing, acting and above all his shareholding in his theatre company, to purchase New Place, the second-largest house in Stratford-upon-Avon (fig. 15). Whereas other successful men of the theatre, such as Edward Alleyn, founder of Dulwich College, accumulated property and influence in London, Shakespeare lived in cheap rented accommodation when in London and used his money to invest in property and status back in Stratford. New Place had an especially fine garden, with a vine that was a talking point even after Shakespeare's death.[24] Shakespeare and his wife doubtless had a gardener to do the hard spadework for them, but his plays are highly sensitive to horticulture and what has been called the 'herbal economy' of the age.[25] Perdita in *The Winter's Tale* refers to using a dibbler used for planting seedlings: 'I'll not put / The dibble in earth to set one slip of them' (4.4.115–16). We have not found Perdita's dibbler, but we can illustrate a spade and a watering pot (figs. 16–17) of the kind used for gardening in the seventeenth century.

16. Drainage spade used for gardening, 1700s.
Ash clad with iron, L. 110 cm.
Shakespeare Birthplace Trust, Stratford-upon-Avon

17. Watering-pot, 1500s.
Lead-glazed earthenware, H. 31.5 cm.
British Museum, London

'streaked gillyvors,
Which some call nature's
bastards'

(*The Winter's Tale* 4.4.93–4)

'The marigold that goes to
bed wi'th'sun
And with him rises weeping'

(*The Winter's Tale* 4.4.121–2)

18–19. *Gillyflower and Privet Hawk Moth* and *Pot
Marigold and Green-veined White Butterfly*, Jacques
Le Moyne, from an album signed and dated 1585.
Watercolour and bodycolour, gillyflower 21.5 x 14 cm;
marigold 20.7 x 14.5 cm. British Museum, London

Perdita's emblematic disquisition on art and nature, in which she prefers simple flowers to hybrids resulting from grafting, points to Shakespeare's eye for native, wild spring flowers. He offers in poetry something akin to what Jacques Le Moyne (*c.* 1533–1588) offered visually in his exquisite contemporaneous drawings. A close observer of nature, Le Moyne and his fellow Flemish and French Protestant immigrants in the Lime Street district of London were laying the ground for modern empirical natural history. Le Moyne's patron, Mary Sidney (1561–1621), was herself an author of dramatic poetry.

The botanist John Parkinson, in his *Garden of all Sorts of Pleasant Flowers* (1629), described gillyflowers, shown here in one of Le Moyne's delicate drawings (fig. 18), as 'the chiefest flowers of account in all our English gardens … the queen of delight and of flowers … they flower not until the heat of the year, which is in July, and continue flowering until the colds of the autumn

'Daffodils
That come before the swallow
dares, and take
The winds of March with beauty'

(*The Winter's Tale* 4.4.136–8)

'There's rosemary, that's for
remembrance'

(*Hamlet* 4.4.180)

20–1. *Daffodil* and *Rosemary and Lackey Moth Caterpillar*, Jacques Le Moyne, from an album signed and dated 1585.
Watercolour and bodycolour, daffodil 21.7 x 14.8 cm; rosemary 21.5 x 14.2 cm. British Museum, London

check them, or until they have wholly outspent themselves, and these fair flowers are usually increased by slips.'[26] But Perdita does not have these flowers of high summer (the time of the sheep-shearing feast) in her garden as she does not like grafting: 'I care not / To get slips of them' (*The Winter's Tale* 4.4.95–6). She sees marigolds (fig. 19) as flowers of 'middle Summer' for middle-aged men, and 'Daffodils / That come before the swallow dares, and take / The winds of March with beauty' (4.4.123, 136–8) as flowers suitable for youth (fig. 20). The same feeling pervades the opening sonnet of Le Moyne's album of plant drawings, dedicated to Mary Sidney and signed and dated 1585: 'La moindre fleurette / Nous demonstre un Prin-temps d'immortelles couleurs' ('The least little flower / shows us a spring of immortal colours'). Ophelia is another character who famously reminds the Shakespearean audience in London of the herbal economy (fig. 21).

The theatres themselves were on the edge of the city, close to nature in a way that London theatres are no longer: the herbalist John Gerard, in his famous *Herball* (1597), noted 'a special double-flowered crowsfoot in a field next unto the Theatre by London'. He also observed pennyroyal growing in a crevice by a door by Chaucer's tomb in Westminster Abbey.[27]

Hamlet's cruel jibe that Ophelia should go to a nunnery creates an aura whereby her plant lore evokes the old religion and its rituals. Modern commentators suggest that the destruction of the great monastic gardens and their tradition of horticulture, and the redistribution of monastic lands, led to new developments in gardening practice and awareness in a wider population.[28] At the same time, gardens were places of spiritual refreshment for Protestant men and women.[29] Meanwhile, the increasing availability of reasonably priced books meant that manuals for housewives on the medicinal uses of plants began to appear.

The embroidering of horticultural motifs, too, was a feminine art. Thus Helena to Hermia in *A Midsummer Night's Dream* (3.2.204–9):

> We, Hermia, like two artificial gods,
> Have with our needles created both one flower,
> Both on one sampler, sitting on one cushion,
> Both warbling of one song, both in one key,
> As if our hands, our sides, voices and minds,
> Had been incorporate.

Needlework forged a close alliance between women.[30] The point of this speech is to show how this bond has been ruptured by rivalry over men.

Pregnancy was also a time when women surrounded themselves with other women, creating a wholly female world: this is beautifully evoked in the figure of Hermione in the early scenes of *The Winter's Tale*. An embroidered linen jacket, unlined and informal, is loose-fitting in a way that suggests it might have been a pregnancy garment worn by a woman at home (fig. 22).[31] This garment has very English naturalistic decoration of a scrolling pattern embroidered in silk and metal threads with strawberries – as on Desdemona's handkerchief – honeysuckle, acorns and peapods, which are all emblematic both of an English garden and of fertility. This particular item was probably made by professionals, but domestic needlework – the image of a woman embroidering in expensive silks on linen – was emblematic of feminine virtue and viewed as a kind of domestic moral discipline.[32] Giles Fletcher's poem of 1610 *Christs Victorie and Triumph* allegorizes the figure of Mercy as wearing an

> upper garment ...
> With needle-woorke richly embroidered,
> Which she her selfe with her own hand had drawne,
> And all the world therein had pourtrayed,
> With threads so fresh, and lively colored
> That seem'd the world she newe created thear.[33]

'Ripeness is all'

(King Lear 5.2.12)

22. Woman's jacket, made of linen, hand-sewn and embroidered with silk thread in a variety of stitches with curling scrolls, flowers, fruits and nuts. Perhaps made loose to wear in pregnancy, and using a uniquely English embroidery style, *c.* 1600–25. The ribbons are modern.

L. (neck to hem) 66.5 cm.

Victoria and Albert Museum, London

The representations on this jacket probably derived from contemporary embroidery pattern books, of which several appeared in the 1590s.[34] One of these pattern books, by De Moynes, *La Clef des Champs* of 1586, shows cowslips, marigolds and strawberries in hand-coloured woodcuts annotated by the book's owner.[35] These in turn were derived from botanical woodcut illustrations of native plants in printed herbals.[36]

Tighter, more fitted versions of these embroidered jackets were also worn by women at home, as seen in portraits such as that illustrated here (fig. 23).[37] But the pregnancy garment (if that is what this is), along with the new genre of the pregnancy portrait, exemplified by a Gheeraerts portrait of about 1595 (fig. 24),[38] seems to point to a new sensibility among women and their husbands as to the dangers of childbirth for both mother and child; an acute awareness of what could go wrong and a strong identification with children.

Shakespeare married Anne Hathaway (1555/6–1623) when she was pregnant with their first child, Susanna; not long after she successfully carried twins, Judith and Hamnet. But the Shakespeares had no more children after this. We do not know whether that was because their marriage cooled and he left home relatively early in the

23. Margaret Laton's embroidered linen jacket,
England, 1610–15 and a portrait of Margaret
Laton, attributed to Marcus Gheeraerts the Younger,
c. 1620, showing her wearing the jacket.
Jacket: linen, embroidered with coloured silks,
silver and silver-gilt thread, L. 51 cm, W. 60 cm
Portrait: oil on panel, 81.5 x 62.5 cm.
Victoria and Albert Museum, London

24. Portrait of an unknown lady,
Marcus Gheeraerts the Younger, *c.* 1595.
Oil on panel, 92.7 x 76 cm. Tate Britain, London

1580s, or (more likely) whether complications following the birth of the twins –
doubly hazardous in an age of frequent death in and after childbirth – meant that
Anne could no longer conceive. Precariously, then, Shakespeare had only one male
heir. The parish register in Stratford records the burial of Hamnet on 11 August 1596.
The boy was eleven.

The Elizabethans were acutely conscious of the sorrow of child mortality. Ben
Jonson wrote one of his most heartfelt poems about his dead son, and Shakespeare is
at his most moving when Macduff hears of the killing of his 'pretty ones' (*Macbeth*
4.3.249) at the hands of Macbeth's henchmen. The dead child portrait was another
new genre, along with the pregnancy portrait. An English school oil-on-panel
painting, dated 1624, shows a dead child of around four, surrounded by flowers in an
embroidered effect (fig. 25).[39] Real flowers were often arranged in the hair, around the
face, and in the clothing and hands of the dead when they were laid out for viewing
by friends and relatives. The custom is symbolically evoked in Gertrude's account of
Ophelia's death in the brook with her 'fantastic garlands' (*Hamlet* 4.6.151).

Ophelia's distraction and death are provoked by Hamlet's rejection of her, which is
dramatized in her account of his visit to her closet in the garb and pose of the lovesick
young man 'with his doublet all unbraced' (2.1.82). The association of love and

'Grief fills the room up of my absent child'

(*King John 3.3.95*)

25. Portrait of a dead child around the age of four, unknown English artist.
Oil on panel, 1624. Berger Collection, Denver

'it is a melancholy of mine own'

(*As You Like It 4.1.11–12*)

26. Portrait of John Donne as a melancholy lover, unknown English artist, *c.* 1595.
Oil on panel, 72.4 x 60 cm.
National Portrait Gallery, London

melancholy is played upon more comically in the encounters between Jaques (the cynical philosopher–melancholiac) and Orlando (the archetypal man in love). 'The lunatic, the lover and the poet', Theseus reminds us in *A Midsummer Night's Dream*, 'Are of imagination all compact' (5.1.7–8).

In the wonderful portrait shown here (fig. 26) the philosophically-minded love poet John Donne poses as the archetypal melancholy lover. The portrait seems to have been a special commission in which the patron was involved in structuring the conceit: as with Jacques, Donne's affectation is 'a melancholy of mine own' (*As You Like It* 4.1.11–12). It is also one of the earliest author portraits of an Englishman, though of a very Italianate type of a kind fashionable with the English from the 1580s. Donne stands deep in the shadows, further shaded by his floppy black hat, drawing attention to his sensuous red lips and delicate ungloved hand. His lace collar is un*done*, indicative of being in a state of fashionable undress and perhaps a pun on his name such as he uses in his poetry ('When Thou hast done, Thou hast not done' ['A Hymn to God the Father']). His arms are crossed over his chest, something also associated with the disaffected melancholy lover: in *The Two Gentlemen of Verona*, Speed observes Valentine's tendency 'to wreathe your arms like a malcontent' (2.1.18). The portrait is inscribed in Latin 'ILLUMINA TENEBR[AS] / NOSTRAS DOMINA' ('O Lady lighten our darkness'), a blasphemous parody of the Psalms, invoking his lover as a goddess. No wonder Donne referred to this portrait in his will rather ambivalently, or even disapprovingly, as 'that Picture of myne wch is taken in Shaddowes and was made very many yeares before I was of this profession [i.e. the profession of divinity]'.[40]

Shakespeare sometimes indulges in, but more often parodies, the conventions associated with the melancholy lover. One thinks of the langorous Orsino in *Twelfth Night* and the comic image in *Love's Labour's Lost* of how Don Armado should present himself as a lover: 'with your hat penthouse-like o'er the shop of your eyes, with your

'the scholar's melancholy'

(*As You Like It* 4.1.8)

27. Portrait miniature of Edward Herbert,
1st Baron Herbert of Cherbury, Isaac Oliver,
c. 1613–14.
Vellum on card, 18.1 x 22.7 cm. Powis Castle, Wales

arms crossed on your thin-belly doublet like a rabbit on a spit' (3.1.10–12).

The great miniaturist Isaac Oliver (*c.* 1565–1617) specialized in figures of melancholy aristocrats. His miniature of the poet and philosopher Lord Herbert of Cherbury (1583–1648) (fig. 27) – kinsman of Mary Sidney and the Pembrokes, and older brother of poet–priest George Herbert (1593–1633) – was painted in about 1613–14. Yet it is strikingly old-fashioned, perhaps deliberately on the part of a self-conscious and vain patron who idealized the medieval cult of chivalry. All the elements of melancholy are here, together with the idealized pastoral location with shady trees and a brook. Sir Thomas Overbury noted that the melancholy individual is rarely found 'without the shade of some grove, in whose bottome a river dwels'.[41] Herbert lies propped on his elbow in meditative pose, as if on a contemporary tomb monument, gazing soulfully out at the viewer. The inscription on his shield refers to sympathetic magic and shows a heart arising from flames or wings as a symbol of creative inspiration. His expensive lace collar is artfully unlaced, as in the Donne portrait: as with Hamlet, a state of undress indicative of informality and melancholy. He is wearing an expensive doublet and breeches, with garters and supple riding boots. In the background are his plumed helmet, up-to-the-minute armour and his horse, for tilting in a chivalric tournament. The most striking element of this portrait, however, is the super-real representation of the trees and their bark, the vivid colouring of the woodland clearing and the sense of aerial distance, inspired by Dutch landscape

painting and quite new in English art. These visual innovations find their echo in the vivid descriptions of landscape in the plays of Shakespeare and the poetry of Edmund Spenser (*c.* 1552–1599).[42]

This type of imagery and posturing had a wider social reach than the two portraits above – which emerge from elite culture – might suggest when seen in isolation. Drama did its work in promoting courtly ideals to a wider audience, but so did vernacular visual media, such as tin-glazed ceramic, something relatively new in England around 1620. The jug seen here (fig. 28) belongs to the middling sort rather than the aristocracy. It shows the standing figure of a young man wearing a large ruff, Italianate breeches, garters, stockings and shoes with rosettes. He stands with his hat in one hand and his other hand on his heart, as if to profess unrequited love as referred to in the inscription in the border around his figure: 'I. AM. NO. BEGGER. I. CAN. NOT. CRAVE. BUT. YU. KNOW. THE. THING. THAT. I. WOULD. HAVE.' Not everyone interprets the figure this way, however; at least one previous owner of the pot thought the youth was asking for a beer! It may be a joke on the part of the ceramic painter, given that ceramic is traditionally a medium for satire or irreverence, particularly in poking fun at desire and lust.[43] The youth's clothing should be melancholic black, but because that is difficult to represent on tin-glazed pottery the potter has used blue instead. The jug is sophisticated and ambitious in its imagery and brightly painted decoration, which is perhaps derived from a print, and it is well fired. It takes its form from a drinking pot made of imported German stoneware and this, along with its quality, suggests that

28. Jug with a portrait of a melancholy lover. Probably made in Southwark, *c.* 1620.
Tin-glazed earthenware, H. 32.2 cm.
Victoria and Albert Museum, London

29. The progress of a scold, showing her mocking, grimacing and gagged, carved on a fifteenth-century wooden misericord, or choir seat.
Church of Holy Trinity, Stratford-upon-Avon

it was probably the work of Dutch immigrant potters in Southwark. The London delftware industry was just starting up at this point and ceramic painters were searching for a British visual style. The melancholic lover was nearly always seen as a quintessentially English type, and yet once again it is the immigrant craftsman who helped to shape the national self-image.[44]

For all he reveals about courtly attitudes to love in *As You Like It*, and about courtly melancholy through Jacques, Shakespeare's imagination remained grounded in the Arden of his early years. He presents Orlando's old country servant Adam with realism and almost biblical dignity of language. There is a strong tradition that Shakespeare acted this part himself. Throughout his comedies, though they are usually set in distant lands and climes, Shakespeare reveals his Warwickshire country boy origins, dropping in dialect words, references to folk customs and a sharply irreverent and never sentimental sense of English rural life in all weathers: 'greasy Joan' keels the pot in *Love's Labour's Lost* (5.2.917) and 'the fat ale-wife of Wincot' (a tiny hamlet just outside Stratford) is name-checked in the induction to *The Taming of the Shrew* (Induction 2.16–17).

30. Woodcut illustration showing Robin Goodfellow, or Puck, from *Robin Goodfellow, His Mad Prankes and Merry Jests*, London, 1639. Page size 17 x 12.5 cm. Folger Shakespeare Library, Washington DC

The world of the latter play – which begins with an English tinker transported to a lord's country house decorated with erotic tapestry hangings – is very much that of the extraordinary fifteenth-century misericords in the chancel of Holy Trinity Church in Stratford, where Shakespeare would have been obliged to worship weekly all through his early years. Lively scenes are carved on to tip-up seats for tired clergy who acted as chantry priests. Here mischievous monkeys play at doctors and the war between the sexes is acted out with a scold or old nag grimacing and mocking, and then being bridled (fig. 29). A man beats a woman-beast's bare buttocks with a bunch of sticks, while a woman grabs a man by the beard and bashes him with a saucepan. Carved in the wood of Shakespeare's church we see the Earl of Leicester's badge of the chained bears – a familiar sight with travelling troupes in Stratford and in the bear-baiting rings in London, which vied with the playhouse as public spectacle. Also represented is the pagan world of harpies (a foretaste of Ariel's transformation in *The Tempest*) and beguiling mermaids. The medieval Green Man of the woods is there too, as well as pagan masks sprouting foliage and garlanded with leaves.[45] Like the great beams in the roof of Snitterfield Church, where John Shakespeare would have worshipped, these carvings attest to the presence of the nearby forests and their ancient culture as a Warwickshire undercurrent. The misericords survived the Reformation, a fact that suggests the conservatism of Stratford and the way in which old ways persisted there.

The old religion coexisted with magic and the real presence of fairies and hobgoblins. In the woodcut illustrated here Robin Goodfellow is depicted as a priapic satyr with goatish thighs, cloven hooves and horns, along with outsize ears (fig. 30).[46] He wears a hunting horn around his neck. Tiny witches cavort around him in a circle as he brandishes a candle and a besom. This Robin is more demonic and serious than the Puck of *A Midsummer Night's Dream*, but revelatory of that character's disturbing

'My horns I bequeath your husbands'

(The Merry Wives of Windsor 5.5.17–18)

31. Headdress made from the antlers and skull of a red deer, *c.* 8000 BC. Excavated at Star Carr, Vale of Pickering in Yorkshire.
H. 15 cm, L. 18 cm. British Museum, London

32. The 'horn dance' at Abbots Bromley, Staffordshire, an annual event recorded from the seventeenth century, though one of the antlers used, which are from a reindeer, has been carbon-dated to the eleventh century.

power, which the play associates with his master Oberon, and with the capacity of ill-tempered fairies and malicious sprites to disrupt the rural economy:

> The ploughman lost his sweat, and the green corn
> Hath rotted ere his youth attained a beard.
> The fold stands empty in the drownèd field,
> And crows are fatted with the murrion flock,
> The nine men's morris is filled up with mud,
> And the quaint mazes in the wanton green
> For lack of tread are undistinguishable.
> (*A Midsummer Night's Dream* 2.1.95–101)[47]

Elsewhere in *A Midsummer Night's Dream* and *The Merry Wives of Windsor* fairies are associated with lighter themes: women, children, human folly and ignorance as elements of comedy. The conjunction of antlers, always evocative of sexual humiliation, and children dressed as fairies in a rural location with symbolic associations ('Herne's Oak' in Windsor Great Park) characterizes the glorious night scene at the climax of *The Merry Wives of Windsor*: 'My horns I bequeath your husbands' (5.5.17–18). Wearing deer antlers as part of ritual had ancient roots in England. Figure 31 shows a headdress made from a red deer antler frontlet, excavated around 1950 at Starr Carr in the Vale of Pickering, 5 miles south of Scarborough in Yorkshire. This was fashioned in the Mesolithic period from the skull of a large stag, and worked with flint tools: it was scraped smooth and the antlers trimmed, with two holes made at the back of the skull probably for threading with leather thongs so that the frontlet could be tied to the head and worn in rituals by a shaman. Similar objects were used in the Abbots Bromley 'horn' dance (fig. 32) which is still performed every year in this Staffordshire village on Wakes Monday in September, using ancient antlers that are otherwise kept in the local church. There is no reference to the dance before Robert Plot's description of 1686, but the horns themselves are reindeer antlers (one has been carbon-dated to the eleventh century). Horns of this kind were probably imported from Scandinavia.[48] It is quite possible that Plot records a practice that was Anglo-Saxon in origin.

There was a forestry tradition too for horn-wearing: in *As You Like It* Jaques and foresters talk about how they will present a dead deer to the duke: 'It would do well to set the deer's horns upon his head for a branch of victory' (4.2.3–4). They sing:

> What shall he have that killed the deer?
> His leather skin and horns to wear.
> Then sing him home,
> The rest shall bear this burden:
> Take thou no scorn to wear the horn,
> It was a crest ere thou wast born,
> Thy father's father wore it,
> And thy father bore it.
> The horn, the horn, the lusty horn,
> Is not a thing to laugh to scorn.
> (*As You Like It* 4.2.8–17)

This is reminiscent of the motto on the African drinking horn in figure 25, Chapter 1, which is dated 1599 and inscribed: 'Drinke you this and thinke no scorne although the cup be much like a horn'. Perhaps the horn had a similar use in tenure rituals.[49]

When Falstaff comes on stage in *The Merry Wives of Windsor* wearing antlers, the stage image has a dual significance. It plays on the classical Actaeon myth of destructive male desire (the hunter metamorphosed to a stag and torn to pieces by his own hounds as punishment for desiring the goddess Diana – see p. 39), but it also alludes to the native tradition of Herne the Hunter and the ritual mockeries of mummers' plays and customs.

Mistress Page tells the story of Herne the Hunter (*The Merry Wives of Windsor* 4.4.24–34) to her husband Page when planning a fitting punishment for Falstaff. The story goes that Herne was a skilled hunter who saved the king from a vicious stag, then wore the stag's horns himself, only to be accused of poaching and hanged from an oak in Windsor Great Park, which he was said to haunt. A block of 'Herne's Oak' (fig. 33) was given by Queen Victoria to the British Museum in 1863: the tree died in 1796 and blew down in a gale in 1863. Queen Victoria had a cabinet made from it and William Perry used its wood to make a box to contain a Shakespeare First Folio. Perry

'Walk round about an oak, with great ragged horns'

(*The Merry Wives of Windsor* 4.4.27)

33. 'Herne's Oak': a fragment from the tree in Windsor Great Park mentioned by Shakespeare in *The Merry Wives of Windsor*. When the tree finally blew down in a gale, Queen Victoria gave this block to the British Museum in 1863. H. 51.5 cm, W. 45 cm. British Museum, London

wrote a book called *Herne's Oak* in 1867, with a picture of the tree as its frontispiece. The chunk of this famous oak in the British Museum has initials carved in it, rather as Orlando carved the name of his beloved in the imaginary trees of Arden.[50]

There appears to be no record of Herne the Hunter before Shakespeare's play. It is possible, then, that he was inventing a folk tradition. We need to question the assumption that references to folk traditions and old customs were always evocative of old times and the old lost faith. The Reformation, it has recently been argued, 'served as much to stimulate the formation of landscape legends as it did to extinguish them'.[51]

Given that Shakespeare's only male heir, Hamnet, was buried in Stratford-upon-Avon in the summer of 1596, it is surprising that only a few months later John Shakespeare, working through William, who was resident in London, made his second attempt to obtain a grant of arms from the College of Arms, in order to give gentlemanly status to the family. This new sense of status was grounded on the Arden inheritance. But who would inherit that status with Hamnet gone?

The process of gaining a coat of arms was not easy, especially as Sir William Dethick (1542–1612), a key official in the herald's office, may well have had his doubts about conferring arms upon someone of such a vulgar trade as 'Shakespeare ye player'.[52] A draft granting John's request was drawn up by Dethick in his capacity as Garter King-of-Arms on 20 October 1596 (fig. 34). It refers to John as having raised the matter before, in around 1576, following his appointment as bailiff of Stratford in 1568. The fair copy of the grant seems to have disappeared, but it was definitely granted, judging by later squabbles among the heralds about the legality of grants that Dethick had made to those (including the Shakespeares) who were either thought not to be of sufficient social status or whose arms were too close to those of other, older families.[53]

In order to prove gentry status, applicants had to review and record what was known of their family's lineage, offices and land held. The Shakespeare application depended on a vague reference to what might have been military service to the first Tudor king, Henry VII, and on the Arden connection through John's marriage. Dethick declared himself willing to grant arms and a crest to John:

> being solicited and by credible report informed that John Shakespeare of Stratford upon Avon in the counte of Warwik, whose parentes and late grandfather for his faithfull and valeant service was advanced and rewarded by the most prudent Prince Henry the Seventh of famous memorie, sythence which tyme they have continewed in those partes, being of good reputacion and credit, and that the said John hath maryed the daughter and one of the heyrs of Robert Arden of Wilmcote in the said counte esquire.[54]

Dethick noted that John Shakespeare had been bailiff and Justice of the Peace in Stratford, that 'he hath lands and tenements of good wealth and substance' amounting

'He's a mad yeoman that sees his son a gentleman before him'

(*King Lear 3.6.9–10*)

34. Draft grant of arms to John Shakespeare, 20 October 1596. One of two drafts drawn up by Sir William Dethick, Garter King-of-Arms at the College of Arms in London.
Manuscript, ink on paper, 29.2 x 29.3 cm.
College of Arms, London

to 500 pounds, and, most importantly that he had married 'a daughter and heyre of Arden, a gent. of worship'. It was on the basis of that marriage that John Shakespeare applied in 1599 for the right to impale the Arden arms with his own (fig. 35). The request led to questioning over the relationship between the Ardens of Wilmcote and the rather grander Ardens of Park Hall in Warwickshire, and the matter was dropped.[55]

The Shakespeare arms ('Gould on a bend sables a Speare of the first steeled argent') shows a chivalric tilting staff rather than a spear. The crest of a falcon shaking its wings in preparation for flight is also an allusion to the family name. The falcon also hints that the Shakespeares are now a family of the right status to participate in the better class of rural sports: William is poacher no more. The motto *Non Sanz Droit* (Not without right) is a bold statement, but one which the family does not seem to have used. Ben Jonson does, however, appear to have mocked Shakespeare over it when he included in his 1599 play *Every Man out of his Humour* a social climber from the country called Sogliardo, whose motto is 'Not without mustard'.

Between 1604 and 1611 Shakespeare spent much of his time at home in Stratford (often engaging in lawsuits over property and money), rather than in London. He was in the capital in 1612 to give evidence in the Belott v. Mountjoy court case, in which he is described as 'William Shakespeare of Stratford upon Aven in the Countye of

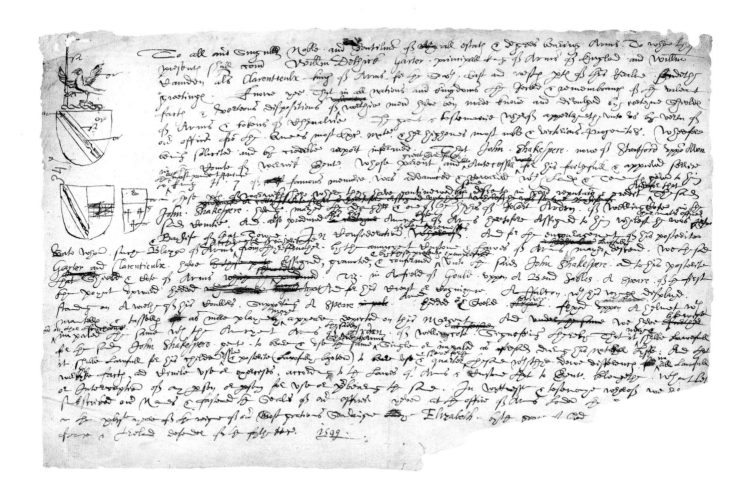

'the Slys are no rogues. Look in the chronicles, we came in with Richard Conqueror'

(*The Taming of the Shrew* Induction 1.3–4)

35. Detail of the draft exemplification of 1599, requesting the right to impale the Arden arms with those of Shakespeare. Drawn up by Sir William Dethick at the College of Arms in London.
Manuscript, ink on paper, 20.5 x 31.5 cm.
College of Arms, London

Warwicke, gentleman of the Age of xlviii [48 years] or thereabouts': not as a fashionable playwright of London fame, but as a man of substance in his own county (see Chapter 1, p. 13–4). The following year he bought a gatehouse in Blackfriars. With the acquisition of New Place in Stratford (see p. 71), his income from investments and his appointment, along with his company, as a King's Man in 1603, Shakespeare's status both in his home town and in court and capital was assured.

As a tithe-holder, whose income from agricultural produce helped to support the church, Shakespeare had the right to be buried at the east end of Holy Trinity Church in Stratford. The arms and the crest are there, above the bust on the wall monument erected by his friends. He was remembered as a gentleman rather than a player. Indeed, when the King's Men came to Stratford in 1622, surely with the intention of paying their respects at the grave of their great colleague, they were – ironically – paid by the Puritan town council *not* to perform in the town: 'To the King's Players for not playing in the hall, 6s'.[56]

'I am Richard,
know ye not that?'

(Statement allegedly made by Elizabeth I in 1601
and recorded by William Lambarde)

1. Portrait of Richard II enthroned,
unknown artist, painted between
7 June 1394 and 15 December 1395
Oil on panel, 213.5 cm x 110 cm.
Westminster Abbey, London

3 'Cry "God for Harry, England and Saint George!"' Kingship and the English Nation

I N THE AUTHORITATIVE LATIN dictionary of the Elizabethan age, published in 1587 just before Shakespeare began his theatrical career, the word 'monumentum' is defined as 'A remembrance of some notable acte, as tombes, sepulchers, books, images, etc., a memoriall, a token, a signe, a testimonie, a monument, a recorde, a chronicle, an historie.'[1] Londoners in Shakespeare's age were surrounded by monuments of many kinds, by embodiments of collective memory. Tombs in Westminster Abbey, volumes of chronicles on the bookstalls in St Paul's churchyard, history plays on the stage of the Rose and Globe Theatres: all served the same purpose, to offer the people lively remembrances of notable acts.

The importance of the past and the lessons it could teach the present were instilled from an early age. Everybody was taught to believe in the histories contained in the Bible and to have faith that the 1,600-year-old story of the life, death and Resurrection of Jesus Christ was the key to their own salvation. History also lay at the centre of the educational revolution that has become known as Renaissance humanism. The humanist ideal was to recover the values of classical antiquity (see p. 123). If the Romans had their national histories, by such authors as Livy and Tacitus, then the English must have theirs. The need was made all the more imperative by King Henry VIII's break from Rome: as the culture of England was severed from the centuries-old traditions of Catholic Europe, the national past became a vital means of establishing and securing a distinct national identity in the present.

Shakespeare made his name as the author of history plays. The two earliest references to his theatrical career concern the cycle of plays in which he dramatized the Wars of the Roses, the battles for succession and influence between the Houses of Lancaster and York that had fractured the nation in the century before his own.

In 1592 a pamphlet appeared under the title *Greenes Groats-worth of Witte, bought with a million of Repentance* by the university-educated playwright Robert Greene (1558–1592). Dying in poverty, he complains of 'an upstart Crow, beautified with our feathers, that with his Tygers hart wrapt in a Players hyde, supposes he is as well able to bombast out a blanke verse as the best of you: and beeing an absolute *Johannes fac totum*, is in his owne conceit the onely Shake-scene in a countrey.' Shakescene is of course Shakespeare. He had clearly become a well-known figure in the London theatre world and successful enough to provoke Greene's jealousy. *Johannes fac totum* – Jack of all trades – suggests that he had gained a reputation as a man who would try his hand at anything: acting, adapting plays in the existing repertoire (to the annoyance of their original authors – 'beautified with our feathers'), and writing poetic drama of his own ('bombast out a blanke verse'). The really interesting detail is the sly misquotation: 'Tygers hart wrapt in a Players hyde' is an allusion to a scene in one of the *Henry VI* plays, in which Queen Margaret puts a paper crown on the head of Richard Duke of York, and he goads her in return with the words:

> She-wolf of France, but worse than wolves of France,
> Whose tongue more poisons than the adder's tooth!
> How ill-beseeming is it in thy sex
> To triumph, like an Amazonian trull,
> Upon their woes whom fortune captivates!
> O, tiger's heart wrapt in a woman's hide!
> (*Henry VI Part 3* 1.4.111–15, 137)

Greene's mocking quotation shows that Shakespeare's scene stuck in the memory. Although the career of 'the upstart crow' from the backwoods of Arden was only just beginning, he was already becoming the maker of famous poetic phrases.

That same year of 1592 Thomas Nashe (1567–*c.* 1601), another playwright and pamphleteer, made reference to Talbot, the hero of *Henry VI Part 1*:

> How it would have joy'd brave Talbot (the terror of the French) to thinke
> that after he had lyne two hundred yeare in his tombe, hee should triumphe
> againe on the Stage, and have his bones new embalmed with the teares of
> ten thousand spectators at least (at severall times) who, in the tragedian
> that represents his person, imagine they behold him fresh bleeding.[2]

The phrase 'at severall times' reveals that the play had established itself as a box office hit, a fixture in the repertoire. What is striking, though, is Nashe's image of brave Talbot coming out from his tomb and beholding a repeat performance of his own death and embalming. Historical drama is clearly imagined as a living monument. The kings and nobles who shaped English history had long been remembered by means of shrines, inscriptions on tombs, effigies and paintings.[3] These were all passive forms, designed to elicit silent spectatorship and absorption in the lessons of the past. Publicly performed plays were something new: active re-presentations that brought alive great events, moving vast audiences to collective emotion and making them believe for the moment that they were witnesses to history. The ghosts of slain princes have major roles in the plays themselves, especially in *Richard III*, but Nashe's image of brave Talbot suggests that all the historical figures in Shakespeare's plays were like ghosts that had risen from their tombs, moving effigies that had stepped out from their monuments.

Shakespeare's first tetralogy of historical plays – the three parts of *Henry VI* and *Richard III* – comes to a harmonious conclusion with the defeat of wicked King Richard at the battle of Bosworth Field in 1485. The victorious Earl of Richmond, who belongs to the house of Lancaster, marries the Princess Elizabeth, of the house of York, thus unifying the nobility and bringing to an end the Wars of the Roses. In the final scene of *Richard III* Lord Stanley places the crown on Richmond's head and he becomes King Henry VII, inaugurator of the Tudor dynasty. The play closes with a speech in which Henry looks back on the civil strife that has been the subject of the tetralogy, and forward to the golden age over which his wife's namesake, Queen Elizabeth, liked to believe that she reigned:

> England hath long been mad, and scarred herself;
> The brother blindly shed the brother's blood,
> The father rashly slaughtered his own son,
> The son, compelled, been butcher to the sire:
> All this divided York and Lancaster,
> Divided in their dire division,
> O, now, let Richmond and Elizabeth,
> The true succeeders of each royal house,
> By God's fair ordinance conjoin together.
> And let thy heirs—God, if thy will be so—
> Enrich the time to come with smooth-faced peace,
> With smiling plenty and fair prosperous days!
> (*Richard III* 5.3.390–401)

On hearing these lines, Shakespeare's audience would themselves have looked both forward and back: back to a bloody period in the nation's history, with relief at how it was providentially ended by the Tudor dispensation; forward to an uncertain future, in the knowledge that the queen was now too old to sustain the line.

Not long after completing his first sequence of history plays, Shakespeare turned to the back story. *Henry VI Part I* had begun with the funeral of King Henry V. There was already an old play in the repertoire that moved rapidly from his misspent youth as Prince Harry through to his famous victory at Agincourt. That would offer Shakespeare enough material for three whole plays – the two parts of *Henry IV* and

2. The interior of the southern end of Westminster Hall, unknown English or Dutch artist, *c*. 1620. Pen and brown ink, with brown wash, over graphite, 29.7 x 19.6 cm. British Museum, London

Henry V – but if he was going to write about the reign of King Harry's father, he would have to begin with the king whose removal from the throne inaugurated that reign: Richard II, the last king of England whom everyone agreed was the legitimate monarch. The trouble was, according to the chroniclers, he was not a very effective king. What is to be done if the divinely ordained ruler of the land is not the best person to maintain a peaceful and prosperous nation? Are there any circumstances in which a monarch can be dethroned? That was a question asked again and again, first in print and then on stage, from the deposition of Richard II in 1399 through the various uprisings, rebellions and assassination plots of Queen Elizabeth's reign to the extraordinary moment in 1649 when King Charles I was beheaded.

A reader of *A Mirroure for Magistrates* (1578), an influential collection of poems written in the voices of the ghosts of fallen princes and other doomed figures from English history, would have gained a very negative impression of King Richard II:

> I was a Kinge, who ruled by Lust
> Without respect of Justice, Right, or Lawe,
> In false Flatterers reposinge all my trust,
> Embracinge sutch as could my vices clawe:
> Fro counsell sage I did always withdrawe,
> As pleasure prickt, so nedes obay I must.[4]

What is more, according to some sources, Richard's 'Lust' was of a homosexual nature.[5] It was certainly a problem for the succession of the crown that, though twice married, he had no children.[6]

In contrast to the negative image of Richard that prevailed in print, the visual iconography available in Shakespeare's London represented him as a figure of exceptional holiness. This was partly his own doing: in order to assert his fragile authority, which was in part the result of his having come to the throne at the age of ten, he cultivated the royal image. He became the first English king to have himself portrayed in panel paintings of great majesty, most notably the huge coronation portrait that is now in Westminster Abbey (fig. 1) and the highly symbolic Wilton Diptych (see further below), a portable work probably intended to accompany Richard on his Irish campaign.

Richard II's magnificent artistic patronage was exceptional – particularly his involvement with Westminster Abbey, its Hall and Palace – and some of the results were still to be seen in Shakespeare's day. A drawing of around 1620 (fig. 2) shows the interior of Westminster Hall with the six statues of English kings placed there in 1385 as part of Richard II's refurbishment of the Norman Hall. We do not know which of the English kings from Edward the Confessor to Richard himself they were intended to portray, but they collectively represented 'our ancestors, Kings of England of famous memory', the kings with whom Richard declared he wished to be buried in Westminster Abbey.[7] In the Hall they form the backdrop to the Court of King's Bench and the Chancery in session, which had their allotted places on the dais at the southern end of Westminster Hall by the end of the fourteenth century. Spectators in a wooden compartment on the left, and the groups of lawyers talking in the foreground, emphasize just how public and on view Richard's kings were. This was the scene of major political trials, and it was where the Earl of Essex (1565–1601) was tried and, later, Guy Fawkes and the Powder Plotters. But the Hall was also thronged on a daily basis with booksellers, seamstresses and chapmen (pedlars) hawking their wares.[8] And it was where the Shakespeare family attorney, John Harborne, took the case of Shakespeare v. Lambert, concerning the mortgage and debt on property at Barton-on-the-Heath, in 1588.[9]

Could Shakespeare have taken in the two wonderful portraits of Richard II and his tomb in Westminster Abbey when forming his concept of Richard?[10] Shakespeare's poetic martyr and victim is very much the kneeling figure presented by St John the Baptist to the Virgin and Child in the Wilton Diptych, which is dated by its heraldry to 1395–9 (fig. 3). The painting is a masterpiece of self-presentation.[11] Behind Richard are the two English royal saints: St Edmund, the last King of East Anglia (r. 855–869/70) who was martyred by the Danes, and St Edward the Confessor (r. 1042–1066). Richard is just off-centre, but the focus is very much on him as he kneels in his coronation robes. Ten of the eleven angels around the Virgin gaze or point at him. Nine of them – and Richard himself – wear his personal device of the white hart. This bold way of presenting his device suggests divine support for Richard, and implies that the angels are in some kind of feudal relationship with him: 'Heaven for his Richard hath in heavenly pay / A glorious angel' (*Richard II* 5.2.55–6).[12]

The device, a white hart with a coronet and chain worn around its neck, takes the

'Heaven for his Richard hath in heavenly pay A glorious angel'

(*Richard II* 5.2.55–6)

3. The Wilton Diptych, a portable altarpiece painted for the private devotion of Richard II. The outside bears Richard's arms and his personal emblem of a white hart chained with a crown around its neck. By an unknown French or English artist, *c.* 1395–9.
Egg on oak panel, 53 x 37 cm. National Gallery, London

form of an enamelled gold badge worn on the breast. The Dunstable Swan of around 1400 (fig. 4) gives us the best idea of what the exquisite white hart badges worn in the Wilton Diptych would have looked like in reality.[13] The swan of the De Bohun family took the place of the white hart when Henry of Lancaster took over the throne from Richard II.[14] According to the *Historia Vitae et Regni Ricardi Secundi* (1377–90), Richard is said to have adopted the hart emblem at the Smithfield Tournament in October 1390, and he is thought to have distributed badges of his device in the last nine years of his life.[15] A charming lead livery badge of a white hart, now missing its antlers, indicates that these were widely worn by Richard's retainers at a lower level (fig. 5). Badges were fashionable decorative devices, too, in denoting ownership, as engraved on the quadrant dated 1399 which belonged to Richard II (fig. 6). Similarly a plaster cast at the Soane Museum of a sculpted corbel which was formerly built into Westminster Hall (rebuilt by Richard II) shows the hart with the royal arms.[16] The hart appears again at Westminster, delicately pouncing on Richard's gilded robes on his tomb, and much more crudely in a mural painted in the Muniment Room there.

4. The Dunstable Swan Jewel,
made in England or France, c. 1400.
Gold with enamel, H. 3.4 cm. British Museum, London

5. White hart badge of Richard II, c. 1390–9.
Lead alloy, L. 3.91 cm. British Museum, London

6. Horary quadrant engraved with the white hart
emblem of Richard II, dated 1399.
Brass, engraved and originally gilded, H. 9.2 cm.
British Museum, London

'This precious stone set in the silver sea'

(*Richard II* 2.1.46)

7. Detail from the Wilton Diptych (fig. 3) showing
the orb on the top of the banner of St George.

But perhaps the most tantalizing detail of the Wilton Diptych is the little orb of a green island set in a silver leaf sea on the banner of St George on the right-hand panel (fig. 7). It is an evocation of what Shakespeare would later describe as 'this little world, / This precious stone set in the silver sea' (*Richard II* 2.1.45–6). It is this detail which has led more than one art historian to speculate as to whether Shakespeare could have seen the Wilton Diptych, and to try to establish its ownership and location in his day. Even if this idea is wildly far-fetched, it is telling that when this detail was first seen under a microscope at the National Gallery in 1993, the people present thought back to this quotation, which demonstrates its hold on the national imagination even now.[17] Richard was buried first at Langley in Hertfordshire, but in 1413 Henry V brought his body back to Westminster and buried it in the tomb illustrated here that Richard had commissioned for his wife, Anne of Bohemia, in 1395 (fig. 8). It is the first royal double tomb in England, with portraits of both husband and wife.[18] Richard's portrait shows him as frail and ageing and – anticipating Philip Larkin's lovely poem 'An Arundel Tomb' – they were originally holding hands, at Richard's specific request in the 1395 contract for the tomb. Hentzner describes the tomb, so it must have been on the tourist trail in Shakespeare's day. And Shakespeare, in sharp contrast to the suggestion in some of his sources that Richard II (like Edward II) reserved his deepest love for his male hangers-on, duly evokes tenderness in the relationship between the king and his queen: 'Hand from hand, my love, and heart from heart' (5.1.82) he says as they part, she to exile in France, he to imprisonment in the Tower of London.

The Westminster Abbey portrait is over-life-size, painted in a linseed oil medium on a panel (see fig. 1).[19] It dates from the mid-1390s. Portraits on panel from the fourteenth century are exceptionally rare north of the Alps and this full-length, frontal image has no parallels. It was unprecedented in offering a large-scale monumental portrait of a king in majesty, wearing royal robes, ermine collar and crown, and holding the orb and sceptre.[20] There is a disquieting element of portraiture in the

'Hand from hand, my love, and heart from heart'

(*Richard II* 5.1.82)

8. Tomb of Richard II and Anne of Bohemia in Westminster Abbey, commissioned by Richard in 1395, the effigies cast by Nicholas Broker and Godfrey Prest. The couple were originally shown holding hands as stipulated in the contract for the tomb, but these have been broken off. Henry V reburied Richard II's body here in 1413.
Westminster Abbey, London

painting, which presents both an individual who can be held responsible for his actions – and found wanting – and at the same time an icon of majesty.[21] This duality opens the way for one of the key themes of Shakespeare's play: the idea of the 'king's two bodies', the conflict between the monarch as embodiment of the royal line, the majestic representative of God on earth, and the king as a person – a self, a personality, a human individual.

To become a monarch and take on the 'body politic',[22] a king or queen had to go through the highly theatrical public ritual of being crowned. Coronation scenes – and in the case of *Richard II* an extraordinary de-coronation – offered moments of high spectacle in many plays of the time. Strikingly, the crossing of Westminster Abbey's

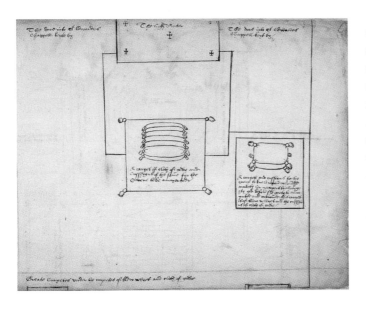

9. Drawing showing the staging of the coronation of Elizabeth I in Westminster Abbey, 1559, with the siege royal.
Graphite and ink on paper, 28.7 x 38.1 cm.
British Library, London

nave, which was designed as the site of the coronation of successive kings and queens of England, has become known as the Coronation Theatre.[23] A contemporary drawing (fig. 9) shows how the Abbey was prepared for Elizabeth I's coronation in January 1559. A special stage was constructed with the 'siege royal', the chair for the queen, raised at its centre. When seated after anointing, Elizabeth faced the altar and the coronation chair made by Edward I (r. 1272–1307) to hold as a relic the Stone of Scone, brought down from Scotland in 1296.[24] The ritual itself was a clever compromise between the Catholic practices of Queen Mary's reign and the Protestant ones that Elizabeth intended to introduce: she was crowned in Latin by a Catholic bishop but parts of the service that followed were read twice – in Latin and English. James I's coronation forty-five years later was the first to be conducted entirely in English. Understanding the force of the symbolism of sacral kingship, and the moral covenant that the ruler makes on behalf of their people in the presence of God, makes the effect of Richard's unthroning in Shakespeare's play even more shattering.

Richard's portrait from the 1390s is also in a sense a blown-up icon of kingship, of the kind seen on a smaller scale on the great seals of successive English kings and queens, those symbolic instruments of royal power. Richard showed his fierce concern for the royal prerogative and its emblems in the Latin inscription on his tomb at Westminster Abbey, which says he laid low anyone who violated them.[25] He was also known to be precise in marking distance and status: in 1398 he was described as presenting himself to his courtiers in this silent pose with the crown and regalia, and if 'he looked at anyone, that man had to bow the knee'.[26] Richard had a marked devotion to Westminster Abbey, especially to the tomb of Edward the Confessor. It has been suggested that the painting was intended to represent his presence in perpetuity in the sacred space of the Choir, where it was recorded as hanging in 1631, although its formality and its hieratic quality would perhaps have made it more suitable for a royal palace, maybe Westminster itself.[27]

An argument for the painting having been in the Palace of Westminster in Shakespeare's day is strengthened by the testimony of William Lambarde. He noted the apparent assertion by Elizabeth I that the antiquarian Lord Lumley (c. 1533–1609) had found it 'fastened to the backside of a door of a base room' and that he brought it to her attention.[28] Lambarde recorded, as if it had actually happened, a revealing conversation he had had with the queen in the Privy Chamber at east Greenwich on 4 August 1601:

So her Majestie fell upon the reign of King Richard II saying, 'I am Richard, know yet not that?'

WL 'Such a wicked imagination was determined and attempted by a most

10. 'Coronation portrait' of Elizabeth I, unknown artist. Probably a copy of a lost original of *c.* 1559, and dated by tree-ring analysis of the panel to *c.* 1600.
Oil on panel, 127.3 x 99.7 cm.
National Portrait Gallery, London

unkind gent. The most adorned creature that ever your Majestie made.'

HER MAJESTIE 'He that will forget God, will also forget his benefactors; this tragedy was played 40tie times in open streets and houses.'

… Then returning to Richard II she demanded, 'Whether I had seen any true picture, or lively representation of his countenance and person?'

WL 'None but such as be in common hands.'

HER MAJESTIE 'The Lord Lumley, a lover of antiquities, discovered it fastened on the backside of a door of a base room; which he presented unto me, praying, with my good leave, that I might put it in order with the ancestors and successors; I will command Tho.Kneavet, Keeper of my house and gallery at Westminster, to shew it unto thee.'[29]

Scholars have too often jumped to the false conclusion that here Elizabeth was referring to the performance of *Richard II* by Shakespeare's acting company, which was commissioned by the Earl of Essex's followers on the eve of his abortive rebellion.[30] They have, by contrast, paid less attention to the significance of the reference to Lord Lumley and none to Lambarde's remark about true pictures or lively representations of Richard II being 'in common hands'.

The Portrait of Elizabeth I at her Coronation (fig. 10) was actually painted around 1600 (according to tree-ring analysis of the panel on which it is painted) and appears to copy an earlier miniature now at Welbeck Abbey in Nottinghamshire.[31] Like the panel of Richard, it displays the same frontal presentation and formality, and the same uneasy blend of portrait and icon of majesty which may derive from an intricate web of imagery of former rulers in the form of seal-dies and illuminated miniatures that is for the most part lost to us.[32] Conventional though the form of presentation had become, the figure of Richard II remained the archetype, the iconic (in the proper sense) representation of English majesty. The fact that Lord Lumley – mentioned by Lambarde – commissioned a variant copy of the portrait of Richard II indicates the gaining popularity of royal portraits in the 1580s, at a time when it was crucial to secure a sense of national identity and unity in the face of the threat from Spain abroad and Catholic dissent at home. Lambarde's reference also reveals that the Richard II panel now in Westminster Abbey was known at the time of Shakespeare's play.

Lumley made Lumley Castle in County Durham a pantheon to his ancestors and the lost pre-Reformation glories of his Catholic lineage. An inventory of 1590 records a series of 'statuaries of sixteen ancestors from the Conquest' which were probably paintings, including a portrait showing the 1st Lord Lumley kneeling before Richard II and receiving the writ of Parliament: 'The statuary of Richard II delivering the writ of parliament to Ralph, the first Baron Lumley' (fig. 11).[33] James I didn't approve of Lumley's genealogicial obsession: 'I did'na ken Adam's ither name was Lumley'.[34]

As for Lambarde's reference to representations of Richard II being familiar 'in common hands', it may refer to the kind of standardized painting of kings' heads that had become common as pub signs. It had, after all, been King Richard who in 1393

passed an act making it compulsory for taverns and inns to have a sign in order to
identify them to the official Ale Taster. One of the most popular signs, still seen in
Shakespeare's time and ours, was Richard's own emblem: The White Hart. From the
Abbey to the theatre to the tavern, the signs and symbols of kingship were everywhere
in Shakespeare's London.

Drama has a peculiarly rich capacity to convey several contradictory messages
simultaneously. The English are notorious for getting their theology from Milton and
their history from Shakespeare, rather than from more orthodox sources. *Richard III*
is one of those core Shakespearean plays that everybody has heard of, even if they
have never read it. The endurance of the image of a Richard who is 'determinèd to
prove a villain' (*Richard III* 1.1.30) is testimony to the power of drama as being more
memorable than written history. The success of two film versions – first Sir Laurence
Olivier's in 1955 and subsequently in 1995 Sir Ian McKellen's dazzling update to
the fascist 1930s – has assured its continuing life. But the real Richard III has proved
equally fascinating: historians still debate the question of how villainous he really was,
and in particular whether he personally ordered the slaying of the princes in the Tower.
What is not in doubt is that it was convenient for the Tudors to paint him as a
villain in order to make his opponent, the future Henry VII, into a hero and a saint.
Sir Thomas More began the process with his *History of King Richard III*, written
at the court of Richmond's son, Henry VIII. Shakespeare finished the work,
immortalizing Richard as the scheming Crookback, in the public theatre of
Henry VIII's younger daughter.

Nowhere is the fluctuation of Richard III's reputation shown more clearly than
in the portrait of him shown here from the Society of Antiquaries (fig. 12). It is a
prime example of Tudor propaganda, probably painted around the middle of the
sixteenth century. It presents him as a usurper with a broken sword – probably a
sword of state, representative of royal authority – as a symbol of broken kingship.[35]
Some sense of what this symbol means is given by a large surviving sword of state,
dating to around 1473–83, associated with a Prince of Wales as Earl of Chester in the
British Museum (fig. 13). The arms on the copper panels on the grip (fig. 14) show
that the sword could only have belonged to one of two Princes of Wales, both called
Edward: the future Edward V (r. April–June 1483), who became Prince of Wales and
Earl of Chester in 1473, or Edward (*c.* 1473–1484), son of Richard III, who received
both titles in 1483. A sword of state was carried before the future Edward V as Prince
of Wales in a state procession in Chester in 1475. It may have been this very sword.[36]
It is this powerful emblem of the sword of state to which Shakespeare refers when
Richard claims his hold on power through a series of rhetorical questions:

> Is the chair empty? Is the sword unswayed?
> Is the king dead? The empire unpossessed?
> What heir of York is there alive but we?

'Every tale condemns me for a villain'

(*Richard III* 5.3.199)

12. Portrait of Richard III with
a broken sword, unknown artist, mid-1500s.
Oil on oak panel, 48.5 x 35.5 cm.
Society of Antiquaries, London

'Is the sword unswayed?
Is the King dead? The empire
unpossessed?'

(*Richard III* 4.4.484–5)

13. Sword of state of a Prince of Wales as
Earl of Chester. Perhaps made in Germany,
though the hilt was decorated and perhaps
made in England, *c.* 1473–83.
Steel, copper alloy, enamel and lead, L. 181.4 cm.
British Museum, London

14. Detail of the hilt of the sword in fig. 13
showing the enamelled arms of a Prince of
Wales as Earl of Chester.

And who is England's king but great York's heir?
(*Richard III* 4.4.484–7)

The portrait of Richard III shown here is a posthumous portrait of a villainous king, painted closer to Shakespeare's time than to Richard's. It was politically necessary for the Tudors to portray Richard III as a villain in order to justify Henry VII as a heroic founder of a new dynasty at Bosworth in 1485. Richard is shown here with (under repaint) a withered *left* shoulder and arm, as described by Thomas More in his *History*, suggesting that this painting is almost an illustration to More's book, published in 1557: 'And therwith he plucked up his doublet sleeve to his elbow upon his left arm where he showed a weirish withered arm and small, as it was never other.'[37] John Rous, writing in *Historia Regum Angliae* around 1485–91, mentions a raised right rather than left shoulder: 'He was small of stature, with a short face and unequal shoulders, the right higher and the left lower.' This is how he is shown in the portrait that was probably in the possession of Henry VIII at Whitehall Palace and inventoried in 1542.[38] It is possible that the slight deformity shown in that portrait was added in the Tudor period, when this particular type became the prototype for sixteenth-century images of the king. Perhaps More made the unevenness on the left side instead to make a moral point about Richard's sinister quality, always associated with left-sidedness (the very word *sinister* derives from the Latin word for left). We cannot know when this manner of denoting Richard's inner villainy entered common currency: an early portrait of Richard, dating to around 1510, also in the Society of Antiquaries (fig. 15), follows an original of his own reign between 1483 and 1485, and is rare in showing no deformity.[39]

The mid-sixteenth-century Antiquaries portrait is a fascinating palimpsest of changes in Richard's reputation as it was overpainted, to reduce evidence of deformity and a negative reading of Richard's character. This was perhaps done in the eighteenth century, and certainly before it was given to the Society in 1828. It is possible that this makeover followed on the publication of Horace Walpole's *Historic Doubts on the Life and Reign of Richard III*, published in 1768, which revived Richard's reputation.

15. Portrait of Richard III, unknown artist, probably soon after 1510.
Oil on oak panel, 39.5 x 28 cm (including frame).
Society of Antiquaries, London

Like Richard II, Richard III had his own heraldic devices. The white boar was Richard III's personal emblem, frequently referred to in contemporary literature. This identification is the reason for the scurrilous rhyme put on the door of St Paul's Cathedral by William Collingbourne on 18 July 1484, casting Richard III as 'the hog': 'The Cat, The Rat and Lovell our Dog / Rule all England under the Hog.'[40] The resonance of the identification of Richard III with the savage boar was one with a particular political meaning for Tudor readers and play audiences.

The boar was used by Richard as his own device, and given to his retainers and supporters as livery badges. Accounts of the royal wardrobe note thousands of such

'the most deadly boar'

(*Richard III 4.5.2*)

16. Boar badge of Richard III, late 1400s, found at Chiddingly, East Sussex, in 2003. Silver-gilt, 3.2 x 2.35 cm. British Museum, London

17. Boar badge of Richard III, *c.* 1470–85, found near Upton, Leicestershire, in 2009. Silver-gilt, L. 2.8 cm. Bosworth Battlefield Heritage Centre, Leicester

badges being made for his coronation. At the investiture of Richard III's son Edward as Prince of Wales an order was made on 31 August 1483 for 13,000 costume badges of the white boar to be made – perhaps for wear at the investiture ceremony itself in York Minster.[41] Boar badges in copper-alloy, lead and pewter have been found in York, at Richard's favourite castle at Middleham and in London.[42]

The only boar examples made in precious metal are recent discoveries. The silver-gilt badge in figure 16 was found at Chiddingly in East Sussex and acquired by the British Museum through the 1996 Treasure Act. The boar is engraved with a protruding tusk, bristling spine and curled tail above back legs; the front legs are missing, as is the attachment pin on the reverse. The badge was possibly worn as a hat emblem. In 2009 a silver-gilt boar badge (fig. 17), probably worn by one of Richard's knights, was found during a controlled archaeological survey at what has been claimed to be the exact spot where Richard III died at the Battle of Bosworth when his horse got stuck in the mud ('A horse! A horse! My kingdom for a horse' [5.3.361]). This badge was found close to the site of a medieval marsh. The findspot was on private farmland at Upton, Leicestershire, at Fenn Lane, 2 miles away from the Bosworth Battlefield Museum that up until now has been the official site of the battle. The badge was acquired by the Bosworth Battlefield Heritage Centre; the controversy about the actual site of the Battle of Bosworth continues.[43]

A fifteenth-century processional cross, with the Yorkist device of the sunburst engraved on it (fig. 18), was found around 1788 at what was then thought to be the site of Bosworth and aroused considerable scholarly interest when it was first published in 1811.[44] By that time the idea of the Tudors as the saviours of England after the years of division and civil war, and of Henry VII's victory at Bosworth as the dawn of a new age of national greatness, had become fully entrenched in the national consciousness – in large measure as a result of Shakespeare's cycle of history plays.

Henry V – the climax of the sequence of plays that began with *Richard II* – had by the nineteenth century become synonymous with English patriotism. A dashing young king achieves a stunning military victory against all odds, stirring his men to impossible valour through sheer rhetorical force. The phrases have become legendary:

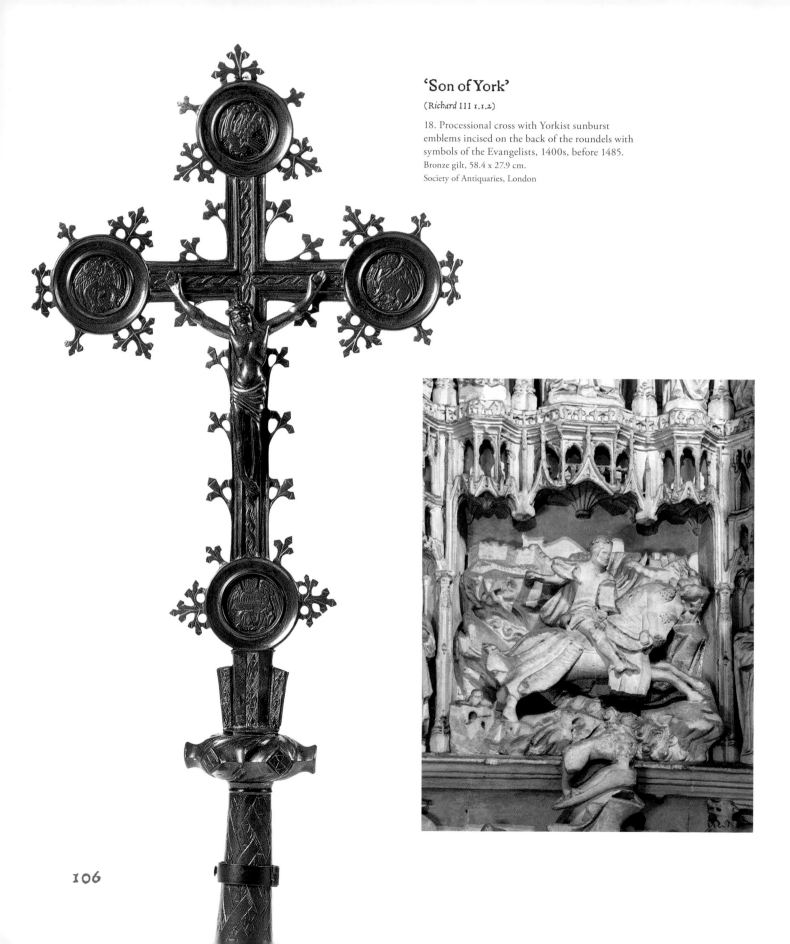

'Son of York'

(*Richard III* 1.1.2)

18. Processional cross with Yorkist sunburst emblems incised on the back of the roundels with symbols of the Evangelists, 1400s, before 1485. Bronze gilt, 58.4 x 27.9 cm.
Society of Antiquaries, London

'Once more unto the breach, dear friends, once more' (3.1.1); 'Cry "God for Harry, England, and Saint George!"' (3.1.34); 'We few, we happy few, we band of brothers' (4.3.62). Whereas all Shakespeare's other history plays of the 1590s portray an England riven by faction and anxiety over rightful succession to the throne, here the nation seems united and all-conquering.

Monks had celebrated Henry V's victory at Agincourt in 1415 by singing a Te Deum in Westminster. Henry contributed money to rebuilding the nave and reburied Richard II in St Edward's Chapel. He also directed in his own will that his tomb should be placed at the east end of St Edward's Chapel – Edward the Confessor was perceived as gatekeeper for successive kings – with a chantry chapel above in which to say masses for his soul. It is all still there. On the north side, clearly visible from the ambulatory as you go up steps into the Henry VII Chapel, is a carving showing Henry on horseback leaping a stream with his soldiers' tents behind him (fig. 19).[45] The silver-gilt tomb effigy with a head of solid silver had already had bits stolen from it by 1467, but the silver plates covering the effigy were stripped and stolen in 1546 so that only the wooden core remained.[46] A new head and hands were made in polyester resin by Louisa Bolt in 1971.[47] Such was the fame of Olivier's Henry V that it was later claimed (incorrectly) that the hands were actually modelled on those of Laurence Olivier, representing a desire to superimpose the celluloid image of Olivier on to Henry's effigy.

When you stand in the Chantry of Henry V you are just beneath a chestnut crossbeam on which were suspended his funeral achievements, clearly visible from almost every point in the Abbey. 'Achievements' were the crested helm and other armour carried in the funeral procession of a dead knight, which were then hung in perpetual memory over his tomb. The custom can be documented back to 1376, with the funeral achievements of the Black Prince at Canterbury Cathedral.[48] Henry V's achievements remained displayed on their crossbeam at Westminster Abbey from the time of his funeral on 6 November 1422 up to 1972 (when they were removed to the Abbey museum for conservation), and were described in 1682: 'The saddle which this heroic Prince used in the wars in ffrance, with his shield and other warlike furniture is to be seen'.[49]

The achievements included a tilting helm, used for jousting (fig. 20), which would originally have had a painted crest, probably a heraldic leopard as in the English royal arms. Although the helm was made for use in jousting, it is fitted with a hook on the back for attachment on to the crossbeam. The silk mantling formerly around the crest would have looked like that on the carved helms on the outside of Henry V's Chantry Chapel, making a link between the permanent monument and Henry's funeral.[50] The shield (fig. 21) may once have belonged to Henry V's father, Henry IV, at the time of his marriage to Joan of Navarre in 1403. The brilliantly coloured silk lining was already of some age then, and was probably woven in China specially for the export market. Four saddles were made for Henry's funeral; that shown here (fig. 22) is almost certainly one of them, though it was probably not part of the achievements. It now

19. Carving showing Henry V on horseback leaping a stream with his soldiers' tents behind him, from the outside of Henry V's Chantry Chapel in Westminster Abbey, viewed from the ambulatory at the entrance into Henry VII's Chapel. Possibly about 1422.
Westminster Abbey, London

'bruisèd helmet'

(*Henry V* 5.Chorus.18)

20. Helm associated with the funeral
of Henry V in 1422. England, early 1400s.
Iron or steel and copper alloy, H. 42.5 cm, W. 25.4 cm.
Westminster Abbey Museum, London

'Lay these bones in an unworthy urn / Tombless, with no remembrance over them'

(*Henry V* 1.2.231–2)

21. Shield associated with the funeral
of Henry V in 1422 (back view).
England, probably late 1300s.
Lime wood and textile, H. 61 cm, W. 39.4 cm.
Westminster Abbey Museum, London

22. Early fifteenth-century saddle, perhaps
associated with the funeral of Henry V in 1422.
Wood, hessian and leather, H. 39.3 cm (front),
H. 33 cm (back), L. 67.3 cm, W. 54.6 cm. Westminster
Abbey Museum, London

'his bended sword'

(*Henry V 5*.Chorus.*18*)

23. Sword, perhaps associated with the funeral
of Henry V in 1422. Probably England,
1400s or early 1500s.
Steel, iron and wood, L. 89.5 cm, L. (of blade) 73 cm.
Westminster Abbey Museum, London

lacks the splendid velvet cover which was described in 1723 as blue velvet with fleurs-de-lis in gold, perhaps the arms of France – suitable for a king who fought for so much of his life in France and married a French princess. The fifteenth- or early sixteenth-century sword (fig. 23) was only found in the Abbey in 1869 and may not have been part of the achievements, though it is likely to have been associated with a burial in the Abbey. The exact constituents of Henry's achievements are not determined, though the helm and the shield were illustrated hanging in the Abbey in 1707, but the force of the assemblage as secular relics is still felt today: 'To see armour and a sword associated with Henry V is sufficiently moving today, but for those who had known or admired the dead king, or who lived shortly after him, the trophy must have elicited a deeper emotional response by evoking the physical presence of that most splendid warrior prince.'[51]

It therefore comes as no surprise that the achievements are actually written into the prologue of act five of *Henry V*, as 'his bruisèd helmet and his bended sword' (Chorus 18). It has been suggested that Shakespeare may have seen them in their original location on the outside of Edmund the Confessor's tomb when he attended Edmund Spenser's funeral in the Abbey in 1599, but whether he did or not is somewhat irrelevant: they were known to be there.[52] This is perhaps implied when Shakespeare has Henry imagine an ignominious defeat for himself in France, charging his listeners to 'lay these bones in an unworthy urn / Tombless, with no remembrance over them' (1.2.231–2). The objects associated with Henry have a special resonance as they were visible in the Abbey from 1422 and were familiar to Londoners as relics of English medieval history. Through his poetic language, Shakespeare metaphorically brings them from the church to the stage, the Abbey to the Globe Theatre, the sacred arena to the secular. The powerful combination of artefacts and words shapes the heroic image of the national past.

Although Shakespeare's play of *Henry V* symbolically unites the four nations of the isles, bringing together an Englishman (Gower), a Scotsman (Jamy), a Welshman (Fluellen, i.e. Llewellyn) and an Irishman (MacMorris), on the battlefields of France, the reality of 1599, when the play was first performed, was not so happy.

The last independent Prince of Wales to have been recognized by the English, named Llywelyn ap Gruffud, had been killed during Edward I's invasion of Wales in 1282. Edward I inaugurated the custom of investing the heir apparent to the English throne with the title Prince of Wales. According to the chroniclers of Shakespeare's time, Edward II (r. 1307–1327), among his many other deficiencies, neglected to confer this title on his son. But Edward III (r. 1327–1377) revived it, naming his eldest son the Black Prince as Prince of Wales. According to William Camden's *Britannia*,

> King Edward the Second conferred not upon his sonne Edward the title of Prince of Wales, but only the name of Earle of Chester and of Flint, so farre as ever I could learne out of the Records, and by that title summoned him to Parliament,

being then nine yeres old. King Edward the Third first created his eldest sonne Edward surnamed the Blacke Prince, the Mirour of Chivalrie (being then Duke of Cornwall and Earle of Chester), Prince of Wales by solemne investure, with a cap of estate and Coronet set on his head, a gold ring put upon his finger, and a silver vierge delivered into his hand, with the assent of Parliament.[53]

The Black Prince (1330–1376) was the original heroic warrior Prince of Wales. His victory over the French at Crécy, against seemingly insurmountable odds, was the prototype for Henry V's victory at Agincourt, and the chronicle play of *Edward III* (*c.* 1592–4), to which Shakespeare contributed several scenes, was in turn the prototype for *Henry V*. From the point of view of the historians of the Tudor era, England's misfortunes began with the unprovidential death of the Black Prince before he ascended the throne. This meant that the throne passed to his son, a minor: Richard II. Since Richard had no son, there was no Prince of Wales at the moment when Henry Bullingbrook took the throne from Richard and became Henry IV. His son, Prince Harry of Monmouth, the future Henry V, was invested as Prince of Wales in the autumn of 1399. But the following year Owain Glyndŵr's followers proclaimed him Prince of Wales, in defiance of the English. Some years later, King Henry IV suppressed Owain's revolt, destroying any hope of Welsh independence.

Shakespeare's *Henry IV Part 1* brings together the Glyndŵr rebellion and that of the northern English earls who had helped Henry IV to the throne, then turned against him. Harry Hotspur and Glyndŵr are both, as it were, rival heirs who must be defeated by the true Prince of Wales and future king of England. Prince Harry triumphs, transforming himself from tavern-frequenting layabout to heroic horseman. He becomes a reincarnation of the Black Prince and prepares himself for his future victory at Agincourt.

The seal-matrix of Henry, Prince of Wales (later Henry V), for the lordship of Camarthen in figure 24 is part of Henry's assertion of power in Wales following the collapse of Owain Glyndŵr's revolt. It shows Henry as an equestrian figure, his horse trappings including the royal arms of England.

> I saw young Harry with his beaver on,
> His cuisses on his thighs, gallantly armed,
> Rise from the ground like feathered Mercury,
> And vaulted with such ease into his seat,
> As if an angel dropped down from the clouds,
> To turn and wind a fiery Pegasus
> And witch the world with noble horsemanship.
> (*Henry IV* 4.1.109–15)

In the Tudor era Queen Elizabeth's father, Henry VIII, had formally united England and Wales, but his only son, Edward VI (r. 1547–1553), became a boy-king

'And witch the world with noble horsemanship'

(*Henry IV Part I, 4.1.115*)

24. Seal-die of Henry Prince of Wales (later Henry V) for the lordship of Carmarthen, England, 1408–13.
Bronze, diam. (excluding lugs) 7.1 cm.
British Museum, London

before he was old enough to be invested as Prince of Wales. And of course Queen Elizabeth had no heir apparent. This, then, was another respect in which the reign of Elizabeth was like that of Richard II: there was no Prince of Wales. The Black Prince and Prince Harry of Monmouth were longed-for heroes of stage, chronicle and iconography precisely because there was no equivalent to them in the present, waiting in the wings to take the throne. That is one reason why there was great national rejoicing in the summer of 1610 when the sixteen-year-old Prince Henry, son of King James, was invested as Prince of Wales. And why there was deep national mourning when this paragon of hope died just two years later in November 1612.

Nevertheless, Wales remained relatively stable in the latter years of Queen Elizabeth's reign. Ireland was another matter. When the Chorus speaks the prologue to the final act of *Henry V*, he refers not only to the past – the evocation of Henry V's funeral achievements – but also to the present:

> Were now the general of our gracious empress,
> As in good time he may, from Ireland coming,
> Bringing rebellion broachèd on his sword,
> How many would the peaceful city quit,
> To welcome him?
> (5.Chorus.30–4)

This is the most specific and resonant topical allusion anywhere in the works of Shakespeare. In the summer of 1599, on the stage of the Globe Theatre, the Chorus refers specifically to what was happening in the real world at that very moment: the Earl of Essex was in Ireland, confronting the rebellion against English rule led by Hugh O'Neill, 2nd Earl of Tyrone (*c.* 1550–1616).

Although the setting for Shakespeare's history plays was the Hundred Years War against France and the Wars of the Roses in England, the backdrop against which many of them were written was the Nine Years War (1594–1603) in Ireland. There is extraordinary contemporary force to the words of the stage Irishman, MacMorris, in *Henry V*:

FLUELLEN Captain MacMorris, I think, look you, under your correction, there is not many of your nation –

MACMORRIS Of my nation? What ish my nation? Ish a villain and a bastard and a knave and a rascal. What ish my nation? Who talks of my nation? (3.2.88–91)

Here there is an implicit recognition that the Irish have had their nation taken away from them by the colonizing English. Later in the play (4.4.3) Pistol misquotes a Gaelic song 'Cailin og a stor', perhaps indicating that a misappropriated Gaelic culture was part of a London playgoer's world, however dimly recognized.[54]

Again and again in Shakespeare's history plays there are shadowy references to the wild Irish rebelling against English rule. The Dauphin in *Henry V* says 'you rode like a kern of Ireland, your French hose off, and in your straight strossers' (3.7.38–9). The Cardinal of Winchester in *Henry VI Part 2* refers to 'The uncivil kerns of Ireland' (3.1.310), while Richard Plantagenet (Duke of York) compares the common rebel Jack Cade to both a Morisco and an Irishman (3.1.360–70). A messenger in the same

'What ish my nation?'

(*Henry V* 3.2.90)

25. Rorie Oge, a wild kerne and a defeated rebel, in the forest with wolves for company, from John Derricke, *The Image of Irelande*, London, 1581, pl. 11.
Woodcut, 17.9 x 31 cm.
Edinburgh University Library, Edinburgh

play describes the Duke of York 'newly come from Ireland', with 'a puissant and a mighty power / Of gallowglasses and stout kerns' (4.9.24–6). That same combination of kerns and gallowglasses is transposed from Ireland to Scotland in *Macbeth*: 'The merciless Macdonald … from the Western Isles / Of kerns and gallowglasses is supplied' (1.2.11–15). And in Richard II the king turns his intention to 'our Irish wars': 'We must supplant those rough rug-headed kerns, / Which live like venom where no venom else / But only they have privilege to live' (2.1.156–9).

So what was a 'kern'? The copy of *The Image of Irelande, with a discoverie of Woodkarne* (1581) by John Derricke illustrated in figure 25 was given by the poet, William Drummond of Hawthornden, to his Edinburgh college.[55] It shows Irish rebels and their subjugation by the English, culminating in the submission of the rebel leader Turlough Lynagh O'Neale and the other kerne to Sir Henry Sidney (1529–1586) as Elizabeth I's Lord Deputy in Ireland. The woodkarne, or woodkerne, whose fate is told in a series of savage woodcuts forming a kind of satirical strip cartoon, were Irish rovers likened to the Border Reivers between Scotland and England who were active during the same period. Given the scarcity of surviving Irish artefacts from the late sixteenth century this book is ironically one of the best sources we have for Irish dress, custom and experience in the period. The woodcut by Derricke of an outlawed Irish woodkern shows him shivering in the forest under his shaggy mantle or cloak with a wolf howling behind him, echoing his own misery. The doggerel below ends:

> O Lamentable thyng to see, ambition clyme so high,
> When superstitious pride shall fall, in twynckling of an eye,
> For such is every rebeles state, and evermore hath bene,
> And let them never better speede, that ryse against our Queene.

The rebel's cloak resembles a type known in Shakespeare's day as an Irish rug or *hiberne*, after the Latin for Ireland, which made and exported these rugs. They were made of shaggy wool pile, sometimes chequered as an early form of tartan. Shag-pile Irish rugs, or mantles, were luxury goods in England as blankets, and in grand houses servants were specially deployed to put 'An Irish rugge' on the bed of important guests.[56] In Ben Jonson's *Irish Masque* of 1613, the cultural and political associations of Irish mantles are made evident when the comic Irish slough them like an old skin and become 'new-born creatures all' in masquing gear, and British to boot.[57]

Elizabethan anxiety about the troubles in Ireland was often focused less on the native Gaels than on the 'old English' who had been there since the Norman invasion of the twelfth century. The colonizer who turns native is a familiar fear: what would be the consequences if a new generation of English came to some accommodation with the rebel O'Neill?

The marvellous portrait seen in figure 26 presents Thomas Lee (1551/2–1601) as an adventurer out (like so many contemporary English gentlemen) to make his fortune in Ireland. He was to be executed with Essex in 1601 following Essex's disastrous Irish

'I found it out by the bogs'

(*The Comedy of Errors* 3.2.107)

26. *Captain Thomas Lee,* Marcus Gheeraerts the
Younger, dated 1594.
Oil on canvas, 230.5 x 150.8 cm.
Tate Britain, London

campaign of 1599 against O'Neill and his attempted *coup d'état* against Elizabeth I.
The portrait is dated 1594, the year in which he faced questioning as a double agent.[58]
Lee's dealings with the Ulster chieftain Hugh O'Neill are referred to in a good light
in the Latin tag from Livy in the tree at upper left. In his pose as a peacemaker who
can straddle English and Irish worlds, Lee's portrait is carefully literary and classical
in reference, but there is no doubting the urgency of the message.[59] Fraternizing with
the enemy was risky.

The portrait's artist Gheeraerts presents an ambiguous melding of Irish and
English dress, and it is interesting that even now commentators cannot agree on how
much of this allegorical portrait is 'Irish' in reference, other than the spear and the bare
legs, bravely bared for bog-trotting – one recalls the reference to finding Ireland out
'by the bogs' in the globular comic exchange in *The Comedy of Errors* (3.2.107). Lee's
costume also shows interesting correspondences with that of a couple of men labelled

27. Irish men and women, the men labelled as
'wilde Iresche', from Lucas de Heere's illustrated
manuscript *A Short Description of England, Scotland
and Ireland*, 1573–5.
Pen and ink and watercolour with bodycolour,
31.7 x 20.4 cm. British Library, London

'Bringing rebellion broachèd on his sword'

(*Henry V* 5.Chorus 32)

28. Robert Devereux, 2nd Earl of Essex on horseback, with Cadiz, the Azores and Ireland in the distance. Published by Thomas Cockson between the Irish campaign in 1599 and Essex's fall in 1600.

Engraving, 33.2 x 26.3 cm. British Museum, London

'a beard of the general's cut'

(*Henry V* 3.6.60)

29. Robert Devereux, 2nd Earl of Essex, Marcus Gheeraerts the Younger, *c.* 1596–9.

Oil on panel, 110 x 80.5 cm. Trinity College, Cambridge

'wilde Iresche', on fol. 34 of Lucas de Heere's *Short Description of England, Scotland and Ireland* (1573–5) (fig. 27).[60] The sophisticated pistol, helmet and blackwork shirt look Continental European or English, but the buckler and spear may be intended to be read as Gaelic.[61] It is a recognizable picture of the English in Ireland and it was an issue that was never going to go away. As a captain in Essex's army complained, 'I am sorry that when I am in England, I should be esteemed an Irishman, and in Ireland, an Englishman.'[62]

Whatever Shakespeare's views of Irish Gaelic culture there is no doubting his sympathy for the English soldiers on the Irish campaign who accompanied Essex: a stage direction in *Henry V* reads 'Enter the King and his poor soldiers' (3.6.67.1).[63] Feeling ran high in London where conscription weighed heaviest, but even in Cheshire it gave rise to a new proverb: 'Better be hanged at home than die like dogs in Ireland'.[64] War veterans like Pistol often turned to crime: in 1601 Stratford-upon-Avon tried to turn out one ex-soldier who had served in Ireland, a Lewis Gilbert, who embodied the psychological as well as physical maiming of the Irish war.[65]

Shakespeare was playing on anti-Irish feeling in London in his direct allusion to the Earl of Essex's campaign. Essex was keenly aware of publicity and self-promotion through portraits and prints (fig. 28).[66] Half-length versions of Essex's portrait like that in figure 29 exist in large numbers of varying quality.[67] They were workshop productions given to Essex's friends, clients and contacts.[68] Shakespeare expresses hope for a victory for Essex in Ireland when he compares Essex to Henry V on his triumphant return from France as 'a conqu'ring Caesar', defeating 'rebellion broachèd on his sword' while in the service of 'our gracious empress'. But he is not certain: 'as in good time he *may*' (*Henry V* Chorus 5.28–32). This is a rare moment when, like a freeze-frame in a movie, the drama of history stops and dramatist, actor and audience alike wait with bated breath upon the outcome of contemporary events.

LONDINIVM

Maximus hic Rex est
V luce serenior ipsa
Princeps quæ falcem
Cernit in Vrbe ducem
Cuius Fortunā superat
sic Vnica Virtus. Ve

PAR · DOMVS · HAEC · COELO · SED · MINOR · EST · DOMINO

1 2 3 4 5   10

S   H Excud·

4 'Beware the Ides of March': the Legacy of Rome

W E DO NOT KNOW FOR CERTAIN which play opened the new Globe Theatre in Southwark in the summer of 1599, but there are two strong candidates. One is *Henry V*, with its prologue referring self-consciously to the capacity of the bare stage of a theatre to evoke a battlefield. The other is *Julius Caesar*.[1] Either way, the Chamberlain's Men chose to stage a play set in the past but relevant to the present. They were as conscious of the ancient Roman influence on their world as they were of the country's own past. And indeed, on emerging from the Globe, audience members could have looked across the Thames and seen a visible sign of that influence in the form of what Shakespeare called 'Julius Caesar's ill-erected Tower' (*Richard II* 5.1.2): it was erroneously believed that the Tower of London was erected by Julius Caesar. Furthermore, public events such as royal triumphs were self-consciously based on Roman models. The chorus to the fifth act of *Henry V* imagines the triumphant return of the Earl of Essex from his Irish campaign, with Londoners lining the streets to welcome their 'conqu'ring Caesar' (*Henry V* 5.Chorus.28). Caesar had conquered the Gauls and Essex was out to conquer the Gaelic Irish as Henry V had the French.[2]

An impressive classical triumph was put on in honour of James I on 15 March 1604 which would take the king in procession from the Tower to the City of London through a series of seven triumphal arches, designed by Stephen Harrison and all paid for by the City of London, apart from two arches paid for by 'strangers' – the Dutch and Italian merchants. It had originally been planned for James's coronation in March 1603, but an outbreak of plague had forced a postponement. The arches were only temporary stage-prop constructions but were nonetheless massive and splendid, heavy with symbolism and royal flattery on the best classical model.

1. Plate from Stephen Harrison, *Arches of Triumph*, London, 1604, entitled 'Londinium'. One of seven arches put up in London in 1604 in honour of James I's accession. Engraving by William Kip, taken from the third edition of the book, printed before 1618.
26.8 x 23.1 cm. British Museum, London

The first arch at Fenchurch Street took the form of a representation of London itself, titled in Latin LONDINIVM. The letterpress text accompanying the plate in the 1604 edition of the *Arches of Triumph* explained how the arch was designed to support 'the goodliest Houses, Turrets, Steeples, &c. within this City … And those Models, stood as a Coronet on the forehead or Battlements of this Great and Magnificent Edisice [Edifice]' (fig. 1). The River Thames and the Genius of the City were also personified, beneath the figure symbolizing 'the British Monarchy'. As the royal procession approached, the Genius of London, played by the actor Edward Alleyn, addressed the king and the people. The spectacle was witnessed by what Thomas Dekker, who scripted the event with Ben Jonson, described as 'a sea of people so that the street could not be seen, women and children crowding every casement'.[3] As an evocation of imperial Rome in Jacobean London, mapping the ancient on to the modern city, it could hardly be bettered.

Shakespeare's interest in ancient Rome goes back to the beginning of his career. His other early box office hit, in addition to his sequence of dramas about the Wars of the Roses, was the gory tragedy *Titus Andronicus*. Probably revised from an earlier play by George Peele, it is an invented history of the late Roman Empire and the wars between the Romans and the Goths. Published in 1594, it was the earliest Shakespeare play to appear in print. The classical setting is used in order to explore a series of contemporary late Elizabethan questions: the succession of the crown, the ethics of revenge, the insider and the outsider, civilization and barbarity.

In the mind's eye of Shakespeare and his audience, it was possible for a play to be set simultaneously in ancient Rome, medieval England and the present. This sense of what we might call temporal syncretism is apparent in the earliest surviving illustration of a Shakespearean play, the drawing attributed to Henry Peacham that is now at Longleat House (fig. 2). There has been intense scholarly debate over many aspects of this drawing: its date (perhaps 1594, the year of the play's publication); the relationship between the drawing and the text below (which conflates speeches from different parts of the play and adds in some extra lines); whether the sketch is intended to represent a moment or moments in the play, or is more of a composite or emblematic representation of the drama and its characters; and whether it was a memory of a viewing of the play on stage or an invention based on a reading of the text.[4] These questions all remain unresolved, but what can be said with certainty is that in sketching his view of the play Peacham saw no incongruity in the juxtaposition of Roman accessories (toga, laurel crown), medieval-looking features (armour, Tamora's dress), and elements of contemporary Elizabethan costume and prop (hose, halberd). Modern stage directors who dress their Shakespeare one part Elizabethan, one part Roman and two parts modern dress can point to this drawing as a precedent for their eclecticism. For our purposes, what is revealing is that both on stage and in the mental theatre of the age, the world of ancient Rome – like the city of Venice, to be discussed in Chapter 5 – was a mirror held up to modern London. The evidence of the Peacham drawing tallies with the anachronisms that worried eighteenth- and nineteenth-century

2. Recollection of *Titus Andronicus*,
Henry Peacham, 1594?
Manuscript, pen and ink on paper, 29.6 x 40.3 cm.
Longleat House, Wiltshire

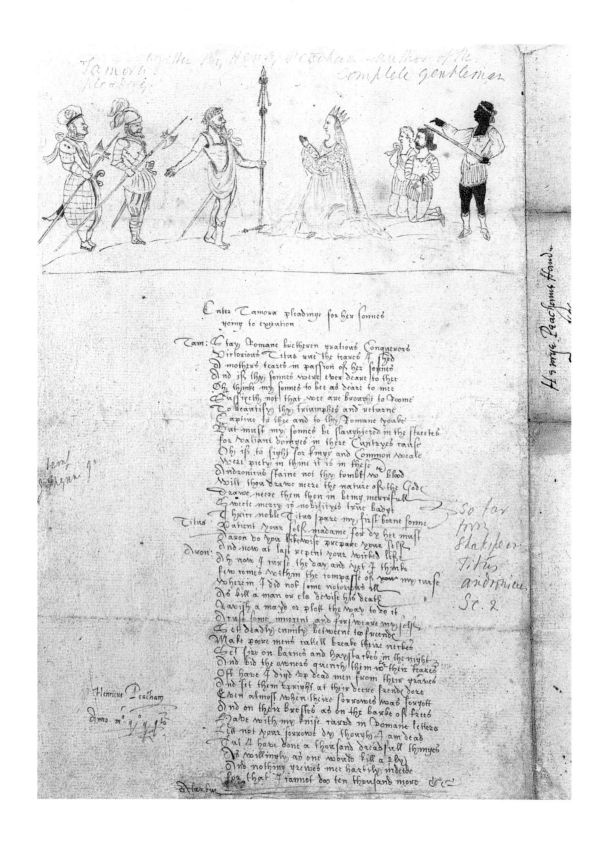

Enter Tamora pleadinge for her sonnes
goinge to execution

Tam: Stay Romane brethren gratious Conquerors
Victorious Titus rue the teares I shed
A mothers teares in passion of her sonnes
And iff thy sonnes were euer deare to thee
Oh thinke my sonnes to bee as deare to mee
Sufficeth not that wee are brought to Roome
To beautify thy triumphes and returne
Captiue to thee and to thy Romane yoake
But must my sonnes be slaughtered in the streetes
for valiant doynges in there Cuntryes cause
Oh iff to fight for kinge and Common weale
Were piety in thine it is in these
Andronicus staine not thy tombe wth blood
Wilt thou draw neere the nature off the Gods
Drawe neere them then in beinge mercifull
Sweete mercy is nobilityes true badge
Thrice noble Titus spare my first borne sonne

Titus Patient your self madame for dye hee must
And now do you likewise prepare your self

Aron: And now at last repent your wicked life
Ah now I curse the day and yet I thinke
few comes within the compasse of my curse
wherein I did not some notorious ill
As kill a man or els deuise his death
Rauish a mayd or plott the way to do it
Accuse some innocent and forsweare my self
Set deadly enmity betweene two freinds
Make poore mens cattell breake theire neckes
Set fire on barnes and haystackes in the night
And bid the owners quench them wth their teares
Oft haue I digd vp dead men from their graues
And set them vpright at their deere frendes dore
Euen almost when theire sorrowes was forgott
And on their brestes as on the barke off trees
Haue with my knife carued in Romane letters
Let not your sorrow dy though I am dead
But I haue done a thousand dreadfull thinges
As willingly as one would kill a fly
And nothing greues mee hartily indeede
But that I cannot do ten thousand more &c

Hoc est nusquam simile.

Effigiavit georgius Hoefnaglius Anno 1568

3. *The Progress of Queen Elizabeth I to Nonsuch Palace*, Joris Hoefnagel, 1568.
Pen and brown ink, with grey-brown, blue and red wash, 21.6 x 45.6 cm. British Museum, London

editors of Shakespeare: there are books with leaves, a chiming clock and a reference to chimneypots in *Julius Caesar* not because Shakespeare was ignorant of ancient history, but because the Rome of the play is also London.

The reading of the present through the lens of the classical past was at the core of education and elite culture in Shakespeare's England. A romantic vision of the classical past is expressed in Joris Hoefnagel's drawing of 1568, which shows the imagined progress of Queen Elizabeth I to Nonsuch Palace (fig. 3).[5] The queen in a carriage in the foreground is surrounded by soldiers with pikes, while we see the palace behind, with trees and fields beyond.[6] The timber-framed outer court of the palace was covered with stucco panels framed by intricately carved plaques of dark grey slate, the design picked out with gilding. The decorative scheme covered an area of 2,055 square metres, and depicted the Roman emperors, the gods and goddesses of classical mythology, and scenes from the life of Hercules with the liberal arts and virtues. Their original position is shown in the Hoefnagel watercolour. It was here that Elizabeth was holding court in September 1599 when Essex, sick and muddied from his disastrous Irish campaign (see pp. 113–16), burst into her private apartments unannounced, before the queen was properly wigged, made up or gowned. Ben Jonson evoked the scene in Elizabeth's bedchamber in *Cynthia's Revels* (1600): 'Seems it no crime / To brave a deity?'[7] The backdrop for this extraordinary encounter was the romantic classicism of Nonsuch itself, a fit setting for an anecdote reminiscent of Diana being chanced upon by Actaeon (see p. 39).

The splendid stucco relief of a Roman soldier from the Nonsuch Palace illustrated here (fig. 4) is a vivid embodiment of the classical legacy. The stuccoes were largely the work of Nicholas Bellin of Modena, who formerly worked at Francis I's palace of

4. Stucco panel carved with a Roman soldier
with spear and shield, attributed to Nicholas Bellin
of Modena, *c.* 1541–7, and excavated from the site
of Nonsuch Palace.
H. (of stucco panel) 136.8 cm. Reconstruction drawing
by David Honour. Museum of London, London

Fontainebleau in France but then left under a cloud to work for Henry VIII. His crossing-over was a cultural propaganda coup for the Tudors. Hoefnagel shows the Nonsuch reliefs in detail in his drawing: there is a sense of national pride in the image of an English royal palace matching the decorative panache of the great Renaissance buildings on the Continent.

Although the term 'Renaissance' was an invention of the nineteenth century, the idea that cultural and political greatness could be achieved through a rebirth of classical ideals was pervasive in the sixteenth century. At the basis of education was the humanist ideal that the study of the ancients could teach rationality, eloquence, virtue and political wisdom. The foundation of Shakespeare's classical education would have been laid at grammar school, but he would have begun around the age of six by learning 'his A B C' (*The Two Gentlemen of Verona* 2.1.20) from a hornbook. This comprised a wooden frame designed to be held in the hand, with a single printed sheet tacked on to the front beneath a protective layer of cow's horn. Very few of these learning tools have survived, in spite of the fact that they were once so common, as they were so heavily used. The sheet on the seventeenth-century example illustrated here (fig. 5), which can hardly be made out beneath the warped and clouded horn, is printed with the Lord's Prayer and the alphabet.[8] As one of the first generations of English schoolchildren to be brought up entirely in the Protestant faith, and with the liturgy in English, William Shakespeare's contemporaries took in the building blocks of their native language at the same time as absorbing the basic tenets of their religion.

Thanks to his father's position on the town council, Shakespeare was entitled to a free education at the King's New Grammar School in Stratford-upon-Avon. Grammar meant Latin grammar: that was what the young Shakespeare studied from dawn to dusk, six days a week, all the year round (though Thursdays and Saturdays were half days). Figure 6 shows a rare survival of an early edition of the standard Latin grammar of the sixteenth century, instituted for use by Edward VI in grammar schools, from which Shakespeare too would have begun his first studies in Latin.

His masters were Simon Hunt and then Thomas Jenkins. Although the latter came to Stratford from London, his name suggests that he was from a Welsh family. In *The Merry Wives of Windsor* a Welsh schoolmaster called Hugh Evans gives a Latin lesson to a clever but cheeky boy whose name can hardly have been chosen thoughtlessly: William. The scene reveals how Shakespeare learnt his Latin through rote and double translation, backwards and forwards between English and Latin, day in, day out. Having learnt the basics of grammar, William would then have gone on to construe Latin sentences. A caricature of Ovid as a Latin master teaching in class (fig. 7) gives a vivid sense of the learning process from a pupil's point of view. It is drawn into a late sixteenth-century edition of Ovid's *Metamorphoses*, of the kind Shakespeare's contemporaries used as a school text, and is perhaps copied from a print of the type found on title pages of schoolbooks.[9] The annotations, pen flourishes and owner inscriptions in the book, as well as the details of the schoolmaster's dress,

'his A B C'

(The Two Gentlemen of Verona 2.1.20)

5. Horn-book from the late 1600s, comprising a paper sheet printed with the alphabet and the Lord's Prayer, protected by a layer of horn. Papered wood with horn sheet fixed by bronze strips, L. 10.3 cm. British Museum, London

suggests that this is a late seventeenth-century drawing, perhaps drawn when the book was used in a Scottish school, but the method of learning, and the nature of the experience, varied little over time and place.

Ben Jonson, sometime bricklayer's apprentice, sneered at Shakespeare's 'small Latin', but a few years in an Elizabethan grammar school would have yielded enough Latin to last a lifetime. Shakespeare's initiation into the dramatic arts came with the schoolroom exercise of writing Latin epistles that imagined a particular situation or impersonated the style of a figure from classical history or mythology. And the desire to create poetic imagery, shape narratives of love and death, develop memorable characters and animate imaginative worlds would have been stimulated by study of the great authors of ancient Rome such as Virgil and Ovid.

In the absence of what we now call the mass media, the two primary locations for the communication of big political ideas to the people were the pulpit and the theatre. Both were dependent on the arts of language. The purpose of all that Latin grammar at school was to make boys skilled in rhetoric, the persuasive use of words for the purposes of argument. Rhetoric meant learning how to order a speech, and how to hone metaphors and develop elaborate figures of verbal symmetry. Grammar school rhetoric was intended to prepare the boys for a life of service to the church or the state, but in practice some

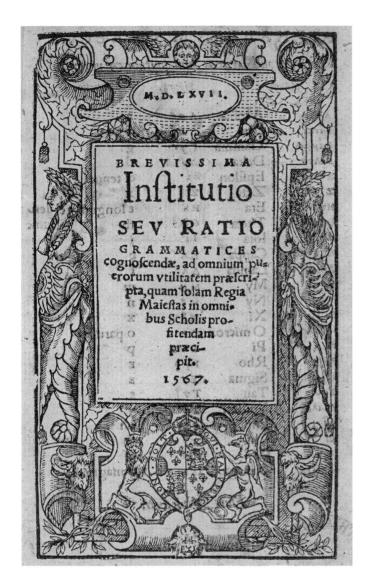

'I pray you, have your remembrance, child, *accusativo, hing, hang hog*'

(*The Merry Wives of Windsor* 4.1.33)

6. *A Shorte Introduction of Grammar*, William Lily, London, 1567. A rare survival of an early edition of the standard Latin grammar instituted for use in grammar schools by Edward VI, and the basis of Master William's Latin lesson with his Welsh schoolmaster Sir Hugh Evans in *The Merry Wives of Windsor*.
Printed book, leaf 18.5 x 13.4 cm, closed 19 x 14.3 cm.
Bodleian Library, Oxford

'What is the focative case, William?'

(*The Merry Wives of Windsor* 4.1.35)

7. Caricature of a Latin master teaching in class, drawn in ink by a seventeenth-century schoolboy in his copy of Ovid's *Metamorphoses*.
Pen and ink on paper, 7.6 x 11.9 cm.
Eton College Library, Eton

'Does thou love pictures? We will fetch thee straight Adonis painted by a running brook'

(*The Taming of the Shrew* Induction 2.43–4)

8. *Venus and Adonis*, workshop of Titian, *c.* 1554. There are more than thirty painted and engraved versions of this painting, some of which were painted by Titian himself, while others were produced by members of his workshop, and still others were the work of later copyists.
Oil on canvas, 177.9 x 188.9 cm.
National Gallery, London

of the brightest of them, such as Christopher Marlowe and William Shakespeare, turned instead to the nascent entertainment industry. The orator's art was equally apt for politics and for theatre. Player and politician are alike: each depends for his living on the ability to work a crowd. The close analogy between theatrical oration and politically driven public preaching – Elizabeth I was keen to 'tune the pulpits' as a propaganda tool – is nicely apparent from the way that Brutus's famous oration to the Roman crowd in *Julius Caesar*, 'Friends, Romans, countrymen, lend me your ears' (3.2.70), is delivered from a 'pulpit' (3.1.245).

No book worked upon Shakespeare's imaginary force more vigorously than Ovid's *Metamorphoses*, the source of most of his mythological imagery. *Venus and Adonis*, the poem with which he made his name in 1593 (see Chapter 2, pp. 68–9), was based on an Ovidian story that was well known and frequently illustrated in the period. Venus was the embodiment of sexual desire, Adonis beautiful but reluctant to indulge (he would rather be hunting). In the Induction of *The Taming of the Shrew*, a servingman offers Christopher Sly a tantalizing promise of the delights of the Lord's picture gallery:

> Dost thou love pictures? We will fetch thee straight
> Adonis painted by a running brook,
> And Cytherea [i.e. Venus] all in sedges hid,
> Which seem to move and wanton with her breath,
> Even as the waving sedges play with wind.
> (Induction 2.43–7)

The most famous visual representation of the story of Venus and Adonis, known throughout Europe and frequently copied, was Titian's. Illustrated here is a workshop copy of around 1554 (fig. 8), not one of the finest versions, but it makes our point: the prevalence of copies reveals how widely this treatment of the story was known and admired. The fresh underdrawing and the head of Adonis are attributed to Titian himself, though it is thought the painting may have been a preliminary sketch that Titian kept in his workshop as the basis for copies.[10] Like Shakespeare, Titian takes the story from Ovid but changes various elements: this scene, in which Venus attempts to restrain Adonis, is not directly based on a moment in the original poem. And, as so often in both Renaissance art and Shakespearean dramaturgy, motifs are imported from other sources in another form of creative syncretism. So, for example, the twisting figure of Venus is derived from a famous Roman marble relief known as the Bed of Polyclitus, which was much admired by collectors and patrons alike.[11] Shakespeare's poem shares with the painting a particular emphasis, absent from Ovid, on Venus trying to restrain Adonis from leaving her. This might suggest that Shakespeare had seen a version of the painting or one of the many engraved copies of it that were circulating by the 1590s (fig. 9), but it is equally possible that painter and poet developed the image independently. Variation and expansion of an original

9. Print of Titian's composition in a vertical format by Giulio Sanuto, dated 21 September 1559 and approved by the aritst.

Engraving, 53.8 x 41.5 cm. British Museum, London

source was a key part of creative *imitatio* in both painting and writing.

The picture epitomizes a new kind of mythological painting that was an essential accessory to the fashionable noble patron. An ostentatious lord would want such a piece in his gallery, just as he would take pleasure in having an eloquent and fashionable work of poetry dedicated to him. English patrons were no exception: there were probably paintings on this theme in late sixteenth-century British collections.[12]

The figure of Adonis, whose face was probably painted by Titian's own hand (fig. 10), is suggestively androgynous. A contemporary observer, Ludovico Dolce, described it in a letter of 1554 to Alessandro Contarini:

This history-piece of Adonis was painted a short time ago and sent by the good Titian to the King of England [i.e. Philip of Spain, who was King of England by his marriage to Queen Mary]. But to begin with the figure. He has made it

'Stain to all nymphs,
more lovely than a man'

(Venus and Adonis 9)

10. Detail of Adonis's face in fig. 8

of a stature suitable to a boy of sixteen or eighteen years, well-proportioned, graceful, and charming, and in every part light and airy, with a fine complexion, plainly showing that he is extremely delicate and of royal blood; and we see in the air of the face that this wonderful master has endeavoured to express a certain engaging beauty, which though it participates of the female face, yet is not unmanly or effeminate. I would say that it is a lady with something I know not what of masculine beauty, or rather a man with all the beauty of a lovely woman, a mixture difficult, pleasing, and especially (if we may rely on Pliny) prized by Apelles [the ancient Greek painter].[13]

The idea of Adonis's sexually ambiguous beauty is developed in the *Metamorphoses* itself. Venus tells Adonis the story of Atalanta and of how 'when Hippomenes saw Atalanta's face and unclothed body – a body like my own, or like yours, Adonis, if you were a woman – he was struck with wonder' (*Metamorphoses* 10.578–80).[14] Shakespeare, who was already beginning to show an interest in the androgynous beauty of the boy actors who played the female parts in his plays (see, for example, *The Taming of the Shrew* Induction 1.126–7 and *The Two Gentlemen of Verona* 4.4.142–56), makes much of this quality in Adonis: 'Stain to all nymphs, more lovely than a man' (*Venus and Adonis* 9). It can reasonably be assumed that he wrote this in the knowledge that the prospective patron to whom he dedicated the poem, Henry Wriothesley, 3rd Earl of Southampton, had a certain androgynous beauty himself (fig. 11). If, as is likely, some of Shakespeare's early *Sonnets* were also written with Southampton in mind, then the theme was further developed: 'A woman's face with Nature's own hand painted / Hast thou, the master-mistress of my passion' (*Sonnet* 20.1–2).

'What I have done is yours, what I have to do is yours, being part in all I have, devoted yours.'

(*The Rape of Lucrece* Preface)

11. Portrait of Henry Wriothesley, 3rd Earl of Southampton, unknown artist, *c*. 1600. Southampton is shown with the suit of armour in fig. 12.
Oil on canvas, 204.5 x 121.9 cm.
National Portrait Gallery, London

Southampton's fair face, tumbling locks and feminine charm were combined with a strong sense of his masculine accomplishments. Around the time that Shakespeare sought his patronage, he was painted wearing armour, suggestive of commanding presence and high courtly ambition. In the portrait illustrated here Southampton is shown wearing the collar of the armour, with the cuirass on the floor to his left and the helmet, with plumes, on a plinth to his right. The portrait is thought to have been painted around 1600, when he was a key figure in the circle of the Earl of Essex.[15]

The armour in the portrait survives (fig. 12). It used to be considered Flemish and comparable to a number of pieces of armours attributed to the so-called 'Master of the Snails and Dragonflies' from Antwerp, but recent scholarship suggests that it is French, and may have been acquired during the Earl's diplomatic mission to Paris in 1598.[16] The distribution of the delicately etched design (fig. 13) over the whole armour surface, and the use of hatched grounds in the foliage borders seem to be characteristic French features of the period.[17]

One of the great themes in Renaissance art and poetry is the battle between Venus and Mars or desire and duty, the pursuit of love and the pursuit of honour. Adonis's preference for hunting – a form of mock-battle – over dalliance with the goddess of love is a playful manifestation of this theme. The second poem that Shakespeare dedicated to Southampton in 1594, *The Rape of Lucrece*, explores the darker side of the conflict. Shakespeare turns from the witty poetry of Ovid to the political history of Livy. Collatine is a soldier who makes the mistake of boasting of his wife Lucrece's sexual purity to a more powerful man, Sextus Tarquinius, the son of the Roman king. Tarquin sets out to test the claim and, having failed to seduce Lucrece with silver words, violently rapes her. Shamed by her dishonour, she commits suicide. In revenge, Collatine joins with other soldiers, led by Lucius Junius Brutus, in overthrowing the Tarquin monarchy and turning Rome into a republic.

The language of the dedication to Southampton (fig. 14) suggests that Shakespeare had gained some access to, or benefit from him as a result of his first bid for patronage: 'The warrant I have of your honourable disposition, not the worth of my untutored lines, makes it assured of acceptance. What I have done is yours, what I have to do is yours, being part in all I have, devoted yours'. If the first poem made the flattering but

12. Three-quarter field armour of Henry Wriothesley, 3rd Earl of Southampton. Probably French, and possibly acquired by the Earl when on a diplomatic visit to Paris in 1598. He is shown in fig. 11 wearing the collar, with the cuirass on the floor and the helmet on the table beside him. Steel, gilded and etched, H. (top of helmet to bottom of knee defence) 136 cm. Royal Armouries, Leeds

13. Detail of the etched decoration on the armour in fig. 12.

14. Shakespeare's dedication of his poem *The Rape
of Lucrece* to the Earl of Southampton, London,
1594. Printed by Richard Field for John Harrison.
17.8 x 11.6 cm. British Library, London

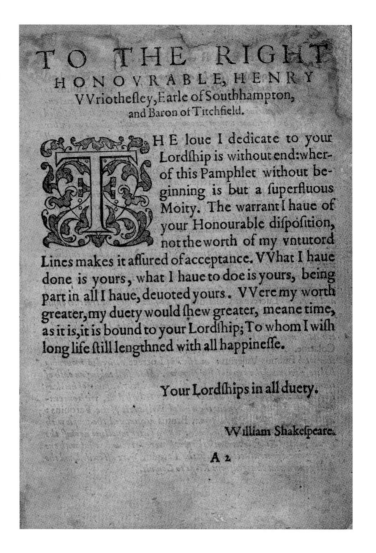

TO THE RIGHT
HONOVRABLE, HENRY
VVriothefley, Earle of Southhampton,
and Baron of Titchfield.

THE loue I dedicate to your
Lordship is without end:wher-
of this Pamphlet without beginning is but a fuperfluous
Moity. The warrant I haue of
your Honourable difpofition,
not the worth of my vntutord
Lines makes it affured of acceptance. VVhat I haue
done is yours, what I haue to doe is yours, being
part in all I haue, deuoted yours. VVere my worth
greater, my duety would fhew greater, meane time,
as it is, it is bound to your Lordfhip; To whom I wifh
long life ftill lengthned with all happineffe.

Your Lordfhips in all duety.

VVilliam Shakefpeare.

A 2

risky insinuation that Southampton was an Adonis in beauty, the second appeals
more to his devotion to the code of honour. It gives due prominence to arms and
armour, whether in a long digression describing a painting of the Trojan War, or the
vivid image of Tarquin's 'falchion' (curved sword) (176) smiting sparks of fire from
a flint in order to light a torch, symbolic of the heat of desire. If *Venus and Adonis*
was meant for Southampton the lover, *The Rape of Lucrece* was directed at
Southampton the soldier.

Some time in the 1590s, perhaps in Southampton's library or perhaps thanks to a
discount copy from his schoolfriend Richard Field, Shakespeare began reading Sir
Thomas North's translation of Plutarch's *Lives of the Noble Grecians and Romanes*
(fig. 15). Each life in Plutarch was prefaced by a coin-like portrait, 'the face of an
old Roman coin, scarce seen' (*Love's Labours Lost* 5.2.629). Coins and numismatic

evidence were beginning to be used in England as an historical source, as had long been the case in Italy.[18] *Julius Caesar* was the first of three plays that Shakespeare based closely on Plutarch, the subsequent ones being *Antony and Cleopatra* and *Coriolanus*. Although the narrative follows Plutarch closely, many elements of characterization are Shakespeare's invention. Could the way in which Julius Caesar is portrayed as somewhat petulant and past his prime, almost the old maid, have offered a whispered suggestion of Queen Elizabeth at the end of her life, fearful of conspiracy and assassination?[19] And could the attribution to Brutus of various weaknesses with no historical warrant from Plutarch – deafness, poor swimming, wavering and superstitious fears – be symptoms of a politically subtle desire to humanize but not over-idealize the soldier–conspirator?

The epoch-making historical events that form the plot of the play were known to all educated men and women in Elizabethan England. On 15 (or 'ides') of March 44 BC Julius Caesar was assassinated by a group of twenty-three conspirators, who were angered by the Roman general and politician's rise to power, and persistent rumours that he wished to become king – a concept abhorrent to the ideology of republican Rome. One of the assassins, Marcus Junius Brutus, had been considered a trusted ally by Caesar. The betrayal felt by Caesar is captured for all time in the invented line in Shakespeare's *Julius Caesar*: 'Et tu, Brute?' (3.1.84). The conspiracy sparked an extended period of civil war, during which Gaius Octavius (later Rome's first emperor, Augustus) and Mark Antony fought and defeated the assassins, before eventually turning against each other in a confrontation that led to the downfall of the republic.

Perversely to the modern eye, Brutus himself chose to commemorate Caesar's murder through the commissioning of coinage, which carried his portrait, the date, as well as images of the assassins' daggers and a *pileus* or freedman's cap, symbolic of Rome's escape from tyranny (fig. 16). The coin was produced in 43–42 BC at the mobile mint of Brutus and his fellow conspirators, who had by this time fled Rome for Greece. Brutus is named as BRVT IMP on the coin, with IMP being an abbreviation of *Imperator*, a title awarded to generals by their armies. Unusually the coin's significance – and its completely new iconography – was recognized in antiquity, being described by Cassius Dio in the second century AD: 'Brutus stamped upon the coins which were being minted his own likeness and a cap and two daggers, indicating by this and by the inscription that he and Cassius had liberated the fatherland.'[20]

Silver *denarii* of this type are unusual enough, but gold examples (*aurei*) are extraordinarily rare.[21] Fascinatingly, this particular coin has been pierced. Close analysis suggests that this is likely to have taken place shortly after it was struck. If so, it takes on a new significance, as it would have been pierced so that it could be worn as a pendant around the neck. Wearing this coin would have been a powerful symbol of support for the conspirators and their cause. Given that gold coins were of high value – perhaps the equivalent of a month's pay for an ordinary Roman legionary – it is likely that its owner was a wealthy and powerful supporter of the conspirators. It requires only a small leap of faith to suggest that this coin was once owned and worn

THE LIFE OF
Marcus Brutus.

A **M**Arcus Brutus came of that *Iunius Brutus*, for whome the auncient Romanes made his statue of brasse to be set vp in the Capitoll, with the
images of the kings, holding a naked sword in his hand: bicause he had
valliantly put downe the Tarqvines from their kingdom of Rome.
But that *Iunius Brutus* being of a sower stearne nature, not softned by
reason, being like vnto sword blades of too hard a temper: was so sub-
iect to his choller and malice he bare vnto the tyrannes, that for their
sakes he caused his owne sonnes to be executed. But this *Marcus Brutus* in contrarie maner, whose life we presently wryte, hauing framed
his manners of life by the rules of vertue and studie of Philosophie, and hauing imployed his
B wit, which was gentle and constant, in attempting of great things: me thinkes he was rightly
made and framed vnto vertue. So that his verie enemies which wish him most hurt, bicause
of his conspiracy against *Iulius Cæsar*: if there were any noble attempt done in all this conspiracie, they referre it whollie vnto *Brutus*, and all the cruell and violent actes vnto *Cassius*, who
was *Brutus* familiar frend, but not so well geuen, and condicioned as he. His mother *Seruilia*,
it is thought came of the blood of *Seruilius Hala*, who, when *Spurius Melius* went about to
make him selfe king, and to bring it to passe had entised the common people to rebell: tooke
a dagger and hid it close vnder his arme, and went into the market place. When he was come
thither, he made as though he had somewhat to say vnto him, and pressed as neere him as he
could: wherefore *Melius* stowping downe with his head, to heare what he would say, *Brutus*
C stabbed him in with his dagger, and slue him. Thus muche all writers agree for his mother.
Now touching his father, some for the euil wil & malice they bare vnto *Brutus*, bicause of the
death of *Iulius Cæsar*, doe maintaine that he came not of *Iunius Brutus* that draue out the Tarqvines: for there were none left of his race, considering that his two sonnes were executed
for conspiracie with the Tarqvines: and that *Marcus Brutus* came of a meane house, the
which was raised to honor and office in the common wealth, but of late time. *Posidonius* the
Philosopher wryteth the contrarie, that *Iunius Brutus* in deede slue two of his sonnes which

*The parentage
of Brutus.*

*Brutus ma-
ners.*

*Seruilia M.
Brutus mo-
ther.*

*Brutus paren-
tage by his
father.*

'the face of an old Roman coin, scarce seen'

(*Love's Labour's Lost* 5.2.629)

15. Brutus, from Thomas North's translation of Plutarch's *Lives of the Noble Grecians and Romanes*, London, 1579. Each life is prefaced by engraved coin-like images such as this one. A later edition was printed by Shakespeare's friend and schoolmate Richard Field, who also printed *Venus and Adonis* and a Latin edition of Ovid's *Metamorphoses*.
Printed book, 31.8 x 21 cm.
British Library, London

'Beware the Ides of March'

(Julius Caesar 1.2.21)

16. Gold coin (*aureus*) commemorating the murder of Julius Caesar. Minted by Brutus and his fellow conspirators in 43–42 BC when they had fled Rome for Greece. The coin is pierced to be worn as a token, perhaps by one of the conspirators or their immediate supporters soon after the event.
Diam. 2.01 cm. British Museum, London

by one of the conspirators themselves. Shakespeare could not have known this, but he grasped the importance of money in the purchase of allegiance in ancient Rome: Mark Antony buys the people's loyalty to Caesar's memory by telling them that he has left 75 drachmas to every citizen and when Brutus falls out with Cassius it is partly over 'certain sums of gold' (*Julius Caesar* 3.2.239 and 4.2.134).

In Shakespeare's time riots often broke out on holidays, when the people were not confined at work. Instability and civic unrest are evoked at the beginning of *Julius Caesar* with a motley assortment of workers out on the streets. *Coriolanus* also begins with a dangerous scene of mass unrest. In that play, the plebeian crowd – fickle, easily manipulated, but still a force to be reckoned with – remains prominent in later scenes. 'You are they / That made the air unwholesome when you cast / Your stinking greasy caps in hooting at / Coriolanus' exile (4.6.157–60). Those caps are contemporary, not Roman (fig. 17).[22] The chronicler of London, John Stow, talks about a fashion for knitted caps among 'youthful citizens' in the time of Henry VIII. A later woodcut of the burning of a martyr, John Rogers, in 1555 shows the crowd wearing these caps (fig. 18). Later, the fashion declined and with it the woollen industry. In order to improve the market conditions for wool a statute was enacted in 1571 to enforce the wearing of woollen caps by everyone over six years of age on Sundays and holidays. Shakespeare's uncle was fined under the act for not doing so – enforcement was locally policed and is frequently mentioned in royal proclamations. So it is no surprise that Shakespeare refers to 'plain statute-caps' in *Love's Labour's Lost* (5.2.300). The statute was repealed in 1597, but Coriolanus's reference suggests that they were still common holiday wear in the early Jacobean years. The woollen cap of artisans and apprentices would have characterized Hamlet's groundlings in the yard, the lowest status area of the playhouse.[23]

At the beginning of the second act of *Julius Caesar*, a sleepless Brutus is troubling himself over whether he should participate in the conspiracy. He asks his serving boy

'plain statute-caps'

(Love's Labour's Lost 5.2.300)

17. In 1571 a statute was enacted to enforce
the wearing of woollen caps by everyone over
six years of age on Sundays and holidays. This
knitted woollen man's cap, made in England
in the mid- to late sixteenth century, was found
in Moorfields, London.
Wool, knitted and felted, and silk, diam. 24 cm.
British Museum, London

to check the calendar in order to establish whether the next day is the first of March.
After a soliloquy in which he *pieces out* what he should do ('piece it out' 2.1.51),
coming towards a resolution by citing the example of his ancestor who overthrew
the Tarquins, the boy returns and tells him that it is actually the fifteenth, not the
first. Brutus is pleased: it is the ides of March, the day of which the Soothsayer has
told Caesar to beware. All the auguries, Brutus now believes, are in place for the right
outcome. But why does his initial instinct get the date wrong by two full weeks?
Nowadays this would seem a somewhat implausible error, but in Shakespeare's time
the calendar was not a given: it was subject to political and religious pressures, and
to corruption over time.

A solar year is approximately 365.25 days long. The original Roman calendar
divided the year into twelve months, with a total of 355 days and the occasional
'intercalary' month of twenty-two days inserted between February and March. In
45 BC Julius Caesar improved this reckoning by introducing what became known as
the Julian Calendar: 365 days in the year, with an extra day at the end of February
once every four years. The Julian Calendar was adopted by the Christian Church at
the Council of Nicaea in AD 325 to ensure that Easter was celebrated at the same time
everywhere. But this did not entirely solve the problem, since the solar year is not
exactly 365.25 days long: it is about eleven minutes shorter, which meant that the
Julian calendar gained about three days every four centuries. This difficulty was tackled
by Gregory XIII (r. 1572–1585) in a papal bull of 1582, the year of Shakespeare's
marriage. The Gregorian reforms proposed a new method of calculating Easter,
removed ten days from October 1582, and modified the system of leap years. These
reforms were accepted by the Catholic Church but rejected by most Protestant states.

Sir Francis Walsingham, Queen Elizabeth's Secretary of State, and an arch-
Protestant, received details of the reforms in diplomatic correspondence and asked
John Dee, the court magus, to comment.

Dee's ambition in framing a new Christian calendar is made visually clear in

The burning of Maiſter Iohn Rogers, vicar of Saint Pulchers, and Reader of Paules in London.

Lord receiue my ſpirite,

'Is this a holiday?'

(*Julius Caesar* 1.1.2)

18. Caps are worn by the crowd at the burning of John
Rogers for heresy under Mary Tudor in 1555. In *Julius
Caesar*, Brutus implores the crowd not to 'hew him
[Caesar] as a carcass fit for hounds', which refers
Shakespeare's audience back to the visceral theatre of
punishment as experienced at the executions of traitors
who were hanged, drawn and quartered in public.
Woodcut from a sixteenth-century edition of Foxe's
Book of Martyrs, 12.6 x 17.4 cm. British Museum, London

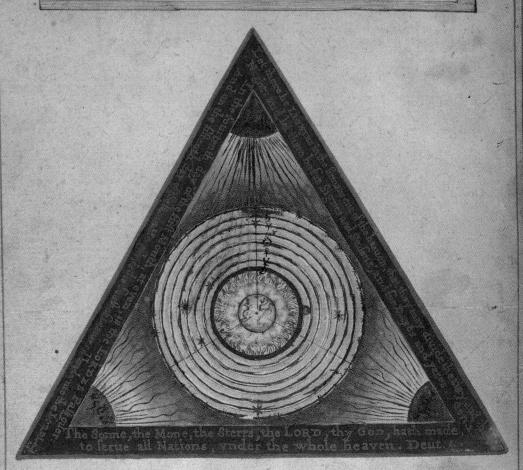

'Is not tomorrow, boy, the first of March?'

(*Julius Caesar* 2.1.40)

19. The illuminated frontispiece of John Dee's unpublished treatise on calendar reform, 1583. Page 29.4 x 20.5 cm, closed 31.9 x 22.9 cm. Bodleian Library, Oxford

the illuminated preface to the treatise that he produced in response (fig. 19). It takes the form of an emblem that has cosmic, national and personal significance. The title, *Primi Quatridui Mysterium* (*The Mystery of the First Four Days*), refers to God's creation of the lights – sun, moon and stars – that separate light from darkness and mark days, seasons and years. This is the mystery described in Genesis 1:14, one of three quotations from the Old Testament inscribed in gold on the triangular blue border. In the diagram divine rays pour in from the godhead (identified with the Hebrew 'Elohim'), passing through the planetary spheres of the Ptolemaic universe and converging on the earth at the centre of the system: they seem to meet at the North Pole, lending divine support for the Arctic exploration that Dee put at the heart of his project for a new British Empire under Elizabeth. And Dee's role as shaper of this ambitious scheme is acknowledged by the triangular design of the diagram, which forms a *delta*, the fourth letter of the Greek alphabet and one of Dee's favourite puns on his own name.[24]

His treatise ended with a poem petitioning the queen to alter the English calendar by eleven days, not ten. In the poem, he refers to Elizabeth as the new Caesar, and himself as the new Sosigenes (Sosigenes of Alexandria, the astronomer consulted by Caesar to help construct the Julian calendar).

A reformation of eleven days as opposed to ten would have the political advantage of keeping the identity of the Church of England separate from that of Rome. In time, Dee argued, the Romans would discover that his calculation, not theirs, was correct, and they would fall into line. Dee dreamed that there would one day be a British Empire – an 'incomparable Islandish monarchy', as he called it – stretching across the world, rivalling the power of ancient Rome. There would be a lot of potential practical problems in living globally with three ever-diverging calendars – the Julian, the Gregorian and his proposed 'Elizabeth's perpetual Kalendar' – but he was sure that the English would eventually be proved right and that his scheme would in time be adopted universally. A new and correct Elizabethan calendar anchored on the London meridian would be the temporal and 'cosmographical' centrepiece of a mathematically coherent new world order in which Protestantism reigned and Britannia ruled the waves. In the light of the international adoption of Greenwich as the prime meridian in 1884, at the height of the British Empire, Dee was in a certain sense proved prophetically right.

The pragmatic Lord Burghley, Elizabeth's chief minister, thought that the best course of action would be to adopt the new calendar, but negotiate to persuade Rome to make a change of eleven days rather than ten. But the Bishops objected to any change: since the Pope was Antichrist, there could be no negotiation with him and England should have nothing to do with any reform emanating from Rome. The outcome was that England remained outside the Gregorian system for another 170 years.[25] Thus in 1599, the date in Rome was significantly different from that in London, a discrepancy which Shakespeare plays upon in Brutus's uncertainty over the date.

The calendar, then, was an area of contention between church and state. The fact that the reforms were not adopted, despite Burghley's desire that they should be, reveals that the church still held considerable political sway in Shakespeare's England. The players had to be very careful in drawing implicit parallels between Roman history and contemporary affairs. The writer Fulke Greville (1554–1628) destroyed his own play on the subject of Antony and Cleopatra for fear that the story of a queen seducing a soldier-hero to 'forsak[e] empire to follow sensuality' would elicit parallels with Elizabeth and Essex.[26] It was only after Elizabeth's death that Shakespeare's acting company brought the Cleopatra story to the public stage. The playing cards shown here (fig. 20) reveal that the parallel between the ancient and the modern queens as famous female world rulers was made visually by the 1640s in Europe. Shakespeare's Cleopatra is not in any sense a direct allegorical representation of Queen Elizabeth, but audiences would have been provoked into seeing the parallels: a woman ruler in an overwhelmingly male world, the identification between the queen and her country. Cleopatra is referred to as 'Egypt', while Elizabeth in her famous oration at Tilbury compared her body to the body politic of England: 'I know I have the body of a weak, feeble woman; but I have the heart and stomach of a king – and of a king of England too.'

In each case, the mythologizing of the queen involved identifying her with a goddess – or, in Elizabeth's case, a range of goddesses, among them Diana (the embodiment of chastity) and Astraea (the symbol of a golden age of justice). Queen Elizabeth's virginity was central to her image in many portraits and poems (see Chapter 1, p. 37 and fig. 27), and in the famous gold medal (fig. 21) in which she is

20. Two playing cards from a set entitled *Le Jeu des Reynes Renommées* (*The Game of Famous Queens*) etched by Stefano della Bella, 1644. Cleopatra with the asp is labelled: 'Queen of Egypt: she won the good graces of Caesar'; while Elizabeth I is labelled: 'Queen of England: she governed her realm wisely'. Etchings, Elizabeth 8.9 x 5.5 cm; Cleopatra 8.7 x 5.5 cm. British Museum, London

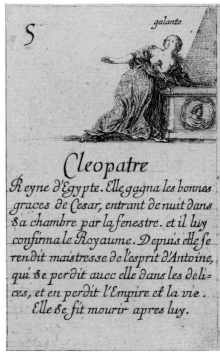

21. The 'Phoenix Jewel': pendant with a cut-out bust of Queen Elizabeth I on the front and the phoenix arising from the flames on the back, under the royal cipher. England, *c.* 1570–80.
Gold and enamel, 6.1 x 4.6 cm (including suspension loop). British Museum, London

compared to the phoenix that, according to legend, rose out of its own ashes and lived once more.[27] The Christian mind came to associate that regeneration of the phoenix with Christ himself, and with chastity. The crowned monogram of the queen appears on the reverse above the image of the phoenix rising from the flames, but on a silver version of the medal dated 1574 the Latin legend pities 'the wretched English', as their phoenix, the queen, could not come to life after death.[28] Another version of the medal, is inscribed 'The single Phoenix is all in all, and the glory of England'.[29]

Manipulating their own image was equally important to both queens in a man's world. But there were obviously profound differences. Cleopatra, in contrast to Elizabeth, identified herself with Isis, who was associated above all with fertility, and worshipped as the ideal mother and wife as well as the matron of nature and magic. Cleopatra was also linked in the Roman mind with Aphrodite. A Hellenistic gold pendant (fig. 22), said to have been found in Egypt, presents Aphrodite seated on a high-backed throne, accompanied by a small winged Eros. She turns her head sensuously over her bare shoulder. Her thin tunic (*chiton*) has slipped off one shoulder and clings to her breasts. The erotic mood of this delicate medallion evokes Plutarch's description – taken up by Shakespeare – of Cleopatra in her barge, with boys like little Erotes fanning her (2.2.222–37).[30]

Cleopatra's actual appearance remains elusive. One of the first marble heads to be identified as a portrait of her, on the basis of comparison with her coin portraits, is now thought to be that of one of her entourage in Rome who modelled herself on Cleopatra's image (fig. 23). It is indeed very close in profile to the coin portraits of the queen, but the Roman informality and lack of royal diadem or insignia is out of character with what we know about the real Cleopatra and her sense of her own regal status.[31]

The paradox and the fascination of Cleopatra, which Shakespeare plays upon so powerfully, was her double identity as both goddess and courtesan. In early modern slang, 'quean' was a term for a prostitute: Cleopatra is represented as both 'queen' and 'quean', supreme in regality yet voracious in sexual appetite. Cleopatra's erotic cross-dressing with Antony (2.5.21–6) is just the kind of act associated with contemporary courtesans, as well as her eloquence and the attention she commands through her speech. In the *Life of Antony*, Shakespeare's source for his play, Plutarch emphasizes the charm of Cleopatra's voice, of her speech and the grace of her presence. This must be the model for the way in which Tullia d'Aragona, a sixteenth-century Roman courtesan, was described by one of her admirers: 'She talked with such a grace and rare eloquence when joking or when she was debating serious subjects so that she drew and conquered the soul of her listeners, like another Cleopatra.'[32]

The same identification is apparent in a sixteenth-century portrait of a courtesan in the guise of Cleopatra, attributed to Paris Bordone (fig. 24). Leading Renaissance courtesans fashioned themselves on the *hetairai* of classical antiquity. But they were women who dominated their own, contemporary world in striking ways. Several of them – Tullia and Veronica Franco, for example – showed themselves to be adept at profiting from the expansion of the world of learning through cheaper print and the

22. Medallion with Aphrodite and Eros. Hellenistic, *c*. 200–100 BC, said to be from Egypt. Cleopatra liked to associate herself with Aphrodite, the Greek goddess of love. Julius Caesar had a gold statue of Cleopatra placed in the temple of Venus (the Roman name for Aphrodite) in Rome.
Gold, diam. 4.4 cm. British Museum, London

23. Head of a woman resembling Cleopatra. Roman, *c*. 50–40 BC. Close in profile to Cleopatra's coin portraits, but lacking the royal diadem or insignia, this sculpture perhaps represents a woman who modelled herself on Cleopatra in Rome.
Limestone, H. 28 cm. British Museum, London

new status of Italian vernacular as a dignified language. Women without a classical education could now publish not only their letters, as Latin-educated noblewomen had done in the fifteenth century, but also their works in poetry and prose.

Bordone's portrait is a very special portrayal of an unknown Venetian courtesan in the classical mould.[33] It shows her finely dressed in a luxurious and stately interior – probably the bedchamber in which she received her important clients. All the details matter in conveying the message: the panels of embossed and gilt leather on the walls, the fine table carpet, the gilt mirrorframe carved with a classical mask, the lace edgings to her sheets, as well as the X-frame chair of a kind associated with princes and popes. Her rich silk dress and all her accessories – high chopines, diadem, pearls, heavy gold chain and gem-set bracelets – demonstrate her imperiousness and social standing. Her sensuality is eminently apparent, but at the same time there is a sense of dignity, of cultured confidence and of independent resolve of the kind with which the most famous Italian Renaissance courtesans were associated.[34] The crown on the table suggests her role in the guise of the queen of Egypt. Like Cleopatra in the play, the courtesan looks as if she is professing that she will die for love, with the asp grasped firmly like a trophy in her fist.

Cleopatra's suicide was an iconic image. In figure 25 the sixteenth-century Sienese artist Neroni sets the scene in a contemporary Italian interior: as in Shakespeare's plays, there is a creative illusion whereby antiquity exists simultaneously with the present. The pose of Cleopatra here is reminiscent of classical sculpture; indeed, the posture of her upper body is imitated from a famous Roman statue of Ariadne that was identified from the early sixteenth century as Cleopatra merely because the figure is languorous and wears a snake bracelet, which was taken for an asp. Pope Julius III (r. 1550–1555) installed the statue in a special room in the Belvedere at the Vatican called the Cleopatra room – poems were written about it and the identification was only changed to Ariadne in the late eighteenth century.[35] George Eliot in her great novel *Middlemarch* (1871–2) talks about her heroine Dorothea in her Quaker grey silk standing by 'the reclining Ariadne, then called the Cleopatra' in 'the marble voluptuousness of her beauty, the drapery folding around her with petal-like ease and tenderness' – a description which beautifully catches the eroticism of the statue.[36]

The link between Cleopatra as the tragic heroine of antiquity and the fashionable contemporary woman of Renaissance Italy is also apparent in the sixteenth-century cameos seen here (fig. 26). They show Cleopatra with the asp, bare-breasted, combining ancient and modern details of fashionable dress in the antique style. Her grace and fortitude at the moment of death, which the play dramatizes so forcefully, are also caught in Guercino's beautiful drawing from the 1630s (fig. 27), as poised and serene as it is erotic. Striking as these visual analogues with Shakespeare's play may be, the artistic tradition does not catch every aspect of the 'infinite variety' (*Antony and Cleopatra* 2.2.272) with which Cleopatra is portrayed on stage. For one thing, the women who are portrayed as her are all white. Historically, Cleopatra was from the Ptolemaic dynasty of Macedonia, so she was not strictly Egyptian, let alone 'black'. But Shakespeare identifies

25. *The Death of Cleopatra*, Bartolommeo Neroni,
called Riccio, *c.* 1550–73.
Pen and brown ink, with grey-brown wash, over black
chalk, 40.4 x 26.8 cm. British Museum, London

24. *Portrait of a Woman in the Guise of Cleopatra*,
attributed to Paris Bordone, Venice, mid-1500s.
Oil on canvas, 146.5 x 126 cm.
Walters Art Gallery, Baltimore

her less with her origin than her geographical location: in his imagination, the
heat of the North African sun has given her a 'tawny front' (1.1.6).[37]

Within the dialogue of the play, she is also compared to a 'gipsy' (1.1.10).
This was a connection made by Shakespeare's contemporary, a future Archbishop
of Canterbury, in a book of global reach published in that key year 1599:

Although this country of Egypt doth stand in the self same climate that
Mauritania doth, yet the inhabitants there are not black, but rather dun,
or tawny. Of which colour Cleopatra was observed to be; who by inticement,

'The stroke of death is as a lover's pinch / Which hurts and is desired'

(*Antony and Cleopatra* 5.2.331–2)

26. Two cameos with the suicide of Cleopatra. Northern Italian, late 1500s. Cleopatra is shown both as seductress and ancient heroine, a fanciful combination of ancient and modern.
Sardonyx, top H. 3.5 cm; bottom H. 4.3 cm.
British Museum, London

so won the love of Julius Caesar, and Antony. And of that colour do those runagates (by devices make themselves to be) who go up and down the world under the name of Egyptians, being indeed but counterfeits and the refuse of rascality of many nations.[38]

'Tawny' was an orange-brown colour, associated with the sun, but clearly differentiated from the blackness of the Moors of Mauritania. It was the colour of 'gipsies', who claimed to come from Egypt. Whereas Iago insults Othello with racial abuse of sub-Saharan African features, the Romans insult Cleopatra by calling her a gipsy, associating her with a tribe famous for indolence, vagrancy, theft, fortune-telling and verbal wiles, magic and counterfeiting – exactly the characteristic of Shakespeare's representation of Cleopatra's court.

Gipsies were often associated with beggars, and part of the paradox that is Cleopatra comes from the sense in which the opposite poles of regality and beggary meet in her. Antony begins his journey with the claim that 'There's beggary in the love that can be reckoned' (1.1.15), while Cleopatra ends hers by recognizing that the dungy earth is both 'The beggar's nurse and Caesar's' (5.2.8). Refusing to demean herself by begging in supplication to Caesar, she welcomes the beggar-like clown instead and purchases the asp that she will nurse at her breast. It seems that her main reason for refusing to surrender to Caesar is a refusal to undergo the shame of public display:

> Saucy lictors
> Will catch at us like strumpets, and scald rhymers
> Ballad us out o'tune. The quick comedians
> Extemporally will stage us and present
> Our Alexandrian revels: Antony
> Shall be brought drunken forth, and I shall see
> Some squeaking Cleopatra boy my greatness
> I'th'posture of a whore.
> (5.2.254–61)

'Rascality', Bishop Abbott's word for gypsies, was applied, again in the year 1599, to players in a puritan anti-theatrical polemic called *Th'overthrow of Stage-playes*.[39] Cleopatra's scathing references to playing constitute one of Shakespeare's most daring self-allusions: he is the scald rhymer, his actors the quick comedians extemporally staging the revels. Antony has been brought drunken forth in the person of Richard Burbage and the 'squeaking Cleopatra' who speaks these lines – in the full knowledge that boy actors were sometimes described as the players' whores – is Burbage's cross-dressed apprentice, a young man in his late teens or at most his very early twenties. That is a sobering thought, given that in modern times the part has been considered the supreme Shakespearean role for a mature female actor, but it is also indicative of the way that Shakespeare's Cleopatra embodies the fluidity of the characteristics of race, colour and gender in the early modern world.

'I have
Immortal longing in me'

(Antony and Cleopatra, 5.2.316–7)

27. *Cleopatra*, Giovanni Francesco Barbieri,
called Guercino, late 1630s.
Red chalk, 29.2 x 21.5 cm. British Museum, London

'I may speak of thee as the traveller
doth of Venice:
Venetia, Venetia,
Chi non ti vede non ti pretia.'

(*Love's Labour's Lost* 4.2.73–5)

1. *Bird's-eye View of Venice from the South*,
Jacopo de' Barbari, 1498–1500.
Woodcut, 134 x 280 cm. British Museum, London

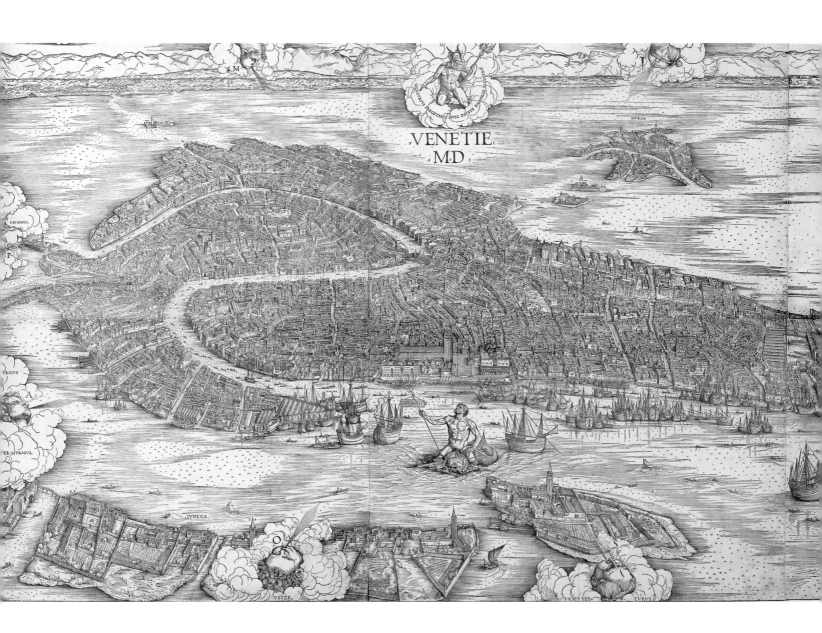

5 'A FAIR CITY ... POPULATED WITH MANY PEOPLE': VENICE VIEWED FROM LONDON

*Vederete vna bella, ricca, sumtuosa, forte, citta ben fornita, adorna di belle
done, populosa di ogni gente, abundante, e copiosa di tutte le bone cose.*
You shal see a fayre citie, riche, sumptuous, strong, wel furnished, adorned
with fayre women, populated of many people, abundant, and plentiful of
al good things.

John Florio, *Florio his First Fruites* (1578), chapter 8

Italy was one of the most important of Shakespeare's imagined places. And within Italy
Venice had a special hold on the English. A fair city, an open society grown rich on
maritime trade, a multicultural population, a place of fashionable innovation and
questionable morals: in Venice Londoners saw an image of their own desires and fears,
their own future.

'I may speak of thee as the traveller doth of Venice: "*Venetia, Venetia, / Chi non
ti vede non ti pretia*"' ('Venice, Venice, who sees you not values you not') (fig. 1).
Holofernes (*Love's Labour's Lost* 4.2.73–5) quotes this well-known proverb of a kind
that was commonly used for learning colloquial language.[1] Like the costume books
of the late sixteenth century, which aimed to bring the world's cultures within the
compass of one theatre of the world, collections of proverbs were tools for ordering
experience. A proverb could instantly define the ethos of a foreign city.[2] And by
defining what was foreign or 'alien', the English began to know themselves as a nation.

The phrasebook from which Shakespeare borrowed was probably *Florio his First
Fruites which Yeelde Familiar Speech, Merie Proverbes, Wittie Sentences, and Golden
Sayings* (1578), which claimed to offer 'a perfect induction to the Italian, and English,
tongues'. The author, John Florio, was a resident alien in London who earned a living

2. Glass ewer, mould-blown with white cane decoration (*vetro a retorti*). Murano, Venice, 1550–1600.
H. 27.5 cm. British Museum, London

'the trade and profit of the city Consisteth of all nations'

(*The Merchant of Venice 3.3.33–4*)

3. *Bird's-eye View of Venice*, Odoardo Fialetti, 1611.
Oil on canvas, 215.9 x 424.2 cm. Eton College, Berkshire

as language tutor to the nobility. Shakespeare may well have met him in the household of the Earl of Southampton. Holofernes, the pedant in *Love's Labour's Lost*, does not quote the second half of the proverb: '*Ma chi ti vede, ben gli costa*' ('But he who sees you pays dearly for it').[3] Nevertheless, in Shakespeare's Venetian plays, *The Merchant of Venice* and *Othello*, there is ample demonstration of English ambivalence towards Venice, the archetypal modern city.

There was a perceived affinity between Venice and London, derived from their dynamism and attractiveness to strangers, their maritime trade and the quantity of human traffic. Venice had many roles in the English imagination: as a republic with a famous constitution and supposedly high ideals of public service, as a bulwark against the Ottoman Turk, and as a critic of the papacy, which gave it additional merit in the eyes of Protestant Europe. Lewis Lewkenor, translating a contemporary treatise on Venice's constitution in 1599, transmitted to English readers a highly idealized picture of the city's government, with its legally defined estates or orders of society, each with specific privileges, and corporations with particular functions.[4] It was a rigid system in which each individual, including the carefully classified stranger, was expected to know his or her place under the law. Only then could harmony be maintained. Whether or not Shakespeare knew Lewkenor's book, he had enough regard for the Venetian legal system to imagine a private suit – Brabantio's against Othello over Desdemona – being heard in the middle of a threatened Turkish invasion of the frontier territory of Cyprus.[5]

Admiration for Venice's famous crystalline glass, made in Murano, drew eager consumers to the annual fair, La Sensa, to see the latest styles and techniques: trying one's hand at glass-blowing was already on the tourist itinerary by 1611, when Thomas Coryat, who travelled from Somerset to Venice on foot, had a go (fig. 2).[6] The city had always astounded pilgrims and travellers, but appreciation of its urban spaces, architecture and painting developed at the very end of the 1500s as part of the vogue for virtuoso travel, which took an aesthetic approach to European cities and would later develop into the Grand Tour.[7] Connoisseurship in all things Venetian was largely led in England by Sir Henry Wotton (1568–1639), who was appointed in 1604 as the first post-Reformation English ambassador to Venice.[8] In a letter of 22 April 1606 Wotton refers to a painter and printmaker, Odoardo Fialetti, who had studied under Tintoretto and stayed in Venice.[9] Fialetti painted Wotton receiving an audience from the then Doge of Venice, Leonardo Donato, as a kind of ambassadorial souvenir. He also painted a series of Venetian doges for Wotton: these were similarly elite tourist items.[10] Most impressive of all was Fialetti's bird's-eye view of Venice itself, signed and dated 1611 (fig. 3).[11] Based on earlier views of Venice – not least Jacopo de' Barbari's – this is early modern Venice laid out before the viewer, as it was encountered by the foreign dignitary and merchant, the tourist and the stranger. The view reaches from the Arsenal to the segregated Jewish enclave in the Ghetto. Fialetti adds figures and ships as well as gondolas and *traghetti* (fig. 4), the public ferries that still operate today over sections of the Grand Canal. Portia incorrectly refers to the ferries that plied between the islands as *traghetti* as she prepares to dress up as a lawyer before travelling

4. Detail from Odoardo Fialetti's *Bird's-eye View of Venice* (fig. 3) showing *traghetti*.

from her villa in Belmont to try Shylock's case in Venice:

> Bring them, I pray thee with imagined speed
> Unto the traject, to the common ferry
> Which trades to Venice.
> (*The Merchant of Venice* 3.4.53–5)

Wotton's pride in his magnificent painting of Venice prompted him to have a tablet made (now missing) inscribed in Latin to commemorate his gift of the picture to Eton College, of which he was elected provost in 1629. The inscription was intended as a tribute both to Venice and to Eton: 'Henry Wotton, after serving three times as ambassador to Venice, grew old in the happy bosom of Eton College. After twelve years as provost, passed in most agreeable amity with the Fellows, he hung in 1636, near the Fellow's table in memory of himself, this picture of a wonderful city that seems to float.'[12] This remarkable record of the English love affair with Venice was seen in College Hall by Samuel Pepys in 1665: it has remained at Eton to this day.[13]

Shakespeare held up Venice – as did other playwrights – as a mirror to London. Using Venice in this way gave playwrights a certain psychological distance at which to probe issues of concern to London audiences. One of these was the sex trade and its impact

'the virtuous Desdemona'

(Othello 2.3.296–7)

5. Portrait of a Venetian lady, called *La Bella Nani*, Paolo Veronese, *c.* 1560. The sitter's pearl necklace and hairstyle suggest she might be a recent bride, like Desdemona.

Oil on canvas, 119 x 103 cm. Louvre, Paris

'their best conscience Is not to leave't undone, but kept unknown'

(Othello 3.3.226–7)

6. *A Couple Embracing in a Gondola*, from *Vere imagini et descritioni delle piu nobili citta del mondo*, Donato Bertelli, Venice, 1578.

Engraving, W. 25 cm. New York Public Library, New York

7. The print shown in fig. 6, modified in Erckenprecht Koler's friendship album, dated 1588.

Watercolour heightened with gold, 19.4 x 14 cm.

British Library, London

on wider society, for one of the first associations that Venice had for Londoners was with sex and its availability: the famed beauty of Venetian women, the numbers of prostitutes operating openly in the city and the supposed licentiousness of Venetian wives. This is the understood context for *Othello*, in which 'the virtuous Desdemona' (2.3.296–7) (fig. 5) stands apart from the sexual stereotypes traded by Iago, Roderigo and Cassio until the distinct categories of whore and wife dissolve into one in the latter part of the play. The presence of 'BIANCA, a courtesan' (List of Roles), Cassio's mistress, is a key element in the sexual traffic that pervades the play. Iago comments:

> In Venice they do let heaven see the pranks
> They dare not show their husbands: their best conscience
> Is not to leave't undone, but kept unknown.
> (*Othello* 3.3.225–7)

A Venetian print of 1578 plays up to this voyeuristic view of Venetian women. It shows a gondola with a closed canopy, which the viewer can lift to show a canoodling couple hidden from public view (fig. 6). This image appealed to a German student so much that he had the print copied into his souvenir album in 1588, flap and all (fig. 7).[14] However, the couple are not shown embracing but singing to the accompaniment of a lute player. This particular adaptation sanitizes the interface between the way in which Venetians translated their city to the visitors, and the way in which those visitors wished to perceive it. The Venetian Council of Ten, a major governing body in the city, was concerned enough about courtesans' antics in gondolas to patrol the canals in 1578, the year of the print.[15] This degree of uncertainty about a woman's apparent virtue and transgressive inner nature is revealed in Othello's desperate remark to Desdemona when he accuses her of being a whore: 'I took you for that cunning whore of Venice / That married with Othello' (4.2.98–9).

8. *A Venetian Gentlewoman at Lent* from *Degli habiti antichi et moderni di diverse parti del mondo*, Cesare Vecellio, Venice, 1590, facing f. 133. Woodcut, 15.3 x 9.5 cm. British Library, London

9. Glass goblet enamelled with a figure of a Venetian woman after a Venetian print (see Figs 8 and 14), and with a Germanic coat of arms. 'Façon de Venise', Venice or Northern Europe, 1590–1600. Blown glass, with enamelling and gilding, H. 21.5 cm, diam. 12.6 cm. British Museum, London

The Venetian sex-trade took place in full public view. A printed catalogue of 1570 listed 215 names of available women with prices and locations. At the top were the high-ranking courtesans.[16] Lower down the scale were the women who lived independently in their own apartments, as the courtesan Bianca in *Othello* appears to do.[17] There were also prostitutes operating in the city's many brothels.[18] The very openness of the trade blurred social distinctions. Coryat, used to the English custom of having boys play the female parts, was shocked to see women on stage,[19] and Sir Henry Wotton, visiting in the 1590s, wondered at the challenge in distinguishing respectable married women from whores in the street. 'Both honest and dishonest wemen are *Lisciate fin'alla fossa*, that is paynted to the very grave', as the English traveller Fynes Moryson noted.[20]

'Lend me thy handkerchief'

(Othello 3.4.50)

10. Detail of a handkerchief belonging to either a man or woman, embroidered with a pattern of honeysuckle and grapevines and the initials 'EM'. England, *c.* 1600.
Linen, embroidered with silk and trimmed with silver-gilt lace, 37 x 37 cm. Victoria and Albert Museum, London

The smallest gestures and tokens took on great significance, as documented by Cesare Vecellio in his costume book of 1590 (fig. 8). Vecellio delights in talking about Venetian betrothal and marriage rituals,[21] but is caustic about courtesans, who, by means of what Iago calls 'a seeming' (*Othello* 3.3.234), were known to emulate 'respectable' women in their dress. Their noisiness in public usually gave them away,[22] as with Cassio's concern to pacify Bianca after a tiff, 'she'll rail in the streets else' (*Othello* 4.1.163). Giacomo Franco's *Costumes of Venetian Women* followed Vecellio's book in 1609 and also had a wide currency. These visual types of Venetian women were widely diffused, copied and collected in Northern Europe, and formed an image bank for the outsiders' view of Venetian society (fig. 9).[23] Courtesans in these images convey just that feisty independence which even the virtuous Desdemona reveals in banter with Iago. All the women in *Othello* are branded as whores. Iago gives Desdemona plenty of provocation in his description of women:

> Come on, come on: you are pictures out of door, bells in your parlours, wild-cats in your kitchens, saints in your injuries, devils being offended, players in your housewifery, and housewives in your beds.
> (*Othello* 2.1.121–3)

Courtesans make a great play on their ungloved hands, and the elegant accessory of the handkerchief (fig. 10). The fact that a handkerchief – a love token as well as a fashion accessory – could be a moral indicator in London as in Venice is shown by a single incident involving Elizabeth I and her favourite, Robert Dudley, the Earl of Leicester. In 1565 Leicester seized Elizabeth's handkerchief to mop his brow after a tennis match, only to be challenged to a duel by the Duke of Norfolk to protect the queen's reputation.[24] This is the context for the obsession with Desdemona's handkerchief in *Othello* and its journey from hand to hand. Iago only has to evoke its embroidered design, 'spotted with strawberries', to break Othello (3.3.479).[25]

Venetian women were known to take the shocking step of dyeing their hair. Blondness in women was something of a Venetian obsession,[26] and was particularly fashionable as a preparation for marriage, when blonde tendrils on the forehead and loose curls on the shoulders set off the bridal dress. Do Portia's 'sunny locks', compared to Jason's golden fleece (*The Merchant of Venice* 1.1.171), take on a special significance in this respect as the characteristic of the desirable Venetian patrician bride?

'But since she did neglect her looking-glass / And threw her sun-expelling mask away, / The air hath starved the roses of her cheeks / And pinched the lily-tincture of her face / That now she is become as black as I'

(*The Two Gentlemen of Verona* 4.4.136–40)

11. Vizard mask worn by gentlewomen in the sixteenth and possibly into the seventeenth century to protect them from the sun when travelling. The mask was secured by a glass bead attached to a string and held in the wearer's teeth. Found folded in half and concealed within the wall of a sixteenth-century building in Northamptonshire in 2010.
Velvet, lined with silk and strengthened with a pressed-paper liner, H. 19.5 cm. Private collection

'sunny locks'

(*The Merchant of Venice* 1.1.171)

12. *A Venetian Woman Bleaching her Hair*, from *Degli habiti antichi et moderni di diverse parti del mondo*, Cesare Vecellio, Venice, 1590, facing f. 145. Woodcut, 15.3 x 9.6 cm. British Library, London

Desdemona is described as 'fair' (*Othello* 4.2.228), a word that equates blondness and pallor with beauty (see fig. 5).[27] Fashionable and high-status European women took trouble not to tan, sometimes wearing a vizard mask when outside in summer: a wonderful example was found in June 2010 in an inner wall of a sixteenth-century building in Northamptonshire (fig. 11).[28]

Dyeing one's hair was an occupation for a Saturday afternoon as one sat on the roof-top platform known as an *altana*.[29] Vecellio's illustration seen here shows a woman with her high platform shoes, or chopines, by her side (fig. 12). These were worn as overshoes, but they had erotic associations since they were copied from the slippers worn in the Ottoman Turkish hamam (baths).[30] Venetian brides took pains to learn how to walk and dance in them, so that they could show off their skills, rather than their chopines (which they took great care to hide), at their wedding.[31] Dancing, like music-making, was a desirable social accomplishment in a bride, as Othello recognizes when he agonizes about Desdemona's virtue:

'Your ladyship is nearer heaven than when I saw you last, by the altitude of a chopine'

(*Hamlet* 2.2.376–7)

13. Chopines, Venice, *c.* 1600.
Wood covered with punched kid leather (not identical),
L. 24 cm and 23.5 cm, max. H. of sole 19.5 cm
and 18 cm. Victoria and Albert Museum, London

'Tis not to make me jealous
To say my wife is fair, feeds well, loves company,
Is free of speech, sings, plays and dances:
Where virtue is, these are more virtuous.
(3.3.206–9)

But that was just the point, for these were also the kinds of skills that were thought to distinguish the courtesan from the common prostitute.

As an English visitor, Coryat had no time for chopines. When he saw a woman fall 'downe the staires of one of the little stony bridges with her high Chapineys alone by her selfe', he did nothing to help her, 'because shee wore such frivolous and (as I may truly terme them) ridiculous instruments, which were the occasion of her fall' (fig. 13).[32] Coryat was probably aware that teetering platforms were associated with loose virtue, but quite how confusing these kinds of indicators could be is demonstrated in a Venetian print by Pietro Bertelli of a very special interactive kind, dating from around 1588 (fig. 14). This might almost have been designed as an advertisement for the Venetian courtesan as a tourist attraction.[33] The print shows a well-dressed Venetian woman with her hair worn in two twisted peaks or 'horns', a fashion of the late 1580s and 1590s intended to resemble the crescent moon worn by the chaste goddess Diana, but satirized as a cuckold's horns.[34] She stands with her expensive fan, pearls and handkerchief in a recognizably watery Venetian landscape. Cupid above her indicates an amorous purpose, and her sidelong expression is at least

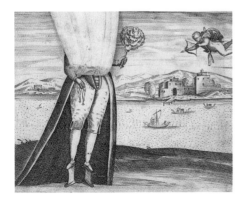

14. *Courtesan and Blind Cupid* (flap print with liftable skirt), Pietro Bertelli, *c.* 1588.
Engraving and etching, 14 x 19.1 cm.
Metropolitan Museum of Art, New York

'I fear me it will make me scandalized'

(*The Two Gentlemen of Verona 2.7.61*)

15. *Courtesan and Blind Cupid*, unknown artist after Pietro Bertelli (fig. 14). From the friendship album of Sir Michael Balfour, 1596–9, f. 128r. Manuscript, 16 x 27 cm. National Library of Scotland, Edinburgh

'I do adore thy sweet grace's slipper'

(*Love's Labour's Lost 5.2.677*)

16. Pair of slippers (chopines, *pantoble, pianelle*)
Venice, *c.* 1600
Wood, velvet, leather, silver-gilt braid, lace,
L. 20.5 cm, W. 10.7 cm, H. 9 cm.
Victoria and Albert Museum, London

suggestive. When the viewer lifts the front panel of her dress, her chopines and masculine-style breeches (*braghessi*), which she is wearing as underwear, are revealed.[35] One Scots visitor on the Grand Tour in Venice in 1596–9 had the print copied into his souvenir album as a permanent memento of his visit to the city (fig. 15).[36] When Julia decides to set off for Milan to search for Proteus in Shakespeare's *Two Gentlemen of Verona*, her maid Lucetta counsels her to dress as a man in breeches and codpiece.[37] Julia is shocked: 'how will the world repute me / For undertaking so unstaid a journey? / I fear me it will make me scandalized' (2.7.59–61). She is the first of a long line of cross-dressed heroines, played by a boy dressing up as a girl, dressing up as a boy. The full charge of this experiment is only felt in the shock and titillation associated with real women dressing up as men, even if only in their underclothes, as in Bertelli's print.

This is the spirit in which Hamlet jokes about chopines in teasing the young boy who is to act the queen in the play-within-a-play about how he has grown: 'Your ladyship's nearer to heaven than when I saw you last by the altitude of a chopine' (*Hamlet* 2.2.376–7). Chopines would have been familiar to Shakespeare's audiences as elite accessories: the English poet Lady Falkland (1585–1639) mentions ones 'which she had ever worne, being very low, and a long time very fatte' in her memoirs.[38] In 1591 Elizabeth I had made for herself two pairs of delicate *pantobles*, open at the toes and 'laid on with silver lace', which may have resembled the pair illustrated here (fig. 16).[39] Similar slippers are shown with other Italian or specifically Venetian fashions in the portrait of Anne of Denmark in figure 17.[40] She holds an Italian feather fan like the Venetian one in figure 18, and she is also wearing an expensive Italian silk woven with a repeating design of peacock feathers, suitable for a woman described by her husband, King James, as 'Our earthlie Juno'. The panel of surviving silk in figure 19 is of the same type. Anne was not unusual in being an eager consumer of Italian

17. *Queen Anne of Denmark*, Marcus Gheeraerts the Younger, *c.* 1611–14.
Oil on canvas, 221 x 131 cm. Woburn Abbey, Bedfordshire

'lost the handle of her fan'

(*The Merry Wives of Windsor* 2.2.7–8)

18. Handle for a feather fan, similar to that in fig. 17. Venice, *c.* 1550.
Gilt brass, H. 17.8 cm, W. 8.2 cm.
Victoria and Albert Museum, London

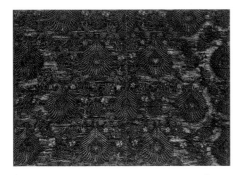

'Enrobe the roaring waters with my silks'

(*The Merchant of Venice* 1.1.35)

19. The Venetian merchant Salanio worries about shipwrecks ruining silks in his cargo. Panel of silk dress fabric woven with a peacock feather design, like that worn by Queen Anne of Denmark in fig. 17. Italy, 1600–20.
L. 142.5 cm, W. 49 cm.
Victoria and Albert Museum, London

and specifically Venetian luxury goods, but this portrait demonstrates that she was an Italophile with an Italian motto, 'My greatness comes from above' ('La mia grandezza dal eccelso').[41] She employed John Florio as Italian tutor to her daughter, Princess Elizabeth; the 1611 edition of his Italian–English dictionary was entitled in her honour *Queen Anna's New World of Wordes*.[42]

Apart from luxury and licence, Venice was also associated in the English imagination with wealth derived from commerce: 'the wonderful concourse of strange and foreign people … as though the city of Venice onely were a common and generall market to the whole world'.[43] As a model of an open maritime city, it was renowned for the fact that 'the trade and profit of the city / Consisteth of all nations' (*The Merchant of Venice* 3.3.33–4). Commerce demands credit and the Venetian solution to this – one which shocked many English commentators and Christian critics – was to turn to the Jews. Christians acted as moneylenders too, but it was still perceived as a Jewish speciality.

Usury – lending money at interest – was inextricably linked with Jews in the contemporary English imagination, for although usury was widely practised in England in the late sixteenth century, exploitative rates of interest were still associated with Jewish moneylenders, as they were elsewhere in Europe. Apart from their usefulness, Jews and prostitutes were easily identified outsiders and scapegoats when things went wrong.[44] The travel writer Samuel Purchas wrote of how 'the beastly trade of courtesans and cruel trade of Jews is suffered for gain' in Italy, and Venice was considered the most obvious example of this.[45] Venice was known to be a society in which Jews were allowed to profess their faith openly, yet they could only be accepted if they were in Venetian society but not of it, contained within a segregated community that was a condition of their toleration.[46] This was very different from the way in which a tiny number of Iberian Jews lived in London, as converts (Marranos) whose Christianity was always in doubt and who were thought to practise Judaism in secret. The fact that they were Spanish or Portuguese Jews made them even more suspect, regarded as potential spies highly placed in court and city.[47] At this period there was no acknowledged Jewish community in England, as a result of the first expulsion of a Jewish community in Europe in 1290 (see further below, p. 159).[48]

Religious conversion was a major issue in Venice, as in London.[49] Shakespeare's two Venetian plays, *The Merchant of Venice* and *Othello*, are both dramas of conversion, in which individuals are 'turned' from one religion or identity to another.[50] Both plays consider difference and otherness – religious, national, racial, sexual – and fears about how encounters with such differences test, threaten or transform a society's values.

It was understood in the late sixteenth century in England that 'Antwerp and Venice could never have been so rich and famous but by entertaining of strangers and by that means have gained all the intercourse of the world'.[51] And it was widely known, and often commented upon by English visitors, that Venice offered aliens a carefully defined legal status in order to make coexistence possible. Dated 1552,

'our tribe'

(*The Merchant of Venice* 1.3.101)

20. Bronze portrait medal of Elijah de Lattes, Jewish physician, and his mother, Rica. Veneto, 1552.
Cast bronze, diam. 4 cm. British Museum, London

the medal in figure 20, probably made in the Veneto, is not only the first Italian Renaissance medal commemorating a Jew, but one of the earliest portraits of a European Jew, in which the name of the individual – the papal physician and astronomer Elijah de Lattes – is proudly accompanied by 'EBREO' or Jew. It is a hundred years earlier than other European medals commemorating Jews.[52] It was commissioned by a mother and son together, making it a confident tribute to Jewish lineage and family in a Christian context – two generations of the family had been doctors to the Pope.

Nothing like this was to be seen in London in the 1550s. Just how difficult coexistence with 'strangers' was in London, and what a live issue it was in the 1590s, is shown in the libel pinned on the door of the city's Dutch church in 1593 when tensions between native artisans and immigrants were high. The Dutch libel showed how swiftly anti-alien feeling compared foreigners to the legendary, predatory Jew: 'And like the Jews you eat us up for bread'.[53]

The story of the Jews' expulsion from England in 1290 is an ugly one. Jews followed William the Conqueror in 1066 as the king's money-collectors and lenders, a conveniently alien group whose financial usefulness was continually tested. Although they made up less than 1 per cent of the population it is estimated that they owned up to one third of the mobile wealth of England at the end of the 1100s.[54] Antagonism towards them flared up in the first charge of ritual murder in Europe, the case of St William of Norwich in 1144 (see fig. 26), which involved the claim that Jews murdered Christian children and used their blood to bake bread.[55] Continental charges of ritual murder followed, including that of Simon of Trent in 1475, accompanied by executions and massacres of Jews. Increasing government pressure and popular anti-Semitism culminated in the Edict of Expulsion of Edward I in 1290.[56] It was not until 1656 that Jews were officially readmitted to England by Oliver Cromwell (1599–1658).[57]

'Our sacred nation'

(*The Merchant of Venice 1.3.35*)

21. Sabbath lamp (?), 1200s–1300s,
found in Windsor in 1717.
Bronze, H. 13 cm, W. 16.2 cm.
Society of Antiquaries, London

The bronze oil lamp illustrated here (fig. 21) is probably a medieval Jewish Sabbath lamp from the period before the Expulsion. It can be compared with a similar lamp excavated in Bristol on the site of the thirteenth-century settlement of New Jewry in Peter Street.[58] The Sabbath lamp is a key element in Jewish domestic rituals, as it is lit by the housewife on Friday evening, the eve of the Sabbath or day of rest, and on the eve of major festivals. Women played a vital role within the Jewish household, especially in the observation of the dietary and culinary traditions that maintained a sense of identity over the generations.[59] Jessica's responsibilities, following the death of her mother, Leah, are acknowledged in *The Merchant of Venice*: the loss of Jessica is, for Shylock, the loss of his Jewish posterity. The woodcut seen here, taken from a book of Jewish customs printed in Venice in 1600 with a Yiddish commentary (fig. 22), shows a well-dressed woman blessing the Sabbath lamp, similar to the medieval English one illustrated in figure 21.[60] If that identification is correct for this lamp, it speaks of the lost medieval Jewish community in England more powerfully than any text can do.[61]

The expulsion of Jews from Granada in 1492 following the Spanish re-conquest led to forced conversions and pre-emptive migration through Europe.[62] Jews who converted or whose ancestors had converted were called Marranos, but their Christian beliefs and political allegiance were always doubted as it was thought that they had made 'a counterfeit profession'.[63] Nowhere is this seen more clearly than in the fortunes of the Portuguese Marrano family, the Nasi, to use their Hebrew name.

'Jessica, my girl, Look to my house'

(*The Merchant of Venice 2.5.16–17*)

22. The lighting of the Sabbath lamp, from *Sefer Minhagim* (*Book of Customs*), Venice, 1600. This *Minhagim* is a key text for our understanding of Venetian Jewry at this date. It was produced in Yiddish for Ashkenazi Jews in Venice by a Christian printer, employing a Christian artist who did not understand all the details of Jewish ritual from the inside. These sophisticated woodcuts offer a visual parallel to the manner in which Shakespeare portrays a Jewish household. Woodcut, 7 x 9.5 cm. Bodleian Library, Oxford

'Most beautiful pagan, most sweet Jew'

(*The Merchant of Venice* 2.3.10)

23. Bronze portrait medal of Grazia Nasi, by Pastorino de' Pastorini. Probably Ferrara, 1558–9. Diam. 6.6 cm. British Museum, London

'The villain Jew'

(*The Merchant of Venice* 2.8.4)

24. *Lopez Compounding to Poyson the Queene*, Friedrich von Hulsen, from George Carleton, *A Thankfull Remembrance of Gods Mercy*, London, 1627.
Printed book, 20 x 14.5 cm. British Library, London

Joseph Nasi (d. 1579) was a professing Jew who became Duke of Naxos and Prince of the Cyclades in service to the Ottoman Turkish Empire at a time of increased English commercial and political activity there. The Italian medal of the 1550s in figure 23 records Joseph's sister-in-law, Grazia Nasi.[64] She is presented, probably at the time of her marriage, as a young and fashionable Italian noblewoman. She is also shown as a Jewess, for her name is proudly proclaimed only in Hebrew, for the first time on a European medal.[65] The Nasi had international political and trading links, including with the London Marrano community.[66] All Marranos were identified with international conspiracy, counterfeit Christianity and anti-Spanish prejudice. It was a powerful mix, as demonstrated in the trial and execution of the Marrano Roderigo Lopez, Queen Elizabeth's doctor, on a charge of trying to poison her in 1594. Lopez was imprisoned 'for intelligence with the king of Spaine' (fig. 24).[67] He was famous enough in London life to have been given a name-check, long before his execution, in Marlowe's *Dr Faustus* (1592?), but his execution gave a new lease of life to

performances of Marlowe's *Jew of Malta* while licensing more general anti-Semitism.[68] Prints showing Lopez busy with his plots had a long life in arguing for the special character of the English nation and its divine deliverance from internal and external threats.[69]

By 1600 many English Protestants saw themselves as God's chosen people in place of the Jews: when the clergyman Lancelot Andrewes called for an annual commemoration of discovery of the Gunpowder Plot he referred to it as 'our Passover'.[70] In 1616 he used the biblical story of Esther, the young Jewess who secured the delivery of her people from the death decree of Haman by her intercession with Ahasuerus, King of Persia, as the text for his sermon recalling James's survival from the Gowrie Plot of 1600.[71] Much of this sense of identification was based on the renewed study of Hebrew essential for a proper understanding of the Bible, promoted through Regius Professorships in Oxford and Cambridge following the establishment of Protestantism as the state religion in England. The emphasis on the Old Testament was part of a return to ancient values, and it had its political uses in making the case for Henry VIII's divorce and for his royal supremacy.[72] The contribution of Jewish law is acknowledged in the Hebrew inscription referring to him as 'supreme head' on the Supremacy Medal of 1545 (fig. 25).[73] Such was the respect for Hebrew scholarship that the 1611 Authorized Version of the Bible was to draw on the translation skills of twenty-five English Hebraists.[74] But much of the genuine interest in the language was rooted in a sense of Christian, and specifically Protestant, superiority.[75]

In the later seventeenth century, respect for Hebrew as one of the two central languages of the Bible was to lead to greater tolerance towards Jews themselves, but in Shakespeare's lifetime popular anti-Semitism remained. The charge of ritual murder remained long after the Jewish community had been forced to leave, promoted in histories, sermons and, for those who could not read, painted on the walls of churches (fig. 26).[76] Usury was common practice among Jews and non-Jews alike by the late sixteenth century – Shakespeare's father, John, was accused of it – and attitudes were changing as credit was widely recognized as an essential underpinning for business.[77] But financial exploitation remained in the popular imagination associated with Jewish moneylenders, even though they had not existed in England for 300 years.[78] Folk prejudice lived on in anti-Semitic tales, ballads and proverbs. Thomas Coryat glosses one of the latter: 'to looke like a Iew (whereby is meant sometimes a weather-beaten warp-faced fellow, sometimes a phreneticke and lunaticke person, sometimes one discontented)', stereotyping that relates interestingly to Shylock's rancorous disposition. Yet Coryat also notes that the Jews he saw in the Venetian Ghetto were 'most elegant and sweete-featured'.[79]

Shakespeare refers to a number of pejorative proverbial phrases in several plays in a way that suggests that his presentation of Shylock partly depends on this kind of verbal culture. But Shylock's own language is a key to his identification, such as his exotic and outlandish lament on hearing that his daughter has exchanged his wife's ring for a monkey: 'It was my turquoise, I had it of Leah when I was a bachelor. I would not

25. Supremacy Medal of Henry VIII, 1545, inscribed in Hebrew, Latin and Greek.
Gold, diam. 5.4 cm. British Museum, London

'if it will feed nothing else,
it will feed my revenge'

(*The Merchant of Venice* 3.1.37)

26. Painted rood screen panel depicting the
ritual murder of St William of Norwich by Jews,
early 1400s.
Oil on panel. Holy Trinity Church, Loddon, Norfolk

have given it for a wilderness of monkeys' (*The Merchant of Venice* 3.1.79–81). It is obvious that Leah's ring was not a marriage ring. Jewish marriage rings were not set with stones, as a ring's value in gold alone was assessed before it was used as part of the marriage ceremony. Shakespeare and his audiences were unlikely to know what a Jewish marriage ring looked like anyway.[80] Leah's ring was instead a love token of a kind familiar to Shakespeare's audiences. Mined in Persia and Tibet, turquoises were prized for their exoticism, their unique colour and their amuletic properties. They were thought to preserve the sight, and to protect the wearer from poisoning, drowning and riding accidents. Contemporary treatises also state that turquoise preserved harmony between husband and wife, which is presumably the association evoked by Leah's gift. Small sixteenth-century rings set with turquoises show that they were thought, like coral, suitable for children as amulets; other rings demonstrate that turquoises were linked with love and marriage in sixteenth-century culture.[81]

Shylock's reported rant when he loses both his daughter and his Venetian ducats in one night makes it quite clear which property he values most: 'My daughter! O my ducats! O my daughter!' (*The Merchant of Venice* 2.8.15) is a touch taken from Marlowe's stock villain, Barabas, in *The Jew of Malta*.[82] The mention of ducats (fig. 27), like the mention of the Rialto as both an exchange market and a building, adds Venetian colour that Shakespeare's audience would have understood, but much of Shylock's presentation shows Shakespeare's apparent lack of concern about authenticity.[83] Shakespeare is more interested in cultural interchange between Jew and Christian in urban society, and in where the virtual boundaries lie, than in obvious physical markers such as dress. Hence the confusing mention of Shylock's 'Jewish gaberdine' (1.3.103) as a marker of difference, when Caliban's fishy cloak is described as a gaberdine too (*The Tempest* 2.2.31) (see p. 245). It may be that this kind of covering garment was a stage prop for outsiders and that it had much wider associations with difference, from Levantine Jews trading in Mediterranean markets to Gaelic woodkerns shivering in their shaggy cloaks in Ireland (see p. 112).[84] By making Shylock a figure who moves freely in Venetian society and who is not constrained within a ghetto, Shakespeare creates a far more disquieting and pervasive presence, one which his audiences would have associated with the wealthy, well-connected and highly placed Marranos they knew in London.

Italian Jews were integrated into the wider Christian society around them in fascinating ways, as shown by the Purim scroll in figure 28. The story of Purim is taken from the Book of Esther, an historical event that is commemorated every year in the

'My daughter! O my ducats! O my daughter!'

(The Merchant of Venice 2.8.15)

27. A brass coin balance and weights, made by Guillaum de Neve, 1600–54, Amsterdam; and ducat issued by Andrea Gritti, Doge of Venice, 1523–38.

Wood and brass, balance H. 15 cm, W. 11 cm; box L. 15 cm, W. 9 cm. Ducat, gold, diam. 2 cm.

British Museum, London

synagogue at the Feast of Purim, when a reading from a plain undecorated scroll is made.[85] However, embellished scrolls with decorated borders began to be made in late sixteenth-century Italy for use at home, and the engraved borders, which bore no relation to the sacred text, show the whole variety of grotesque ornament that was fashionable at the time.[86] The scroll shown here is one of three surviving ones of around 1573, the borders of which were designed by a Christian, Andrea Marelli, for use in Latin books. The Esther scrolls were specially commissioned: they are printed on a heavy parchment of a type used for this distinct purpose. It looks as if a Jewish patron would have commissioned the scrolls with their borders from a bookseller, probably in Rome, and then had them inscribed.[87] This confidence in adapting contemporary classical motifs for private ritual argues for a level of cultural exchange and social interaction that is otherwise hard to document for the sixteenth century. And it is a reminder that the distinctive features of Italian Jewry cannot be understood – as Shakespeare intuited – other than within the context of the wider society.[88]

Shakespeare explores the deep inner hatred and prejudice between Antonio, the

המלך מה לך אסתר המלכה ומה בקשתך עד | המלך ותאמר לו זרש אשתו וכל אהביו יעשו עץ
חצי המלכות ונתן לך ותאמר אסתר אם על המלך | גבה חמשים אמה ובבקר אמר למלך ויתלו את
טוב יבוא המלך והמן היום אל המשתה אשר | מרדכי עליו ובא עם המלך אל המשתה שמח
עשיתי לו ויאמר המלך מהרו את המן לעשות את | וייטב הדבר לפני המן ויעש העץ
דבר אסתר ויבא המלך והמן אל המשתה אשר | בלילה ההוא נדדה שנת
עשתה אסתר ויאמר המלך לאסתר במשתה היין | המלך ויאמר להביא את ספר הזכרונות דברי
מה שאלתך וינתן לך ומה בקשתך עד חצי המלכות | הימים ויהיו נקראים לפני המלך וימצא כתוב אשר
ותעש ותען אסתר ותאמר שאלתי ובקשתי אם | הגיד מרדכי על בגתנא ותרש שני סריסי המלך
מצאתי חן בעיני המלך ואם על המלך טוב לתת | משמרי הסף אשר בקשו לשלח יד במלך
את שאלתי ולעשות את בקשתי יבוא המלך | אחשורוש ויאמר המלך מה נעשה יקר וגדולה
והמן אל המשתה אשר אעשה להם ומחר אעשה | למרדכי על זה ויאמרו נערי המלך משרתיו לא
כדבר המלך ויצא המן ביום ההוא שמח וטוב לב | נעשה עמו דבר ויאמר המלך מי בחצר והמן בא
וכראות המן את מרדכי בשער המלך ולא קם ולא | לחצר בית המלך החיצונה לאמר למלך לתלות
זע ממנו וימלא המן על מרדכי חמה ויתאפק המן | את מרדכי על העץ אשר הכין לו ויאמרו נערי
ויבוא אל ביתו וישלח ויבא את אהביו ואת זרש | המלך אליו הנה המן עמד בחצר ויאמר המלך
אשתו ויספר להם המן את כבוד עשרו ורב בניו | יבוא ויבוא המן ויאמר לו המלך מה לעשות באיש
ואת כל אשר גדלו המלך ואת אשר נשאו על | אשר המלך חפץ ביקרו ויאמר המן בלבו למי
השרים ועבדי המלך ויאמר המן אף לא הביאה | יחפץ המלך לעשות יקר יותר ממני ויאמר המן
אסתר המלכה עם המלך אל המשתה אשר | אל המלך איש אשר המלך חפץ ביקרו יביאו לבוש
עשתה כי אם אותי וגם למחר אני קרוא לה | מלכות אשר לבש בו המלך וסוס אשר רכב עליו
עם המלך וכל זה איננו שוה לי בכל עת | המלך ואשר נתן כתר מלכות בראשו ונתן הלבוש והסוס
אשר אני ראה את מרדכי היהודי יושב בשער | איש משרי המלך הפרתמים והלבישו את האיש אשר

'My sober house'

(*The Merchant of Venice* 2.5.34)

28. A panel from an Esther scroll for use at home, with Hebrew text and hand-coloured marginal engravings by Andrea Marelli, Italy, *c.* 1573. Engraving and watercolour on vellum, panel 17 x 28 cm. British Library, London

Christian merchant of the title, and Shylock, the Jewish trader. He shows these forces to be damaging. Shylock's refusal to 'eat with you, drink with you, nor pray with you' (*The Merchant of Venice* 1.3.25–6) creates a division between business and a civility built on shared values. It was just this segregation in the practice of Jewish and Muslim traditions that most aroused antagonism in Christian communities across Europe.[89] Most chilling of all is that Shylock's famous plea for a common humanity ends with how he has learnt revenge from Christian hatred of Jews, most obviously shown by Antonio in the play: 'The villainy you teach me I will execute, and it shall go hard but I will better the instruction' (*The Merchant of Venice* 3.1.48–9). Shakespeare turns the reputed vengefulness of Jews back on the Christian audience. Shylock's internalized revenge is far more disturbing to the society around him than the rants of Marlowe's Barabas. When Portia enters the courtroom she takes care to ask who is the merchant, who the Jew, which might indicate that she is pleading for time, or that the two protagonists look alike, or that she is reminding her audience that Venetian justice is

'Christian fools with varnished faces'

(*The Merchant of Venice 2.5.31*)

31. *An Italian Carnival*, Arent van Bolten, Netherlands, *c.* 1588–1633.
Pen and brown ink, and brown wash, over black chalk, 44.3 x 61 cm. British Museum, London

would have seen carnival as a time of licence and sexual escapade. An engraving showing Venetian carnival (fig. 32) is inscribed in Latin: 'if they are fleeing the light, then what may they be up to?'[95] Jessica uses the cover of carnival to elope at night, dressed as a boy, from the window in Shylock's absence.

The play deals with every kind of traffic and merchandise. It opens with the Venetian merchant Salerio worrying about his ship, 'my wealthy *Andrew*', being wrecked, a detail which enables the text to be dated to late 1596–7 since the ship was real, a Spanish prize captured at Cadiz (1.1.28).[96] Shylock lists all the threats to ships at sea, from piracy – which was becoming increasingly familiar to British merchants – to natural dangers, in a way that would resonate with London audiences.[97] One of Antonio's ships is later wrecked on 'the Goodwins, I think they call the place' (3.1.3), a reference to the treacherous sands off the Kentish coast.[98] Shakespeare's Antonio (unlike the wealthiest Venetian merchants of the day) evidently lacked insurance, which would make these losses ruinous.[99]

Just as perilous and real to a contemporary London audience was the result of human traffic and trading. The servant Lancelet's affair with a black African slave, which occurs offstage, results in a pregnancy, the fate of which, like Aaron and Tamora's mixed-race child in *Titus*, is just too hot to handle within the play.[100] Shylock holds the issue of miscegenation up for questioning in his eloquent bid for the legality of his bond:

LARVATAE INCEDVNT VENETAE, CVR LVCE PVELLAE! LVXVRIANT ANIMI REBVS PLERVMQVE SECVNDIS,
AN FVGITANT LVCEM, SI BENE QVID FACIVNT? DIVITIIS ALITVR LVXVRIOSVS AMOR.

32. *A Venetian Carnival Scene on a Terrace*, Pieter de Jode the Elder after Pozzoserrato, *c.* 1595–8. Engraving, 37.4 x 50.2 cm. Rijksmuseum, Amsterdam

You have among you many a purchased slave,
Which, like your asses and your dogs and mules,
You use in abject and in slavish parts,
Because you bought them. Shall I say to you,
Let them be free, marry them to your heirs?
(4.1.91–5)

Shakespeare gives this critique of slavery to Shylock, which might have surprised London audiences given that Marranos, because of their Iberian origins, were particularly (though not exclusively) associated with black-slave-owning in contemporary London.[101] Shylock knows that no white Christian Venetian, however much lip service they pay to mercy and tolerance, will agree to miscegenation. Nor would Londoners have condoned it, even though (or perhaps because) it appears to have been happening around them. Only four apparently cross-racial marriages are documented in London in the 1570s, but it is clear that whites and blacks did have sex and/or marry in real life as they were portrayed fictionally in *Titus* and *Othello*. This was something new, and babies born to these unions challenged the theory that environment decided skin colour, as expressed by one George Best in 1578: 'I my selfe have seene an Ethiopian as black as cole brought into England, who taking a faire English woman to wife, begat a sonne in all respects as blacke as the father was, although England were his native country, and an Englishwoman his mother.'[102]

6 THE NOBLE MOOR

OTHELLO, AS A COMPOSITE FIGURE who combines elements of a
North African Moor, an Ottoman Turk and a sub-Saharan African, shows
Shakespeare exploring Moorish, Turkish and black African identity. The fact
that the ill-defined word 'Moor' had these connotations for contemporaries, and that
Moors had a stage history independent of any historical reality, gave Shakespeare and
his fellow playwrights a relatively free hand in presenting Moors as outsiders.[1]
Shakespeare had already presented Aaron the Moor in *Titus Andronicus*, a scheming
villain who reveals only a streak of humanity in his protectiveness towards his baby
son. Henry Peacham's drawing (see Chapter 4, fig. 2) presents an emblematic reading
of the whole of *Titus*, showing Aaron on the extreme right as a sub-Saharan African.[2]
Peacham imagines him played by an actor 'in blackface'. The Prince of Morocco in
The Merchant of Venice represents an entirely different figure, as a courtly North
African and a potential ally, with the gold of Africa at his disposal. In evoking the
prince, described in the stage directions as 'a tawny Moor all in white', Shakespeare
drew on precise detail.[3] In creating Othello, too, every detail is telling in its
associations for a contemporary audience.

Nowhere is this more evident than in Othello's choice of weapon when,
discovering Desdemona's innocence of the adultery for which he has mistakenly
murdered her, he decides to kill himself:

'noble moor'

(*Othello* 3.4.20)

See fig. 9, p. 180.

> I have another weapon in this chamber:
> It was a sword of Spain, the ice-brook's temper.
> (*Othello* 5.2.288–9)

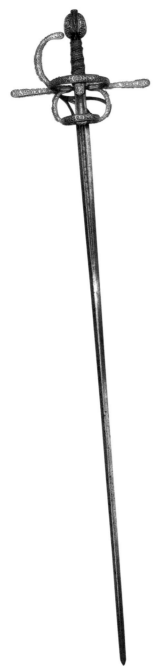

'a sword of Spain'

(*Othello 5.2.289*)

1. Rapier with blade signed by the smith Francesco Ruiz of Toledo; hilt made in France, possibly by Claude Savigny, *c.* 1590.
Steel, the hilt encrusted and inlaid with silver chains, L. 111 cm. Victoria and Albert Museum, London

The weapon is carefully chosen to be fit for purpose and inherently noble. Shakespeare here refers to a Spanish sword, a rapier with a Spanish blade, famed for its quality. Blades were made in Toledo where this lucrative export trade was carefully policed: a royal decree of 1567 stipulated that blades made there should 'wear the mark and sign of the master who made it' in an attempt to control the manufacture and marketing of fakes.[4] German swordsmiths in Solingen sometimes put faked Toledo marks on their blades to increase their value. Surviving weapons combine blades that have faked Toledo marks with swept hilts made in Germany, France or England. The Spanish sword in figure 1 is a rare example from around 1590 of a genuine Toledo blade signed by a known Toledo swordsmith, Francesco Ruiz, with a French hilt. This kind of rapier was heavily associated with ideas of honour – and perhaps with Italian honour killing – as demonstrated by the Italian inscription on the blade of another Spanish sword with a German hilt: 'NON TITUBARE SE TURBAR TI DEVI' ('Hesitate not where duty calls').

But in emphasizing the Spanishness of Othello's chosen blade, Shakespeare was not just reminding the audience of the weapon's killing power. It was also a fashion statement, since a Toledo mark was an early form of brand identity with which Shakespeare and his audiences would have been familiar. Rapiers with real or faked Toledo blades are to be seen in innumerable portraits of fashionable civilians in Shakespeare's England, posing as adventurers (see, for example, Chapter 3, fig. 29). It is hardly surprising that Shakespeare's contemporary Robert Greene noted that it was easy for English cutlers to pass off on an unsuspecting client 'a sword or rapier new over glased, and sweare, the blade came either from Turky, or Toledo'.[5] Blades on some surviving swords bear marks for more than one famous centre – Milan as well as Toledo on one example – but this might have been too much of a good thing even for a gullible English customer.[6]

Othello's rapier would have been an immediately recognizable stage prop.[7] But Shakespeare is not content to leave it at that. He inverts the weapon's name from the prosaic 'Spanish sword' to the more poetic 'sword of Spain' with a purpose, for Othello's carefully selected blade had other resonances for contemporary audiences. The 'ice-brook's temper' is another reference to the high quality of Spanish blades, since the steel used to make them was tempered, or reheated and quenched in icy water, to make it hard and durable. Shakespeare may have thought that the icy streams of Innsbruck, flowing down from alpine glaciers, would be especially suitable for this.[8] Or 'ice-brook' might be a misprint for 'Innsbruck', also known for its armourers. Either way, it all adds to the romance of the rapier as Othello's chosen suicide weapon.

Othello's insecurity about Desdemona's virtue shades into ethnic and religious anxieties about 'turning Turk'.[9] As he prepares to die, he metamorphoses from 'noble moor' to 'a malignant and turbaned Turk', referring to himself in the third person as a 'circumcisèd dog' before killing himself. His suicide is almost an act of judicial violence, for he carries out his own punishment and secures his own damnation according to Christian doctrine right in front of our eyes. As a former Christian

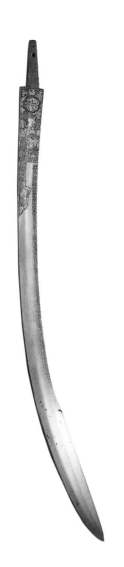

convert, he is 'double damned' (4.2.41).[10] Part of that reversion to a Muslim identity is revealed by his choice of sword, for Eastern cultures traditionally revered the sharpness, precision and craftsmanship of the blade rather than the ornateness of the hilt.

It is for this reason that Shakespeare's Prince of Morocco swears by his scimitar in *The Merchant of Venice* (2.1.25–32). The blade of the scimitar of Ali Pasha, supreme commander of the Ottoman Turkish fleet, was one of the prizes taken by Don John of Austria at the Battle of Lepanto in 1571. The blade, which is now in Madrid, has lost its hilt and bears an intricate Arabic inscription (fig. 2).[11] A contemporary German broadside of Ali Pasha shows how this scimitar was a key element in his identity as seen by his opponents (fig. 3). These resonances of what was seen as a religious battle between Christianity and Islam would have held for *Othello* in the early 1600s, especially since James I had written a poem (reprinted at his accession in England) commemorating Lepanto as a battle 'Betwixt the baptis'd race, / And circumcised

2. Blade of the scimitar of Ali Pasha, captured at the Battle of Lepanto in 1571 from the supreme commander of the Turkish fleet and taken by the Austrians as a trophy.
Steel with gilded inlay, L. 88.5 cm. Real Armería, Madrid

'By this scimitar'

(*The Merchant of Venice* 2.1.25)

3. Rare German broadside of *c.* 1571 showing Ali Pasha alive in the foreground, wearing his scimitar (see fig. 2) and, behind, his head impaled on a spike.
Letterpress and woodcut with stencil and hand-colouring, 42.6 x 33 cm.
Victoria and Albert Museum, London

'Nay, it is true, or else I am a Turk'

(*Othello* 2.1.125)

4. *A Warrior Adoring the Infant Christ and the Virgin*, Vincenzo Catena, after 1520. Oil on canvas, 155.3 x 263.5 cm. National Gallery, London

Turband Turkes', which Shakespeare apparently echoed in Othello's own self-description.[12] Even Othello's name recalls that of Othman I, the founder of the Ottoman Turkish dynasty.[13] *Othello* is recognizably a drama of conversion, for the word 'Moor' was principally a religious rather than racial classification for English playhouse audiences, and the issue of conversion was crucial to the relationship between European Christianity and the Ottoman Empire.[14]

It is in this intellectual context that Vincenzo Catena's enigmatic painting of a warrior abasing himself before the Virgin and Child takes on a particular meaning (fig. 4).[15] Probably dating to the 1520s, it has the format of a picture designed to hang in the portico or hall of a Venetian palace, and it belongs to a long and distinguished tradition of Venetian votive paintings. The central figure's greaves and fluted breastplate suggest that he is a warrior. His silk headcloth is not a turban, but can be matched with the headdress of a black African in a Flemish portrait miniature of much the same date. A very similar headdress can also be seen worn by John Blanke, a trumpeter documented in the service of Henry VIII in London, in the Great Tournament Roll of 1511 (fig. 5). 'John Blanke, the black trumpet' wears royal livery and his trumpet is hung with the arms of Henry VII, just like his fellow white musicians. Unlike them, however, he wears a rich silk headcloth which, given the uniform of the rest of his dress, must have been officially permitted as a badge of distinction.[16]

5. Miniature showing John Blanke, the black African trumpet, in the household of Henry VIII. From the Great Tournament Roll of Westminster, 1511.
Gold, silver and colours on vellum, whole roll 1813.5 x 37.5 cm. College of Arms, London

6. Headstall (part of a bridle or halter that encompasses a horse's head) like that shown in fig. 4. Attributed to Nasrid royal workshops, Granada, Spain, late 1400s.
Copper-gilt and enamel, L. (of largest assembled piece) 38.6 cm, W. 21.4 cm. British Museum, London

The rich accessories and goatee beard of Catena's warrior all suggest that he has Moorish or other wealthy Islamic connections. He is an individual of high status, as shown by his well-dressed Venetian servant and horse with fine trappings (fig. 6), of a kind which match those attributed to the Nasrid royal workshops of Moorish Granada.[17] His dagger, with its curving blade and tooled leather pouch, is also probably Moorish. Although he almost lies at the feet of the Virgin and Child, and places his right hand on his heart in homage, this is not apparently a conversion portrait. If it were, we would expect the presence of a saint as sponsor, presenting the convert to the Virgin and Child. Here all we have is the slightly disapproving figure of St Joseph. The picture would, however, appear to be a portrait, as it is the warrior's head as patron which appears at the centre and as the focus of the composition. Behind his head, a church appears in the distance, and his Moorish dagger is juxtaposed with a small white dog, emblematic of faith and faithfulness. If this is not a conversion portrait, it might instead be a portrait of someone who is making a statement of Christian orthodoxy and wishes to promote this view of himself. Several suggestions – none of them convincing – have been made as to his identity among liminal figures on the Western and Eastern margins of the Venetian Empire. One idea is that he might be a commander of Albanian mercenaries.[18] Or he could be a member of a powerful Venetian patrician family who worked closely with Muslims in Istanbul; a man regarded with ambivalence by his Venetian contemporaries.[19]

Although the painting is considerably earlier than either *Othello* or Shakespeare's source, the *Gli Hecatommithi* of 1565 by Giovanni Battista Giraldi Cinthio, it offers a unique window into the special context of the threatened borders of the Venetian Empire that Shakespeare sketches in so vividly for Othello as his own additions to his source. It evokes aspects of Othello's world – particularly its proximity to the Muslim world – like no other. It raises far more questions than it answers, and in that, too, it expresses the kind of questioning of religious and racial identity that is such a feature of Shakespeare's Venetian plays. If what we see here is a profession of faith rather than a conversion, then it matches Othello's insistence on his own Christian values when he breaks up the brawl between Montano and Cassio: 'Are we turned Turks? … For Christian shame, put by this barbarous brawl' (2.3.152–4). Othello is a baptized Moor, who, like the Marranos (see Chapter 5, p. 160), in London is assumed to be a convert. His allegiance and his very identity is questionable or at least unstable, as 'an extravagant and wheeling stranger / Of here and everywhere' (1.1.143–4).[20]

Shakespeare's particular interest in 'strangers' is demonstrated in passages attributed to him in the manuscript of *Thomas More* (see Chapter 1, p. 15), in which he suggests that Englishmen might try to imagine what it means to be judged an alien and infidel.[21] The English imagining of outsiders or strangers was formed by the playhouse. This was a two-way traffic. However emblematic a black character such as Othello, Cleopatra or Aaron the Moor might appear on stage, play texts show how the real European encounter with Africans helped to shape a cultural definition of whiteness in this period.

Muslim North Africans were perceived quite differently from sub-Saharan black Africans in England in Shakespeare's lifetime. North Africans were regarded as potential allies against Spain and the Ottoman Turks, as well as gatekeepers to African gold, whatever prejudice or fear they aroused as Muslims. The portrayal of Moors on stage in late sixteenth-century London followed upon visits from Moroccan delegations and, most famously, the six-month diplomatic visit by seventeen 'noble Moors' who aroused a mixture of hostility, fear and admiration in Londoners (see Chapter 1, pp. 34–5).[22] Contemporary commentators refer to the 'strangely attired and behavioured' group of men, who kept themselves apart and 'kild all their own meate within their house … and they turne their faces eastward when they kill anything'.[23] The unique portrait of the Moroccan ambassador, Abd-el-Ouahed ben Messaoud ben Mohammed Anoun, in Chapter 1 (fig. 26) is the visual legacy of this encounter.[24] There is a strong likelihood that he and his delegation witnessed a court performance by Shakespeare's theatre company, giving the playwright and his actors an image of North African nobility that fed into the creation of *Othello*. Elizabeth I's shrewd anti-Spanish manoeuvring with the Moroccans was just one example of her overtures to potential Muslim allies across the globe, wherever she and her subjects wished to operate commercially.[25]

Black Africans arrived in Britain from the 1500s by a variety of routes, often via Portugal, Spain or Italy, and only directly from Africa from the middle of the century. One well-documented high-status black visitor was Dedery Jaquoah, son of a king on the Pepper Coast in Guinea (now Liberia). He came to London in 1611 in the company of an English merchant trading with his father in order to learn English ways and trading customs, and to be baptized. The baptism was recorded in London as an important public event, as much for commercial as religious reasons.[26]

Offstage, around and beyond the London playhouses, the arrival of significant numbers of sub-Saharan Africans shaped language itself. 'Black' and 'white' had come into common linguistic use with reference to skin colour in Europe in the fifteenth century, when black skin was regarded as fascinating, exotic and erotic. It was also to be appraised in contrast to white skin. When Isabella d'Este sought a young black slave girl in 1491 she wanted the girl to be 'as black as possible' to set off her own prized pallor.[27] Contemporary paintings juxtapose white goddesses, mistresses and rulers with black maids or pages for much the same reason, setting off black beauty against white beauty,[28] and Anne of Denmark's wish to play at court 'in blackface' in the 1605 *Masque of Blacknesse* shows how this courtly fashion operated (see further Chapter 8, p. 220).[29] Like the black children paired with white children in the masque in Sir Henry Unton's memorial picture (see Chapter 1, fig. 43), these representations offer a visual parallel to the patterning of black against white in the language of Shakespeare's *Othello*, in showing off whiteness by contrast.[30] There was even a custom of calling things by their opposites, whereby black Africans were given variants of a name which incorporated notions of whiteness: John Blanke, Zuan Bianco, Jehan Blanc.[31]

The way in which this new element in European visual and literary culture related to an actual black presence is elusive. It probably owed as much to European court taste as it did to the reality of contacts with Africa or the slave trade.[32] The latest archival research suggests that there might have been around 900 black Africans out of a population of 200,000 in Elizabethan London, living mainly as slaves, servants, free men and women, many of whom were in domestic service, or acting as artists, artisans, or prostitutes.[33] They were concentrated in what were then the suburbs, where they had higher visibility in the vicinity of the playhouses.[34] In the diary of Simon Forman, who lived in Philpot Lane near London Bridge, is a reference in 1597 to 'Polonia the blackamor maid at Mr Piers of 12 yeare old' whom he diagnosed with 'a fainte harte full of melancholy'. Polonia was brought to him by her English employer.[35] Forman's diagnosis evokes Dürer's sensitive drawing of a named sub-Saharan slave in the service of the Portuguese agent João Brandão in Antwerp in 1521 (fig. 7). Dürer labelled the drawing with her name, Katherina, and her age, twenty at the time of the drawing in 1521, and described in his diary how he had drawn 'his [Brandão's] black African woman'.[36]

The English court was the focus for black Africans, who were evident in Elizabeth's royal household and in those of highly placed courtiers, such as her favourite Robert Dudley and her trusted servant William Cecil.[37] It could hardly have escaped Shakespeare's notice, through his contacts with adventurers and the Inns of Court backing the latest trade ventures, that English merchants were dealing in slaves as commodities. In 1565 the English adventurer John Hawkins added to his crest a black African slave, 'bound in a cord as bonde and captive' complete with gold armlets and

9. *Portrait of an African Man* (detail),
Jan Jansz. Mostaert, *c.* 1525–30.
The sitter was a Christian courtier.
Oil on panel, 30.8 x 21.2 cm. Rijksmuseum, Amsterdam

'were't to renounce his baptism'

(*Othello* 2.3.307)

10. Pilgrim badge of the Madonna of Hal, Belgium,
or the Netherlands, probably early 1500s, as worn
by the unknown courtier in fig. 9.
Silver-gilt, diam. 3.8 cm. British Museum, London

African descent, and baptisms of the children of slaves, are also documented, using a mixture of African and English names.[45]

Although not all black Africans in Europe were slaves, Europeans continued to classify them as such.[46] The fire-blower in figure 8, made in Venice around 1500, presents the common visual stereotype for sub-Saharan Africans. He takes the form of the bust of a young sub-Saharan African boy, who is richly dressed in a velvet tunic worn close around his neck in the manner of Venetian dress of about 1500. One earring survives in place; the hole for the other exists. Earrings were associated with black Africans, especially slaves, at the time when this object was made. This fire-blower would have been filled with water and placed in front of a fire; steam would be forced through the pierced lips of the puffing boy into the heart of the fire to make it burn more brightly.[47] We cannot know for certain whether this boy is intended to represent a slave, or a freed slave working as a domestic servant. There were many black Africans working in Renaissance Venice – as slaves, freed slaves and servants – and in other Italian ports, as well as in courts and urban households. Slave or free, they were often domestically employed: visual and archival evidence from Venice suggests that many worked as gondoliers.[48] The maker of this fire-blower was self-consciously picking up on the way in which black Africans were portrayed in ancient Roman bronze vessels in the shape of heads, as revived in Italian Renaissance bronze oil lamps. Some of these representations of Africans – both ancient and Renaissance – tend towards caricature and the demeaning of their subjects as someone's human property.[49]

This is what makes Jan Mostaert's portrait of a sub-Saharan African man as an exemplary Christian courtier all the more surprising (fig. 9). The portrait dates to around 1525–30, when Mostaert is documented as working at the court of Margaret of Austria in Mecheln,[50] though the painting could have been made in Antwerp, with its Portuguese links to Africa (see fig. 7). The subject's stance and self-presentation are recognizably European, fitting into a well-known genre of contemporary portraits. One finely gloved hand rests on a rapier and another on a purse, embroidered with the fleur-de-lis in silver, which might argue for an association with the Valois kings of France. But the only specific detail in the painting, which must be an item of significance to the subject of the portrait and which was intended to be readily identified, is the medallion sewn on to his cap. This is a pilgrim badge showing that the subject had been on pilgrimage to a famous site, the black Madonna of Our Lady of Hal in Belgium. Such badges, made of lead or silver, were sold at the shrines for pilgrims to wear with pride on their return home. Mostaert has rendered the badge precisely, so that the words 'Ave Maria' can be made out on the angels' scrolls and 'de Hal' can be read on the base of the Virgin's throne.

Three silver-gilt examples of this pilgrim badge survive, including one in the British Museum which exactly matches that worn by Mostaert's subject (fig. 10).[51] The badge marks this individual out as a Christian and one of high rank, since the shrine was one associated with the Hapsburgs and the Valois in particular. Could he have been a visiting Christian dignitary from sub-Saharan Africa wearing European

11. *Portrait of Ne-Vunda, Kongolese ambassador to the Pope*, attributed to Rafaello Schiamossi, 1608. Etching, 27.5 x 19.7 cm. British Museum, London

clothes, as was the common practice? With the accession of Afonso I (r. 1506–43) as Christian King of Kongo in 1506, Kongolese youths were sent to Portugal and Rome to be educated.[52] Ne-Vunda, the Christian Kongolese ambassador to the Pope in 1608, is shown in contemporary Italian and German prints in European dress (fig. 11). The printmakers obviously thought that there was a market interested in the physical appearance of black Africans as well as in the current news aspect of the story. The German broadside telling of his embassy to Rome explains how he was both exotic and Christian:

He was the very first ambassador sent from the Kingdom of Congo to the Papal Throne by King Alvardo, who is the fourth Christian king of Congo, a kingdom in the most distant part of Africa, mightily rich in gold … in place of coin they use shells, and because it lies in Ethiopia or the land of the moors this kingdom's inhabitants are completely black, like this ambassador, and go

doubting its moral seriousness, or the fact that it presents an extraordinary integration of a black African into an official Venetian visual format.

A developing aesthetic of blackness, reaching towards something new, is shown in European sculpture around 1600. In small-scale sculpture such as cameos, the different coloured brown and black layers within agate or sardonyx were used to present convincing images of black Africans in relief.[58] A sensuous example is seen in figure 13, designed to be mounted into a brooch or ring or displayed in a cabinet of curiosities as a miniature showpiece. The head of a black African rendered in marble by Nicholas Cordier in Rome around 1610 is closely based on classical prototypes (fig. 14). Cordier restored ancient Roman sculptures, sometimes incorporating ancient fragments into a new figure.[59] When he sculpted a bust of a Moorish woman, now in the Borghese Gallery in Rome, he was reproached in a poem of 1613 for not giving such a beauty a white complexion. How could a beauty be black?[60] The head illustrated here, made of a type of black marble called *bigio morato*, would probably have attracted the same criticism. It recalls the dignity of some of the finest ancient Greek and Roman prototypes in bronze and marble which are clearly Cordier's models, even down to the taut concentration of the subject's gaze, accentuated by the white marble around the pupils in his eyes.[61]

The silver-gilt cup in figure 15 in the form of a Moor's head is chivalric and obviously courtly in purpose. German goldsmiths had a long tradition of making silver-gilt heraldic drinking cups in ever more fantastic and intricate forms that were displayed and occasionally used for formal dining. This cup was made by the leading Nuremberg goldsmith, Christoph Jamnitzer, around 1595–1600, probably for the wedding of the Elector of Saxony, Christian II, to Hedvig of Denmark.[62] It is unique in that the hollow silver bust – which opens so that you can drink either from the head or the upturned cover – takes the form of the head of a sub-Saharan African. The headband and one surviving earring possibly link it to heraldic imagery of Moors' heads, as on the arms of the Pucci family of Florence, and may indicate the subject's slave status.[63] The gilded foot and details make a striking contrast with his blackened skin and the rock crystal gems in the aigrette on his head. The aigrette copies a kind of feathery hat jewel fashionable in Renaissance European courts[64] and was

'far more fair than black'

(*Othello* 1.3.308)

14. Bust of a black African, Nicolas Cordier, Rome, *c.* 1610.
Black *bigio morato* marble and white marble, H. 34 cm.
Staatliche Kunstsammlungen, Dresden

associated with exoticism, from Indian and Turkish to African (fig. 16).[65] The whole Jamnitzer bust has sculptural presence and poise, particularly suitable for a cup which might have been a sports trophy at a Saxon court tournament in 1602 celebrating Christian's wedding.[66]

In portraying Africans, both in art and in drama, Europeans defined themselves through difference. Although these were independent imaginative creations, they owed something, however misunderstood or manipulated, to the actual European encounter with Africa and Africans.[67] Shakespeare uses Venice – the open, modern city – as a setting for plays that explore very English anxieties about shifting racial and religious identity and allegiance in a period of global expansion.[68]

15. Moor's head cup, Christoph Jamnitzer.
Nuremberg, *c.* 1602.
Embossed silver, partially gilt, and rock crystal, H. 52.2 cm.
Bayerisches Nationalmuseum, Munich

16. Hat jewel with military trophies. Germany or the Netherlands, early 1600s.
Gold, enamelled and set with diamonds, rubies and emeralds, L. 8.59 cm. British Museum, London

King James 1st

7 'FOR REBELLION IS AS THE SIN OF WITCHCRAFT': THE SCOTTISH PLAY

THE SMOOTH ACCESSION OF JAMES I in March 1603 was something of a national triumph (fig. 1). One French commentator, looking back on the repression and political unease at the end of Elizabeth's reign, described England as 'a theatre filled with the most horrible and bloody tragedies which one could expect in an entirely disordered and ravaged state'.[1]

James I was welcomed, as an experienced male ruler with two male heirs to succeed him, after more than forty years of rule by a single and autocratic woman who refused to allow any public discussion of the succession.[2] John Fenton expressed the national mood:

> I must confess that in Eliza's prime
> We never did enjoy a happier time …
> Now may we proudly boast we neede not feare,
> We have a King, and this same King an heire.[3]

Across the religious spectrum, from Catholics to Presbyterians, King James's subjects looked to the new Supreme Governor of the Church for leadership and a new beginning, after decades of mounting tension and division. Faced with several irreconcilable agendas, James set out on a difficult and dangerous path as he sought to create unity and toleration – though one of his assets was the new international identity that could be created for 'Great Britaine', as England and Scotland were brought together with Ireland and Wales under the same monarch for the first time. A new sense of nationhood could be forged and there were the first stirrings of imperial ambition.

1. Portrait of James I wearing the Feather Jewel in his hat, attributed to the studio of John de Critz the Elder, *c.* 1606. John de Critz was a Protestant exile from the Netherlands who settled in London and was appointed Sergeant Painter to James I in 1605 and 'his Majestie's Painter' in 1611. There was demand both in Britain and abroad for an official portrait of the new king. De Critz was paid for a full-length portrait of James in 1606 and is thought to have created the official portrait type that was used until the king sat for Paul van Somer in 1618. This half-length version shows James as the scholar-king, a man of poetic and literary ambition.
Oil on panel, 56 x 43 cm. Parham House, Sussex

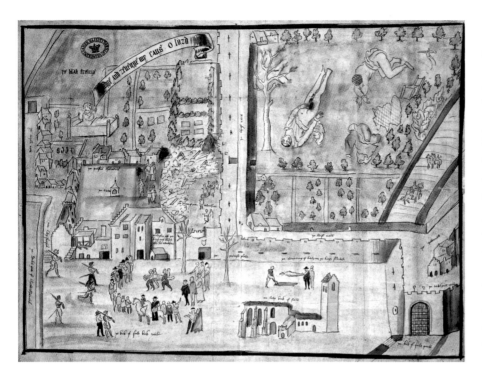

2. Lord Darnley's murder at Kirk o'Field, Edinburgh, 10 February 1567. This vivid contemporary drawing was sent to William Cecil in England just after the event.

Pen and ink, 44 x 52.3 cm. National Archives, Kew

On 19 May 1603 Shakespeare's acting company was proclaimed the King's Men, 'freely to use and exercise the Art and faculty of playing Comedies, Tragedies, Histories, interludes, Morals, pastorals, Stage plays and such others … for the recreation of our loving Subjects as for our Solace and pleasure when we shall think good to see them'.[4] This confirmed their status as the most prestigious acting company in the land. As royal servants the King's Men had formal status in the royal household as Grooms of the Chamber in Ordinary without fee. This was an honorary position that entitled the wearer to parade in livery on court occasions and to serve as ushers at important diplomatic events.[5] This experience of life at court feeds into Shakespeare's creation of the dangerous world of *Macbeth*. It is tempting to see this new position in the king's presence in the gruesome scene in which the Macbeths smear the drugged grooms attending on King Duncan with his blood in an attempt to frame them for his murder. Shakespeare had earlier conveyed the surveillance and electric unease of life at court in *Hamlet*, with spies hiding behind the wall hangings, but when he wrote this scene, he was himself a Groom of the Chamber. Could this have given the players – if not their viewers – an added frisson or dramatic edge in performing the scene at court?[6]

King James I was far from confident in his rule. Even in the womb he had been threatened at the murder of his mother's lover, Riccio, in 1566.[7] When he was a few months old he survived the murder of his father, Lord Darnley (1545–1567) (fig. 2). His mother, Mary, Queen of Scots, was deposed for her part in this murder and James succeeded to the throne of Scotland at the age of one in 1567.[8] He survived an alleged assassination attempt – though the details remained mysterious – in the Gowrie conspiracy in 1600, and then the Bye and Main Plots of 1603, the latter of which aimed to set his cousin Arbella Stuart (1575–1615) on the throne. Writing about such threats directly was out of bounds, as the King's Men discovered to their cost when they attempted a play about the Gowrie conspiracy in 1604: the show was banned after two sell-out performances.[9] The spectacular fiasco of the Gunpowder Plot or Powder Treason in 1605 – a Catholic act of terrorism allegedly designed to blow up the king, his family, Parliament and the judiciary – provided the essential backdrop for Shakespeare's *Macbeth*, which deals with 'dire combustion and confused events'

'dire combustion and confused events'

(Macbeth 2.3.52)

3. Lantern traditionally associated with Guy Fawkes, given to the University of Oxford in 1641 as a memento of the Gunpowder Plot. Made of sheet iron, it would originally have had a horn window and could have been closed completely to hide the light of the single candle within. Sheet iron, H. 34.5 cm. Ashmolean Museum, Oxford

(2.3.52).[10] This is the only time that Shakespeare uses the word 'combustion', and it is in this play that he introduces the word 'assassination' into English literature (1.7.2).[11]

However the precise significance of the Gunpowder Plot is interpreted, there is no doubt that it changed the British national psyche forever and put an end to any possibility of a reversion to Catholicism as the state religion.[12] The preacher Lancelot Andrewes referred to it in a famous sermon of 5 November 1606 as 'our Passover', the salvation of a people by the direct intervention of God, which required 'a yearly acknowledgement to be made of it through all generations' in the manner of the Jewish festival of Passover.[13] The Plot inspired ballads, broadsides, plays and sermons within the year following its discovery, and in the following decades it was paired with the defeat of the Armada in written and visual propaganda.[14] In each event, the ruler had been promoted as the saviour of the nation, divinely protected and justified. Both events were seen as a national victory for Protestantism against an international Catholicism that threatened England's very survival.

'Guy Fawkes' lantern', a secular relic now in the Ashmolean Museum, Oxford, takes us close to the Gunpowder Plot and its legacy (fig. 3). Fawkes was identified with his lantern in the popular imagination and in contemporary images, and a number of lanterns with alleged links to him survive. This one was reputedly given to Oxford University in 1641 by Robert Heywood of Brasenose College. His father was the Justice of the Peace who had arrested Fawkes underneath the Palace of Westminster as he was about to set off the explosion. It was shown in the Bodleian Library as a document of British history and as a testament to anti-Catholicism and Catholic exclusion from the time of its gift into the 1880s, when it was transferred to the Ashmolean Museum. The fact that an ordinary lantern of this kind was kept as a talisman or icon – whether or not it was indeed associated with Fawkes – testifies to the role of the Plot in the British imagination.

For Shakespeare the immediate impact of the Plot must have been inescapable since the main plotters, Catesby, Tresham and Winter, had Stratford links, with a safe house just outside Stratford at Clopton.[15] The trials of the conspirators, once they had been hunted down, made sensational news, playing on deep national anxieties about the Catholic enemy within. Events were followed closely by the public, not just in Britain, but abroad. It was dangerous, though, to make direct reference to the events in print or image. Tensions remained high for most of 1606: in March of that year a rumour flew round in London that James had been murdered on a hunting trip. The Venetian ambassador commented: 'the news spread to the city and the uproar was amazing. Everyone flew to arms, the shops were shut, and cries began to be heard against Papists, foreigners and Spaniards'[16] – that is to say, the usual trio of suspects was rhetorically rounded up. James was informed of the rumour and swiftly returned to London: bells were rung and fireworks set off in celebration of his safety. Ben Jonson even wrote a poem to commemorate the event, 'Upon the happy false rumour of his death, the two and twentieth day of March, 1606', which ends:

remained a figure in the popular imagination in England and abroad in both Protestant and Catholic circles for some years: in 1608 Thomas Coryat, on seeing portraits of Garnet on sale in Cologne, referred to him as 'our famous English Jesuite Henry Garnet'.[22]

The political immediacy of the Gunpowder Plot within the texture of *Macbeth* is heightened by Lady Macbeth's welcome to the night that will cloak the murder of Duncan: 'That my keen knife see not the wound it makes, / Nor heaven peep through the blanket of the dark, / To cry, "Hold, hold!"' (1.5.50–2). That last phrase was the very command made by the crowd to the hangman when they ran forward to pull on Garnet's legs to hasten his death as he was hanged: an unusual sign of compassion on the part of the crowd at the execution of a traitor. Sympathy with Garnet as a state target went further, the Jesuit Father Gerard noted: 'For when he was cut up and his bowels cast in the fire, and his heart pulled out and showed unto the people with these words, that are ever used in such cases, "Behold the heart of a traitor", there was not heard any applause, or those that cried "God Save the King", which is always usual when the heart or head is held up in that kind.'[23]

Edward Oldcorne, another Jesuit executed for his faith and his perceived part in the Plot, was offered no such clemency. He was hanged, then drawn and quartered while still alive at Worcester on 7 April 1606.[24] A member of the crowd fished his right eyeball out of the pot in which the quartered body was boiled before being spiked on a pole for public display. The silver reliquary (fig. 7) in which this gruesome relic was displayed beneath its eye-shaped aperture is roughly contemporary.[25]

Oldcorne's eyeball is the most vivid reminder imaginable of the public spectacle of execution, one which vied with the playhouse as popular spectacle (over which it

'Out, vile jelly!
Where is thy lustre now?'

(*King Lear* 3.7.88–9)

7. Silver reliquary made around 1606 to contain the right eye of the Jesuit priest Blessed Father Edward Oldcorne, which was collected at his execution at Worcester in 1606. The relic was smuggled out to the Jesuit College in St Omer, France, in the seventeenth century, and returned to Stonyhurst in 1794.

Silver, diam. 4.6 cm. Stonyhurst College, Lancashire

8. Drawing by Claes Jansz. Visscher showing the execution of eight of the Gunpowder Plotters on 30–31 January 1606. Set in an imaginary city, this is a preparatory drawing for Visscher's print, which reproduces the scene in reverse with inscriptions as a piece of anti-Catholic propaganda. Both can be dated to around 1606.

Pen and brown ink, brown wash, with lines indented for transfer, 23.9 x 34.2 cm. British Museum, London

had the advantage of being free instead of costing at least a penny). Execution brought the nature of mortality and the frailty of flesh brutally home to spectators. The Duke of Cornwall's relish in plucking out the Earl of Gloucester's eyes in *King Lear* seems to owe its force to the experience of torture and public execution: 'Out, vile jelly! / Where is thy lustre now?' (3.7.88–9). It appears that Shakespeare coined the word 'eyeball' in English (*The Tempest* 1.2.356). Executioners, many of whom normally worked as butchers, regularly handled bits of bodies in front of the crowd.[26] Claes Jansz. Visscher's drawing of the execution of eight of the Gunpowder Plotters in St Paul's churchyard on 30–31 January 1606 sets the scene not in London, but in an imaginary contemporary city (fig. 8). However fictive the setting, the details of the execution of traitors are real enough and were familiar to people all over Europe. Audiences at the London playhouse expected a high degree of authenticity when similar violence was enacted on stage: George Peele's *The Battle of Alcazar* (*c.* 1591) sees three characters disembowelled, which required '3 violls of blood & a sheep's gather [organs and entrails]' to be supplied for each one.[27]

Shakespeare made mention of the practice of public execution as torture and spectacle in his plays. The language of torture was recognizable in the wider culture of

Imprinted at London for W.B.

A most strange and true report of a monsterous Fish, who appeared in the forme of a Woman, from her waste vpwards.

'a fish that appeared upon the coast'

(The Winter's Tale 4.4.278)

11. 'A most strange and true report of a monsterous fish', 1604.
Woodcut, 17.5 x 13.5 cm.
National Library of Wales, Aberystwyth

The anti-Catholic writer Samuel Harsnett satirized the kind of Catholic priest who travelled the country 'as Tynkers doe [with] their bitches … a peddling Exorcist of the rascal crue, who wandered like a chapman of small wares'.[41] The chest illustrated here is the kind that a chapman or pedlar would have taken on a packhorse, though these were less common than backpacks. A pedlar's chest of the early seventeenth century is rare enough in itself (a Catholic one rarer still), and on one level it offers a parallel to the pack used by the thieving Autolycus in *The Winter's Tale*, who declares 'My traffic is sheets' (4.3.23) – items he steals off the hedges where they have been put to dry in springtime. Autolycus carries a list of wares, which were the stock in trade of contemporary chapmen, as inventory evidence demonstrates. He advertises courtship gifts, textiles, dress pins, and ballads on monstrous births and fabulous fish, talking up each item with a bawdy sales banter to match.[42] One of the ballads mentioned by Autolycus concerns 'a fish that appeared upon the coast … it was thought she was a woman and was turned into a cold fish for she would not exchange flesh with one that loved her' (4.4.278–82). This contemporary print has recently been identified (fig. 11).[43]

The Stonyhurst chest is particularly special, however, in that it contains patched Catholic vestments made from women's clothing, handkerchiefs for use as corporals on which to celebrate Mass, a simple rosary, an altar stone and a small pewter chalice for celebrating the Mass in secret.[44] These were the same kinds of recriminating items as those sent in a cloakbag from another safe Catholic base, Clopton House near Stratford, by the Grant family following the arrest of Guy Fawkes in November 1605.[45] The chest illustrated here was found in the mid-nineteenth century walled up in a compartment in a well-known Catholic house, Samlesbury Hall, near Preston in Lancashire. The house was a safe refuge for Catholic priests in the late Elizabethan and Jacobean periods, and it is thought that the contents of the chest might possibly be linked with the Jesuit Edmund Arrowsmith, who operated locally and was executed at

Lancaster in 1628.[46] Nothing conveys more clearly the way in which Catholic priests lived on the margins.

During the Garnet trial reference was frequently made to Jesuits as male witches, cooking up a hellish plot which, as Lancelot Andrewes preached in his anniversary sermon on the Plot in 1606, could only have been devised by the Devil and those in league with him.[47] Witchcraft was political. Distinct from witchcraft, but linked to it, was the issue of demonic possession, which was argued over at James's accession in a flurry of high-profile cases, sensational pamphlets and London sermons (fig. 12).[48] People knew that James had had personal experience of witches (see below, p. 198) and had written a treatise on witchcraft, *Daemonologie*, in 1597, which was twice reprinted in England at his accession in 1603 (fig. 13).[49] But James expressed some scepticism about the idea of demonic possession. More extreme doubts were voiced by Samuel Harsnett, chaplain to the then Bishop of London. Harsnett's polemical *Declaration of Egregious Popish Impostures*, printed in 1603, exposed the way in which exorcisms were orchestrated as theatrical events by those at both ends of the religious spectrum, from Jesuit priests to Puritan ministers.[50] The parodic language of demonic possession in Harsnett's book was borrowed by Shakespeare for Edgar's assumed madness in *King Lear*, with direct quotation of the imaginary spirits' names: 'The prince of darkness is a gentleman: Modo he's called, and Mahu' (3.4.117–18).[51] There may have been a Stratford connection too, in that one of the priests castigated by Harsnett was Richard Debdale of Shottery, near Stratford, who was possibly a kinsman of Shakespeare.[52]

12. *The most wonderfull and true storie, of a certaine Witch named Alse Gooderidge*, London, 1597. An account of demonic possession and exorcism which drew on the testimony of witnesses and confessions at trials. This is one of the witchcraft tracts collected by Richard Bancroft as Bishop of London from 1597 to 1604, which he regarded as essential documentation on an important matter of religious politics. They were part of his founding collection at Lambeth Palace Library in 1610.
Printed book, 17.7 x 13 cm. Lambeth Palace Library, London

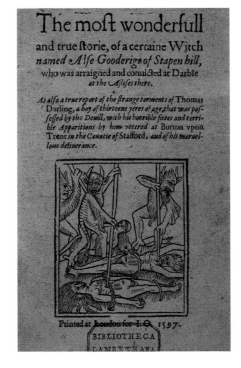

The text is accompanied by a woodcut showing several scenes, including four witches of Berwick cooking up a charm in their cauldron, and the storm they have concocted causing the shipwreck at left. Details of the witches' indictments in *Newes from Scotland* may lie behind Shakespeare's weyard sisters, including the First Witch's claim that she will set sail in a sieve (1.3.9): Euphame MacCalzean was another of the accused in the North Berwick trial, for going to sea in a sieve or riddle to raise storms.[65] In *Macbeth* the First Witch talks of adding 'a pilot's thumb, / Wrecked as homeward he did come' (1.3.29–30), which may also refer back to Agnes Sampson's confession to 'jointing' corpses, or others like it.[66]

The crime of witchcraft was perceived to be a serious one and punished accordingly. The iron 'witch's collar' or jougs with serrated edge in figure 16 was used to encircle the neck of an individual accused in a local Scottish kirk session of immorality, breach of the peace or other misdemeanours within the community. This could include 'flyting' or slander, the victims often being women. It has traditionally been asserted that they were used in the torture and punishment of witches, but recent research does not bear this out.[67] This jougs is one of the few examples to enter a public collection with a specific reference to its use in witchcraft.[68] It has a ring to attach by a chain to the kirk wall or gate. In both Scotland and England punishment

'If you prick us, do we not bleed?'

(*The Merchant of Venice* 3.1.44)

16. Witches were thought not to bleed when pricked. Top: iron gag known as a 'branks' or witches' bridle. Both pieces have chains attached to fasten the woman captive in a public place. Above and right: iron jougs placed on the neck of a woman accused in a local kirk session of being a witch. North-east Fife, Scotland, 1600s.
Jougs diam. 15.5 cm. Branks H. 19.2 cm.
National Museums Scotland, Edinburgh

in a public, designated space – such as a town tollbooth in Scotland – was common for first offences, but the presbytery in Scotland worked with criminal courts in policing 'superstition' at kirk sessions before they got to court.[69] This jougs is from the seventeenth century and comes from the kirk in Ladybank, Fife. The serrated edge on the collar may not have just been intended to wound, but to prove a witch's identity, as they were thought not to bleed when pricked. Shylock the Jew refers to this superstition when he argues for the humanity of his own people, differentiating them from the witches with whom Jews were often compared in the popular imagination: 'If you prick us, do we not bleed?' (*The Merchant of Venice* 3.1.44). This jougs is shown underneath an iron gag known as the 'branks' or witches' bridle that passed over a woman's tongue and gagged her. It has a chain attached to fasten the woman captive in a public place.

Given the political resonances of witchcraft at the time in which he was writing, Shakespeare is cautious, even equivocal, in the use of witchcraft in *Macbeth*.[70] His weyard sisters are not directly typecast as witches, but as mysterious female prophets or sibyls of classical and biblical antiquity – perhaps close to the well-dressed women in the woodcut illustrating their encounter with Macbeth in Holinshed's *Chronicle*

17. Macbeth and Banquo encountering the three weyard sisters. From Raphael Holinshed, *Chronicles*, London, 1587. This expensive three-volume edition is the one Shakespeare used as source material for *Macbeth*, *King Lear* and *Cymbeline*.
Woodcut, 7.8 x 13.8 cm. Folger Shakespeare Library, Washington DC

'supernatural soliciting'

(Macbeth 1.3.140)

20. The Glenorchy Charmstone, which belonged to the Campbell family of Glenorchy and Bredalbane, Argyllshire, Scotland. Used for curing sickness and murrain in cattle, this charm is probably the one recorded in the *Black Book of Taymouth* of 1640.
Rock crystal set in a seventeenth-century mount of silver and red coral. H. 7 cm, W. 4.5 cm.
National Museums Scotland, Edinburgh

21. The Ballochyle Brooch, *c.* 1610. This silver brooch, set with a rock crystal and inscribed 'De Serve and Haif the Hevin Bebeif' ('Deserve and have the Heaven above'), belonged to the MacIver Campbells of Ballochyle, Scotland, and was used as a charm against disease or the working of witchcraft in people or animals. Marked VS for the goldsmith William Stalker of Glasgow.
Diam. 13.8 cm. National Museums Scotland, Edinburgh

before the entrance of the supposedly possessed Poor Tom: 'O, nuncle, court holy-water in a dry house is better than this rain-water out o'door. Good nuncle, in, ask thy daughters' blessing: here's a night pities neither wise men nor fools' (*King Lear* 3.2.10–12). Typically, Shakespeare complicates the image received out of popular custom: in a play that offers a devastating critique of the flattery and falseness of the courtier's arts, 'court' holy water is a tainted oxymoron.

Another brooch illustrated here is one of a group of four passed down as family heirlooms and worn as cloak brooches.[80] The Lochbuie Brooch (fig. 22) and the Brooch of Lorn (fig. 23) are so similar that they must have been made by the same silversmith, working in Scotland around 1600. On both, it is the mesmeric quality of the cabochon rock crystal at the centre that dominates, changing colour from milky opaque to transparent, and from blue-grey to mauve, as you turn it in the light. Both have a central reliquary section under the rock crystal, perhaps for a prayer, fragment of bone, skin or textile, which would draw the wearer closer to a holy person or saint.[81]

Each brooch is intimately tied up with the history of the clan to which it belonged and can be said to represent the distinctiveness of the history of the Highlands. The Western Highlands, the Highlands and Ulster, just over the narrow sea, were to King James I ungovernable Gaelic borderlands beyond the civility promised by the Union of the crowns of Scotland and England. These three brooches represent everything that

22. The Lochbuie Reliquary Brooch, made for the Macleans of Mull, *c.* 1600. The brooch is of silver set with local pearls and an earlier rock crystal, which unscrews to reveal an inner compartment, now empty.
Diam. 12.2 cm. British Museum, London

23. The Brooch of Lorn is similar in design and construction to the Lochbuie Brooch (fig. 22) and probably by the same maker. Said by tradition to have been captured from Robert the Bruce by the MacDougalls of Lorn at the battle of Dalrigh in 1306, the brooch as we see it now dates from *c.* 1600. Rock crystal set in a silver mount decorated with pearls.
H. approx. 40 cm, W. 10 cm. MacDougall of Dunollie Preservation Trust, Dunollie House, Oban

James found ungovernable and 'alluterly barbares' in the Western Highlands and Isles, for they are the last in the line of great medieval clan brooches that embodied the standing and power of their wearers.[82] When, at the end of *Macbeth*, the righteous Malcolm talks of a new order in Scotland, it would have had special meaning for James I: 'My thanes and kinsmen, / Henceforth be earls; the first that ever Scotland / In such an honour named' (5.7.107–9). The transformation from the Scottish term 'thanes' to the English title 'Earls' symbolizes the union of Scotland and England that comes simultaneously within the play – when Malcolm makes his alliance with the English King Edward the Confessor – and the moment of the play's first performance, when James united the thrones at Scone and at Westminster.

Shakespeare builds an image of goodness, legitimate rule and kingly majesty through contrast. The presentation of the witches is part of the way in which malevolence is pitched against legitimacy. Macbeth's hidden and occult relationship with the weyard sisters is set against the role of the radiantly holy English king, Edward the Confessor, who is able to cure people miraculously from scrofula:

Such sanctity hath heaven given his hand –
They presently amend …
'Tis called the Evil:

24. Gold coin minted in London in 1605–6, known as an 'angel' because the obverse has an image of the Archangel Michael. Coins such as these were used in touching for the King's Evil, or scrofula. This coin was evidently used, as it is pierced to be worn round the neck. It was almost certainly distributed by James I at the touching ceremony at Whitehall Palace in 1605–6.
Diam. 2.6. British Museum, London

25. *Macbeth*, Jacob de Wet the Younger, from a series of portraits of real and legendary Scottish kings in the Great Gallery at the Palace of Holyrood house, Edinburgh, 1684–6.
Oil on canvas, 79 x 81 cm. Royal Collection, Edinburgh

A most miraculous work in this good king,
Which often, since my here-remain in England,
I have seen him do. How he solicits heaven
Himself best knows: but strangely-visited people,
All swoll'n and ulcerous, pitiful to the eye,
The mere despair of surgery, he cures,
Hanging a golden stamp about their necks
Put on with holy prayers: and 'tis spoken,
To the succeeding royalty he leaves
The healing benediction. With this strange virtue
He hath a heavenly gift of prophecy,
And sundry blessings hang about his throne
That speak him full of grace.
(*Macbeth* 4.3.159–76)

The 'golden stamp' was a gold coin known as the angel, a coin distinguished by the Archangel Michael on the obverse and the ship of state on the reverse, first minted by Edward IV (r. 1461–1470 and 1471–1483) from 1461. Small issues of 'angels' were minted by James I for ceremonial uses, including touching. The angel was probably chosen for this role as it was made of gold of high purity and bore no portrait of a king or queen, unlike most coins. It was also the most common coin in England, hence the number of times it is mentioned by Shakespeare in his plays. The iconography of the Archangel Michael was also particularly appropriate for its use as a touchpiece. It was a sign of a true English king or queen who ruled by right of legitimate succession that they could heal in this way, and the coins were themselves considered amulets or charms with healing powers.[83] Figure 24 shows a touchpiece almost certainly used by James I in 1605–6 in touching for the King's Evil at Whitehall Palace, though the king himself was a bit anxious about this recourse to magic as superstitious. The Latin inscription points to God's will: 'This is the Lord's doing and it is wonderful in our eyes' [Psalm 118]. The Venetian ambassador wrote home recording the practice in 1604, adding sceptically that 'it remains to be seen with what result'.[84]

Macbeth as a play speaks to James I's insecurity about his own status and right of legitimate succession (fig. 25). His mother was a Stuart, the Catholic Mary, Queen of Scots, beheaded by Elizabeth I in 1587 and viewed by Catholics as a martyr. James himself was a Protestant and a Stuart, as well as being the head of a new dynasty in England. The early years of his reign saw attempts to convince his subjects that he was no foreigner but a genuine Protestant descended through the Tudors. James I stressed not only his claim through Margaret Tudor, but also his Welsh royal blood, which was supposedly due to the legendary Fleance, son of Banquo, marrying the Prince of Wales's daughter. It was their son who became the founder of the House of Stuart. This useful invention of a Stuart ancestor in Banquo was that of the Stuart apologist,

85. MACBETHVS

'shall Banquo's issue ever Reign in this kingdom?'

(*Macbeth* 4.1.110–11)

26. The Lyte Jewel, enamelled gold with diamonds set in the royal cipher of James I and containing the king's miniature by Nicholas Hilliard. Made in London and presented to Thomas Lyte in 1610–11 in thanks for his royal genealogy tracing James's descent from Brutus, the mythical Trojan founder of Britain.
H. 6.5 cm, W. 4.8 cm. British Museum, London

Hector Boece; but it was George Buchanan, James's tutor, who portrayed Macbeth in his *History of Scotland* (1582) as 'a man of penetrating genius, a high spirit, unbounded ambition' and who noted that aspects of the Macbeth legend were 'more adapted for theatrical representation … than history'.[85] In *Macbeth* Shakespeare contrived to introduce Banquo and Fleance into the play and to portray them as wronged characters. Macbeth manages to have Banquo murdered, but Fleance escapes and it is his lineage, not Macbeth's, that will produce future kings of Scotland.[86] In doing this, taking the story and its atmosphere from Holinshed's *Chronicles* and possibly from Buchanan's *History*, he rewrote history for his royal patron in extending the line of succession from Banquo and Fleance to James himself.

The Lyte Jewel (fig. 26) tells us much about James I's contribution to the making of British identity in the early years of his reign, and the political will that lay behind it.[87] It is a diamond-studded locket, made in London around 1610 to hold a miniature by Nicholas Hilliard of James I of England. It was presented by the king to Thomas Lyte of Lytes Cary, Somerset (fig. 27), at the Palace of Whitehall between 12 July 1610

27. Anonymous portrait of Thomas Lyte wearing the Lyte jewel, dated 14 April 1611.

Oil on panel, 57 x 44 cm. Museum of Somerset, Taunton

and 14 April 1611, in thanks for writing a fantastic genealogy claiming that James was 'a second Brutus' as a descendant of Brute, the mythical Trojan founder of the British nation (fig. 28).[88] The genealogy was Lyte's personal take on the Galfridian myth derived from Geoffrey of Monmouth's *Historia Regum Britanniae* (*c*. 1136), known as 'the British History'. Four of the original nine memranes of the genealogy are now missing from the outer corners. One of these traced the origins of the Stuart line and would almost certainly have made clear – given its importance to James – his descent from Banquo and Fleance, and the link with Welsh royal blood through Fleance's marriage to a Welsh princess. The genealogy, started at James's acession, had taken Lyte seven years of careful research. By 1610 the year of its completion, the myth had been discredited by William Camden, the author of *Britannia* (1586), and other authorities, but its appeal and usefulness was undiminished at court, so much so that Camden apparently signed up to it.[89] The presentation copy of Lyte's genealogy was displayed at Whitehall Palace and was mentioned by several commentators who saw it there in 1611, until it became so grubby from fingering that James ordered it to be engraved and printed. No printed copy survives today: the only record we have is Lyte's unfinished and unilluminated copy.

The expensive jewel, its origin and its presentation at court in an apparently spontaneous gesture to a loyal courtier in front of foreign ambassadors, was all a carefully managed exercise to shore up James's position both at home and abroad. Shakespeare seems to have understood this very clearly indeed, as if he knew it from inside. When the weyard sisters show Macbeth the prophetic line of kings culminating

28. *Brittans Monarchie*, Thomas Lyte's genealogy of James I, *c*. 1605. Detail showing the English (left) and British (right) line of descent. From an uncoloured and unfinished copy on vellum from Lytes Cary manor, Somerset, of the illuminated genealogy presented at court to James I on 12 August 1610. The presentation and its significance was highly sensitive politically and Lyte was rewarded by the king with 'his picture in gold, set with diamonds, with gracious thanks'. Lud, Lear and his daughters Goneril, Regan and Cordelia – names resonant for Shakespeare – appear in the detail (right).

Pen and ink on vellum, five membranes (four now missing), 189 x 212 cm. British Library, London

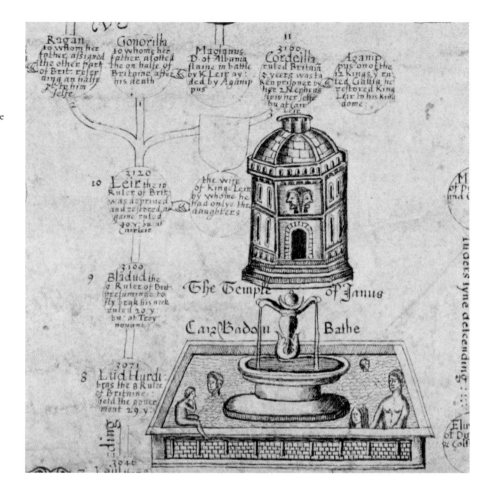

in the bloodied Banquo, the aim is to enforce the answer to Macbeth's desperate quest for certainty: 'shall Banquo's issue ever / Reign in this kingdom?' (4.1.110–11).

Macbeth, then, is steeped in the preoccupations of the new king: the relationship between England and Scotland, the rights of royal succession, anxiety about high treason and Roman Catholic plots, the reality of witchcraft and the sacred powers of the monarch. The Lyte genealogy, meanwhile, also traced James's line of descent through Lud, Lear and his three daughters – names resonant for Shakespeare. Whereas his historical dramas in the reign of Queen Elizabeth had focused on her predecessors on the English throne, from Richard II through Henry V to the advent of the Tudor dynasty after the defeat of Richard III, the new phenomenon of a king on the throne of two previously divided kingdoms led in turn to new subject matter: the history of Britain as opposed to that of England.

A BRITAINE

A ROMANE

A SAXON

BRITANNIA

A DANE

A NORMAN

THE
THEATRE
OF THE EMPIRE
OF GREAT
BRITAINE:
Presenting
AN EXACT GEOGRAPHY
of the Kingdomes of ENGLAND,
SCOTLAND, IRELAND,
and the ILES adioyning:
With
The *Shires, Hundreds, Cities* and
Shire-townes, within y Kingdome
of ENGLAND, divided and
described
By
IOHN SPEED.

IMPRINTED AT LONDON

Anno
Cum Privilegio
1611

And are to be solde by Iohn Sudbury & Georg
Humble, in Popes-head alley at y signe of y white Horse.

8 THE MATTER OF BRITAIN: PAST, PRESENT AND FUTURE

WILLIAM SHAKESPEARE IS A REGULAR FIXTURE in lists of national icons, Great Britons and the like. But was he an English dramatist or a British one? The answer to this question is surprisingly simple but all too often neglected. It is that during the reign of Queen Elizabeth I Shakespeare thought of himself as English, and indeed devoted a large portion of his writing time to plays that dramatized the history of England, but in the early years of the reign of James VI of Scotland as James I of England he began writing about 'British' matter, notably in *Cymbeline*, because James had hopes of creating a British state. Whereas Elizabethan Shakespeare cried 'God for Harry, England, and Saint George' (*Henry V* 3.1.34), Jacobean Shakespeare, in *King Lear* and *Cymbeline*, asked what it meant to be an inhabitant of Britain. Falstaff in *Henry IV* refers to 'our English nation' (*Part 2* 1.2.186 [Quarto text]), while Edgar in *King Lear* speaks of 'a British man' (3.4.162) and the queen in *Cymbeline* dreams of having 'the placing of the British crown' (3.5.78).

On his accession as king of England in 1603, James ruled over a new international entity: 'Great Britain'. This combined four realms: his native Scotland; England, with its old lordship of Ireland (ruled from 1541 as a distinct kingdom); Wales (belonging to the English Crown from 1536); and a nominal claim to France.[1] The two states of England and Scotland remained separate, though James dreamed of full union.[2] His impassioned speech to his first Parliament in 1604 made this clear using the words of the Church of England marriage ceremony:

> What God hath conjoined then, let no man separate. I am the husband, and all the whole Isle is my lawful wife; I am the head, and it is my body; I am the

'Britain's A world by itself'

(Cymbeline 3.1.14–15)

1. Title page from John Speed, *Theatre of the Empire of Great Britain*, London, 1611. The title expresses a theatrical sense of British history and origins. An ancient Briton stands at the centre of a contemporary stage-like structure in the antique style. He is flanked by a Roman, a Saxon, a Dane and a Norman.
Printed book, 48.5 x 30.5 cm (closed).
Queens' College, Cambridge

'His honour and the greatness of his name
Shall be, and make new nations'

(*Henry VIII* 5.4.55–6)

2. Designs for the Union flag of 'Great Britain', *c.* 1604, combining the flags of Scotland and England to symbolize their union through James VI and I.

Watercolour, pen and ink on paper, 29 x 43 cm.
National Library of Scotland, Edinburgh

Shepherd, and it is my flock: I hope therefore no man will be so unreasonable as to think that I that am a Christian king under the Gospel, should be a polygamist and husband to two wives; that I being the head, should have a divided and monstrous body; or that being the shepherd to so faire a flock (whose fold hath no Wall to hedge it but the four seas) should have my flock parted in two.[3]

This aim was thwarted by Scotland and England when commissioners from both parliaments met in 1604, and although James continued to press for it, union of the two kingdoms had to wait over a century – until 1707. This did not prevent James from promoting and publicizing his wish to make his peoples one nation through the new royal arms and 'Our title' as 'King of Great Britain'. In his proclamation of 20 October 1604 he referred to:

the blessed Union, or rather Reuniting of these two mightie, famous and

ancient kingdoms of England and Scotland, under one Imperiall Crowne …
that the Isle within it selfe hath almost none but imaginarie bounds of
separation without, but one common limit or rather Gard of the Ocean Sea,
making the whole a little World Within itself.[4]

James's words echo those of John of Gaunt in Shakespeare's *Richard II*:

This fortress built by nature for herself
Against infection and the hand of war,
This happy breed of men, this little world,
This precious stone set in the silver sea …
(2.1.43–6)

Shakespeare plays more ambivalently with the same theme in *Cymbeline*, in the evil
Cloten's assertion 'Britain's / A world by itself' (3.1.14–15) (fig. 1).

In 1604 James explored the possibility of a new flag for Great Britain, which would
combine the red and white cross of St George for England with the blue and white
saltire of St Andrew for Scotland. A fascinating set of designs to commemorate what
James called 'this happy marriage' was considered by the Earl of Nottingham in his role
as Earl Marshal (fig. 2). The submitted designs presented several possible combinations,
with one flag superimposed on another in various ways, which would have implied
dominance and subjection to one or other of the two nations. This was a live issue even
for those Scots in favour of the Union: as John Russell explained, it was important that
Scotland should not be 'subalterne to Ingland … the ane to command, the uther to
obey, thair by ancienne Scotland to loss hir beautie for evir!'[5] The chosen flag design was
the one which, read heraldically and in accordance with contemporary values, suggested
that England had dominance over Scotland, like a husband over his wife. The Earl of
Nottingham, echoing James I in his marriage metaphor for political union, wrote under
his choice: 'In my poure opinion this wyll be the most fetest, for this is like man and
wife wtout [without] blemesh on to other'.[6] James promoted the new flag 'to all the
subjects of this Isle and kingdom of Great Britain' through a royal proclamation of 10
April 1606, and it was used by civil and military ships. One of the ships shown sailing
on the Thames in John Gipkyn's *Diptych of Old St Paul's* of 1616 shows a very early
representation of the Union flag being flown (fig. 3).[7]

'a British ensign'

(*Cymbeline* 5.4.564)

3. Detail from *Diptych of Old St Paul's*, John
Gipkyn, 1616, showing the Union Flag flown
by ships on the Thames. See Chapter 1, fig. 9.

King James valued coins and medals above painted portraits as forms of self-promotion
in his role as unifier and peacemaker. The silver coronation medal of 1603 (fig. 4), the
first made for an English king, showed him with the titles and costume of a Roman
emperor, indicative of imperial ambition. Just to make this explicit, the Latin legend
states 'James I, Caesar Augustus of Britain, Caesar the heir of the Caesars, presents this
medal'. On the reverse James makes a further claim for himself as saviour of his
people: 'ECCE . PHAOS ; POPVLIQ' . SALVS' ('Behold the beacon and safety of

4. Silver medal struck to commemorate the coronation of James VI of Scotland as James I of England, 1603. The king appears in the costume and with the titles of a Roman emperor.
Diam. 2.85 cm. British Museum, London

5. Gold medal of James I designed by Nicholas Hillard and commemorating peace with Spain, concluded by the Treaty of London of 1604.
Diam. 3.7 cm. British Museum, London

the people').[8] James was keen to draw attention to the parallels between himself and the first emperor of ancient Rome, Augustus. He saw himself as the founder of a new dynasty, and ruler and rebuilder of a great world city. In a proclamation of 1615 concerning his plans to improve London he refers to himself ambitiously as 'Wee whom God hath honoured to be the first King of Great Britaine'.[9] Equally assertive, though different in style, is the medal made to commemorate peace with Spain in the Treaty of London in 1604 (see further below, pp. 228–9) (fig. 5). This shows him in contemporary dress, wearing the hat jewel known as the Mirror of Great Britain, which symbolized the union of England and Scotland, while the legend proclaims James king of England, Scotland, France and Ireland. The inscription on the reverse – 'HINC . PAX . COPIA . CLARAQ . RELIGIO' – translates as 'Hence peace, plenty and pure religion'. This medal was cast in gold with a loop so that it could be presented and worn as a badge of allegiance.[10]

James further promoted his role as unifier of his kingdoms through his second English coinage of 1604, which was coordinated with his Irish and Scottish coinage to buttress his role as king of Great Britain. All the inscriptions on gold and silver coins in his English second issue are new and refer to the union of the kingdoms; the silver crown and shilling even use the wording of the Latin marriage service, 'Those whom God has joined together let no man put asunder'. The large gold sovereign in this issue became known as the 'unite' (fig. 6). This had James's portrait and Latin title as king of 'Great Britain' with, on the reverse, the royal arms and Latin biblical inscription from Ezekiel 37:22: 'I will make them one nation'.[11]

James claimed in his proclamation of 20 October 1604 that his new title as 'King of Great Britaine' was one 'which God and Time have imposed upon this Isle, extant and received in Histories, in all Mappes and Cartes, wherein this Isle is described … and other records of great Antiquitie'. This appeal to a national mythology was not lost on playwrights, for the playhouse was the arena for explorations of British history and cultural identity.[12] James's aim of full union – and peaceful harmony – between his two

'There is no more such Caesars'

(*Cymbeline* 3.1.38)

6. James I's ambition to revive British *imperium* is demonstrated on this English gold unite of 1612–13 with James's Latin title as 'King of Great Britain, France and Ireland'.
Diam. 3.7 cm. British Museum, London

kingdoms remained a personal ambition with limited reach rather than a political reality, but it appears to have had a resonance for Shakespeare. In his Elizabethan history plays of the 1590s, Shakespeare had always referred to his own country as England. With James's accession, England is differently conceived: in *Macbeth*, which was first performed in 1606, England is portrayed as an orderly, hierarchical kingdom by contrast with lawless, wild Scotland, a place of 'dire combustion' (2.3.52) and regicide. In *Cymbeline*, which dates from about 1610, Shakespeare provides a historical fantasy exploring the ancient legacy of 'the British crown' (3.5.78), which would seem to indicate a degree of support for James's wish to recreate a kingdom of Britain, unifying his two realms into a single state. As James I had reminded his subjects in his 1604 speech to Parliament: 'Do we not remember, that this Kingdome was divided into seven little kingdoms, besides Wales? And is it not now the stronger by their union? And hath not the union of Wales to England added a greater strength thereto?' In *Cymbeline, King of Britain* – the title given in the First Folio of 1623 – Shakespeare uses the word 'Britain' or 'Britains' nearly fifty times.[13] *King Lear* presents a king and the disastrous division of his kingdom into three: is this some kind of prompt towards support for a unifying king?

Geoffrey of Monmouth (*c.* 1100–1155) had written the classic account of the national myth of a glorious Trojan past in Britain in his *History of the Kings of Britain*. In this narrative the British are given the same origin as the Romans. Brutus, the great grandson of Aeneas, accidentally kills his father and goes into exile. He meets up with the last remnants of the Trojan race, frees them from the Greeks and leads them on a voyage to the distant northern island of Albion, which was then uninhabited save for the last few of an old race of giants. They land at Totnes in the west country and Brutus renames the island after himself; his followers become Britons. Geoffrey then outlines two thousand years of mythic British history. The line of kings inaugurated by Brutus includes many who would be featured in Elizabethan and Jacobean drama, such as Locrine, Gorboduc, Ferrex and Porrex, Lear and Cymbeline. The *History* ends with the death of Arthur, the greatest of these kings, and the prophecy that his line would one day be revived. Cue the Tudor propagandists four centuries later: they pointed to Henry VII's Welsh ancestry as evidence that this new dynasty was made of true Arthurian, and ultimately Brutish/Trojan stock.

The line of Brutus was, of course, a myth, but Geoffrey's narrative drew at various points on true history. Before the Romans renamed it Londinium, Britain's first city took its name from a powerful local tribe, the Trinovantes. Trinovantium could thus be reinterpreted as Troynovantum, new Troy. So Edmund Spenser in the third book of the Elizabethan *Faerie Queene* (1590): 'For noble *Britons* sprong from *Troians* bold, / And *Troynouant* was built of old *Troyes* ashes cold'. Despite Spenser's enthusiasm, growing scepticism over this narrative was widespread, particularly after it had been carefully but rather regretfully discounted by the historian William Camden in his *Britannia* of 1586.[14] Shakespeare was certainly not idealizing the Trojan line when he wrote *Troilus and Cressida* in the last years of Queen Elizabeth's reign. But he offers no

217

'Camden! ... to whom
my country owes
The great renown and name
wherewith she goes!'

(Ben Jonson, Epigrams XIV, 1616)

7. *William Camden*, Marcus Gheeraerts the
Younger, 1609. Camden is shown as the author
of the bible of British archaeology, *Britannia*.
Oil on panel, 76 x 58 cm. Bodleian Library, Oxford

alternative source of loyalty or allegiance, certainly not in the
cynical Greeks or in the figure of the scabby satirist, Thersites,
who acts as commentator on the action of that play.[15]

Rejections of the traditional story, both on- and offstage,
led to questions as to who the national ancestors really were.
There appears to have been an unspoken agreement that a new
identity for James I's 'Great Britaine' demanded a new history,
but there was no agreement about what that history was to be.
Growing antiquarian interest, led by William Camden (fig. 7),
in the Roman invasion of Britain prompted a series of questions
about the identity and culture of the native British tribes that
the Romans had overcome. Had they been as barbarous and
wild as classical authors described them? Did civil society in
Britain originate with the Romans? If so, was there a parallel
to be drawn with the English plantation of Virginia? Could an
alternative model be found for the making of the nation that
became England?

The formative influence of the Anglo-Saxons, rather than
the Romans, was just beginning to be understood and studied
in antiquarian circles.[16] There was a self-declared nationalist
agenda at work here. Camden thought that an emphasis on
Anglo-Saxon influences offered a new sense of nationhood for
a united England and Scotland: 'wee growe united in one
bodie, under one most Sacred head of the Empire, to the joy,
happinesse, welfare and safetie, of both Nations, which I
heartily wish and pray for'.[17] The image of the nation as a body,
united under a benign ruler, recurs in Shakespeare's 'British' plays: when the tyrant
Macbeth is decapitated, Malcolm, a Scot working in concert with the English,
becomes the new head of the nation.

As so often in Shakespeare's world, the historical and the geographical imagination
were yoked together. News from the New World of the Americas led to reflections on
how the island off the coast of Gaul must have seemed a strange and alien place to the
Romans when they established their colonial settlements here. John White (c. 1540–
c. 1593) played as important a role in the English imagining of their ancient origins
and history, as he did in creating a vision of Virginia as a 'brave new world' (*The Tempest*
5.1.205). He was one of a small group of Englishmen who set up a new colony in
Virginia in Roanoke in 1585. White was the gentleman amateur artist on several
voyages to America, and his watercolours of North Carolina Algonquians introduced
Europe to the landscape, wildlife, plants and native people of North Carolina at the
first point of contact between the Old and New Worlds (fig. 8). White's watercolours
were the basis for engravings produced for Theodor de Bry (fig. 9) to illustrate Thomas
Harriot's *A Briefe and True Report of the New Found Land of Virginia*, which was

9. Self-portrait aged sixty-nine, Theodor de Bry, 1597. De Bry was a key figure in promoting the concept of the theatre of the world.
Engraving, 18.5 x 16 cm. British Museum, London

'O brave new world'

(Tempest 5.1.205)

8. *An Indian Werowance, or Chief, Painted for a Great Solemn Gathering*, John White, 1585–93.
Watercolour over graphite, touched with bodycolour, white (altered) and gold, 26.3 x 15 cm. British Museum, London

published in Frankfurt in four languages in 1590.[18] This volume, aimed at English and other traders, merchants and entrepreneurs interested in investing in the colony, shaped the European image of America. De Bry published an appendix to the Virginia volume, containing further images which he said he had received from White showing ancient Picts 'which in the old tyme did habite one part of the Great Bretainne'. White's declared aim, according to de Bry's broken English, was 'to showe that the Inhabitants of the Great Bretannie have bin in times past as savage as those of Virginia'.[19]

The most striking feature in White's depiction of Algonquian Indians is the way in which they painted their bodies. It was this that made the visual link to the ancient Britons, who were always described by ancient authors as people who painted their bodies with blue woad as a distinguishing feature.[20] William Camden quoted such accounts by Dio Cassius, Herodian and Pliny the Elder in his Latin edition of *Britannia* of 1586; the English translation of his book in 1610 made these Greek and Latin sources widely available to Shakespeare and his audiences.[21] Camden even suggested that the 'Brit' in Britannia means 'to paint', which made body-painting an integral element in British national identity.[22]

John White shows an awareness of these debates in his images of Picts of both sexes. One of his women (fig. 10) illustrates Pliny the Elder's statement that women as well as men had painted themselves blue with woad, 'resembling by that tincture the colour of Aethiopians', as Camden explained.[23] Black skin was compared to make-up. Camden implies that ancient Picts blacked up, which made them resemble black Africans. Anne of Denmark and her ladies performed 'in blackface' in Ben Jonson's *Masque of Blacknesse* in 1605 (fig. 11).[24] In the masque the River Niger comes to London with his alluring and exotically dressed black daughters, hoping that the waters of Albion will 'blanch an Ethiop'. This was the prompt for a miraculous transformation when the queen and her ladies removed their disguises and became once again white. The Venetian ambassador was particularly shocked by this conceit, partly because it implied that the queen and her ladies were as sexually available as black African women were generally perceived to be in the contemporary European imagination.[25] Courtly dressing-up and role playing seems to have worked in favour of old stereotypes. As Ben Jonson put it in describing the jewels that the Daughters of Niger should wear in his masque, they should be 'interlaced with ropes of pearle … best setting off from the black'.[26] Blackness and whiteness could best be defined and explored through contrast.[27] Inigo Jones's costume drawing for a Daughter of Niger draws on the tradition of the theatre of the world costume books, showing how theatre and masque shaped British views of aliens and strangers.[28]

There is a strong element of fantasy and theatricality to White's drawings of Picts, of a kind that anticipates stage performance and the masque tradition. The woman's woad-painted body is treated as a ground for delicate decoration that almost forms a kind of skin-tight costume.[29] Her pose is taken from the classical model of Diana the huntress – all that is missing is her bow and arrows, and the accompanying hunting dogs, while Diana's crescent moon is worn on the breast rather than in the hair.[30] Sunbursts are painted on her breasts and stomach, with griffins on her shoulders and lion masks on her knees. Diana was a chaste goddess, sister to the moon: White's Pictish woman is also a virginal nymph with flowing hair who seems to dance across the page. There may be a link with the new territory of Virginia, named after the Virgin Queen, Elizabeth I, in White's image.[31]

White's drawing of a Pictish male warrior holding a human head (fig. 12) is based on two ancient Greek authorities, Dio Cassius and Herodian, whose descriptions of

10. *A Pictish Woman*, John White, 1585–93. Watercolour over graphite, touched with bodycolour and white (altered) and pen and ink, 23 x 17.9 cm. British Museum, London

'Is black so base a hue?'

(*Titus Andronicus* 4.2.73)

11. *Masquer, A Daughter of Niger*, costume sketch
for Ben Jonson's *Masque of Blacknesse*, Inigo Jones.
Performed at the Old Banqueting House,
Whitehall, on 6 January 1605.
Watercolour with gold and silver, 29 x 15.5 cm.
Chatsworth House, Derbyshire

ancient Britons refer to their penchant for torcs, nakedness and body-painting, and
head-hunting.[32] The visual sources informing White's Pictish warrior are equally
classical in inspiration. The body-painting is derived in its detailing from the kind
of parade armour in the modern take on classical style (*all'antica*) designed in Italian
Renaissance courts from the mid-sixteenth century.[33] The grotesque masks on the
Pict's thighs and knees evoke the kind of parade burgonets (helmets) attributed to
the workshop of the Negroli brothers in Milan in the mid-sixteenth century. A good
match is an example in the form of a lion mask, inspired by ancient Roman armour,
in the Fitzwilliam Museum, Cambridge (fig. 13).[34] The aim of this parade burgonet
was to give the wearer the manner and appearance of a Roman emperor, or one of the
heroes of Greek and Roman mythology, such as Hercules. This kind of armour always

'And Britons strut with courage'

(*Cymbeline 3.1.36*)

12. *A Pictish Warrior Holding a Human Head*,
John White, 1585–93.
Watercolour and bodycolour over graphite, touched with
pen and ink, 24.3 x 16.9 cm. British Museum, London

13. Parade burgonet made in the workshop
of Filippo Negroli, Milan, mid-1500s.
Embossed steel with gilt details, H. 31 cm.
Fitzwilliam Museum, Cambridge

had a theatrical quality and was matched by the costumes for Italian court masques, known through engravings, which in turn informed the masques designed by Inigo Jones for James I's court at Whitehall.[35]

White's figure carries other, more troubling associations. He wears a scimitar-like weapon, associated with the ferocity of the contemporary Ottoman Turk, and brandishes the head of a captive as a trophy. The Pict is presented as a naked barbarian, his mouth open in a grimace and his eyes rolled upwards as he brandishes his enemy's head. This is the aspect of White's watercolour that was taken up in Theodor de Bry's

223

engraving of 1590, accompanied by a text in English which emphasizes that 'In tymes past the Picts, habitants of one part of Great Britain, which is now named England, were savages' (fig. 14). De Bry adds a second decapitated head to emphasize the point. The idea that the Picts – anciently based in the modern kingdom of Scotland – could stand in for ancient Britons was revolutionary enough and seems to have derived from Camden's assertion that 'the Picts … were verie naturall Britons themselves, even the right progenie of the most ancient Britans'.[36] Contemporary interest in the theme of the Romans in Britain made *Cymbeline*, with its encounter between a Roman and a British army, one of Shakespeare's most topical plays. This vision of ancient Britain had a powerful political resonance for modern Britain with its imperial aspirations. If the

'I have ta'en His head from him'

(*Cymbeline* 4.2.190–1)

14. *The True Picture of One Pict*, Theodor de Bry after John White. Engraving from Thomas Harriot, *A Brief and True Report of the New Found Land of Virginia*, Frankfurt, 1590. 30.3 x 41.5 cm. British Library, London

ancient Britons had been civilized by the ancient Roman Empire, could not a modern British Empire civilize the Algonquin Indians of Virginia, the wild Irish kerns and the Gaels in the 'alutterly barbares' Highlands and Isles of Scotland?[37] Plantation was the test of empire. James I's 1610 articles of plantation for Ulster stress that the colonists were new Britons, melding and subsuming all ethnic differences into one new nation.[38]

De Bry's commentary to White's drawings emphasizes the aggressive spirit of the ancient Britons, as Shakespeare does in *Cymbeline*, albeit through the mouth of the evil queen at the opening of the play (fig. 15):[39]

> Remember, sir, my liege,
> The kings your ancestors, together with
> The natural bravery of your isle, which stands
> As Neptune's park, ribbed and paled in
> With oaks unscalable and roaring waters,
> With sands that will not bear your enemies' boats,
> But suck them up to th'topmast. A kind of conquest
> Caesar made here, but made not here his brag
> Of 'came, and saw, and overcame': with shame –
> The first that ever touched him – he was carried
> From off our coast, twice beaten: and his shipping –
> Poor ignorant baubles – on our terrible seas
> Like eggshells moved upon their surges, cracked
> As easily gainst our rocks. For joy whereof
> The famed Cassibelan, who was once at point –
> O giglot fortune! – to master Caesar's sword,
> Made Lud's town with rejoicing fires bright,
> And Britons strut with courage.
> (*Cymbeline* 3.1.19–36)

Shakespeare contrasts the evil queen's fortress Britain with the very different view put by the play's heroine, who is named after Innogen, wife of Brutus, the mythical Trojan founder of Britain. Exiled from her native land, Innogen (Imogen, her name in the original printed text, appears to be a misprint), muses: 'Hath Britain all the sun that shines? Day? Night? / Are they not but in Britain?' (3.4.150–1).[40]

Shakespeare had a fairly free hand in his imagining of ancient British history as so little was known about the

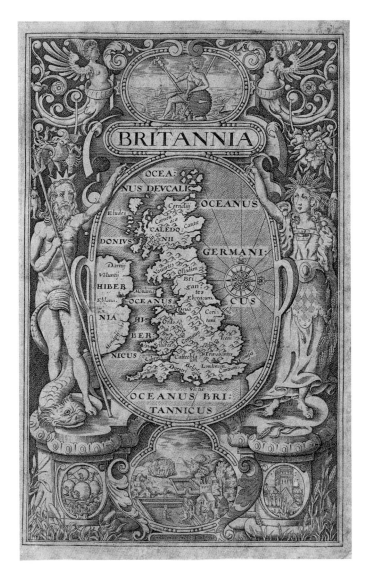

'The natural bravery of your isle'

(*Cymbeline* 3.1.21)

15. Fortress of Britain as it appears on the frontispiece of Camden's *Britannia*, 1610. The fact that Julius Caesar had been blown off course from his invasion of Britain, like the Spanish Armada in 1588, was not lost on Shakespeare's audiences for *Cymbeline*.

Printed book, 48 x 34 cm Society of Antiquaries, London

historical Cunobelin, the Cymbeline of the play.[41] The name, the setting for the play in the opposition to the Roman invasion of AD 43, and the story of the British king and his sons, Guiderius and Arviragus, are all derived from Holinshed's *Chronicles*. The idea that Cymbeline had been reared by Caesar Augustus (fig. 16) in Rome is in Holinshed and in Geoffrey of Monmouth's *History of the Kings of Britain*. Nothing was known of Cunobelin's personality. It has only been through the excavation of settlements and the study of coinage that historians have more recently been able to work out how he came to be awarded the title of king of the Britons (*Britannorum rex*) by the ancient writer, Suetonius. That was indeed the name given to Shakespeare's play in the First Folio of his collected works: *Cymbeline, King of Britain*.

Some of the coin evidence for Cunobelin was being assembled by William

'Thy Caesar knighted me'

(*Cymbeline* 3.1.70)

16. This cameo is a fragment of a larger portrait of the first Roman emperor, Augustus (27 BC–AD 14). 'Great Augustus' was known to Shakespeare's audience to have been emperor when Cymbeline reigned in Britain. Roman, *c.* AD 14–20.
Sardonyx, L. 9.3 cm, H. 12.8 cm.
British Museum, London

17. Plate showing 'Coines of the Britans' from the 1610 English edition of Camden's *Britannia*, p. 89.
Printed book 43 x 24 cm (closed). British Library, London

226

'Cymbeline, King of Britain'

(*Cymbeline*, title)

18. Gold stater of Cunobelin, *c.* AD 10–40, inscribed on the obverse 'CAMV' (Camulodunum, modern Colchester) combined with a corn ear; on the reverse is a classical-style horse with the inscription 'CVNO' (Cunobelin). Diam. 1.8 cm. British Museum, London

'I saw Jove's bird, the Roman eagle'

(*Cymbeline* 4.2.416)

19. *Ignis* (Fire), Johann Sadeler I after Dirck Barendsz., 1587. *Cymbeline* presents the Romans in Britain under the auspices of Jupiter: Jupiter's appearance on an eagle in the play evokes this well-known classical image of the god. Engraving, 17.5 x 22.8 cm. British Museum, London

Camden during the very period in which Shakespeare was writing.[42] Camden was the first to look at native mints as part of a county-by-county survey of Britain's historical geography, and he published this evidence in successive editions of his *Britannia*. Engraved plates of 'Coines of the Britans' appear in the 1610 English edition of his book, including the obverses and reverses of two coins of Cunobelin (fig. 17). One of these is a stater (fig. 18) with a rearing classical horse and the first four letters, CAMV, for Camulodunum (Colchester) – the principal site of the Trinovantes, a people dominated by Cunobelin by AD 10.[43] The imagery and inscriptions on this coin suggest a powerful king and a southern Britain close to Rome, not far from the entirely imaginary intellectual world of Shakespeare's play.

Cymbeline evokes Britain as a satellite state to Rome, under the auspices of the god Jupiter (fig. 19). The decisive battle for Britain, fought against Rome, occurs offstage. The play ends with something like parity between Britain and Rome through an Augustan peace: a peace which could be compared to that negotiated between Spain, the most powerful European Christian empire, and Britain in the Treaty of London of 1604. Is this the harmonious vision of the future envisaged by Cymbeline at the end of the play: 'Never was a war did cease, / Ere bloody hands were washed, with such a peace'? (5.4.568–9).[44]

Shakespeare, as one of the King's Men, may have been one of the ten players who attended on the Spanish ambassador, Don Juan Fernandez de Velasco, Duke of Frias, when he came to negotiate the 1604 treaty after nearly twenty years of open and covert war with Spain which had been highly profitable to English privateers.[45] A painting

IGNIS

Iupiter in Coelo regit omnia lumine clara
Atq; creata suo tunc ta Calore fouet

Ille manu magna spargit tela aspera, et idem
Igne micans summa fulgurat arce Deus.

'Publish we this peace
To all our subjects'

(*Cymbeline* 5.4.562–3)

20. *The Somerset House Peace Conference*, unknown
artist, *c.* 1604. Spanish and Flemish (on the left)
and British negotiators (on the right) conclude
peace after two decades of covert and open war.
Juan Fernández de Velasco, Duke of Frias and
Constable of Castile, is shown seated nearest
to the window on the left.
Oil on canvas, 205.7 x 268 cm.
National Portrait Gallery, London

commemorating the signing of the Treaty of London in August 1604 (fig. 20) shows the Flemish and Spanish party on the left and the British contingent on the right, seated soberly around the negotiating table in Old Somerset House.[46] At the signing of that treaty, a splendid medieval gold cup was given by James I to Juan Fernández de Velasco as a peace pledge to the Spanish (fig. 21).[47] De Velasco recognized the importance of the gift as an object imbued with a sense of history as well as financial value. A medieval cup and English royal treasure played an acknowledged role in the making of modern history. Shakespeare may well have witnessed the ceremonial handover of this object at Somerset House in 1604. Peace with such an imperial power as Spain marked a coup for James's role as peacemaker, even if it was brought about by the fact that Spain was exhausted by fighting on so many fronts. This propaganda win is perhaps obliquely celebrated in the masque-like ending of *Cymbeline*, which culminates in a peace in which 'Th' imperial Caesar, should again unite / His favour with the radiant Cymbeline, / Which shines here in the west' (5.4.557–9). Britain is portrayed as establishing something like parity with Rome in a western empire.

'Pardon's the word to all' (5.4.503): Cymbeline's words share the tone of James I's opening speech to his first Parliament in 1604, promising union between his kingdoms, using the metaphor of the confluence of rivers in the ocean:

> For even as little brookes lose their names by their running and fall into great Rivers, and the very name and memorie of great Rivers swallowed up in the Ocean: so by the conjunction of divers little Kingdomes in one, are all these private differences and questions swallowed up.[48]

When he witnessed a court performance of the play, James I could have seen himself as both this ancient king of Britain, Cymbeline, and the Roman emperor, Augustus, promising peace, unity and harmony. Shakespeare's *Cymbeline* meditates with great sensitivity and awareness on these contemporary debates about national history and origins, and the political incentive behind them. It is as much a fantasy about the present, and the promise of the future, as the past.

21. The Royal Gold Cup, made in Paris, *c.* 1370–80, and enamelled with scenes from the legend of St Agnes. The cup was a peace pledge at the Somerset House Conference negotiating the treaty between Spain and Britain in 1604. Shakespeare may well have seen this precious medieval cup given to de Velasco to seal the peace; de Velasco added an inscription to the stem recording the gift.
Gold with enamel and pearls, H. 23.6 cm.
British Museum, London

230

9 'O BRAVE NEW WORLD THAT HAS SUCH PEOPLE IN'T'

THE FIRST FOLIO OF SHAKESPEARE'S collected plays begins with *The Tempest*, his last solo-authored work, first performed in 1611. Unusually among the early printed texts, it is furnished with information as to the play's setting: 'the scene, an un-inhabited island'. But where is that island located? And where did the characters, sounds and objects that inhabit it come from? The shipwreck that opens the play occurs on a voyage from North Africa to Italy, suggesting a Mediterranean setting. But a series of references to the Bermudas, to the Patagonian god Setebos, to an essay by Michel de Montaigne about the 'cannibals' of South America and to a 'brave new world' (5.1.205) unequivocally evoke the Americas. The uninhabited island is both the New World and the Old, it is everywhere and nowhere, it is both the world and the theatre itself.

But it is the New World aura that has given *The Tempest* peculiar prominence in the twentieth and early twenty-first centuries.[1] Shakespeare was familiar with the contemporary anthropology and travel literature of the New World; the debates within the play about the nature of sovereignty, plantation and colonization still have powerful resonance today. As the Cuban writer Roberto Fernandez Retamar commented, 'What is our culture, if not the history, and culture of Caliban?'[2] However, the interpretation of *The Tempest* as a play dealing with the early English colonization of America only developed retrospectively, relatively late in the play's theatrical and critical history.[3]

Anyone watching one of the recent biopics of Elizabeth I might be tempted to think of her as the founder of a great maritime empire, but the idea that England had an empire in Shakespeare's lifetime, beyond the highly contested island of Ireland, is historically inaccurate.[4] English hold over Ireland was always patchy and insecure beyond

'Had I plantation of this isle'

(*The Tempest* 2.1.131)

1. Nicholas Hilliard's design for Elizabeth I's Great Seal of Ireland, made just before the Virginia voyages, *c.* 1584–5. The design promotes the concept of a new plantation or colonization in Munster, south-west Ireland.
Pen and black ink, with grey wash, over graphite on vellum, diam. approx. 12.4 cm. British Museum, London

ELIZABETA D. G. ANGLIÆ. FRANCIÆ. HIBERNIÆ. ET VERGINIÆ
REGINA CHRISTIANAE FIDEI VNICVM PROPVGNACVLVM .

Immortalis honos Regum, cui non tulit ætas *Queis ipsæ tantum superant reliqua omnia regna,*
Vlla prior, veniens nec feret vlla parem, *Quantum tu maior Regibus es reliquis,*
Sospite quo nunquam terras habitare Britannas *Viue precor felix tanti in moderamine regni,*
Desinet alma Quies, Iustitia atque Fides, *Dum tibi Rex Regum cælica regna paret .*

In honorem sereniss.æ suæ Maiestatis hanc effigiem fieri curabat Ioannes Woutnelius belga. Anno 1596.

the Pale and was ultimately backed by force, particularly during O'Neill's rebellion from 1594 to 1603 and the disastrous retaliatory campaign of the Earl of Essex. As far as the English were concerned, a potentially or actually rebellious Ireland was always too close for comfort.

One of Elizabeth's most ambitious long-term projects to pacify the southwest, the Munster Plantation of 1586, is commemorated in the design for the Great Seal of Elizabeth I in Ireland (fig. 1), which was made just before the Virginia voyages, around 1584–5. It was at this point, following the defeat of the Earl of Desmond's rebellion in Ireland (his head was sent to Elizabeth I in a bag), that a survey was made of his lands in Munster and a plan for English colonization was drawn up. Only tenants of English birth would be allowed to settle; no Gaelic Irish tenants were to be permitted as 'undertakers' of the confiscated lands.[5]

Hilliard's design for the new Great Seal of Ireland was never executed, but there is no doubting the message of English royal authority that it transmits in the subjection of Munster. It shows Elizabeth seated in Parliament robes on a throne, holding the orb and sceptre as head of state. Two divine hands at either side hold back her mantle, and her head is set against an arcade which makes it appear that there is almost a halo around her head, or a sacred aura to her presence. She is flanked by two shields bearing Irish emblems, the Irish harp on the left[6] and the three crowns, the symbol of Munster, on the right.[7] The message is that Munster is ripe for plantation as a way of anglicizing the region and bringing it under English control.

'Had I plantation of this isle, my lord' (2.1.131): Gonzalo's use of the new word 'plantation', passed around as a joke by his companions Sebastian and Antonio, takes us straight to Ireland. It was the first use of the term in the context of the establishment of a colony with specific reference to English attempts to subdue Ireland to English

2. Caliban calls Prospero a usurper. Elizabeth I is shown here as ruler of a maritime empire which claimed England, Virginia, France and Ireland (listed along the bottom). Crispijn de Passe the Elder, published by Hans Woutneel, London, 1596. Engraving, 35 x 25.8 cm. British Museum, London

'Yet he would be king on't'

(*The Tempest* 2.1.146)

3. Sir Walter Ralegh's arms as Governor of Virginia, 1584. Seal-die (shown in reverse to make the legend legible). Silver, diam. 5.7 cm. British Museum, London

rule.[8] The Munster Plantation was the model for the attempted colonization of Virginia. The print in figure 2 proclaims Elizabeth I as ruler of an English empire that included Virginia. Her title there is listed with her titles to Ireland – despite the threat of O'Neill's rebellion – and to France – despite the loss of Calais in 1558. Colonial, imperial and global aspirations were nascent but unrealized: the formal composure of the print has a certain tension about it as a cover-up for national anxiety about England's status at the end of Elizabeth's reign.[9]

The first English attempts at colonizing Virginia had begun in 1584, with an outpost at Roanoke that Ralegh intended to use as an American base for attacks on Spanish fleets returning laden with treasure.[10] Ralegh persuaded the queen to name the new territory in her honour, and the seal-die in figure 3 proudly proclaims him 'Lord and Governer of Virginia' in Latin, together with his arms and the date 1584. Ralegh is advertising very much a private fiefdom here, of the kind that Antonio and Sebastian mock in Gonazalo's dreams of colonization of the island in *The Tempest*: 'Yet he would be king on't' (2.1.146).[11] As Governor, Ralegh had a monopoly on American Indians brought to England from 1584 to 1603, and it was through his circle that they were made part of the transatlantic cultural exchange at Elizabeth I's court and beyond.[12]

The Roanoke settlement had mysteriously disappeared by 1588, and no one from the lost colony was ever seen again. Even though John White did not find the Virginian colonists when he finally returned to Virginia in 1590, he, Ralegh and the queen clung to the belief that they were still alive. English sovereignty over Virginia depended on it. White recorded the ruin of his precious possessions – the nightmare of any gentleman colonist – which he found exposed to the elements in the ruins of the city of Ralegh: 'about the place many of my things spoyled and broken, and my books torne from the covers, the frames of some of my pictures and Mappes rotten and spoyled with rayne, and my armour almost eaten through with rust'.[13]

In both Ireland and Virginia the model was the same. Lands were confiscated from their native owners and repossessed by English 'planters', ultimately backed by military force. The similarities went further, in that the English patronized the Irish much as they did Native Americans, viewing them as wild men, savages – bestial and idle people to whom they, the English, could bring civilization.[14] The model was one based on the developing sense that the warlike ancient Britons had themselves been brought into civil society first by the Romans and then, more distinctively, by the Saxons. Even the Virginians' penchant for body-painting linked them with ancient Britons (see Chapter 8, p. 220). William Strachey wrote of native Virginians in 1612:

Wild as they are, accept them, so were we
To make them civill, will our honour bee,
And if good works be the effects of minds
That like good Angells be, let our designes

233

As we are Angli, make us Angells too
No better work can Church or statesmen doe.[15]

He added to his history a fascinating *Dictionarie of the Indian Language*, which would show his readers 'how to truck and trade with the people'. After the foundation of Jamestown (named after James I) as a permanent English settlement in Virginia in 1607, colonization could take off with the development of greater local control and proprietary colonies from 1632.[16] Only then could the writer Samuel Purchas's dream of 'Another hope of a Great Britain' ('*Magnae spes altera Britanniae*') be realized.[17]

For all the future promise of America for English markets, the focus of most English adventuring, piracy, trade and diplomacy remained the eastern Mediterranean and North Africa.[18] The expulsion of the Moriscos from Spain in 1610 had created an autonomous pirate state on the island of Salé on the Atlantic coast of Morocco, which menaced Moroccan and British coasts alike. The gold treasure of what was probably a Moroccan ship sailing from Morocco to England between 1631 and 1640, recently excavated in Salcombe Bay in Devon, seems to fit in to this picture (fig. 4).[19] Among the broken pieces of gold ingots and jewellery in the cargo were hundreds of gold coins minted by the ruler of Morocco, Muley Hamet, known as 'the golden one' (r. 1578–1603), whose ambassador came to England for six months in 1600 (see Chapter 1, pp. 34–5). Another copper coin of 1627 is Friesian, representing perhaps the small change in the pockets of one of the sailors on board.[20] The Dutch competed with the English in trade with Morocco, and this could have been a Dutch ship. But the third possibility is that this could have been a Barbary pirate ship from North Africa, marauding along the western shores of England and Ireland, a phenomenon that is well documented between 1616 and 1642.[21] The anxiety aroused by these attacks demonstrated the dangers that non-Christians were thought to represent to early modern Britons as trading networks expanded.

4. *Above and right* Artefacts from the wreck of a ship in Salcombe Bay, Devon, England, which sank around 1631 to 1640. Probably a Moroccan pirate ship, given its cargo of broken pieces of gold for bullion.
Gold jewellery, ingots and coins. British Museum, London

5. The robes of a Mediterranean pirate (?), England *c.* 1610. Thought to have belonged to Sir Francis Verney, an English gentleman who 'turned Turk' and became a Mediterranean pirate.
Italian silk velvet, silver braid and silk shag.
Claydon House, Buckinghamshire

English pirates teamed up with Barbary corsairs in the Mediterranean, using Marmora (in Greece) and Tunis (in North Africa) as their bases, and demonstrating a propensity for 'turning Turk' or converting to Islam.[22] A fascinating exemplar of this practice is Sir Francis Verney (1584–1615), 'the (sometimes) great English Gallant' who left England as a discomfited squire having spent his inheritance, joined a North African pirate fleet and converted to Islam in 1609.[23] He was captured and served as a galley slave before dying in poverty in a Christian hospital in Messina (Sicily) in 1615.[24] His turban, two pairs of Turkish slippers and silk robe were sent back with a death certificate to his family in 1615.[25] What is claimed to be these very pieces are still to be seen at Claydon House in Buckinghamshire as secular relics of a chequered career (fig. 5).[26] The story is genuinely the stuff of contemporary drama: Robert Daborne's 1612 play, *A Christian Turn'd Turk*, is based on the similarly sensational life of one of Sir Francis's fellow English pirates, John Ward.[27]

Several pirates of the Mediterranean are present in the hinterland of Shakespeare's plays. In *Henry VI Part 2* there is a reference to 'Bargulus the strong Illyrian pirate' (4.1.110). The allusion is to a bandit from Roman times, but Shakespeare's Mediterranean is always the world of the present, even when it is refracted through the past, so audience members would have been led to think of contemporary piracy too.[28] *Antony and Cleopatra* also imagines an ancient Mediterranean scourged by pirates ('Menecrates and Menas, famous pirates' – 1.4.52). In *Twelfth Night*, which is actually set in Illyria, Antonio is accused of being a pirate. In *Measure for Measure* the death in prison of 'Ragozine, a most notorious pirate' (4.3.54) helps to bring the plot to its conclusion. His name is evocative of Ragusa (now Dubrovnik), a successful Adriatic port in what was then Illyria. Further north, Hamlet is famously assisted by pirates. Marina in *Pericles*, the play that voyages all around the Mediterranean, is abducted by pirates and sold into a brothel in Mytilene.[29] Most strikingly, Shylock in *The Merchant of Venice* stresses the dangers from piracy that are faced by Antonio's trading ships:

> Yet his means are in supposition: he hath an argosy bound to Tripolis, another
> to the Indies, I understand moreover, upon the Rialto, he hath a third at
> Mexico, a fourth for England, and other ventures he hath squandered abroad.
> But ships are but boards, sailors but men. There be land-rats and water-rats,
> water-thieves and land-thieves — I mean pirates — and then there is the
> peril of waters, winds and rocks. (1.3.12–17)

The views expressed on piracy in Jacobean drama are particularly curious given James I's antipathy to pirates who, like witches, he regarded as enemies of both God and king, as well as the state.[30] It is against the backdrop of this uncertain, freebooting Mediterranean world, subject to pirates orchestrated by the Moorish king of Tunis, that Shakespeare sets *The Tempest*.[31]

Shakespeare is careful, however, not to locate his setting for *The Tempest*. The island seems to hover somewhere between Old and New Worlds. It is very much a

Mediterranean drama, and the Old World legacy of Virgil and Ovid is at least as important as the material that Shakespeare borrows from Montaigne and tales of modern adventuring in the New World. The open texture of the play, which artfully interweaves ancient and modern sources, also resists attempts to place it in a particular geographical and political context.[32] The long-term geopolitical shift from the Mediterranean to the Atlantic was begun by the Portuguese in the sixteenth century, but spurred on by the English and the Dutch only in the later seventeenth century. Englishmen were relative latecomers to the exploration of the Atlantic world, although they had long recognized that they needed to master the seas.[33] As Sir Walter Ralegh put it in 1615: 'whosoever commands the sea, commands the trade, whoseoever commands the trade of the world commands the riches of the world, and consequently the world itself'.[34]

The rhetoric was there long before the reality. The 'Renaissance Man' John Dee – often considered a possible model for Prospero (see below, pp. 256–7)[35] – was among the first to coin the phrase 'the British Empire' in 1577, a concept based on maritime supremacy that would allow for the colonization of new territories and the entering of global markets.[36] Dee is traditionally thought to have owned an obsidian mirror from the New World, a Mexica trophy of the kind brought back from Mexico to Europe by the Spanish conquistador Hernán Cortés (fig. 6).[37] If Dee did in fact own it – perhaps as something picked up on his scholarly travels in Continental Europe – he was quite

6. 'Dr Dee's magic mirror'. Mexica, *c.* 1325–1521. Whether Dee actually owned this mirror, let alone used it for 'scrying' or divination, is unproven. There is an intriguing link – probably not known in his lifetime – between this tradition and the way in which the Mexica god of destiny and divination, Tezcatlipoca, was thought to use obsidian mirrors as 'speaking' stones.
Obsidian, wooden case covered in tooled leather, mirror, L. 22 cm, diam. 18.4 cm. British Museum, London

unlikely to have known its origins even if it had come with a story attached. But it would be hard not to associate such an intriguing object with other worlds and other ways of seeing. A sixteenth-century scholar such as Dee would have discerned that it was some kind of instrument, shaped to be held in the hand, carved in the form of a mirror like those known from classical antiquity, but one with only dim, smoky reflections on its black surface. These qualities in themselves made it a rare and exotic scholarly prize, and an object of wonder. Curiosities like this, however challenging to interpret, made it possible to discover and know the world in a new way.

Scientific instruments similarly offered new means by which to explore and understand the world. New World ambition, as Dee recognized, depended on building knowledge of the art of navigation.[38] As English adventurers ventured further afield, new ways of understanding the world developed, from maps and globes (see Chapter 1, p. 52) to scientific instruments.[39] Frobisher's voyagers took instruments supplied and made specifically for them by Humfrey Cole in their first expedition to search for the Northwest Passage in 1576. Cole repaired the instruments on their return from North Atlantic buffetings.[40] He also helped to develop the specialist trade in scientific instruments in London, which coincided with the publication of books on navigation backing English maritime ambition. A particularly fine example of his work is the astrolabe he made in 1574, which may have belonged to Henry Frederick, Prince of Wales (1594–1612), a cultivated patron and collector, who died in 1612 (fig. 7).[41]

Both globes and scientific instruments were essential tools for understanding the modern world, but they were also courtly toys and gentlemanly accessories, things to play with, show off and discuss. Elizabeth I's troubled favourite, the Earl of Essex, owned one of the latest scientific instruments, an astronomical compendium, as discussed in contemporary treatises of navigation (fig. 8). It has been described as the universe in a box. It is made up of several leaves including a nocturnal, a latitude list, compass, sundial, perpetual calendar and lunar age or phase indicator, all of which had practical functions when on campaign. The bitter inscription on the instrument would seem, however, to relate to the earl's frustrations at home, at court. The compendium was made for or given to Essex at a time when, constantly in debt and fighting for preferment, he was making a concerted challenge to the power and authority of the new rich, epitomized by William Cecil, Lord Burghley, in asserting his will 'to intend matters of state'.[42] Read in this light, the inscription, which is hidden inside the lid and coiled around his arms, takes on a new significance: 'HE THAT TO HIS NOBLE LINNAGE ADDETH VERTV AND GOOD CONDISIONS IS TO BE PRAISED / THEY THAT BE PERFECTLI WISE DESPISE WORLDLI HONOR WHER RICHES ARE HONORED GOOD MEN ARE DESPISED'.[43]

Globes made it possible to envisage the world in the round, to feel the earth's curved surface beneath one's hands, and trace the interconnectedness between continents and oceans with a finger (see Chapter 1, p. 52). There was an obvious synergy between the terrestrial globe and the round, purpose-built playhouse, so that when Prospero speaks of 'the great globe itself' (*The Tempest* 4.1.166) he might be

7. Gilded brass astrolabe made by Humfrey Cole, London, 1574. This may later have belonged to Henry Frederick, Prince of Wales, who died in 1612. Used for surveying, timekeeping and determining latitude.
Diam. 8.8 cm. British Museum, London

8. Astronomical compendium of gilded copper alloy made by James Kynvyn, London, 1593. Made for the 2nd Earl of Essex and engraved with his arms and an inscription.

Gilt copper alloy, diam. 6 cm. British Museum, London

referring both to 'this wooden O' (*Henry V* Prologue 13) of the playhouse and to the planet itself.[44] Both provided new spaces in which human experience could be mapped and explored, and both informed Shakespeare's theatre of the world. Shakespeare uses the language of exploration and mapping in his plays in new ways, often comically and playfully. In *The Merry Wives of Windsor* Falstaff jokes about how he will ply between Mistress Page and Mistress Ford: 'They shall be my East and West Indies, and I will trade to them both' (1.3.50).

For all its lack of a specific context, *The Tempest* seems to encapsulate the spirit of European maritime adventuring, even down to the precise nautical commands shouted out by the sailors on the doomed ship at the play's opening.[45] A vivid ink sketch (fig. 9) would seem to be a metaphor for the perils of early modern voyaging and for the rule of the goddess Fortune over seas wracked by storms and studded with hidden reefs like the infamous 'still-vexed Bermudas' of Shakespeare's imagination

'the still-vexed Bermudas'

(*The Tempest* 1.2.267)

9. *Fortune; Sea Goddess* Wenceslaus Hollar, *c.* 1625. The Bermudas were notorious for storms and reefs; the wreck of the *Sea Venture* in 1609 appears to have inspired the opening storm scene in *The Tempest*.
Pen and black ink, 13.4 x 15.7 cm. Victoria and Albert Museum, London

(1.2.267).[46] Shakespeare had contacts with members of the Virginia Company, and it is likely that he drew the details of the opening storm in his play from William Strachey's unpublished account of the wreck of the *Sea Venture* in 1609 on Bermuda.[47] The manuscript would have passed through the hands of William Leverson, a business associate of Shakespeare's who was in charge of attracting investors for the Virginia enterprise; of Dudley Digges, a key member of the company board, who in 1610 visited his stepfather in Stratford, a close friend of Shakespeare's; and of Sir Henry Rainsford of Clifford Chambers, whose doctor was Shakespeare's son-in-law and who was intimate with Shakespeare's friends the Combe family. Shakespeare coins new

10. *A Wife of an Indian Werowance or Chief of Pomeiooc, and her Daughter*, John White, 1585–93.
Watercolour over graphite, touched with bodycolour, white (altered) and gold, 26.3 x 14.9 cm.
British Museum, London

compound words – 'sea-sorrow' (1.2.199), 'sea-change' (1.2.464), 'sea-swallowed' (2.1.253) and 'sea-marge' (4.1.75) – to characterize the island as a place apart, one subject to sudden changes of mood and irresistibly powerful forces of transformation.

The *Sea Venture* had been backed by a consortium of investors in the trade and colonization of the New World. Whatever the insecurity of the English in America before 1607, there was a keen interest from the 1580s in the new market for English goods that Virginia offered.[48] John White's drawings (see Chapter 8, pp. 219–24) offer the first English view of America, and it is significant that one drawing shows the wife of a chief of Pomeiooc and her young daughter apparently welcoming friendly commerce with strangers from overseas, wearing necklaces and holding a doll which they have been given by the English (fig. 10).[49] Thomas Harriot describes in his *Briefe and True Report of the New Found Land of Virginia* (1590) 'babies brought oute of England' as desirable presents 'which wee thought they delighted in'.[50] The status and significance of the doll in White's watercolour is evident by comparison with the print from 1630 in figure 11 showing a mother and daughter at an urban toy stall in Europe, in which similar luxurious dolls are on display. The engraving illustrates the Dutch emblem 'well set out is half sold', and the verse underneath talks about the art of wooing.[51]

Miranda in *The Tempest* sometimes acts as intermediary between Prospero and Caliban. A Virginian woman who certainly played a crucial role as mediator and peacemaker between Native Americans and settlers was the Powhatan Indian woman known as Pocahontas (*c.* 1595–1617). Following her capture in 1613 as a pawn in the colonist's struggles with her father, Powhatan, she was taught English and baptized with the Old Testament name Rebecca.[52] Her visit to England a month after Shakespeare's death in 1616 as the wife of one of the English settlers, John Rolfe, is commemorated in the print in figure 12. Like that of the Moroccan ambassador in 1600, her visit caused quite a stir: she was granted an audience with Queen Anne at Whitehall, and invited to a dinner at Lambeth Palace and a Twelfth Night masque. Pocahontas is correspondingly shown off as a European trophy in her engraved portrait in a consciously theatrical way. Her clothes are all-important in that process of translation and acculturation:

11. *Mother and Child at a Toy Stall*, anonymous artist after Adrien van de Venne, *c.* 1630. The girl holds a doll like that held by the Virginian girl in fig. 10, a present from English traders. From *Spiegel van den ouden ende nieuwen tijdt*, The Hague, 1632.

Engraving, 13.4 x 13.4 cm. British Museum, London

she is shown to have been converted through her Northern European clothing as well as through her Christian faith.[53] She wears a tall hat, stiff lace collar and carries an ostrich-feather fan. The Latin and English inscriptions describe her as having been 'converted and baptised to the Christian faith', give her name, Matoaka, in her own language, and define her as daughter of Powhatan, Emperor of Virginia. Her marriage to John Rolfe – commemorated in English on the print – seems to have been fundamental to the maintaining of peace between the settlers and the Powhatans until her sudden death in England in 1617.[54]

12. Portrait of Pocahontas (Matoaka/Rebecca Rolfe), Simon van de Passe, London, 1616. Engraving, 17 x 11.7 cm. British Museum, London

MATOAKA ALS REBECCA FILIA POTENTISS · PRINC · POWHATANI IMP · VIRGINIÆ ·

Ætatis suæ 21 A.
1616.

Matoaks als Rebecka daughter to the mighty Prince
Powhatan Emperour of Attanoughskomouck als virginia
converted and baptized in the Christian faith, and
wife to the wor.th Mr. Joh. Rolff.

S. Pass: sculp: Compton Holland exc.

'Now I will believe That there are unicorns'

(*The Tempest* 3.3.24–5)

13. Narwhal tusk in a sixteenth-century case. Narwhal tusks were traded and collected in Europe as horns of the mythical beast, the unicorn.
L. (of tusk) 224 cm, H. (of case) 272 cm.
Parham House, Sussex

The Tempest reveals the wonder of the early literature of travel and exploration, and the kind of cultural indigestion which it caused in European readers at home: how much of this stuff could they believe, and how were they to understand this 'brave new world' that was opening up all around them? The playhouse was the place in which such cultural encounters could be safely explored. Faced with Prospero's magic banquet, Sebastian finds himself inclined to believe the wildest traveller's tale: 'Now I will believe / That there are unicorns' (3.3.24–5). The 'unicorn horn' from Parham House, Sussex, in figure 13 is, like all so-called unicorn horns to be seen in cabinets of curiosities in Renaissance Europe, the tusk of an Arctic whale, the narwhal. The name 'narwhal' is perhaps derived from 'corpse whale' in Old Icelandic. Only the male has an astonishing tusk like this, which is in fact a spirally formed incisor tooth. Narwhal live in the eastern Arctic where they are still hunted by Inuit and Greenlanders for

their skin, which provides the vitamin C that for Europeans often comes from fruits and vegetables.[55] The Frobisher voyage to Baffin Island in 1577 provides the first scientific reference to narwhal, but the story of its discovery shows that old legends and habits of magical thinking die hard, even in the face of new evidence.[56] The voyagers recounted how they found a rare whale thought to be a sea unicorn:

> Upon another small island there was also founde a greate dead fishe, which, as it should seeme, had bin embayed with ise, and was in proportion rounde like to a porpose, being about twelve foote long, and in bignesse answerable, havyng a horne of two yardes long growing out of the snoute or nostrels. This horne is wreathed and strayte, like in fashion to a taper made of waxe, and maye truly be thought to be the sea Unicorne. This horne is to be seene and reserved as a jewel, by the Queen's majesties commandement in hir wardrop of robes.[57]

Elizabeth I's horn was probably presented in a sixteenth-century case, specially made for it as a treasured curiosity, like the one at Parham.[58]

Frobisher did not just bring back trophies like this, or quantities of useless iron pyrite (fool's gold) in the ceaseless search for gold.[59] Living people, described by George Best in 1578 as 'this new prey', were also collected as prizes and curiosities in early modern Europe.[60] And when they died, usually swiftly of European diseases to which they had no immunity, even their dead bodies might be a source of profit. Trinculo in *The Tempest* refers to this practice, perhaps even to Frobisher's bringing back of the Inuk known as Kalicho, who had been captured with a woman, Arnaq, and baby, Nutaaq, on Baffin Island in 1577 (fig. 14).[61] Fun is made of their fishy-smelling garments in which they hunted seal:

> A man or a fish? Dead or alive? A fish, he smells like a fish: a very ancient and fishlike smell: a kind of not-of-the-newest poor-John. A strange fish! Were I in England now – as once I was – and had but this fish painted, not a holiday fool there but would give a piece of silver: there would this monster make a man: any strange beast there makes a man: when they will not give a doit to relieve a lame beggar, they will lay out ten to see a dead Indian.
> (2.2.22–8)

Kalicho's death was compassionately recorded by his English doctor, Edward Dodding, who noted how Kalicho 'recognised us as people he knew… And he sang clearly that same tune with which the companions from his region and rank had either mourned or ceremonially marked his final departure when they were standing on the shore (according to those who heard them both)'. Apart from his deathsong, his last words in English were 'God be with you'.[62] Kalicho was in fact buried in Bristol in November 1577, whereas the burial of Nutaaq and Arnaq, who died shortly afterwards in London, is not recorded in parish records.[63]

Of the thirty-five or more North American natives who came to England in Shakespeare's lifetime, some did manage to return home after their visit. The Virginian Indian Eiakintamino is thought to have stayed in London for a year or more around 1615–16: he is shown with 'Indian' birds and animals in St James's Park in a delightful miniature from a German student's tourist album in figure 15.[64] But the departure or burial of around twelve of these North American Indians is not apparently recorded. As 'heathen' their bodies may well have been displayed after death since they were exempt from the kinds of religious taboo and legal constraints governing Christian burial.[65] Even their portraits had a posthumous celebrity value: Platter mentions at Hampton Court 'life-like portraits of the wild man and woman whom Martin Frobisher, the English captain, took on his voyage to the New World, and brought

'When they will not give a doit to relieve a lame beggar, they will lay out ten to see a dead Indian.'

(*The Tempest* 2.2.27–8)

14. *Kalicho, an Inuk from Frobisher Bay*, after John White, 1585–93. Kalicho was captured by Frobisher in 1577.
Watercolour with pen and grey ink on paper, 39 x 26 cm. British Museum, London

Een Jongheling uyt de virginis

dese Jndiaense Vogelen en Beesten, met den Jongheling
syn A:1615:1616 Jn St James Parck of diertgarden
by Westmunster voorde Stadt London te sien geweest.

15. *Eiakintomino, a Virginian Indian Pictured
with American Animals in St James's Park, c.* 1616.
From Michael van Meer's friendship album.
Watercolour, approx. 8.5 x 17.5 cm. Edinburgh University
Library, Edinburgh

16. Doit, minted in the Netherlands, early 1600s.
Alloy, diam. 2 cm. British Museum, London

back alive to England', indicating that Inuit were regarded as wild men.[66] Trinculo's cheerful cynicism is underlined by the casual reference to ten doits as a suitable entrance fee to view a body. Doits were the currency of low-value celebrity entertainment (fig. 16). The Dutch word *duit* became anglicized as *doit*, in a similar way to the Dutch coin, the *mijt*, which became anglicized as the *mite* (it appears in the Authorized Version of the Bible in 1611 as 'the widow's mite' in the famous parable about true charity – Mark 12:42). Trinculo is referring to a low-value little coin, which was not even English, that Shakespeare's audiences would have understood perfectly in this comic context of Europeans in holiday mood.[67]

What Trinculo has tripped over in the scene quoted above is not a fish, but the strangely monstrous figure of Caliban, 'a salvage [sic] and deformed slave' (List of Characters) in his smelly 'gaberdine' (2.2.31).[68] Sebastian and Trinculo are quick to exchange alcohol for survival skills in exploiting Caliban as a natural slave, someone who lives in the borderlands of civilization as a kind of wild man. Cranach's drawing of Hercules fighting nude wild men shows them as the bestial hairy figures of late medieval European imagination (fig. 17). Because they were associated with dark and

'Caliban, a salvage [sic] and deformed slave'

(*The Tempest* List of Characters in the First Folio, 1623)

17. *Armoured Knight, Perhaps Hercules, Fighting Wild Men in a Wood*,
Lucas Cranach the Younger, *c*. 1551.
Pen and black ink with grey and pink wash,
18.1 x 21.8 cm. British Museum, London

mysterious borderlands, wild men were sometimes said to have a taste for human flesh. In Constantinople in 1590 an English traveller, Edward Webbe, claimed that he had seen two wild men chained to 'a post, each of them having a Mantell cast about their shoulders and all over their bodies they have wonderfull long haire. They are Chained fast by the necke and will speedily devour any man that commeth in their reach'.[69] Webbe's descriptions of captive wild men in public places are likely to be fanciful – he also claims to have sported with unicorns – but they echo the sinister study of the corpse of a hairy man, attributed to Michel le Blon, perhaps made to illustrate an early seventeenth-century travel book like Webbe's (fig. 18). Wild men were also thought to abduct children and eat them.[70] Cranach's crawling monster (fig. 19) is a kind of werewolf who emerges from the forest to prey on lone cottages. Werewolves were the subject of learned fascination as well as popular credulity: no less a scholarly divine than John Donne owned one of the first serious treatises on werewolves, Claude Prieur's *Dialogue de la lycanthropie* of 1596, and proudly wrote his name on the title page.[71]

Caliban's name, an anagram of cannibal, has associations with both the Old World and the New. Cannibalism was thought to be a feature of some New World cultures. The Tupinamba of eastern Brazil, who fought French and Portuguese attempts to gain colonial domination there in the sixteenth century, hunted and fished but were also recorded as ceremonial cannibals.[72] Caliban is not however presented as a cannibal, though his temper as 'a born devil, on whose nature / Nurture can never stick' (4.1.204–5) reveals itself in his brutal suggestions as to how to kill Prospero with a nail driven into his forehead. He has also made a reported attempt to rape Miranda so as to people the island with Calibans in order to challenge the usurper, Prospero, who has made himself king. But Caliban's skills as an islander are those of the classic wild man, particularly his fishing and wood-gathering, showing how he is at one with the natural world: 'I'll show thee the best springs: I'll pluck thee berries: I'll fish for thee and get thee wood enough' (2.2.124–5).[73]

The image of Caliban fetching firewood is one which goes to the heart of the wild man's European identity, as shown in the German artist Albrecht Altdorfer's expressive drawing of 1508 (fig. 20). Wild men and their families living in the extensive Central European forests played an important part in German mythology, and were a popular theme in medieval and Renaissance German and Swiss art.[74] Altdorfer shows a wild man, oblivious to any observer, unselfconsciously carrying a tree he has just felled for fuel. These are exactly the traditional wild man pursuits to which Caliban sings a drunken goodbye – drunkenness being another feature of the classic wild man[75] – in celebrating a new life with Stephano and Trinculo: 'No more dams I'll make for fish, / Nor fetch in firing at requiring' (2.2.137–8).

18. *Study of the Corpse of a Long-haired Man*,
Michel le Blon, 1602–30, perhaps made to
illustrate an early seventeenth-century travel book.
Pen and brown ink with brown and yellow-brown
wash, touched with bodycolour, 13.9 x 7.4 cm.
British Museum, London

'A born devil, on whose nature Nurture can never stick'

(The Tempest 4.1.204–5)

19. *The Werewolf*, Lucas Cranach the Elder,
c. 1510–15.
Woodcut, 16.2 x 12.6 cm. British Museum, London

John White's watercolour of the native Virginians of Secotan and Pomeiooc in figure 21 shows 'The manner of their fishing'. It includes a variety of methods, such as netting, including weirs or traps using currents and tides, which were an Indian speciality on which the English colonists depended.[76] His Virginians are also shown spearing fish on foot and night-fishing with a fire from a dug-out canoe.[77] Different crabs, sharks and fish are shown so as to be readily identified by the potential colonizer as a kind of pictorial inventory of the natural resources waiting to be harvested. Some of them are native to Virginia; others have been imported from other New World contexts by White in a fit of fantasy.

The manner in which New World animals, as well as people, were brought back to Europe as prizes is also reflected in *The Tempest*. Caliban is sometimes described in terms that suggest New World resonances, as when Prospero chides him for his slowness and compares him to a tortoise: 'Come, thou tortoise! When?' (1.2.372). John White's drawing (fig. 22) of 'A land Tort wch the Sauages esteeme above all other Torts' accords with Harriot's description of how Virginian tortoises 'both of land and sea kinde' were valuable and how their eggs provided food. Indians used the box turtle

'get thee wood enough'

(*The Tempest* 2.2.125)

20. *Wild Man Carrying an Uprooted Tree*, Albrecht Altdorfer, 1508.
Pen and black ink, 21.4 x 14.6 cm.
British Museum, London

'I'll fish for thee'

(*The Tempest* 2.2.124)

21. *Indians Fishing*, John White, 1585–93.
Watercolour over graphite, touched with bodycolour
and gold, 35.3 x 23.5 cm. British Museum, London

The manner of their fishing.

in particular for food, medicine, ceremonies and hunting. Like Caliban, this kind of marsh turtle had amphibious qualities and could be found in woodlands and meadows with ponds.[78] Caliban himself advertises his New World credentials in one phrase, when he tells his new master how he will 'instruct thee how to snare the nimble marmoset' (2.2.129–30). This is the play's only specific mention of a New World animal. Marmosets are small, squirrel-like primates from the Atlantic rainforests of south-east Brazil. They were brought back to Europe as pets for princes: Don John of Austria famously sported one on his shoulder at the Battle of Lepanto in 1571.[79] The marmoset in the late sixteenth-century sheet of studies illustrated here (fig. 23) sits on

'Come, thou tortoise! When?'

(*The Tempest* 1.2.372)

22. *Common Box Turtle*, John White, 1585–93.
Watercolour over graphite, 14.4 x 19.7 cm.
British Museum, London

'how to snare the nimble marmoset'

(*The Tempest* 2.2.129–30)

23. *Four Studies of a Marmoset* (*Hapale jachus*),
unknown artist, German, *c*. 1520–50.
Pen and grey ink with watercolour and bodycolour,
heightened with white, partly silhouetted, 39.6 x 28 cm.
British Museum, London

a post in someone's menagerie or private house, and is clearly drawn from life in several different poses. It is a remarkably vivid and freshly preserved record of the European fascination with the New World, which echoes Caliban's promise to show his new masters 'all the qualities o'th' isle' (1.2.395). The drawing closely resembles those commissioned by Philip II of Spain of the exotic animals in his menagerie in the

'We may then well call them barbarous ... but not in respect of us that exceede them in all kinde of barbarisme'

(Michael de Montaigne, *Of the Caniballes*, translated by John Florio, 1603)

24. *Standing Black Youth Dressed in a Feather Skirt, and Holding an Axe*, Hans Burgkmair the Elder, 1520–30.
Pen and black ink with grey, brown and green wash, 24 x 16.1 cm. British Museum, London

1560s.[80] The drawings were both souvenirs and aids to study of the New World over which he was emperor; he hung them in his private quarters at the Escorial palace.

Debates about what to make of the peoples of the New World and how to interpret them centred on the Tupinamba of Brazil in the early to mid-sixteenth century.[81] The works that European artists produced reveal something of this process: they tended to combine genuine Tupinamba and other South American artefacts in fanciful ways to make entirely new composite figures. This is apparent in Hans Burgkmair's drawing of a standing black man with a fanciful feather skirt holding a recognizable battle axe (fig. 24). Another Burgkmair drawing (fig. 25) shows a black

man holding a shield that can be matched to a surviving Mexica shield given by the Mexica ruler Moctezuma to Cortés, now in Vienna.[82] Another more battered example of this rare kind of shield is in the British Museum (fig. 26).[83] This method of visual representation – piecing together exotic associations and references to make a new composite figure of fantasy – is suggestively analogous to Shakespeare's subtle way of presenting Caliban. He is evoked by interleaving other ways of being, thinking, imagining and talking with a kaleidoscope of animal and fishy forms.

As Shakespeare knew, contemporary European interest in the Tupinamba went deep. The French writer Michel de Montaigne (1533–1592) not only had Tupinamba artefacts at home: he had also talked to Tupinamba Indians in Rouen in 1562, recorded their impressions of European manners and men, and had even written down and analysed the lyrics of one of their love songs.[84] His purpose in writing his famous essay on cannibals was primarily moral and political: to criticize European thinking and customs by contrast. The local setting for Montaigne was civil war in France. Shakespeare read Montaigne in John Florio's translation:

'This damned witch Sycorax'

(*The Tempest* 1.2.311)

27. Two views of a black-figured pot (*skyphos*) showing Circe (as a black African woman) with Odysseus and one of his sailors, transformed into a pig beyond her loom. Inscribed 'KIRKA'. Boeotia, Greece, 450–420 BC, H. 19.05 cm, diam. 19.05 cm. British Museum, London

I thinke there is more barbarisme in eating men alive, than to feed upon them being dead; to mangle by tortures and torments a body full of lively sense, to roast him in peeces, to make dogges and swine to gnaw and tear him in mammocks (as wee have not only read, but seene very lately, yea and in our owne memorie, not among ancient enemies, but our neighbours and fellow-citizens; and which is worse, under pretence of pietie and religion) than to roast and eat him after he is dead.[85]

By this, Montaigne was referring to the theatre of punishment regularly staged in early modern Europe, one which produced such grisly relics as the Jesuit Edward Oldcorne's eye (see Chapter 7, pp. 192–3).[86] Shakespeare had read Montaigne closely. In *The Tempest* he quotes and paraphrases Florio's translation in Gonzalo's speech about how he would order this island in a new commonwealth:

> For no kind of traffic
> Would I admit: no name of magistrate:
> Letters should not be known: riches, poverty,

'make thyself like a nymph o' th' sea'

(*The Tempest* 1.2.354)

28. *A Harpy*, Peter Paul Rubens, *c.* 1625.
Black chalk with some yellow chalk, 26 x 36.5 cm.
British Museum, London

And use of service, none: contract, succession,
Bourn, bound of land, tilth, vineyard, none:
No use of metal, corn, or wine, or oil:
No occupation, all men idle, all:
And women too, but innocent and pure:
No sovereignty.
(2.1.137–45)

The island is not, however, virgin territory, but the former domain of the witch Sycorax in her banishment from Algiers for witchcraft. She came to the island allegedly pregnant by the Devil with Caliban, and bound Ariel into a pine tree, whence he was rescued by Prospero. He tells the audience that she died on the island, and he sets himself and his magical powers up in direct opposition to her feminine black arts, but her presence still seems to linger in the island atmosphere. Her name recalls not only

'Enter Ariel, like a harpy:
claps his wings upon the table,
and, with a quaint device, the
banquet vanishes'

(The Tempest 3.3.63.1–2)

29. *A Harpy or Siren*, Melchior Lorck, 1582.
Woodcut, 23.2 x 16.2 cm. British Museum, London

the raven (Latin 'corax'), bird of ill omen, but also Circe, the ancient enchantress of Homer and Ovid who had famously turned Odysseus's men into swine.[87] The Greek pot in figure 27 shows Circe as a black African woman, labelled 'KIRKA', offering Odysseus a drugged drink. On the right is her loom, emblematic of feminine wiles and subtlety, at which the travellers first hear Circe 'singing in her beautiful voice as she went to and fro at her great and everlasting loom, on which she was weaving one of those delicate, graceful and dazzling fabrics that goddesses make'. Beyond the loom, the painter shows the consequences of Circe's drugged drink: one of Odysseus's crew has been turned into a swine. Here the painter of the pot has followed Homer very closely in showing the moment of transformation of the head, body and skin complete with bristles, but still with human legs. The swine-man on the pot visually expresses Homer's description of how the enchanted men felt that 'Their minds were as human as they had been before' as Circe keeps them 'penned like pigs in their crowded sties'.[88] They are trapped within the enchantment, as the human Caliban is penned by Prospero in *The Tempest*: 'you sty me / In this hard rock' (1.2.400–1).[89]

Like Circe's island of Aeaea, Prospero's island is a place of unnerving transformations. Ariel, a spirit of indeterminate sex, can be an alluring 'nymph of the sea' (1.2.354), as in Rubens' erotic sketch for the apotheosis of Charles's I's favourite, the Duke of Buckingham, which owes much to the European masque tradition (fig. 28). Or he/she can affectionately be 'my Ariel, chick' (5.1.353), or the snatching, clawed harpy of classical antiquity described in the stage directions: 'Enter Ariel, like a harpy: claps his wings upon the table, and, with a quaint device, the banquet vanishes' (3.3.63.1–2). Melchior Lorck's Turkish harpy – definitely female – in a print of 1582 is a sinister hybrid, standing before an Ottoman mosque sporting a fez and an acanthus-plumed tail (fig. 29).

The figure of Prospero as a magus who works these enchantments in order to dominate the island is one which depends above all on the power of the book. The secret book to which Prospero refers that will allow him to 'perform / Much business appertaining' (3.1.113–14) is never seen but exerts some mysterious force in the 'art' of the play.[90] When Prospero renounces magic he talks of drowning this book, as if it were a living thing:

I'll break my staff,
Bury it certain fathoms in the earth,
And deeper than did ever plummet sound
I'll drown my book.
(5.1.59–62)

Prospero's books are so important an element in his power that Caliban stresses again and again that an assault on them should be the first act of rebellion:

thou mayst brain him,
Having first seized his books …
… Remember
First to possess his books; for without them
He's but a sot, as I am, nor hath not
One spirit to command: they all do hate him
As rootedly as I. Burn but his books.
(3.2.72–9)

It is the emphasis on these books, as records of Prospero's 'secret studies' (1.2.91), that makes the Elizabethan magus John Dee a possible model for Prospero.[91] Secret books were usually manuscripts as they were private and personalized.[92] By incorporating these texts into the appropriate ritual and using the right instruments or props, such as Prospero's staff and his 'magic garment' (1.2.29), one could communicate with and command supernatural beings – Prospero's spirit, Ariel, or one of Dee's angels, Uriel. Dee's 'instruments of conjuration' were inscribed wax discs or 'seals' (see below). They bear a striking similarity to the instructions given by the angels Uriel and Michael during a scrying session held on the afternoon of Saturday 10 March 1582. Dee recorded the vision as a diagram in his own secret book (fig. 30):

URIEL: … you must use a fowre square Table, two cubits square: Where uppon must be set Sigillum Divinitatis Dei …, which is allready perfected in a boke of thyne: Blessed be God, in all his Mysteries, and Holy in all his works. This seal must not be loked on, without great reverence and devotion. This seale is to be made of perfect wax. I mean, wax, which is clean purified: we have no respect of cullours. This seal must be 9 ynches in diameter: The rowndnes must be 27 ynches, and somewhat more. The Thicknes of it, must be of an ynche and half a quarter, and a figure of a crosse, must be on the back side of it, made thus [a diagram of AGLA inscribed in crosses sketched by Dee].[93]

The surviving objects associated with Dee include one large wax disc (fig. 31) and four smaller discs inscribed with the diagram as instructed by the angels, to be used as instruments in future sessions. The larger disc, the Great Seal, was to be placed in the

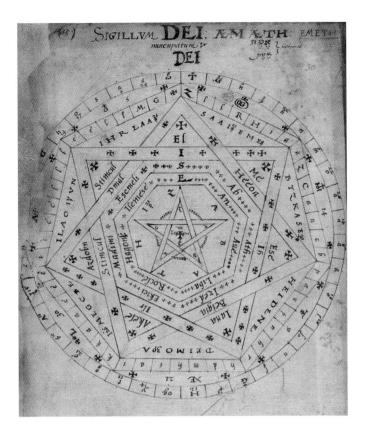

'rapt in secret studies'

(*The Tempest* 1.2.91)

30. John Dee's diagram of a scrying session
of 10 March 1582 in his manuscript book.
Approx. 30 x 20 cm. British Library, London

'By my so potent art'

(*The Tempest* 5.1.55)

31. The Great Seal: the largest of three surviving
wax discs inscribed with the diagram recording
Dee's vision of 10 March 1582.
Engraved wax, diam. 23 cm. British Museum, London

centre of a table made from sweetwood with the four legs balanced on smaller versions of the seal, as sketched by Dee on the same page of his manuscript book.[94]

Shakespeare's audiences lived in a world shot through with magic. As they watched Prospero trace a circle in the sand with his staff, they would have been familiar with the concept that some kind of magic book, like Dee's, was essential in order for Prospero to exert the kinds of command he has over Ariel and the spirits of the island, from the initial storm to vanishing banquets, frozen conspirators, and a masque of goddesses and farmhands. Ariel describes the enchantment Prospero has cast upon Alonso, King of Naples, and his men:

> Just as you left them; all prisoners, sir,
> In the line-grove which weather-fends your cell:
> They cannot budge till your release …
> … but chiefly
> Him that you termed, sir, the good old lord Gonzalo:
> His tears run down his beard, like winter's drops
> From eaves of reeds.
> (5.1.11–19)

257

Prospero as shaman is a figure recognizable in many world cultures, as is often brought out in contemporary productions of the play. The Taíno wooden figure from around 1500 of a male spirit-being standing rigid in a drug-induced trance (fig. 32) evokes aspects of Ariel's description of enchantment, even down to the gilded tear channels. The figure is carved from a dense tropical hardwood, polished with pebbles to give a deep shine to the surface.[95] This symbol of male potency linked living people with the spirit of their dead ancestors and may have been used in shamanic rites.[96] In Taino culture this figure embodied the life force, or *cemi*, which has many natures and forms and could work powerful magic in a similar manner to a shaman. The sculptor has seen the form of the straining figure within the curve of the trunk and carved through to it; the spirit is within the wood.[97] The sculpture expresses the nature of enchantment.[98] The concept of the tree spirit present within the wood itself is implicit in Shakespeare's description of the entranced figures standing in the lime grove, 'which weather-fends your cell' (5.1.12). It is also implicit in the story of Ariel's long imprisonment in a cloven pine. Prospero threatens him with the memory: 'it was mine art, / When I arrived and heard thee, that made gape / The pine and let thee out' (1.2.340–2). If Ariel does not do his master's bidding, 'I will rend an oak / And peg thee in his knotty entrails till / Thou hast howled away twelve winters' (1.2.344–6).

Prospero gives up his 'rough magic' (5.1.55), leaving the island to Caliban and spirit magic to Ariel, and putting on his courtier's costume of hat and rapier. In abjuring magic he borrows a speech from one of the great enchantresses of classical antiquity, Medea's incantation from Ovid's *Metamorphoses*:

> the strong-based promontory
> Have I made shake and by the spurs plucked up
> The pine and cedar. Graves at my command
> Have waked their sleepers, oped, and let 'em forth
> By my so potent art.
> (5.1.51–5)[99]

We are back with the witches of folklore. Audience members hearing the allusion would have been less confident than Prospero himself that his art was that of white, or good, magic, despite his attempts to present himself in the play as the

**'His tears run down his beard, like winter's drops
From eaves of reeds.'**

(The Tempest 5.1.18–19)

32. Taíno wooden figure of a male spirit-being standing rigid in a drug-induced trance.
Jamaica, 1400s–1500s.
Guayacan wood, H. 104 cm. British Museum, London

antidote or counterbalance to the witch, Sycorax, with her dark arts and allegedly devilish pedigree.

The idea that *The Tempest* was Shakespeare's last play and that Prospero's farewell to his magical art was Shakespeare's valediction to the stage is a myth that emerged during the romantic period of the early nineteenth century. It was Samuel Taylor Coleridge who described Prospero as 'the very Shakespeare himself, as it were, of the tempest'.[100] In fact, Shakespeare co-wrote *Henry VIII*, *The Two Noble Kinsmen* and the lost play, *Cardenio*, with John Fletcher, in the years 1612–14. Nevertheless, his fellow actors regarded *The Tempest* as a showcase of his poetic and dramatic arts. At least, we may assume this from the fact that they placed it first, in an exceptionally well-edited text, in the First Folio of his collected plays, which they prepared as a monument to his memory after his death, and which began the process whereby Shakespeare became a figure of unprecedented literary power and influence across the globe.

259

10 LEGACY

HOW DID SHAKESPEARE BECOME a 'classic' and when did he first achieve his global fame? In the spring of 1616 two dramatists, Francis Beaumont and William Shakespeare, died within a few weeks of each other. Beaumont became the first theatre-writer to be honoured with burial in the national shrine of Westminster Abbey, beside the tombs of Geoffrey Chaucer (the father of English verse) and Edmund Spenser (the greatest poet of the Elizabethan era). Shakespeare, by contrast, was laid to rest in his native Stratford-upon-Avon. The burial of 'Will. Shakspere, gent.' (that respectable title which he had fought so hard to obtain) was recorded in the parish register of Holy Trinity Church. His gravestone in the chancel was inscribed with a rhyme cursing whomsoever might move the bones beneath, and a monument on the north wall of the chancel recorded that Shakespeare died on 23 April 1616, in his fifty-third year. That same monument credited him with the wisdom of Socrates and the art of Virgil, while claiming that 'quick nature died' with him and yet 'all that he hath writ / Leaves living art, but page, to serve his wit'. These are high claims, but in a very provincial setting.

That same year of 1616, Ben Jonson became the first English dramatist to publish a collected edition of his own plays written for the public stage. He was much mocked for his presumption in doing so, especially under the title of *Works*, suggestive of an edition of a classical author such as Virgil. We now think of Shakespeare as unique, the embodiment indeed of the very idea of artistic genius, but in his own time, though widely admired, he was but one of a constellation of theatrical stars. His contemporaries admired him greatly, but no more than they admired Beaumont or Jonson. How is it, then, that when we reach the eighteenth and nineteenth centuries Shakespeare's fame has outstripped that of all his peers? Why was he the sole dramatist

1. Detail from the title page of *Mr. Wiliam Shakespeares Comedies Histories, & Tragedies. Published according to the True Originall Copies*, the 'First Folio', printed by Isaac Jaggard and Ed. Blount, London, 1623.
Printed book, 32 x 21.8 cm.
Stonyhurst College, Lancashire

of the age who would eventually have a genuinely international – ultimately a worldwide – impact?

In 1619, three years after Shakespeare's death, there appeared unauthorized new editions of ten of his plays. With the assistance of the Earl of Pembroke, who was Lord Chamberlain and a good friend to the actors, the King's Men obtained a blocking order against further productions of a similar kind. Soon after, they began the work of gathering the materials for their own edition of *Mr. Wiliam Shakespeares Comedies, Histories, & Tragedies*, 'Published according to the True Originall Copies'. The great book appeared in 1623, in large double-columned 'folio' format, adorned with Martin Droeshout's engraving of Shakespeare and an array of preliminary matter, including Ben Jonson's commendatory poem praising his fellow playwright as 'soul of the Age', as a rival even to Sophocles, and as a dramatic artist whose works were 'for all time'. Without the Folio, half of Shakespeare's output would have been lost forever, and much of the rest would only have remained available in error-strewn texts. It was a book cherished by readers as various as King Charles I and the radical republican John Milton. With the Folio, the canon of Shakespeare's works was laid down and the author's classic status roundly asserted.

Not all book collectors, however, were equally enthusiastic. Sir Thomas Bodley was reluctant to include playbooks in his new library at Oxford University, saying that barely one in forty of them would be worth keeping. The Bodleian got rid of its copy of the First Folio when it acquired a Third Folio in the 1660s, only to buy it back at great expense in 1905. A more cherished copy was that now in the library at Stonyhurst College (fig. 1). It was purchased soon after publication by Lord William Howard (1563–1640), third son of the Duke of Norfolk, whom Queen Elizabeth had executed for treason. Howard bequeathed his library to a relative, Thomas Arundel, 2nd Baron Arundel of Wardour (1583–1643), in whose (Catholic) family the Folio remained until it was presented to Stonyhurst in 1837.[1]

Arundel was perhaps the first English art collector in the European model. In 1612 he visited Italy with Ben Jonson's artistic collaborator Inigo Jones, and in the 1620s he built up a collection of sculpture, using agents such as the traveller the Reverend William Petty, who made a number of excellent deals in the Mediterranean. When his acquisitions were shipped home to London in January 1627 they caused a sensation. Henry Peacham commented that 'this angle of the world oweth the first sight of Greeke and Romane statues' to Arundel. The English had arrived as cultivated Europeans, connoisseurs of the relics of antiquity.[2] Among the highlights of the collection was a bronze head found by Petty in a well in Smyrna (now Izmir), Turkey (fig. 2). In the eighteenth century it became known as the 'Arundel Homer' – how could a figure of such dignity and antiquity be anyone other than the founding father of Western literature? – and in the twentieth century it was identified with Sophocles, but at the time it was thought to represent a Macedonian king. A recently discovered eyewitness account describes the collection that Arundel kept in his London garden:

2. Sophocles (?), 'the Arundel Homer',
Hellenistic Greece, *c.* 496–406 BC.
Bronze, H. 29.2 cm. British Museum, London

That sculpture and casting had reached a very high point amongst the ancients
is clear from the Arundel marbles, brought from Greece and Italy, which have
been erected in the gardens of the illustrious Lord Arundel in London. Amongst
several inscriptions, urns and statues, we saw a statue of Caius Marius, seven-times
Consul of Theseus, and of the young Hercules: we saw as well busts of Scipio
Africanus, Seneca, Socrates, Aesop and others, all sculpted to the life. Everyone
is agreed in praising the eurhythmia of a statue of Hercules and of another of a
certain feminine body, as well as the head of a certain Macedonian King, cast in
bronze, found in a well at Smyrna by Petty, who spent five years there in his search
for such things. The English sculptors almost to a man model their own works
most accurately on this. A certain man most skilled in the art of casting, and by
common agreement a craftsman, confessed himself unable to express himself

sufficiently. The Earl of Pembroke offered three thousand florins for this head, even allowing for its damaged state, but in vain, as that most civilised of men, Franciscus Junius the younger, who showed me these and many other rarities, reported.[3]

Here the Earl of Pembroke, to whom the Shakespeare Folio was dedicated, attempts to purchase an admired relic of antiquity; the Arundel family, meanwhile, had purchased a Folio. When book and bust came together in 1640, a precedent was established for what became a common phenomenon in the eighteenth century: in the library of any self-respecting gentleman of taste, there would be busts of the great writers, thinkers and doers of antiquity together with an edition of Shakespeare.

The eighteenth century was the crucial period for the enshrining of Shakespeare as a true classic. His texts were re-edited, using the principles that had been applied to the Greek and Roman classics. At the same time, he came to dominate the theatrical repertoire, albeit often in versions of the plays in which the script was adapted to suit the taste of the age.

If we had to identify a single decade in which the 'cult of Shakespeare' took root, in which his celebrity and influence came to outstrip that of his contemporaries once and for all, it would probably be the 1730s. At that time, there was a proliferation of cheap mass-market editions of his plays, while in the theatre the plays came to constitute about a quarter of the entire repertoire of the London stage, twice what they had been hitherto. The promotion of Shakespeare was driven by a number of forces, ranging from state censorship of new plays to a taste for the shapely legs of actresses in the cross-dressed 'breeches parts' of the comedies (actresses instead of boy players had taken the female roles since the reign of Charles II, great lover of both theatre and women). After the passing of the Licensing Act of 1737 it became easier to stage political drama indirectly by way of Shakespeare than to satirize the government of Sir Robert Walpole directly, as John Gay had done in his *Beggar's Opera* a decade before. Around the same time, a Shakespeare Ladies Club was formed under the leadership of Susanna, Countess of Shaftesbury, with the aim of persuading the London theatre managers to stage more Shakespeare and less in the way of Harlequinades (the prototype of the modern pantomime) and other such vulgar spectacles. The plays were becoming synonymous with decency and Englishness, even as the institution of the theatre was still poised between respectability and disrepute.

3. White marble memorial to William Shakespeare in Poets' Corner, Westminster Abbey, Peter Scheemakers, 1741.
Wesminster Abbey, London

Shakespeare at last found his way into the national pantheon. In the years immediately after his death there had been some talk of moving his monument, or even his remains, from Stratford-upon-Avon to Westminster Abbey: hence Ben Jonson's reference in his dedicatory poem in the Folio to lodging Shakespeare 'by Chaucer or Spenser' and bidding 'Beaumont lie a little further on to make thee room'. But the idea was abandoned and it was not until 29 January 1741 (1740 in the old-style calendar) that a memorial statue to him was erected in Poets' Corner in Westminster Abbey.[4]

The life-size white marble statue, shown in the dress of his period, was erected by the Earl of Burlington, Dr Richard Mead, Alexander Pope and Tom Martin, cultural opinion-formers with a taste for Shakespeare (Pope had edited the complete works) (fig. 3). Charles Fleetwood of the Drury Lane Theatre and John Rich of Covent Garden Theatre gave a benefit to help raise funds. The monument was designed by William Kent and executed by Peter Scheemakers. The inscription above the head of the statue can be translated 'William Shakespeare [erected] 124 years after [his] death by public esteem'. Carved heads of Queen Elizabeth I, Henry V and Richard III appear on the pedestal: Shakespeare's own queen is thus brought together with the exemplary good and bad kings of his plays. The figure leans his elbow on a pile of books and his left hand points to a scroll on which are painted a variant of Prospero's valedictory lines from *The Tempest*:

> The Cloud capt Tow'rs,
> The Gorgeous Palaces,
> The Solemn Temples,
> The Great Globe itself,
> Yea all which it Inherit,
> Shall Dissolve;
> And like the baseless Fabrick of a Vision
> Leave not a wreck behind.

The Scheemakers statue established an archetypal image of Shakespeare as inspired genius; copies, either life-sized or miniature, were over the years placed in many different locations, whether public shrines or private collections.

David Garrick (1717–79) arrived in London at a propitious moment (fig. 4). Shakespeare was growing into big business and the time was ripe for a new star to cash in on the name of the Bard. As in many a good theatre story, Garrick's first break came when he stepped in as an understudy and outshone the actor who normally took the part. This was followed by a more formal debut, again of a kind that established a pattern for later generations: the revolutionary new reading of a major Shakespearean part. For Garrick, as for Edmund Kean in the following century and Antony Sher in the one after that, it was Richard III. After this, there was no looking back. Garrick

4. *David Garrick*, Robert Edge Pine, *c.* 1765. The greatest Bardolater of the eighteenth century holding a volume of Shakespeare, in the edition of his friend and former schoolmaster Dr Samuel Johnson.
Oil on canvas, 54 x 67 cm. Private collection

did all the things we have come to expect of a major star: he took on the full gamut of Shakespeare, he had an affair with his leading lady (the gorgeous and talented Peg Woffington), and he managed his own acting company, supervising the scripts and directing plays while also starring in them. It was because of Garrick's extraordinary energy in all these departments that he not only gave unprecedented respectability to the profession of acting, but also effectively invented the modern theatre. The 'actor–manager' tradition that he inaugurated stretched down to Laurence Olivier and beyond.

The climax of Garrick's career in Bardolatry was the jubilee that he organized in commemoration of the bicentenary of Shakespeare's birth. The event took place in Stratford-upon-Avon in 1769, on the occasion of the opening of a new town hall, a mere five years later than the anniversary it was supposed to mark. It lasted for three days, during which scores of fashionable Londoners descended on the hitherto obscure provincial town where Shakespeare had been born. The literary tourist industry began here: local entrepreneurs did good business in the sale of Shakespearean relics, such as souvenirs supposedly cut from the wood of the great Bard's mulberry tree. Not since the marketing in medieval times of fragments of the True Cross had a single tree yielded so much wood. The jubilee programme included a grand procession of Shakespearean characters, a masked ball, a horse race and a firework display. In true English fashion, the outdoor events were washed out by torrential rain. At the climax of the festivities Garrick performed his own poem, 'An ode upon dedicating a building and erecting a statue to Shakespeare at Stratford-upon-Avon', set to music by the leading composer Thomas Arne (1710–1778). In the manner of a staged theatrical 'happening', Garrick had arranged for a member of the audience (a fellow actor), dressed as a French fop, to complain – as French connoisseurs of literary taste had complained for generations – that Shakespeare was vulgar, provincial and overrated. This gave Garrick the opportunity to voice his grand defence of Shakespeare. Back in the metropolis after the event, Garrick re-enacted some parts of the jubilee in his theatre at Drury Lane. Although the whole business was much mocked in newspaper reports, caricatures and stage farces, it generated enormous publicity for both Garrick and Shakespeare across Britain and the Continent. The jubilee did more than make Stratford-upon-Avon into a tourist attraction: it inaugurated the very idea of a summer arts festival.

'The whole will conclude with the apotheosis of Shakespeare', the *Gentleman's Magazine* had reported in advance of the event. The jubilee itself was a curious apotheosis in that Garrick's words were a great deal more prominent than those of Shakespeare (none of the plays was actually performed), but in retrospect it may be seen as the point at which Shakespeare was finally transformed from first among equals to, in Garrick's phrase, 'god of our idolatry'. Garrick's own role as high priest at the shrine – as, indeed, the divine Shakespeare's self-proclaimed representative on earth – was summed up a few years later in book six of William Cowper's immensely popular poem, *The Task* (1785):

5. William Poel's model for a reconstructed Globe, unknown photographer, *c.* 1900.

6. San Diego Globe built in 1935 from the same plan as the Chicago Globe of 1934.

For Garrick was a worshipper himself;
He drew the liturgy, and framed the rites
And solemn ceremonial of the day,
And call'd the world to worship on the banks
Of Avon famed in song. Ah! Pleasant proof
That piety has still in human hearts
Some place, a spark or two not yet extinct.

In an age when orthodox religion was facing severe challenges, the cult of Shakespeare was becoming a secular faith.

By the end of the nineteenth century, the grammar school boy from the edge of the forest of Arden had become the supreme deity not just of poetry and drama, but of high culture itself. He had been translated into many languages and, with the spread of the British Empire, was studied and performed across the world. In the theatre there was a growing desire for authenticity – a reaction against elaborate Victorian staging in proscenium arch theatre of a very different design and aesthetic from the bare boards of Shakespeare's original open stage.

William Poel (1852–1934) made the first sustained attempt to reconstruct the playing conditions of Elizabethan drama. In 1897 he sketched plans for a 1:24 scale model of the Globe (fig. 5), intending it as a maquette for a full-scale reconstruction which, he hoped, would be adopted as the venue for a National Theatre, a project then under discussion.[5] Poel's dream was not realized, although a temporary full-size Globe reconstruction, designed by Edwin Lutyens, was built for an exhibition at Earl's Court in 1912 called 'Shakespeare's England'.[6] For a short time Londoners were, it was claimed, 'able to walk straight into the sixteenth century and visualize the environment and atmosphere of Shakespeare's day'.[7] A company called the Idyllic Players performed

LEONARDO DiCAPRIO   CLAIRE DANES

my only love sprung
from my only hate.

WILLIAM SHAKESPEARE'S
ROMEO + JULIET

www.romeoandjuliet.com   IN THEATRES NOVEMBER 1

7. Poster for Australian director Baz Luhrmann's hugely successful Hollywood version of *Romeo and Juliet*, 1996.

8. Poster for James Ivory's 1965 film *Shakespeare Wallah*, about a travelling troupe of Shakespeare players in post-colonial India.

9. Detail of the Robben Island Bible showing the section in *Julius Caesar* marked and signed by Nelson Mandela, 16 December 1977. Printed book, 21.5 x 15 cm (closed). Collection of Sonny Venkatrathnam, Durban

extracts from the plays, and actors wearing Elizabethan costume impersonated Shakespeare's original audience.

In the course of the twentieth century Shakespeare's Globe Theatre was reconstructed in many different places around the globe. At the 1934 Chicago World's Fair, the exhibition entitled 'a Century of Progress' included a full-size Globe built by Thomas Wood Stevens, based on a design by the Shakespearean scholar J.C. Adams. A young man named Sam Wanamaker was among the visitors. The seed was sown for the dream that he realized at the end of the century, a working reconstruction for London audiences on the south bank of the Thames, within a stone's throw of the site of Shakespeare's original theatre. Shakespeare's Globe opened for business in 1997 and without any public subsidy, has triumphantly offered new audiences something of the experience of the open-air thrust stage for which the dramatist wrote.

The year after the World's Fair, the San Diego Globe was built from the same plan as the Chicago Globe (fig. 6). It became the first permanent reconstruction, staging full versions of the plays. Other reconstructions, in Cleveland, Dallas and elsewhere, helped to stimulate the rise of Shakespeare festivals in America. Today there are more than a dozen working reproduction Elizabethan playhouses around the world, in venues as far apart as Tokyo and Rome.

The global spread of Shakespeare in the twentieth century was also made possible by the new medium of the movies. Numerous versions of the plays, together with adaptations and offshoots from them, have been produced ever since the earliest days of silent film. From Hollywood to Bollywood and beyond, directors have made their names with the help of Shakespeare (figs 7–8).

Throughout his posthumous life, Shakespeare has been used to extraordinary political effect. In Eastern Europe during the Soviet era, productions of the tragedies – with their tyrannical rulers, their spies, informers and paranoia – became a way of criticizing party and regime without incurring the wrath of the censor, as would have happened with explicitly contemporary plays. A production of *Hamlet* in Bucharest in the late 1980s implicitly represented Claudius and Gertrude as the Ceauşescus. So potent was the analogy that when the revolution came in 1989, students turned to the actor who had played Hamlet, Ion Caramitru, and persuaded him to lead the popular assault on the state television station.

In Africa, meanwhile, *Julius Caesar* had particular impact, offering as it did a paradigm for rebellion against imperial rule. The first president of Tanzania, Julius Nyerere, translated the play into Swahili. In South Africa in 1944, when a group of young black politicians including Nelson Mandela formed the Youth League of the African National Congress to provide a pressure group for a more militant African nationalism, its first manifesto ended with lines from the play: 'The fault, dear Brutus, is not in our stars / But in ourselves, that we are underlings' (1.2.146–7). When the ANC leaders were imprisoned on Robben Island, they found a common bond and source of solace in Shakespeare.

One of their number, Sonny Venkatrathnam, managed to get hold of a copy of Shakespeare's works, disguising the cover with Indian religious pictures. He circulated the book to all the leading prisoners, asking them to autograph their favourite passages in the margins; and his unique marked volume reveals how individually they approached Shakespeare. Walter Sisulu, Mandela's closest mentor and friend, chose Shylock's 'Still have I borne it with a patient shrug, / For sufferance is the badge of all our tribe' (*Merchant of Venice* 1.3.100–1). But *Julius Caesar* was the favourite, and Mandela chose Caesar's own fateful words, which he underlined with his signature and dated 16 December 1977 (fig. 9):

> Cowards die many times before their deaths,
> The valiant never taste of death but once.
> Of all the wonders that I yet have heard,
> It seems to me most strange that men should fear,
> Seeing that death, a necessary end,
> Will come when it will come.[8]

Shakespeare's life did not cease with the 'necessary end' of his death in 1616: his plays continue to live, and to give life, four centuries on, all the way across the great theatre of the world.

Notes

Chapter 1

1 Charles Nicholl, *The Lodger: Shakespeare on Silver Street*, London 2007, pp. 3–4.

2 Philip Hentzner, *Itinerarium Germaniae, Galliae, Angliae, Italiae, cum Indice Locorum, Rerum atque Verborum*, Nuremberg 1612. English translation by Richard Bentley, *Travels in England During the Reign of Queen Elizabeth*, London 1797. All quotations from online edition at http://ebooks.adelaide.edu.au/h/hentzner/paul/travels/

3 See Steve Sohmer, *Shakespeare's Mystery Play: The Opening of the Globe Theatre 1599*, Manchester 1999, which argues for 12 June 1599 as the date and *Julius Caesar* as the play, though the case is not definitive.

4 Christian F. Feest, 'John White's New World' in Kim Sloan, *A New World: England's First View of America*, London 2007, pp. 65–78, esp. p. 74.

5 See William Young, *The History of Dulwich College, down to the passing of the Act of Parliament dissolving the original corporation, 28th August, 1857; with a life of the founder, Edward Alleyn, and an accurate transcript of his diary 1617–1622*, 2 vols, London 1889, vol. 2, p. 115, for a typical reference.

6 See further Pamela Tudor-Craig with C. Whittick, *'Old St Paul's': the Society of Antiquaries' Diptych, 1616*, London 2004; David Gaimster, Bernard Nurse and Julia Steele (eds), *Making History: Antiquaries in Britain 1707–2007*, London 2007, cat. 19.

7 Karen Hearn (ed.), *Dynasties: Painting in Tudor and Jacobean England 1530–1630*, London 1995, cat. 35; Maurice Howard, *The Tudor Image*, London 1995, cat. 54; Roy Strong, *The Portraits of Elizabeth I*, London 1987, reprinted 2003, pp. 71–7; Michael Snodin (ed.), *Horace Walpole's Strawberry Hill*, New Haven and London 2009, cat. 102 and p. 129.

8 Susan Doran (ed.), *Elizabeth I*, London 2003.

9 Christopher Hartop, *East Anglian Silver*, Norwich 2004, p. 118, and p. 18 for the maker of this cup, Thomas Buttell, and his activity in Norwich.

10 W.H. Frere (ed.), *Visitation Articles and Injunctions of the Period of the Reformation*, Alcuin Club, vol. 16, 1910, p. 16, injunction 23, cited p. 46. Cited in Tara Hamling, *Decorating the 'Godly' Household: Religious Art in Post-Reformation Britain*, New Haven and London 2010, p. 41.

11 See Martina Bagnoli, Holger A. Klein, C. Griffith Mann and James Robinson (eds), *Treasures of Heaven: Saints, Relics and Devotion in Medieval Europe*, New Haven and London 2010, cat. 122, for an example.

12 Hugh Tait, 'The Stonyhurst Salt', *Apollo*, April 1964, pp. 270–8.

13 Eamon Duffy, 'Bare ruin'd quiers' in Richard Dutton, Alison Findlay and Richard Wilson (eds), *Theatre and Religion: Lancastrian Shakespeare*, Manchester 2003, pp. 40–57.

14 R. Savage and Edgar Fripp (eds), *Minutes and Accounts of the Corporation of Stratford-upon-Avon*, 43 vols, Dugdale Society, Oxford 1921–30, vol. 1, pp. 137–41 and vol. 2, p. 54.

15 Duffy 2003, op. cit. in n. 13 above, p. 46. See Val Horsler, Martin Gorick and Paul Edmonson, *Shakespeare's Church: A Parish for the World*, London 2010, p. 151, for the cup.

16 E. Alfred Jones, 'Old plate at the Church Congress', *Burlington Magazine*, vol. 39, 1921, pp. 254–67, esp. p. 261, pl. I, B and C.

17 Referred to also by Peacham: see Katherine Duncan-Jones, 'Sidney's personal imprese', *Journal of the Warburg and Courtauld Institutes*, vol. 33, 1970, pp. 321–4, esp. p. 321.

18 W.H. Clennell, 'Bodley, Sir Thomas (1545–1613)', *Oxford Dictionary of National Biography*, Oxford 2004.

19 Richard Raiswell, 'Mundy, Peter (c. 1596–c. 1667)', *Oxford Dictionary of National Biography*, Oxford 2004.

20 Dora Thornton, *The Scholar in his Study: Ownership and Experience in Renaissance Italy*, New Haven and London 1997, p. 81, fig. 52; Norah Titley, *Miniatures from Turkish Manuscripts*, London 1981, p. 29, no. 7 (1).

21 Philippa Glanville, *Silver in Tudor and Early Stuart England*, London 1990, p. 339; Nurhan Atasoy and Julian Raby, *Iznik*, London and New York 1989, p. 270.

22 Imtiaz Habib, *Black Lives in the English Archives*, Farnham 2008, p. 88; T.S. Willan, 'Some aspects of the English trade with the Levant', *The English Historical Review*, vol. 70, no. 276, July 1955, pp. 399–410, esp. p. 406.

23 Glanville 1990, op. cit. in n. 21 above, p. 342; Stacey Pierson, *Illustrated Catalogue of Underglaze Blue and Copper Red Decorated Porcelains in the Percival David Foundation of Chinese Art*, London 2004, p. 51, no. 695, col. pl. on p. 41.

24 The *Charity* was the first Dutch ship to arrive in Japan in 1600. Most of the crew were dead, so it came in under the command of its pilot, William Adams. The *Leifde* arrived in poor shape and its poop-carving, apparently showing Erasmus, probably washed up separately, or was torn off by a trophy hunter. It is labelled as Erasmus and dated 1598. The carving, which is just over 1 metre in height, was enshrined until modern times in a Zen temple (the Ryûô-ji in Tochigi), where it was identified as the mythical Chinese inventor of ships (called Kateki-son in the Japanese pronunciation). It is now deposited in Tokyo National Museum. Sakamoto Mitsuro (*et al.*), *Nanban bijutsu to yôfûga*, Genshoku nihon no bijutsu, vol. 25, Tokyo 1970, cat. 71. Information kindly provided by Timon Screech.

25 Timon Screech, 'Pictures (the most part bawdy): the Anglo-Japanese painting trade in the early 1600s', *The Art Bulletin*, vol. 87, no. 1, March 2005, pp. 50–72. For Richard Cock's admiring comments on Japanese theatre, which he saw on 31 October 1613, as representing 'the truth it selfe', see Ury Eppstein, 'The stage observed. Western attitudes toward Japanese theatre', *Monumenta Nipponica*, vol. 48, no. 2, Summer 1993, pp. 147–66, esp. p. 150.

26 Michael Strachan, 'Roe, Sir Thomas (1581–1644)', *Oxford Dictionary of National Biography*, Oxford 2004.

27 Susan Stronge, *Painting for the Mughal Emperor: The Art of the Book 1560–1650*, London 2002, pp. 136–9.

28 For the doublet see Tarnya Cooper, *Searching for Shakespeare*, London 2006, cat. 38.

29 See Hearn 1995, op. cit. in n. 7 above, cats 75 and 79, for English miniatures of the 1590s. See Susan Stronge, *Made for Mughal Emperors: Royal Treasures from Hindustan*, London and New York 2010, pp. 140–1 and pl. 103, for European miniatures at Jahangir's court and their influence on painting and jewellery fashions there.

30 Stronge 2002, op. cit. in n. 27 above, p. 138.

31 Stronge 2010, op. cit. in n. 29 above, pl. 103: *Jahangir Preferring a Sufi Shaykh to Kings*, a miniature signed by Bichtitr, c. 1615–20, depicts James I among the rejected rulers.

32 Habib 2008, op. cit. in n. 22 above, pp. 63–150.

33 Ezio Bassani, 'Additional notes on the Afro-Portugese ivories', *African Arts*, vol. 27, no. 3, Memorial to William Fagg, July 1994, pp. 34–45, esp. pp. 39–40.

34 See further Bernard Harris, 'A portrait of a Moor' in Catherine M.S. Alexander and Stanley Wells (eds), *Shakespeare and Race*, Cambridge 2000, pp. 23–36 (first published in *Shakespeare Survey*, 1958).

35 *Calendar of State Papers Domestic*, 21 October 1600.

36 Detailed commentary in Hearn 1995, op. cit. in n. 7 above, cat. 40, and Strong 2003, op. cit. in n. 7 above, pp. 101–8.

37 Angus Patterson, *Fashion and Armour in Renaissance Europe*, London 2009, p. 64: 'Private duel was one consequence of the development of the rapier'.

38 Jayne Elisabeth Archer, Elizabeth Goldring and Sarah Knight (eds), *The Intellectual and Cultural World of the Early Modern Inns of Court*, Manchester and New York 2011.

39 R.M. Fisher, 'William Crashawe and the Middle Temple Globes 1605–15', *The Geographical Journal*, vol. 140, no. 1, 1974, pp. 105–12, esp. p. 107.

40 Lorna Hutson, 'The evidential plot: Shakespeare and Gascoigne at Gray's Inn' and Bradin Cormack, 'Locating *The Comedy of Errors*: revels jurisdiction at the Inns of Court' in Archer, Goldring and Knight 2011, op. cit. in n. 37 above, pp. 245–63 and 264–85 respectively.

41 John Manningham, *The Diary of John Manningham of the Middle Temple, 1602–1603*, edited by Robert Parker Sorlien, Hanover, New Hampshire 1976, p. 48. One detail is wrong: Olivia is mourning her brother, not a dead husband. But Manningham is by no means the only spectator in the play's history to have mistaken this point.

42 This fine painting is recorded in the Middle Temple Hall from 1637, but may well have been commissioned as part of the refit of the hall in the 1570s: see Tarnya Cooper, 'Professional pride and personal

agendas: portraits of judges, lawyers and members of the Inns of Court 1560–1630' in Archer, Goldring and Knight 2011, op. cit. in n. 38 above, pp. 157–78 and 160–1.

43 On Solomon and the significance of this particular biblical story for Protestant audiences see Hamling 2010, op. cit. in n. 10 above, pp. 99–103. On storytelling as a moral education and its relationship to lawgiving see Paul Raffield, *Images and Culture of Law in Early Modern England, Justice and Political Power*, Cambridge 2004, p. 82.

44 Archer, Goldring and Knight 2011, op. cit. in n. 38 above, Introduction.

45 See Tiffany Stern, *Rehearsal from Shakespeare to Sheridan*, Oxford 2000, pp. 46–122.

46 See J. Leeds Barroll, *Politics, Plague and Shakespeare's Theater*, Ithaca 1991; Andrew Gurr, *The Shakespearean Stage*, 3rd edn, Cambridge 1992; Andrew Gurr, *Playgoing in Shakespeare's London*, 3rd edn, Cambridge 2004; see also E.K. Chambers, *The Elizabethan Stage*, 4 vols, London 1923, esp. vol. 1, pp. 287–96, for the question of Sunday playing.

47 See Julian Bowsher and Pat Miller, *The Rose and the Globe – Playhouses of Shakespeare's Bankside, Southwark, Excavations 1988–90*, London 2009, p. 154, p. 155 for analysis and illustration of this pipe (CP7) and pp. 178–80 for details of pipes in the excavation.

48 Gabriel Egan, 'John Hemminge's tap house at the Globe', *Theatre Notebook*, vol. 55, 2001, pp. 72–7; Bowsher and Miller 2009, op. cit. in n. 48 above, p. 146; Andrew Gurr and Mariko Ichikawa, *Staging in Shakespeare's Theatres*, Oxford 2000, p. 5.

49 George Warner, *Catalogue of Manuscripts at Dulwich College*, London 1881, no. 41. See also Cooper 2006, op. cit. in n. 28 above, cat. 30.

50 Platter's manuscript diary was first printed in *Anglia*, vol. 22, 1899, pp. 456–64, transcribed by Gustav Binz. Translation from Chambers 1923, op. cit. in n. 46 above, vol. 1, pp. 365–6.

51 Cooper 2006, op. cit. in n. 28 above, cat. 61.

52 Ibid., cat. 34.

53 Tarnya Cooper, *A Guide to Tudor and Jacobean Portraits*, London 2008, p. 24; Catharine MacLeod, *Tudor Portraits in the National Portrait*

Gallery Collection, London 1996, p. 33; Charles Nicholl, *Insights: Shakespeare and his Contemporaries*, London 2005, p. 14; Roy Strong, *Tudor and Jacobean Portraits*, 2 vols, London 1969, vol. 1, p. 315.

54 John Sugden, *Sir Francis Drake*, London 1996, pp. 89–157.

55 Helen Wallis, 'The cartography of Drake's voyage' in Norman Turner (ed.), *Sir Francis Drake and the Famous Voyage, 1577–1580*, Los Angeles 1984, pp. 121–63.

56 Claire Jowitt, *The Culture of Piracy 1580–1630*, Farnham 2010, pp. 50–67.

57 Susan Reed, 'Notes: Sir Francis Drake', *Print Quarterly*, vol. 26, no. 3, 2009, pp. 274–5.

58 Christopher Harding, '"Hostis Humani Generis": the pirate as outlaw in the early modern law of the sea' in Claire Jowitt (ed.), *Pirates? The Politics of Plunder*, Basingstoke 2007, pp. 20–38; Juan de Castellajanos, *Discurso de el Capitán Francisco Draque*, edited by Angel Gonzalez Palencia, Madrid 1921, p. 91; Jowitt 2010, op. cit. in n. 56 above, p. 9.

59 The visit is recorded in the Archives of the Middle Temple: MT.1/MPA/3, p. 184.

60 Fisher 1974, op. cit. in n. 39 above, p. 108.

61 Ibid., p. 107.

62 Gloria Clifton, 'Globe making in the British Isles' in Elly Dekker (ed.), *Globes at Greenwich*, Oxford 1999, pp. 46–7.

63 Doran 2003, op. cit. in n. 8 above, cat. 131. For insights into Elizabeth I's relationship to maps as political tools see Peter Barber, 'Was Elizabeth I interested in maps – and did it matter?' *Transactions of the Royal Historical Society*, Sixth Series, vol. 14, 2004, pp. 185–98.

64 William Foster (ed.), *The Embassy of Sir Thomas Roe to the Court of the Great Mogul, 1615–1619*, Hakluyt Society, Second Series, London 1899, vol. 1, p. 108. On Jahangir's distinction between ranks in his court architecture see Stronge 2010, op. cit. in n. 29 above, p. 38 and pl. 28.

Chapter 2

1 'This survey of Shakespeare Country has traversed a rich district of middle England that was familiar to the great poet in his boyhood': J. Leyland,

Shakespeare Country, London 1900, p. 92.

2 See Peter Barber (ed.), *The Map Book*, London 2005, p. 112. For a map of Catholic northern Lancashire made entirely with governance in mind in 1590, see p. 130.

3 See Tarnya Cooper, *Searching for Shakespeare*, London 2006, cat. 9; P.D.A. Harvey and Harry Thorpe, *The Printed Maps of Warwickshire 1570–1900*, Warwick 1959, pp. 1–5 and 71–3.

4 Karen Hearn, *Marcus Gheerearts II: Elizabethan Artist in Focus*, London 2002, p. 12, fig. 3, and pp. 11–12 on his immigrant status; Karen Hearn (ed.), *Dynasties: Painting in Tudor and Jacobean England 1530–1630*, London 1995, cat. 45; Jonathan Bate, *Soul of the Age*, London 2008, p. 27.

5 See further *Reproductions of Early Engraved Maps, II, English County Maps in the Collection of the Royal Geographical Society*, London 1932, sheet 21, for another pack in the Royal Geographical Society. For this set see Gerard L'E. Turner, *Elizabethan Instrument Makers: The Origins of the London Trade in Precision Instrument Making*, Oxford 2000, cat. 26; and A.M. Hind, 'An Elizabethan pack of playing-cards', *British Museum Quarterly*, vol. 13, 1938, pp. 2–4.

6 For the bibliography on the tapestries, and debates on their history and origin see Hilary Turner, *No Mean Prospect: Ralph Sheldon's Tapestry Maps*, Tonypandy 2010, pp. 52–3, in addition to Turner 2000, op. cit. in n. 5 above, and Barber 2005, op. cit. in n. 2 above. See also John Humphreys, *Elizabethan Sheldon Tapestry Maps*, Oxford 1929. For the border designs see Anthony Wells-Cole, 'The Elizabethan Sheldon tapestry maps', *Burlington Magazine*, vol. 132, 1990, pp. 392–401 and his *Art and Decoration in Elizabethan and Jacobean England*, New Haven and London 1997, pp. 221–34. We would like to thank Clare Browne, Helen MacLagan, Maggie Wood, Hillary Turner, Nick Millea, Richard Ovenden and Bruce Barker-Benfield for their advice regarding these tapestries.

7 The other most important set of tapestries is the group commissioned by Lord Effingham to show the Spanish Armada in 1593. These do not survive, but they are recorded in J. Pine, *The Tapestry Hangings of the*

House of Lords, representing the several engagements between the English and Spanish Fleets, in the ever memorable year 1588, London 1739.

8 Sheldon was praised by the Earl of Leicester for providing local employment when Leicester recommended him to Warwick Town Council in the 1570s: 'I marvaile you do not devize some ways amongs you to have some special trade to kepe your poore on work as such as Sheldon of Beolye devised ... as a meanes to kepe our poore from Idelnes or making of clothe or capping or some such like' (*Black Book of Warwick*, transcribed and edited by T. Kemp, Warwick 1899, pp. 47–9). See also Hilary Turner, 'Tapestries once at Chastleton House and their influence on the image of the tapestries called Sheldon: a reassessment', *Antiquaries Journal*, vol. 88, 2008, pp. 313–46, for a revisionist argument.

9 Thomas Elyot, *The Book Named The Governour*, edited by S. Lehmberg, London 1962, p. 52.

10 Brendan Minney, OSB, 'The Sheldons of Beoley', *Worcestershire Recusant*, vol. 5, May 1965, pp. 1–17.

11 Michael Hodgetts, 'Coughton and the Gunpowder Plot' in Peter Marshall and Geoffrey Scott (eds), *Catholic Gentry in English Society: The Throckmortons of Coughton from Reformation to Emancipation*, Farnham 2009, pp. 93–122, esp. p. 121. He was also related to Sir Thomas Tresham, who built the triangular lodge at Rushton in honour of the Holy Trinity in 1594–7: see Hilary Turner, '"A wittle devise": the Sheldon tapestry maps belonging to the Bodleian Library, Oxford', *Bodleian Library Record*, vol. 17, no. 5, April 2002, pp. 23–313, esp. p. 308, for these connections.

12 Michael Snodin (ed.), *Horace Walpole's Strawberry Hill*, New Haven and London 2009, cat. 64.

13 They also seem unusually modern: roads are indicated in yellow. These do not appear in Saxton or generally on English maps until the 1670s, so this is a radical departure. Also not from Saxton are the fire beacons and windmills. See Barber 2005, op. cit. in n. 2 above, pp. 128–9. We are grateful to Peter Barber for his help in interpreting the Warwickshire map, and to Maggie Wood.

14 See Hodgetts 2009, op. cit. in n. 11 above, pp. 104–5, for the

Sheldons, the Throckmortons and the Gunpowder Plot.

15 See Peter Thornton, *Seventeenth-century Interior Decoration in England, France and Holland*, New Haven and London 1978, fig. 118, also fig. 126 for a Danish engraving of 1645 showing a bed resembling the Great Bed of Ware, which was mentioned by Shakespeare.

16 Noted by Phil Withington, *Society in Early Modern England*, Cambridge 2010, p. 88.

17 John Gerard, *The Autobiography of an Elizabethan*, translated from Latin by Philip Caraman, SJ, London, New York and Toronto 1951, p. xxiv.

18 See illustrated entry for 17 April in Gregory Doran, *A Shakespeare Almanac*, London 2009, p. 124, though not linked there with the tapestry.

19 *Treasure Annual Report 2005–6*, no. 847.

20 See further Alison Shell, *Shakespeare and Religion*, London 2010, p. 86; also Robert Bearman, 'John Shakespeare: a papist or just penniless?', *Shakespeare Quarterly*, vol. 56, no. 4, Winter 2005, pp. 411–33.

21 See Joseph Strutt, *Sports and Pastimes of the People of England*, London 1801, p. 26, for Milan bells, made of silver, which had a particularly sweet tone.

22 Gerard 1951, op. cit. in n. 17 above, p. 15.

23 Peter Levi, *The Life and Times of William Shakespeare*, London 1988, pp. 8–9; woodcut illustration in Doran 2009, op. cit. in n. 18 above, p. 153.

24 Russell Fraser, *Young Shakespeare*, New York 1988, p. 34.

25 See Bate 2008, op. cit. in n. 4 above, pp. 55–9.

26 Quoted in ibid., p. 57.

27 Quoted from Levi 1988, op. cit. in n. 23 above, p. 62; see Doran 2009, op. cit. in n. 18 above, p. 365, for further references to London flowers cited by Gerard.

28 Alexandra Walsham, *The Reformation of the Landscape*, Oxford 2011, pp. 311–12.

29 See Dorothy M. Meads (ed.), *The Diary of Lady Margaret Hoby 1599–1605*, Cambridge 1930, pp. 66, 117 and 120, for examples; see also Walsham 2011, op. cit. in n. 28 above, p. 249.

30 The Jane Bostocke sampler in the Victoria and Albert Museum, London, T516–1960, has not only Bostocke's name and date 1598,

but also Alice Lee's name with her birthdate of 1596: see Donald King and Santina Levey, *The Victoria & Albert Museum's Textile Collections: Embroidery in Britain from 1200 to 1750*, London 1993, cat. 47; and Lisa M. Klein, 'Your humble handmaid: Elizabethan gifts of needlework', *Renaissance Quarterly*, vol. 50, 1997, pp. 459–93.

31 King and Levey 1993, op. cit. in n. 30 above, cat. 52.

32 Ann Rosalind Jones and Peter Stallybrass, *Renaissance Clothing and the Materials of Memory*, Cambridge 2000, pp. 134–65.

33 Quoted in ibid., p. 143; see Andrew Morrall and Melinda Watt (eds), *English Embroidery from the Metropolitan Museum of Art*, '*Twixt Art and Nature*', New York 2008, p. 174 and cat. 31, for a fine example of a jacket like the one illustrated here.

34 North in Morrall and Watt 2008, op. cit. in n. 33 above, p. 47.

35 One of three copies recorded, British Museum, PD 1952,5-22,1-48; see also Ellen Power's needlework pattern book of the late sixteenth century in the British Museum, PD 1975,U.1589, for which see Kim Sloan, *A Noble Art*, London 2000, no. 36.

36 Avril Hart and Susan North, *Historical Fashion in Detail*, London 1998, pp. 22 and 24.

37 For Margaret Laton and her jacket see North in Morrall and Watt 2008, op. cit. in n. 33 above, p. 42 and figs 3–5; see also Susan North and Jenny Tiramani, *Seventeenth-century Women's Dress Patterns, Book 1*, London 2011, pp. 22–33. William Larkin's portrait of Lady Thornhagh, at the age of seventeen in 1617, shows her wearing a lowcut version with matching skirt (sold on the London art market in 2008). Isaac Oliver's miniature of his wife, Elizabeth Harding, which dates from 1610–15, shows her wearing a higher-necked version, or one tied at the neck with the addition of a lace-edged collar: see Hearn 1995, op. cit. in n. 4 above, cat. 83.

38 She is much more grandly dressed than the woman who wore the pregnancy jacket would have been, but there is no doubting the pregnancy enhanced by the loops of pearls across her belly. See Hearn 2002, op. cit. in n. 4 above, p. 46 for this picture and p. 44 for the jacket.

39 http://www.bergercollection. org/?id=5&artwork_id=74.

40 Roy Strong, *Tudor and Jacobean Portraits*, 2 vols, London 1969, vol. 1, p. 66; Cooper 2006, op. cit. in n. 3 above, cat. 80.

41 Quoted in John Murdoch, Jim Murrell, Patrick J. Noon and Roy Strong, *The English Miniature*, New Haven and London 1981, p. 71. On this celebrated miniature see further Roy Strong, *The English Renaissance Miniature*, London 1983, pp. 180–4.

42 The first landscape painting by an English-born painter is probably Sir Nathaniel Bacon's little oil painting on copper of the 1620s, which owes much to Dutch and Flemish prototypes. It was documented in the Tradescant Collection in Oxford in 1656, part of the founding collection of the Ashmolean Museum in Oxford in 1683. See Hearn 1995, op. cit. in n. 4 above, cat. 114; also Arthur MacGregor, *Tradescant's Rarities*, Oxford 1983, no. 254.

43 See the work of Francesco Xanto Avelli, Italian Renaissance potter, and his followers in Dora Thornton and Timothy Wilson, *Italian Renaissance Ceramics: A Catalogue of the British Museum Collection*, 2 vols, London 2009, vol. 1, cats 157, 167 and 171; for poking fun at lovers and pornographic imagery on ceramic, see Andrea Bayer (ed.), *Art and Love in Renaissance Italy*, New York 2008, cats 21 and 110–11. Something of the imagery of sexually suggestive fruit is hinted at on the London pot here.

44 Michael Archer, *Delftware: A Catalogue of the Collection in the Victoria and Albert Museum*, London 1997, no. C.1. For growth of the delftware industry in London from archaeological evidence see Kieron Tyler, Ian Betts and Roy Stephenson, *London's Delftware Industry*, London 2008, pp. 8–19. Compare the jug in the British Museum with Samson and the Lion, probably made in the same workshop in Southwark, also *c*. 1620: see Aileen Dawson, *English and Irish Delftware*, London 2010, cat. 33.

45 It is curious that scholars do not quite know what to make of the misericords: 'not easily parsed', says Russell Fraser in Fraser 1988, op. cit. in n. 24 above, p. 19; 'broadly humorous or even satirical' says Alison Shell in Shell 2010, op. cit. in n. 20 above, p. 1.

46 *Robin Good-Fellow, His Mad Prankes, and Merry Jests: full of honest mirth, and is a fit medicine for melancholy. Printed at London: By Thomas Cotes,*

and are to be sold by Francis Groue, at this shop on Snow-hill, neere the Sarazens head.

47 See Jonathan Bate in Val Horsler, Martin Gorick and Paul Edmondson, *Shakespeare's Church: A Parish for the World*, London 2010, introduction p. 10.

48 Robert Plot, *The Natural History of Staffordshire*, Oxford 1686, p. 434. James Campbell (ed.), *The Anglo-Saxons*, Oxford 1982, p. 241, fig. 206.

49 For growing antiquarian interest in tenurial objects in the sixteenth century, see John Cherry, 'Symbolism and survival: medieval horns of tenure', *Antiquaries Journal*, vol. 69, 1989, pp. 111–18.

50 For the tree and its history see Esmond Harris, Jeanette Harris and N.D.G. James, *Oak: A British History*, Oxford 2003, p. 183, no. 299. It was at grid ref. SU 672.

51 Walsham 2011, op. cit. in n. 28 above, p. 531, as part of a discussion about invented landscape traditions.

52 For commentaries see Katherine Duncan-Jones, *Ungentle Shakespeare*, London 2001, pp. 91–103; Michael Wood, *In Search of Shakespeare*, London 2003, pp. 167–8; Levi 1988, op. cit. in n. 23 above, pp. 148–50; and Cooper 2006, op. cit. in n. 3 above, cats 54a and b, and 55.

53 Dethick's Grants X, 'A note of some new coates', fol. 28, no. 34 for the arms of 'Shakespeare ye Player by Garter'. See Folger Shakespeare Library, Washington, mss V.a.156 and V.a.350 for York Herald's complaint of 1602. For Garter and Clarenceux's reply to York Herald of 1602 see ms Ashmole 846, f. 50 in the Bodleian Library: for the text of all three mss see Samuel Schoenbaum, *William Shakespeare: A Documentary Life*, Oxford 1975, nos 131–3. For Dethick's careful response of 1602 see *Heralds' Commemorative Exhibition 1484–1934*, London 1936, reprinted 1970, no. 21. We are grateful to Clive Cheesman, Richmond Herald at the College of Arms, and to Robert Yorke, for showing us these documents and discussing them with us.

54 C.W. Scott-Giles, *Shakespeare's Heraldry*, London 1950, pp. 36–8; *Heralds' Commemorative Exhibition*, op. cit. in n. 53 above, cat. 18; Schoenbaum 1975, op. cit. in n. 53 above, pp. 167–71, docs 128–9.

55 Scott-Giles 1950, op. cit. in n. 54 above, pp. 38–9; Schoenbaum 1975,

op. cit. in n. 53 above, docs 130 and 171.

56 Quoted in Doran 2009, op. cit. in n. 18 above, p. 180.

Chapter 3

1 Thomas Thomas, *Dictionarium Linguae Latinae et Anglicanae*, 1587, s.v. Monimentum, vel monumentum.

2 *Pierce Pennilesse, his Supplication to the Devil*, London 1592, reprinted Edinburgh 1966, p. 87.

3 For royal tombs in medieval and Tudor England see Philip Lindley, 'Collaboration and competition: Torrigiano and royal tomb commissions' in his collection of essays, *Gothic to Renaissance*, Stamford 1995, pp. 47–72.

4 *A Mirroure for Magistrates*, London 1578, fol. 17. An interpolated passage absent from the original edition of 1559.

5 The accusation may be traced to a passage, written around the time when Henry Bullingbrook took power, that the chronicler Thomas Walsingham of St Albans inserted in a manuscript of *Historia Anglicana*, concerning Richard's elevation of one of his favourites, Robert de Vere, Earl of Oxford, to the title of Duke of Ireland in 1386: the phrase 'familiaritatis obscoenae' ('obscene familiarities') clearly implies sodomy. See George B. Stow, 'Richard II in Thomas Walsingham's Chronicles', *Speculum*, vol. 59, no. 1, January 1984, pp. 68–102, esp. p. 86.

6 Nigel Saul, *Richard II*, New Haven and London 1997.

7 Richard II's will, dated 16 April 1399: J.H. Harvey, *The Plantagenets*, London 1967, Appendix II, pp. 221–4 (translated from the original Latin).

8 John Cherry and Neil Stratford, 'Westminster kings and the medieval Palace of Westminster', British Museum Occasional Paper 115, London 1995, pp. 68–73.

9 For the high probability that it was William Shakespeare, not his father John, who went to London in 1588 to instruct Harborne in the case, see Jonathan Bate, *Soul of the Age*, London 2008, pp. 318–23.

10 We are grateful to Pamela Tudor-Craig, Lady Wedgwood, for letting us read her unpublished lecture, 'Richard II: the truth and the tragedy', in which she argues that 'Shakespeare could have known, must

have known, the effigies' of Richard and Anne.

11 Dillian Gordon (ed.), *Making and Meaning: The Wilton Diptych*, London 1993. The medieval historian Nigel Saul calls Shakespeare 'Richard's greatest interpreter' in *Richard II and Chivalric Kingship, inaugural lecture series Royal Holloway College London, 24 November 1998*, London 1999, p. 23.

12 Quoted by Caroline Barron, 'Richard II, image and reality' in Gordon 1993, op. cit. in n. 11 above, p. 13.

13 John Cherry, 'The Dunstable Swan Jewel', *Journal of the British Archaeological Association*, vol. 32, 1969, pp. 38–53; Cherry in Jonathan Alexander and Paul Binski (eds), *The Age of Chivalry*, London 1987, cat. 659; and James Robinson, *Masterpieces of Medieval Art*, London 2008, pp. 172–3.

14 Cherry and Stratford 1995, op. cit. in n. 8 above, p. 94.

15 Silke Ackermann and John Cherry, 'Richard II, John Holland and three medieval quadrants', *Annals of Science*, vol. 56, 1999, pp. 3–23, esp. p. 20.

16 The original was destroyed in the 1850s so casts are the only evidence for the corbels: see Cherry and Stratford 1995, op. cit. in n. 8 above, p. 66. The hart also appears on an Ashanti ewer (British Museum, PE 1896,07-27.1), dating to 1377–99, which was found in 1895 at the palace of the Ashanti king Prempeh at Kumasi, in what is now Ghana: see Hercules Read, 'Bronze jug', *Proceedings of the Society of Antiquaries of London*, Second Series, vol. 17, 1898, pp. 82–7.

17 The diptych is first recorded in 1639 in the collection of Charles I who had received it in exchange for a portrait of himself. See Barron 1993, op. cit. in n. 12 above, p. 13; and Pamela Tudor-Craig, 'The Wilton Diptych in the context of contemporary English panel and wall-painting' in Dillian Gordon, Lisa Monnas and Caroline Elam (eds), *The Regal Image of Richard II and the Wilton Diptych*, London 1997, p. 222, as well as p. 19 for the reference in Dillian Gordon's Introduction to the painting's ownership by Charles I. Our thanks to Pamela Tudor-Craig for her memory of seeing the orb under the microscope.

18 For the tomb see Philip Lindley, 'Absolutism and regal image in Riccardian sculpture' in Gordon,

Monnas and Elam 1997, op. cit. in n. 17 above, pp. 61–83, esp. pp. 61–74.

19 Susie Nash (ed.), *Andre Beauneveu, 'No Equal in Any Land' – Artist for the Courts of France and Flanders*, London 2007, pp. 182–3 and fig. 92. She rejects the former attribution to Beauneveu of this portrait.

20 It was heavily restored in 1732 and again in 1866, when it was given its frame, decorated with Richard II's arms and badges, by Sir Gilbert Scott: see Cherry and Stratford 1995, op. cit. in n. 8 above, p. 91. For the portrait see J.H. Harvey, 'The Wilton Diptych, a re-examination', *Archaeologia*, vol. 97, 1961, pp. 1–28, esp. p. 12, n. 2; Frederick Hepburn, *Portraits of the Later Plantagenets*, Woodbridge 1986, pp. 12–3; Pamela Tudor-Craig in Alexander and Binski 1987, op. cit. in n. 13 above, cat. 713, p. 518; Paul Binski, *Westminster Abbey and the Plantagenets: Kingship and the Representation of Power 1200–1400*, New Haven and London 1995, pp. 203–4; Jonathan Alexander, 'The portrait of Richard II in Westminster Abbey' in Gordon, Monnas and Elam 1997, op. cit. in n. 17 above, pp. 197–231.

21 Alexander 1997, op. cit. in n. 20 above, p. 206.

22 See Ernest Kantorowicz's classic study, *The King's Two Bodies: A Study in Medieval Political Theology*, Princeton 1957.

23 Lawrence Tanner, *The History of the Coronation*, London [no date], p. 25; Alice Hunt, *The Drama of Coronation: Medieval Ceremony in Early Modern England*, Cambridge 2008; Janette Dillon, 'The monarch as represented in the ceremony of coronation' in Alessandra Petrina and Laura Tosi (eds), *Representations of Elizabeth I in Early Modern Culture*, Basingstoke 2011, pp. 125–39.

24 Tony Trowles, *Treasures of Westminster Abbey*, London 2008, p. 68.

25 See Barron 1993, op. cit. in n. 12 above, p. 19. For the the text of the epitaph in English see Lindley in Gordon, Monnas and Elam 1997, op. cit. in n. 17 above, p. 72.

26 Quoted in Binski 1995, op. cit. in n. 20 above, p. 204.

27 J. Weever, *Ancient Funeral Monuments*, London 1631. The original position of the panel is, however, unknown. For the suggestion that it might have been in the Palace of Westminster, see Binski 1995, op. cit. in n. 20 above,

p. 203.

28 P. Tudor Craig in Alexander and Binski 1987, op. cit. in n. 13 above, cat. 713, but that might refer to a sixteenth-century copy, not the original painting: see Jonathan Alexander in Gordon, Monnas and Elam 1997, op. cit. in n. 17 above, p. 335, n. 18.

29 *Memoirs of William Lambarde, Esq., an eminent lawyer and antiquary* in *Bibliotheca Topographica Britannica*, London 1780–90, pp. 493–503, Appendix VII, pp. 525–6.

30 On the necessity for a degree of scepticism over the full veracity of Lambarde's report, and for the probable true meaning of the queen's remark (if she made it), see Bate 2008, op. cit. in n. 9 above, pp. 282–6.

31 See Roy Strong, *Artists of the Tudor Court*, London 1983, cat. 211, for the miniature by Hilliard, its basis on a lost portrait miniature, perhaps by Lavinia Teerlinc, and its relationship to the National Portrait Gallery portrait. See also Janet Arnold, 'The "Coronation" portrait of Elizabeth I', *Burlington Magazine*, vol. 120, 1978, p. 7. We are grateful to Tarnya Cooper and Catherine McLeod for these references.

32 Stephen Orgel, 'Prologue: I am Richard II' in Petrina and Tosi 2011, op. cit. in n. 23 above, pp. 1–43, suggests that the portrait of Richard II is the prototype for the portrait of Elizabeth I in her coronation robes.

33 Copies of this portrait are in Lumley Castle and Leeds Castle: see Catherine Macleod, Tarnya Cooper and Margaret Zolles, 'The portraits' in Mark Evans (ed.), *Art Collecting and Lineage in the Elizabethan Age: The Lumley Inventory and Pedigree*, The Roxburghe Club 2010, pp. 59–70, esp. pp. 22 and 61, fig. 36. We are grateful to Richard Scarbrough for his permission to publish a photograph of the Lumley Castle version.

34 Roy Strong, *The Elizabethan Icon*, London and New York 1969, p. 46.

35 David Gaimster, Bernard Nurse and Julia Steele (eds), *Making History: Antiquaries in Britain 1707–2007*, London 2007, cat. 50.

36 Claude Blair in Richard Marks and Paul Williamson (eds), *Gothic: Art for England 1400–1547*, London 2003, cat. 40; Robinson 2008, op. cit. in n. 13 above, pp. 170–1.

37 Quoted in Pamela Tudor-Craig, *Richard III*, London 1973, cat. P40. The account of the portrait

given here is partly derived from the forthcoming *Catalogue of Paintings in the Collection of the Society of Antiquaries of London* by Jill Franklin, Bernard Nurse and Pamela Tudor-Craig. This material has kindly been made available in advance of publication by the Society of Antiquaries and all copyright is reserved by the Society. We are grateful to Pamela Tudor-Craig, Kate Owen and Maurice Howard, President of the Society of Antiquaries, for their assistance.

38 A raised right shoulder for Richard III mentioned by John Herd in Thomas Purnell (ed.), *Historia Quatuor Regum Angliae*, London 1868, p. 133, which was dedicated to William Cecil in 1562. See Tudor-Craig 1973, op. cit. in n. 37 above, cat. P44; and Maria Hayward, *The 1542 Inventory of Whitehall, The Palace and its Keeper*, 2 vols, Society of Antiquaries, London 2004, vol. 1, p. 93, item 746.

39 Gaimster *et al.* 2007, op. cit. in n. 35 above, cat. 49; Hepburn 1986, op. cit. in n. 20 above, pp. 71–89. Another example in The Royal Collection is in Windsor Castle.

40 William Catesby as Cat, Sir Richard Ratcliffe as Rat and Viscount Lovell as Dog: see Marks and Williamson 2003, op. cit. in n. 36 above, p. 205.

41 Tudor-Craig 1973, op. cit. in n. 37 above, p. 60.

42 Brian Spencer, *Pilgrim Badges and Secular Badges: Medieval Finds from Excavations in London*, vol. 7, London 1998, p. 289, no. 281h. For the York example see Marks and Williamson 2003, op. cit. in n. 36 above, cat. 69.

43 W. Scott, LEIC-A6C834, 2009, 'A Medieval badge'. From the report: 'The badge was found during the search for the battle of Bosworth field and provides good evidence for the presence of a member of the king's personal household in the area. It thus adds weight to the other archaeological evidence, which has now located the battlefield.' Treasure case number 2009T480; Museum accession number at Bosworth Battlefield Museum X.A19.2011.

44 Gaimster *et al.* 2007, op. cit. in n. 35 above, cat. 83; John Nichols, *The History and Antiquities of the County of Leicester* 4 (part 2), 1811, p. 557 and pl. 91; Colum Hourihane, 'The processional cross in late medieval England: the Dallye Cross', *Reports of the Research Committee of the Society of Antiquaries of London*, vol. 71,

45 London 2005, p. 99.

45 Trowles 2008, op. cit. in n. 24 above, pp. 70–1.

46 W.H. St John Hope, 'The Funeral, Monument and Chantry Chapel of King Henry the Fifth', *Archaeologia*, vol. 65, 1914, pp. 129–87, esp. p. 152.

47 We are grateful to Tony Trowles and Christine Reynolds for details from the Archive of Westminster Abbey of these alterations and the service held to commemorate them in 1971, at which Laurence Olivier declaimed the St Crispin's Day speech from *Henry V* in the Abbey.

48 Claude Blair in Alexander and Binski 1987, op. cit. in n. 13 above, cats 626–33.

49 Henry Keepe, *Monumenta Westmonasteriensa*, London 1682.

50 See St John Hope 1914, op. cit. in n. 46 above, p. 180 and pl. XVI, for a drawing of 1707 showing Henry's arms surmounted by the leopard crest above the cap of estate, but no helm or saddle, supported on the crossbeam. Lisa Monnas, 'Textiles from the funerary achievements of Henry V' in J. Stratford (ed.) *The Lancastrian Court, Proceedings of the 2001 Harlaxton Symposium*, Donnington 2003, p. 139; Blair 2003, op. cit. in n. 36 above, cat. 54a.

51 For the achievements as a group see St John Hope 1914, op. cit. in n. 46 above, p. 181; Monnas 2003, op. cit. in n. 50 above; Blair 2003, op. cit. in n. 36 above, cat. 54a–c. The quotation is from Monnas 2003, p. 140. For individual pieces see the catalogue section here.

52 James Shapiro, *1599: A Year in the Life of William Shakespeare*, London 2005, p. 82.

53 Camden, *Britannia*, quoted from the 1637 edition of Philemon Holland's English translation, p. 683.

54 Shapiro 2005, op. cit. in n. 52 above, p. 111.

55 See http://www.lib.ed.ac.uk/about/bgallery/Gallery/researchcoll/ireland. html for this specific copy of the text with its original woodcuts. For Drummond and his Shakespeare reading see James Shapiro, *Contested Will: Who Wrote Shakespeare?*, London 2010, pp. 269–70: in his manuscript library catalogue of 1611 Drummond listed *Venus and Adonis* and *Lucrece*, attributing both to 'Shaksp'.

56 See Peter Thornton, *Seventeenth-century Interior Decoration in England, France and Holland*, New Haven and London 1978, pp. 112 and 255, for

'Waterford' or 'Irish rugges'. John Florio glosses the *Bernia* or 'Sbernia' as 'An Irish or seaman's rugge', 'An Irish rug or mantle', 'A kind of friar's poore garment or frocke': see Peter Thornton, *The Italian Renaissance Interior*, London 1991, p. 162.

57 Ania Loomba, *Shakespeare, Race and Colonialism*, Oxford 2002, p. 18.

58 Karen Hearn (ed.), *Dynasties: Painting in Tudor and Jacobean England 1530–1630*, London 1995, cat. 120; and Hearn, *Marcus Gheerearts II: Elizabethan Artist in Focus*, London 2002, fig. 6 and pp. 18–19; Ann Rosalind Jones and Peter Stallybrass, *Renaissance Clothing and the Materials of Memory*, Cambridge 2000, pp. 50–2 and 289, n. 64.

59 Hiram Morgan, 'Tom Lee the posing peacemaker' in Brendan Bradshaw, Andrew Hadfield and Willy Maley (eds), *Representing Ireland: Literature and the Origins of Conflict 1534–1660*, Cambridge 1993, p. 132.

60 Michael Gaudio, 'The truth in clothing: the costume studies of John White and Lucas de Heere' in Kim Sloan (ed.), *European Visions: American Voices*, London 2009, pp. 24–32, and in particular pp. 25–6 for De Heere.

61 For the helmet see Angus Patterson, *Fashion and Armour in Renaissance Europe*, London 2009, pl. 43. For the blackwork shirt see Susan North, '"An instrument of profit, pleasure and of ornament": embroidered Tudor and Jacobean dress accessories' in Andrew Morrall and Melinda Watt (eds), *English Embroidery from the Metropolitan Museum of Art, 'Twixt Art and Nature'*, New York 2008, pp. 39–77, esp. p. 46, and figs 3–9 for the blackwork partlet and sleeves in the Victoria and Albert Museum.

62 Shapiro 2005, op. cit. in n. 52 above, p. 109.

63 Ibid., p. 101.

64 Shapiro 2005, op. cit. in n. 52 above, p. 74.

65 Shapiro 2005, op. cit. in n. 52 above, p. 114.

66 Paul Hamner, *The Polarisation of Elizabethan Politics*, Cambridge 1999, pp. 199–216.

67 For the Cadiz portrait see Hearn 2002, op. cit. in n. 58 above, fig. 4, p. 22, and fig. 13 for the Trinity College portrait.

68 Hearn 1995, op. cit. in n. 58 above, cat. 121.

Chapter 4

1 For an ingenious but highly speculative argument favouring *Julius Caesar* (and a date of 12 July 1599) on the basis of calendrical references, see Stephen Sohmer, *Shakespeare's Mystery Play: The Opening of the Globe Theatre 1599*, Manchester 1999.

2 See further Andrew Hadfield, *Shakespeare, Spenser and the Matter of Britain*, Basingstoke 2004, p. 10.

3 For the print series see Graham Parry, *The Golden Age Restor'd*, Manchester 1981; and Antony Griffiths, *The Print in Stuart Britain*, London 1998, cat. 3a. See also Thomas Dekker, *The Magnificent Entertainment*, London 1604.

4 For a balanced overview of the debate see Richard L. Levin, 'The Longleat Manuscript and *Titus Andronicus*', *Shakespeare Quarterly*, vol. 53, no. 3, Autumn 2002, pp. 323–40.

5 Martin Biddle in *The Renaissance at Sutton Place*, London 1983, cat. 91; Lindsay Stainton and Christopher White, *Drawing in England from Hilliard to Hogarth*, London 1987, cat. 1; Susan Doran (ed.), *Elizabeth I*, London 2003, cat. 96.

6 'Imaginary progress' as there is no evidence that she visited Nonsuch that year, 1568. The British Museum drawing relates to a second, more highly finished, drawing by Hoefnagel which was offered at Christie's, London, on 7 December 2010, lot 11, and exhibited in the Victoria and Albert Museums' *Gothic* exhibition (see Richard Marks and Paul Williamson [eds], *Gothic: Art for England 1400–1547*, London 2003, cat. 352). The elaborate coach in which Elizabeth I is shown in both drawings recalls a coach made in her reign and given by the Muscovy Company as a gift to the Tsar of Russia, Boris Godunov, in 1604: the coach is now in the Kremlin in Moscow: see Julian Munby, 'Queen Elizabeth's coaches: the wardrobe on wheels', *Antiquaries Journal*, vol. 83, 2003, pp. 311–67.

7 James Shapiro, *1599: A Year in the Life of William Shakespeare*, London 2005, p. 300.

8 This, OA 9184, and the other hornbook in the British Museum collection, PE 1937,1108.1, which dates from the sixteenth century, are exceptionally rare survivals. See Tarnya Cooper, *Searching for*

Shakespeare, London 2006, cat. 15. We are grateful to Annemarieke Willemsen of Nederland Middeleeuwen, Leiden, for her help in interpreting the British Museum examples.

9   Eton College Library, Fd.8.19, *Ovidii Nasonis metamorphoseon lib. xv. Ab Andrea Naugerio castigati, & Vict. Giselini scholiis illustrati ... Antverpiae, ex officina Christophori Plantini*, 1575 (though the drawing may belong to the late seventeenth century).

10 Nicholas Penny, *National Gallery Catalogues: The Sixteenth-century Italian Paintings, Volume 2, Venice 1540–1600*, London 2008, p. 278.

11 Phyllis Pray Bober and Ruth Rubinstein, *Renaissance Artists and Antique Sculpture*, London 1986, no. 94.

12 Penny 2008, op. cit. in n. 10 above, p. 286.

13 Dolce's letter to Contarini, in G.G. Bottari, *Raccolta di Lettere sulla Pittura, Scultura e Architettura*, 7 vols, Rome 1754–73, vol. 3, 1759 pp. 257–60. Translation from James Northcote, *The Life of Titian*, 2 vols, London 1830, vol. 1, p. 344. See discussion in C. Ginzburg, 'Tiziano, Ovidio ei codici della figurazione erotica nel '500', in *Tiziano e Venezia: Convegno internazionale di studi veneziani, 1976*, Vicenza 1980, pp. 125–35. Quoted also in Stanley Wells (ed.), *Shakespeare Found!: A Life Portrait at Last*, Stratford-upon-Avon 2011, p. 66.

14 'Ut faciem et posito corpus velamine vidit, / Quale meum, vel quale tuum, si femina fias, / Obstipuit.'

15 It is unlikely to have been painted in 1601–3 when the earl was imprisoned in the Tower, or after 1603 when he was created Knight of the Garter: R.W. Goulding, 'Wriothesley portraits authentic and reputed', *Walpole Society*, vol. 8, 1919–20, pp. 51–2.

16 Thom Richardson of the Royal Armouries, to whom we are extremely grateful for information about the armour, points out that it bears close comparison with a number of armours which are recorded as being of French manufacture. Two suits at Windsor Castle are broadly comparable, one said to have belonged to Charles I as Prince of Wales (no. 577) and the other (no. 786) to Henry, Prince of Wales – it seems to be depicted in a miniature of him limned by Isaac Oliver in

1607. See G.F. Laking, *The Armoury of Windsor Castle*, London 1904, pls 29 and 33.

17 Stuart Pyhrr and Thomas Richardson, 'The "Master of the Snails and Dragonflies" identified', *Journal of the Arms and Armour Society*, vol. 14, no. 4, September 1993, pp. 329–63.

18 See John Cunally, *Images of the Illustrious*, Princeton 1999, chapter 5, on this custom in Northern Europe, including England, in the sixteenth century.

19 Shapiro 2005, op. cit. in n. 7 above, p. 178.

20 Cassius Dio, *Historia Romana*, 47.25.1.

21 The *aureus* went on display at the British Museum in the Rome City and Empire gallery (Room 70) from the 'ides of March' 2010. This account of the coin is mainly provided by Ian Leins, Department of Coins and Medals, to whom we are most grateful. We would also like to thank Michael Winckless, a private collector and owner of the coin (who has generously lent it to the British Museum on a long-term basis), for his encouragement in interpreting it with reference to Shakespeare. An example of this coin once owned by George III and now in the British Museum has for some time been known to have been a fake. Another specimen owned by the Deutsche Bundesbank appears to be genuine.

22 See Maria Hayward, *Dress at the Court of King Henry VIII*, Leeds 2007, p. 278, on bonnets as part of the livery of the hunt. See also Hayward, '"The sign of some degree"?: the financial, social and sartorial significance of male headwear at the courts of Henry VIII and Edward VI', *Costume*, vol. 36, 2002, pp. 1–17; and Jane Malcolm-Davies, '"He is of no account ... if he have not a velvet or taffeta hat": a survey of 16th-century knitted caps', *Dress and Textile Specialists*, April 2011, pp. 21–5. See Cooper 2006, op. cit. in n. 8 above, cat. 13, for another cap found in Moorfields.

23 Andrew Gurr and Mariko Ichikawa, *Staging in Shakespeare's Theatres*, Oxford 2000, pp. 3–4.

24 We are grateful to William Sherman for this explanation of Dee's illuminated frontispiece to this manuscript.

25 See Robert Poole, 'John Dee and the English calendar: science, religion and empire', http://www.hermetic.ch/cal_

stud/jdee.html, further developed in his *Time's Alteration: Calendar Reform in Early Modern England*, London 1998. See also Benjamin Woolley, *The Queen's Conjuror: The Life and Magic of Dr Dee*, London 2002, p. 193. On Dee more generally, and especially his vision of a 'British empire', see William H. Sherman, *John Dee: The Politics of Reading and Writing in the English Renaissance*, Massachusetts 1995.

26 See Jonathan Bate, *Soul of the Age*, London 2008, p. 382.

27 For the imagery of the phoenix in relation to Elizabeth I see Jonathan Bate and Eric Rasmussen (eds), *William Shakespeare, Complete Works*, RSC, London 2007, p. 2,396 for Robert Chester and Shakespeare himself, and p. 2,343 for the mysterious poem now known as 'The Phoenix and the Turtle'.

28 Doran 2003, op. cit. in n. 5 above, cat. 204.

29 British Museum, CM 1856,0701.778.

30 Susan Walker and Peter Higgs (eds), *Cleopatra of Egypt: From History to Myth*, London 2001, cat. 135.

31 Walker and Higgs 2001, op. cit. in n. 30 above, cat. 210: compare with her profile portrait on the bronze eighty-drachma coin of Cleopatra, 51–30 BC, cat. 179.

32 Gaia Servadio, *Renaissance Woman*, London 2005, p. 40. Thomas Coryate admitted that a top Venetian courtesan was likely to prove 'a good Rhetorician, and a most elegant discourser, so that if she cannot move thee with all these foresaid delights, shee will assay thy constancy with her Rhetoricall tongue'.

33 Dora Thornton, *The Scholar in his Study: Ownership and Experience in Renaissance Italy*, New Haven and London 1997, pp. 92–3; Cathy Santore, 'Julia Lombardo, *somtuosa meretrize*: a portrait by property', *Renaissance Quarterly*, vol. 41, 1988, pp. 44–83.

34 Lynne Lawner, *Lives of the Courtesans*, New York 1987, p. 34.

35 Walker and Higgs 2001, op. cit. in n. 30 above, pp. 201–2 and 304 (fig. 11.1).

36 See Francis Haskell and Nicholas Penny, *Taste and the Antique*, New Haven and London 1982, no. 24, p. 187, for the Eliot quote.

37 For the critical history of the idea of Shakespeare's 'black Cleopatra' see Francesca T. Royster, *Becoming Cleopatra: The Shifting Image of an*

Icon, London 2003, chapter 2.

38 George Abbott, *A briefe description of the whole world wherein is particularly described all the monarchies, empires and kingdomes of the same, with their academies. As also their severall titles and situations thereunto adioyning. Written by the most Reverend Father in God, George, late Arch-bishop of Canterbury*, London 1599, reprinted 1636, p. 162.

39 John Rainolds, *Th'overthrow of stage-playes by the way of controversie betwixt D. Gager and D. Rainoldes wherein all the reasons that can be made for them are notably refuted; th'objections aunswered, and the case so cleared and resolved, as that the iudgement of any man, that is not froward and perverse, may easelie be satisfied. Wherein is manifestly proved, that it is not onely vnlawfull to bee an actor, but a beholder of those vanities. Wherevnto are added also and annexed in th'end certeine latine letters betwixt the sayed Maister Rainoldes, and D. Gentiles, reader of the civill law in Oxford, concerning the same matter*, London 1599, p. 77.

Chapter 5

1   Michael Wyatt, *The Italian Encounter with Tudor England*, Cambridge 2005, pp. 178 and 174–85 on the place of proverbs in language teaching in Elizabethan England.

2   John Hale, *England and the Italian Renaissance*, London 1964, pp. 18 and 28.

3   John Florio, *Florio his First Fruites which Yeelde Familiar Speech, Merie Proverbes, Wittie Sentences, and Golden Sayings*, London 1578, p. 34.

4   Lewis Lewkenor, translation of Gaspar Contareno, *The Commonwealth and Government of Venice*, London 1599, pp. 5–6; Brian Pullan, *The Jews of Europe and the Inquisition of Venice*, Oxford 1983, pp. 146 and 166.

5   Hale 1964, op. cit. in n. 2 above, p. 30.

6   Thomas Coryat, *Coryat's Crudities*, London 1611, p. 248.

7   Michelle O'Callaghan, 'Coryat's crudities and travel writing as the "eyes" of the prince' in Timothy Wilks (ed.), *Prince Henry Revived*, Southampton 2007, pp. 85–103.

8   Logan Pearsall Smith, *The Life and Letters of Sir Henry Wotton*, 2 vols, London 1907, vol. 1, p. 46. See also O'Callaghan 2007, op. cit. in n. 7

above, on Coryat's debt to Wotton.

9   Edward Chaney, *Evolution of the Grand Tour*, London and Portland, Oregon 1998, pp. 163–7, esp. 165–6 for the Italian text of the letter.

10 Wotton left these to Charles I: they are still in the Royal Collection. See Laura M. Walters, 'Odoardo Fialetti (1573–*c*. 1638): the interrelation of Venetian art and anatomy, and his importance in England', PhD thesis, University of St Andrews 2009, vol. 1, pp. 156–60 for portraits of Doges left to Charles I by Wotton in his will of 1637. For prints on the same subject see Michael Bury, *The Print in Italy 1550–1620*, London 2001, cat. 124.

11 Chaney 1998, op. cit. in n. 9 above, fig. 20; Walters 2009, op. cit. in n. 10 above, pp. 169–70.

12 'Henricus Wottonius, post tres apud Venetos legationes ordinarias, in Etonensis Collegii beato sinu senescens, eiusque, cum suavissima inter se sociosque concordia, annos iam 12 praefectus, hanc miram urbis quasi natantis effigiem in aliquam sui memoriam iuxta socialem mensam affixit. 1636': Pearsall Smith 1907, op. cit. in n. 8 above, p. 210.

13 The painting has recently been conserved thanks to the generosity of the Friends of Eton Collections.

14 Erckenprecht Coler, friendship album, British Library, Egerton MS 1208, fol. 19.

15 Patricia Fortini Brown, *Private Lives in Renaissance Venice*, New Haven and London 2004, p. 185.

16 John Hale, *The Civilisation of Europe in the Renaissance*, London 1993, p. 499. See Georgina Masson, *Courtesans of the Italian Renaissance*, London 1975, pp. 152–68, on Franco. Montaigne was not all that impressed by them on a visit in 1580: 'and yet he saw the noblest of those who make a traffic of it; but it seemed to him as wonderful as anything else to see such a number of them as a hundred and fifty or thereabouts spending like princesses on furnishings and clothes, having no other funds to live on except from this traffic; and many of the nobles of the place even keeping courtesans at their expense in the sight and knowledge of all.' *Montaigne's Travel Journal*, translated and with an introduction by Donald M. Frame, Stanford 1983, p. 56.

17 Fortini Brown 2004, op. cit. in n. 15 above, pp. 173–87; Cathy Santore, 'Julia Lombardo, *somtuosa meretrize*:

a portrait by property', *Renaissance Quarterly*, vol. 41, 1988, pp. 44–83. The Walens friendship album shows a courtesan leading her client into her bedchamber: British Library, Add. MS 18991, fol. 46.

18 See *Shakespeare's Europe; Unpublished Chapters of Fynes Moryson's Itinerary, Being a Survey of the Condition of Europe at the End of the 16th Century*, London 1903, p. 412, for an excellent analysis of the structure of the sex-trade in Venice.

19 Sara F. Matthews-Grieco with the assistance of Sabina Brevaglieri (eds), *Monaca, moglie, serva, cortigiana: vita e immagine delle donne tra Rinascimento e Controriforma*, Florence 2001, p. 91, with reference to the actress Isabella Andreini of the Gelosi company. See also Kathleen McGill, 'Women and performance: the development of improvisation by 16th century commedia dell'arte', *Theatre Journal*, vol. 43, 1991, pp. 59–69, esp. pp. 65–8.

20 *Shakespeare's Europe* 1903, op. cit. in n. 18 above, p. 412.

21 Margaret F. Rosenthal and Ann Rosalind Jones, *Cesare Vecellio's Habiti Antichi et Moderni: The Clothing of the Renaissance World. Europe, Asia, Africa, the Americas*, London 2008, p. 177. Fortini Brown 2004, op. cit. in n. 15 above, pp. 141–57; Wendy Thompson in Andrea Bayer (ed.), *Art and Love in Renaissance Italy*, New York 2008, cat. 64.

22 Rosenthal and Jones 2008, op. cit. in n. 21 above, pp. 190 and 195.

23 Many of them are dated in the albums, signed and inscribed by local dignitaries and visiting students, which indicate the kind of circulation these images had. See Rosenthal and Jones 2008, op. cit. in n. 21 above, p. 19; M. Nickson, *Early Autograph Albums in the British Museum*, London 1970; J.-U. Fechner, 'Some 16th century albums in the British Library', *Stammbücher als kulturhistorische Quellen*, Munich 1981; I. O'Dell, 'Jost Amman and the Album Amicorum: drawings after prints in autograph albums', *Print Quarterly*, vol. 9, 1992, pp. 31–6. J.I. Nevinson, in 'Illustrations of costume in the Alba Amicorum', *Archaeologia*, vol. 106, 1979, pp. 167–79, contests a relationship between costume prints and albums, which seems counterintuitive when looking at a number of them. See also n. 34 below.

24 Susan North, '"An instrument of profit, pleasure and of ornament": embroidered Tudor and Jacobean dress accessories' in Andrew Morrall and Melinda Watt (eds), *English Embroidery from the Metropolitan Museum of Art, 'Twixt Art and Nature'*, New York 2008, pp. 39–55, esp. p. 53; Will Fisher, *Materialising Gender in Early Modern English Literature and Culture*, Cambridge 2006, p. 36.

25 Fisher 2006, op. cit. in n. 24 above, pp. 181–2; Ann Rosalind Jones and Peter Stallybrass, *Renaissance Clothing and the Materials of Memory*, Cambridge 2000, pp. 203–6.

26 Rosenthal and Jones 2008, op. cit. in n. 21 above, p. 193.

27 Virginia Mason Vaughan, *Performing Blackness on English Stages 1500–1800*, Cambridge 2005, p. 59.

28 For this vizard mask and its find details see J. Cassidy, 'A post medieval mask', NARC-151A67 2010. It is possible that the mask was deliberately concealed within the building to bring good luck or ward off evil influences: see the Southampton University project at http://www.concealedgarments.org/information/. Such masks rarely survived; a later example is in Norwich Castle Museum, F.7.3.

29 Coryat 1611, op. cit. in n. 6 above, p. 261.

30 Elizabeth Semmelhack, *On a Pedestal: From Renaissance Chopines to Baroque Heels*, Toronto 2009, pp. 31 and 44. See also Elizabeth Bernhardt's webpage on Venetian chopines at http://homes.chass.utoronto.ca/~ebernhar/index.shtml.

31 Semmelhack 2009, op. cit. in n. 30 above, p. 56.

32 Coryat 1611, op. cit. in n. 6 above, p. 262.

33 Lynne Lawner, *Lives of the Courtesans*, New York 1987, pp. 20–21; Semmelhack 2009, op. cit. in n. 30 above, fig. 38; Linda Wolk-Simon in Bayer 2008, op. cit. in n. 21 above, cat. 103.

34 Rosenthal and Jones 2008, op. cit. in n. 21 above, p. 182.

35 Her underclothes symbolize the kind of boyish freedom and hermaphrodite appeal that Pietro Aretino archly celebrated in the courtesan La Zufolina: 'You are a man when you are chanced on from behind and a woman when seen from in front.' Fortini Brown 2004, op. cit. in n. 15 above, p. 185; Lawner 1987, op. cit.

in n. 33 above, p. 23.

36 See Peter Humfrey, Timothy Clifford, Aidan Weston-Lewis and Michael Bury (eds), *The Age of Titian: Venetian Renaissance Art from Scottish Collections*, Edinburgh 2004, cat. 169, for the Balfour Album. We are grateful to Jeremy Warren for this reference and to Iain Gordon-Brown for details of this particular miniature.

37 Fisher 2006, op. cit. in n. 24 above, p. 65.

38 Heather Wolfe (ed.), *Elizabeth Cary, Lady Falkland, Life and Letters*, Cambridge and Arizona 2001, p. 186.

39 Janet Arnold, *Queen Elizabeth's Wardrobe Unlock'd*, London 1988, pp. 214–15.

40 Karen Hearn (ed.), *Dynasties: Painting in Tudor and Jacobean England 1530–1630*, London 1995, cat. 130.

41 See Blake de Maria, *Becoming Venetian: Immigrants and the Arts in Early Modern Venice*, New Haven and London 2010, pp. 38–9, on English taste for Venetian objects and the Ragazzoni family presence in England as merchants.

42 Wyatt 2005, op. cit. in n. 1 above, pp. 252–4.

43 Lewkenor 1599, op. cit. in n. 4 above, p. 1.

44 For two German anti-Semitic broadsides of 1618 and *c*. 1615 see British Museum, PD 1880, 0710.895 and 1876, 0510,518. For analysis of the image of the Judensau (Jewish sow) in Frankfurt see Amos Elon, *Founder, Meyer Amschel Rothschild and his Time*, London 1996, p. 33.

45 Quoted in Ania Loomba, *Shakespeare, Race and Colonialism*, Oxford 2002, p. 160.

46 Pullan 1983, op. cit. in n. 4 above, p. 166.

47 Imtiaz Habib, *Black Lives in the English Archives, 1500–1677: Imprints of the Invisible*, Farnham 2008, p. 111.

48 W.D. Rubinstein, *A History of the Jews in the English-speaking World: Great Britain*, New York 1996, pp. 36–41. David S. Katz, *The Jews in the History of England*, Oxford 1994.

49 Pullan 1983, op. cit. in n. 4 above, p. xiv; James Shapiro, *Shakespeare and the Jews*, New York 1996, pp. 131–65.

50 Daniel Vitkus, 'Turning Turk in *Othello*: the conversion and damnation of the Moor', *Shakespeare*

Quarterly, vol. 48, no. 2, Summer 1997, pp. 145–76.

51 Shapiro 1996, op. cit. in n. 49 above, p. 183.

52 Daniel Friedenburg, *Jewish Medals from the Renaissance to the Fall of Napoleon*, New York 1970, p. 42; Philip Attwood, *Italian Medals c. 1530–1600 in British Public Collections*, London 2003, cat. 420.

53 Shapiro 1996, op. cit. in n. 49 above, pp. 184–5.

54 Cecil Roth, *A History of the Jews in England*, Oxford 1963, p. 14.

55 Katz 1994, op. cit. in n. 47 above, p. 108. Depictions of St William of Norwich, thought to have been murdered by Jews in 1144, survived the Reformation and can still be deciphered painted on at least five rood screens in East Anglian churches. The best of these are at Loddon in Norfolk (fig. 26 here), Eye in Suffolk and Maddermarket in Norwich (now in the Victoria and Albert Museum, 24.1894). Of these, only the Loddon screen shows William stretched out in a saltire-type cross on stakes as if crucified. The others show him with his attributes of sets of nails and a hammer. We are grateful to Lucy Wrapson for this information. For the Loddon screen see M.R. James and Augustus Jessop (eds), *The Life and Miracles of St William of Norwich by Thomas of Monmouth*, Cambridge 1896, frontispiece; and M.R. James, *Suffolk and Norfolk*, London and Toronto 1930, pp. 18–19 and 128. See also Andrew Moore and Margit Thøfner, *The Art of Faith: 3,500 Years of Art in Norfolk*, Norwich 2010, cat. 2.8.

56 Rubinstein 1996, op. cit. in n. 48 above, p. 39; see also Shapiro 1996, op. cit. in n. 49 above, pp. 43–88, on the interpretation of the expulsion.

57 Katz 1994, op. cit. in n. 48 above, p. 109; Shapiro 1996, op. cit. in n. 49 above, pp. 62–76. For Jewish rites observed in London within these communities see E.R. Samuel, 'Passover in Shakespeare's London', *Transactions of the Jewish Historical Society of England*, vol. 26, 1974–8, pp. 117–18.

58 This identification of the lamp as a Sabbath lamp is contested, though the argument for its use as a Jewish ritual object is made by Raphael Ralph Emanuel in 'The Society of Antiquaries' Sabbath lamp', *Antiquaries Journal*, 2000, pp. 308–15, by comparison with another lamp excavated in Bristol. Compare also a lamp in the Jewish Museum in New York, which was allegedly found in the Jewish quarter of Deutz, near Cologne: see Maurice Berger, *Masterworks of the Jewish Museum*, New York 2004, p. 94; David Mickenberg (ed.), *Songs of Glory: Medieval Art from 900–1500*, 1985, pp. 180–1; George Schoenberger, 'A silver Sabbath lamp from Frankfurt-on-the-Main' in Oscar Goetz (ed.), *Essays in Honour of Georg Swarzenski*, Chicago and Berlin 1951, p. 156, no. 23. It is to be hoped that a forthcoming publication of this and other lamps by Bruce Watson will illuminate the status and significance of these pieces.

59 Shapiro 1996, op. cit. in n. 49 above, p. 70; Hale 1993, op. cit. in n. 16 above, p. 167.

60 Kapparot, part of the festival of Yom Kippur: see Diane Wolfthal, *Picturing Yiddish: Gender, Identity and Memory in the Illustrated Yiddish Books of Renaissance Italy*, Leiden and Boston 2004, fig. 86b and pp. 96–101, for this 1600 illustrated edition of a Yiddish book of customs and its woodcut illustrations, which may have been designed, if not printed, by a Christian artist.

61 David Gaimster, Bernard Nurse and Julia Steele (eds), *Making History: Antiquaries in Britain 1707–2007*, London 2007, cat. 32.

62 Hale 1993, op. cit. in n. 16 above, p. 167.

63 Shapiro 1996, op. cit. in n. 49 above, pp. 13–42; Peter Berek, 'The Jew as Renaissance man', *Renaissance Quarterly*, vol. 51, 1998, pp. 128–62, esp. p. 128.

64 Katz 1994, op. cit. in n. 48 above, pp. 51–2.

65 For the medal of Grazia Nasi see Friedenburg 1970, op. cit. in n. 52 above, pp. 44–6; Attwood 2003, op. cit. in n. 52 above, cat. 591; and Stephen Sher (ed.), *The Currency of Fame*, New York 1994, cat. 67.

66 For London Marranos see Beverley Nenk, 'Public worship, private devotion: the crypto-Jews of Reformation England' in David Gaimster and Roberta Gilchrist (eds), *The Archaeology of Reformation*, Leeds 2003, pp. 204–20.

67 Katz 1994, op. cit. in n. 48 above, pp. 104–7; Dominic Green, *The Double Life of Dr Lopez*, London 2004; Rubinstein 1996, op. cit. in n. 48 above, p. 44.

68 Green 2004, op. cit. in n. 67 above, p. 4; Shapiro 1996, op. cit. in n. 49 above, p. 185.

69 Prints showing Lopez plotting appeared first in *Popish Plots and Treasons from the Age of Elizabeth* in 1606 and then in George Carleton's *A Thankfull Remembrance of God's Mercy* in 1627. See Shapiro 1996, op. cit. in n. 49 above, p. 250, n. 136; and Katz 1994, op. cit. in n. 48 above, pp. 102–5, for later dramatic references to Lopez as villain.

70 Lancelot Andrewes, 'A sermon preached before the king's majesty at Whitehall on the fifth of November 1606' in *Ninety-Six Sermons by the Right Honourable and Reverend Father in God Lancelot Andrewes*, 5 vols, Oxford 1841, vol. 4, p. 204. For the growing British identification with the Jews as the chosen nation in this period see Achsah Guibbory, *Christian Identity, Jews and Israel in Seventeenth-century England*, Oxford 2010, pp. 21–55.

71 See Lancelot Andrewes, *XCXI Sermons*, London 1629, pp. 844ff., for this sermon. We are grateful to James Shapiro for this reference.

72 Henry invited Marco Raphael, a Venetian Jew, to England in 1530–1 to help him root his divorce from Catherine of Aragon in the Book of Leviticus: see Katz 1994, op. cit. in n. 48 above, pp. 15–48; see also Susan Doran (ed.), *Henry VIII: Man and Monarch*, London 2009, p. 108 and cat. 114.

73 The medal is the first undoubted English official medal, and was significant enough for Noukious Nikander to record its making, weight and inscription in detail: 'from that time forward the English have alienated themselves from the domination of the Roman pontiff and perform their ecclesiastical ceremonies in a peculiar manner'. See G. Lloyd-Jones, *The Discovery of Hebrew in Tudor England: A Third Language*, Manchester 1983, pp. 190–215. For the medal see Mark Jones, 'The medal in Britain', *Médailles*, 22nd Congress, Helsinki 1990, p. 18; Richard Bishop, 'Hebraica Veritas', in *Auction Insider*, Spink, London, Autumn 2009, p. 20; and Barrie Cook in Richard Marks and Paul Williamson (eds), *Gothic: Art for England 1400–1547*, London 2003, cat. 353. In *Gothic* it is attributed to Henry Basse, Chief Engraver at the Royal Mint in London. See also Philip Attwood, 'The medallic tradition – what is it?', *Médailles*, 2010, p. 90.

74 Lloyd-Jones 1983, op. cit. in n. 73 above, p. 272.

75 Alison Shell and Arnold Hunt, 'Donne's religious world' in Achsah Guibbory (ed.), *John Donne*, Cambridge 2006, pp. 65–82, esp. p. 66.

76 Shapiro 1996, op. cit. in n. 49 above, p. 103.

77 Norman Jones, *God and the Moneylenders: Usury and Law in Early Modern England*, Oxford 1989, pp. 145–74; Craig Muldrew, *The Economy of Obligation: The Culture of Credit and Social Relations in Early Modern England*, Basingstoke 1998.

78 Michael Wood, *In Search of Shakespeare*, London 2003, p. 217.

79 Coryat 1611, op. cit. in n. 6 above, p. 232.

80 For Jewish custom and three fourteenth-century rings set with miniature buildings symbolizing the Temple of Jerusalem see Christine Descatoire (ed.), *Treasures of the Black Death*, London 2009, pp. 60–1, cats 1–3. A fine fifteenth-century example has been in the Munich Kunstkammer since it was recorded in an inventory of 1598: *Schatzkammer der Residenz München*, Munich 1992, no. 52. For later rings of a second type with filigree and enamel see Hugh Tait, *Catalogue of the Waddesdon Bequest, The Jewels*, London 1986, cat. 51; and Diana Scarisbrick and Martin Henig, *Finger Rings*, Oxford 2003, pl. 17. Some of these may be seventeenth-century but many may be later, since they were popular with collectors in the nineteenth century.

81 Three sixteenth-century rings in the Victoria and Albert Museum cover this range: see 955-1871 for a child's ring; M-2-1959 for a ring with initials and a heart; and M.281-1962 for a Netherlandish gimmel ring associated with marriage and with an appropriate inscription.

82 Jonathan Bate, introduction to *The Merchant of Venice* in Jonathan Bate and Eric Rasmussen (eds), *William Shakespeare, Complete Works*, RSC, London 2007, p. 415.

83 Shakespeare does not mention the Ghetto or the curfew in Venice, nor the rule that Jews should wear a red cap out of doors, but it is not possible to tell whether this is ignorance, lack

of concern for detail or the absence of fine-tuning. We are grateful to Kate Lowe for her comments here.

84 Shylock refers to 'my Jewish gabardine', which might be a long outer garment like that worn by Sephardic Jews in the Ottoman Turkish Empire or in Spain: see Cecil Roth, *A History of the Jews in Venice*, Philadelphia 1930, p. 171. John Gillies suggests a gabardine resembled Tom's blanket in Lear: see John Gillies, *Shakespeare and the Geography of Difference*, Cambridge 1994, pp. 96–7.

85 Ilana Tahan in Rickie Burman, Jennifer Marin and Lily Steadman (eds), *Treasures of Jewish Heritage, The Jewish Museum, London*, London 2006, p. 62.

86 Ibid., p. 144.

87 Eva Frojmovic, 'The perfect scribe and an early engraved Esther scroll', *British Library Journal*, vol. 23, no. 1, Spring 1997, pp. 68–80; Ilana Tahan, *Hebrew Manuscripts: The Power of Script and Image*, London 2007, cats 137–8. Wolfthal 2004, op. cit. in n. 60 above, also points out that the printing revolution enabled collaboration between Jews and Christians in making books of customs like the one referred to here.

88 Piet van Boxel and Sabine Arndt, *Crossing Borders: Hebrew Manuscripts as a Meeting-place of Cultures*, Oxford 2009, p. 14.

89 Hale 1993, op. cit. in n. 16 above, p. 167; Loomba 2002, op. cit. in n. 45 above, p. 71.

90 Katz 1994, op. cit. in n. 48 above, p. 106, citing A.F. Pollard. Loomba 2002, op. cit. in n. 45 above, pp. 141–2.

91 Jonathan Bate, *Soul of the Age*, London 2008, p. 148.

92 One famous troupe, the Gelosi, acted for Henri III of France when he was in Venice in 1574; he invited them to France as the first of many Italian touring troupes of players in the country, who played to elite audiences: see Charles Sterling, 'Early paintings of the *Commedia dell'arte* in France', *Metropolitan Museum of Art Journal*, vol. 2, no. 1, Summer 1943, pp. 11–32.

93 Teresa J. Faherty, 'Othello dell'arte: the presence of *Commedia* in Shakespeare's tragedy', *Theatre Journal*, vol. 43, 1991, pp. 179–84, esp. p. 181.

94 M.M. Mahood (ed.), *The Merchant of Venice*, Cambridge 2003, p. 12.

95 'An fugitant lucem, si bene quid faciunt!': see Fortini Brown 2004, op. cit. in n. 15 above, p. 186.

96 Mason Vaughan 2005, op. cit. in n. 27 above, p. 59; Joan Pong Linton, *The Romance of the New World*, Cambridge 1998, p. 30.

97 Claire Jowitt, *The Culture of Piracy 1580–1630*, Farnham 2010, pp. 126–7.

98 De Maria 2010, op. cit. in n. 41 above, p. 43.

99 Ibid., p. 43.

100 Loomba 2002, op. cit. in n. 45 above, p. 90.

101 Habib 2008, op. cit. in n. 47 above, pp. 84–5 and 110–11. But see also Jonathan Schorsch, *Jews and Blacks in the Early Modern World*, New York 2004, pp. 56–8.

102 Habib 2008, op. cit. in n. 47 above, pp. 95 and 102.

Chapter 6

1 Virginia Mason Vaughan, *Othello: A Contextual History*, Cambridge 1994, and *Performing Blackness on English Stages 1500–1800*, Cambridge 2005; Alden T. Vaughan and Virginia Mason Vaughan, 'Before *Othello*: Elizabethan representations of sub-Saharan Africans', *The William and Mary Quarterly*, vol. 54, no. 1, 1997, pp. 19–44; Mary Floyd-Wilson, *English Ethnicity and Race in Early Modern Drama*, Cambridge 2003; Ania Loomba, *Shakespeare, Race and Colonialism*, Oxford 2002.

2 Jonathan Bate, introduction to *Titus Andronicus*, Arden Shakespeare, London and New York 1995, p. 41; Mason Vaughan 2005, op. cit. in n. 1 above, p. 48.

3 For tawny Moors in contemporary imagining see John Pory (trans.), *The History and Description of Africa* by Leo Africanus, edited by Robert Brown, 3 vols, Hakluyt Society, London 1896, vol. 1, pp. 131–2.

4 Angus Patterson, *Fashion and Armour in Renaissance Europe*, London 2009, p. 62.

5 See ibid., p. 62, for Greene. We are grateful to Angus Patterson for information on rapiers in the Victoria and Albert Museum and their context.

6 A fine English rapier of around 1600 in the Victoria and Albert Museum bears spurious marks for Toledo and Milan, another famous centre for armourers (M.51-1947).

7 See Tobias Capwell, *The Real Fighting Stuff: Arms and Armour at Glasgow Museums*, Glasgow 2007, pp. 58–64, esp. p. 62, no. 27, for an extremely fine rapier with blade signed by Juan Martinez of Toledo, late sixteenth century.

8 We are grateful to Tobias Capwell for these interpretations; also to Ralph Moffat and Thom Richardson for help both in tracing surviving rapiers for us to consider and finding the relevant literature.

9 Daniel Vitkus, *Turning Turk: English Theatre and the Multicultural Mediterranean*, New York and Basingstoke 2003, p. 78.

10 Daniel Vitkus in 'Turning Turk in *Othello*: the conversion and damnation of the Moor', *Shakespeare Quarterly*, vol. 48, no. 2, Summer 1997, pp. 145–76, esp. pp. 154–5; see also Vitkus 2003, op. cit. in n. 9 above, p. 106.

11 M.J. Rodriguez-Salgado (ed.), *Armada 1588–1988*, London 1988, cat. 2.37.

12 See Vitkus 1997, op. cit. in n. 10 above, p. 149, citing Emrys Jones, '"Othello", "Lepanto" and the Cyprus Wars', *Shakespeare Survey*, vol. 21, 1968, pp. 47–52.

13 See a broadside of around 1570 on the genealogy of Ottoman rulers from Othman I to Selim II, British Museum, PD 1871,0812.811.

14 Jonathan Bate, *Soul of the Age*, London 2008, pp. 294–5.

15 Giles Robertson, *Vincenzo Catena*, Edinburgh 1954, cat. 48; Jill Dunkerton, Susan Foister and Nicholas Penny, *Dürer to Veronese*, New Haven and London 1999, p. 22.

16 Kate Lowe, 'The stereotyping of black Africans in Renaissance Europe' in T.F. Earle and K.J.P. Lowe (eds), *Black Africans in Renaissance Europe*, Cambridge 2005, esp. pp. 39–40; David Bindman, 'The black presence in British art' in David Bindman and Henry Louis Gates, *The Image of the Black in Western Art, from the 'Age of Discovery' to the Age of Abolition*, Harvard 2010, pp. 235–70, esp. p. 236, fig. 124. Compare the headdress worn by a black subject in a Flemish portrait miniature of the first half of the sixteenth century, formerly on the Paris artmarket, www. dejonckheere.fe, to be exhibited at the Walters Art Museum, Baltimore in 2012–13. Also the headdress worn by Katherina, black slave of 'Brandão the factor's clerk', drawn by Dürer in Antwerp in 1521, which has a jewel at the forehead like that in the Flemish miniature: see Jean Devisse and Michel Mollat, *The Image of the Black in Western Art, II, From the Early Christian Era to the 'Age of Discovery'*, New York 1979, p. 253 and fig. 263.

17 Compare a set of enamelled copper horse-trappings in the British Museum, PE 1890,1004.1, for which see O.M. Dalton, *Proceedings of the Society of Antiquaries of London*, Second Series, vol. 21, pp. 376–80; Jay Levenson (ed.), *Circa 1492: Art in the Age of Exploration*, Washington 1992, cat. 55.

18 Fritz Saxl, 'Costumes and festivals of Milanese society under Spanish rule', *Proceedings of the British Academy*, vol. 13, 1936, p. 11; Robertson 1954, op. cit. in n. 15 above, p. 68.

19 Enrico Maria dal Pozzolo, 'Appunti su Catena', *Venezia Cinquecento*, vol. 16, no. 31, 2006, pp. 80–2.

20 Edward Pechter, *Othello and Interpretative Traditions*, Iowa 1999, p. 35.

21 James Shapiro, *Shakespeare and the Jews*, New York 1996, pp. 185–7.

22 See Nabil Matar, *Britain and Barbary, 1589–1689*, Gainsville 2005, pp. 13 and 24–33, for the 1600 visit and its significance for *Othello*. See John D'Amico, *The Moor in English Renaissance Drama*, Gainsville 1992, for commercial and diplomatic relations between England and Morocco.

23 Bernard Harris, 'A portrait of a Moor', *Shakespeare Survey*, vol. 2, 1958, p. 95. See Chapter 1, n. 34.

24 Ibid., pp. 89–97; Matar 2005, op. cit. in n. 22 above, p. 36. We are grateful to Scotford Lawrence for letting us read his unpublished lecture on the portrait and for help in interpreting it.

25 See Robert Markley, *The Far East and the English Imagination 1600–1703*, Cambridge 2006, pp. 37–41, for Elizabeth I's letter to the Sultan of Aceh, Sumatra.

26 Rosalyn Knutson, 'A Caliban in St. Mildred Poultry' in Tetsuo Kishi, Roger Pringle and Stanley Wells (eds), *Shakespeare and Cultural Traditions*, Newark 1991, pp. 110–26.

27 Devisse and Mollat 1979, op. cit. in n. 16 above, p. 187; Paul Kaplan, 'Isabella d'Este and black African women' in Earle and Lowe 2005, op. cit. in n. 16 above, pp. 125–54, esp. p. 134.

28 Devisse and Mollat 1979, op. cit. in n. 16 above, pp. 188 and 194.

For a fascinating English painting believed to show Florence Smyth with her black page, of around 1640, in Bristol Museums, see Nabil Matar, 'The image of the other: England and North Africa in 1607' in *The World of 1607: Artifacts of the Jamestown Era from Around the World*, Virginia 2007, pp. 160–7, esp. p. 162; Pip Jones, *Satan's Kingdom: Bristol and the Transatlantic Slave Trade*, Bristol 2007, p. 27; Bindman 2010, op. cit. in n. 16 above, p. 254, fig. 137, there attributed to Gilbert Jackson.

29   Ben Jonson, *The Complete Masques*, edited by Stephen Orgel, New Haven and London 1969, pp. 47–60 and 509–14. Floyd-Wilson 2003, op. cit. in n. 1 above, pp. 111–31.

30   For Unton see Bindman 2010, op. cit. in n. 16 above, p. 239.

31   Kaplan 2005, op. cit. in n. 27 above, p. 348, n. 23.

32   Bindman 2010, op. cit. in n. 16 above, p. 237.

33   Imtiaz Habib, *Black Lives in the English Archives, 1500–1677: Imprints of the Invisible*, Farnham 2008, pp. 115–19.

34   Knutson 1991, op. cit. in n. 26 above, pp. 110–26; Habib 2008, op. cit. in n. 33 above, pp. 117 and 268–70.

35   Habib 2008, op. cit. in n. 33 above, p. 106. Michael Wood, *In Search of Shakespeare*, London 2003, pp. 210–14.

36   Joseph Leo Kerner, 'The epiphany of the black magus *c.* 1500' in Bindman and Gates 2010, op. cit. in n. 16 above, p. 56 and fig. 17.

37   Habib 2008, op. cit. in n. 33 above, pp. 2 and 72–6.

38   Lowe 2005, op. cit. in n. 16 above, p. 25; Harry Kelsey, *Sir John Hawkins*, New Haven and London 2003, pp. 32–3.

39   Loomba 2002, op. cit. in n. 1 above, p. 52.

40   See Eldred Jones, *The Elizabethan Image of Africa*, Charlottesville, Virginia 1971, p. 19, for a facsimile of the 1601 draft proclamation; for the text see P.L. Hughes and J.F. Larkin, *Tudor Royal Proclamations*, 3 vols, New Haven 1969, vol. 3, pp. 221–2; but see also comments in Habib 2008, op. cit. in n. 33 above, pp. 112–14. However, see also Miranda Kaufmann, 'Caspar Van Senden, Sir Thomas Sherley and the "Blackamoor" project', *Historical Research*, vol. 81, no. 212, 2008, pp. 366–71, which argues that at least one of these proclamations never got beyond the draft stage and that they were put together without Elizabeth I seeing them.

41   Lowe 2005, op. cit. in n. 16 above, p. 21.

42   Jim Sharpe, 'Social strain and social dislocation 1585–1603' in John Guy (ed.), *The Reign of Elizabeth: Court and Culture in the Last Decade*, Cambridge 1995, pp. 192–211.

43   Vitkus 1997, op. cit. in n. 10 above, pp. 145–76, esp. p. 162.

44   Christopher Harding, '"Hostis Humani Generis": the pirate as outlaw in the early modern law of the sea' in Claire Jowitt (ed.), *Pirates? The Politics of Plunder*, Basingstoke 2007, pp. 29–30. Christian corsairs also took Muslim captives: Nabil Matar, 'Piracy and captivity in the early modern Mediterranean', pp. 56–73 in the same volume, quotes an Arabic poem of 1471 on p. 56, describing Muslim victims of a Portuguese raid.

45   Habib 2008, op. cit. in n. 33 above, pp. 88 and 96.

46   Lowe 2005, op. cit. in n. 16 above, p. 21.

47   Only about four fire-blowers of this type survive: this one belonged to Sir Hans Sloane and was part of the founding collection of the British Museum in 1753. See W. Hildburgh, 'Aeolipiles as fire blowers', *Archaeologia*, vol. 94, 1951, p. 48; Jeremy Warren, 'Sir Hans Sloane as a collector of small sculpture', *Apollo*, vol. 159, February 2004, p. 36; Marta Ajmar-Wollheim and Flora Dennis (eds), *At Home in Renaissance Italy*, London 2006, pp. 299–300. For the symbolic use of a fire-blower figure in customary law of land tenure at Hilton Manor up to 1631 see Arthur MacGregor, 'Jack of Hilton and the history of the hearth-blower', *Antiquaries Journal*, vol. 87, 2007, pp. 821–94.

48   Paul Kaplan, 'Titian's "Laura Dianti" and the origins of the motif of the black page in portraiture', *Antichità Viva*, vol. 21, no. 1, 1982, pp. 11–18, esp. p. 14.

49   For an exception see the Hellenistic bronze head of a young African woman on a vessel in Ian Jenkins and Victoria Turner, *The Greek Body*, Los Angeles and London 2009, p. 122.

50   J.P. Filedt Kok and M. de Winkel, 'A portrait of a black African man by Jan Mostaert', *Bulletin van Het Rijksmuseum*, vol. 53, no. 4, 2005, pp. 470–7; Yvonne Hackenbroch, *Enseignes*, Florence 1996, fig. 237 and p. 239; Lowe 2005, op. cit. in n. 16 above, pp. 44–7, fig. 10.

51   Hugh Tait (ed.), *7000 of Jewellery*, London 1986, cat. 520. See Jos Koldewej, *Foi et bonne fortune, parure et devotion en flandre mediévale*, Arnhem 2006, p. 47, figs 3.3 and 3.4, for the Munich badge and portrait, and pp. 55–6 for analysis of its importance in the picture. For the shrine itself see Emile Van Heurck, *Les drapelets de pèlerinage en Belgique et dans les pays voisins*, Antwerp 1922, pp. 170–8.

52   For documents relating to Christianity in the Kongo see Malyn Newitt, *The Portuguese in West Africa: A Documentary History*, Cambridge 2010, docs 41–2. Mostaert could have received the commission in Antwerp, where the king of Portugal's agent, João Brandão was based: see Arnoud Bijl, Marlies Kleiterp (eds), *Black is Beautiful*, Amsterdam 2008, p. 269.

53   See Kate Lowe, '"Representing Africa": ambassadors and princes from Christian Africa to Renaissance Italy and Portugal', *Transactions of the Royal Historical Society*, Sixth Series, vol. 17, 2007, pp. 101–28, figs 5–6, for Italian representations of Ne-Vunda in his tomb monument and on a medal. See also L. Martínez Ferrer and M. Nocca, 'Cose dell'altro mondo', L'ambasceria di Antonio Emanuele, Principe di N'Funta, Vatican City 2003; and Paul Kaplan, 'Italy 1490–1700' in Bindman and Gates 2010, op. cit. in n. 16, pp. 160–5. For the German print see F.W.H. Hollstein, *German Engravings, Etchings and Woodcuts c. 1400–1700*, Amsterdam 1954, cat. 460, (British Museum, PD 1867,1012.393). Inscription translated by David Paisey, to whom many thanks. For the Italian print of 1608 by Rafaello Schiamossi (attr.), published by GA de'Paoli, Rome, see British Museum, PD 1870, 0504.1463.

54   Lowe 2005, op. cit. in n. 16 above, p. 47.

55   Kaplan 2010, op. cit. in n. 53 above, p. 101.

56   Kaplan 1982, op. cit. in n. 48 above, pp. 11–12; and Kaplan 2010, op. cit. in n. 53 above, pp. 109–10 and fig. 44.

57   Kaplan 2010, op. cit. in n. 53 above, pp. 140 and 141, fig. 67. Anne-Marie Eze, in course of publication: our thanks to her.

58   See Renate Eikelmann (ed.), *Der Mohrenkopfpokal von Christoph Jamnitzer*, Munich 2002, cat. 70, for a very similar agate cameo in the Coin Cabinet in Munich, there attributed to Prague or Northern Italy, *c.* 1600.

59   Sylvie Pressouyre, *Nicholas Cordier: recherches sur la sculpture à Rome autour de 1600*, Rome 1984, cat. 21; Eikelmann 2002, op. cit. in n. 58 above, cat. 66.

60   Elizabeth McGrath, 'Goltzius, Rubens and the beauties of Night' in *Black is Beautiful* 2008, op. cit. in n. 52 above, pp. 50–69, esp. p. 58 and n. 43.

61   See Jenkins and Turner 2009, op. cit. in n. 49 above, pp. 120–1, for an ancient Greek bronze of *c.* 300 BC of a North African youth.

62   Eikelmann 2002, op. cit. in n. 58 above; Jorgen Hein, 'Der Mohrenkopfpokal von Christoph Jamnitzer', *Münchner Jahrbuch der Bildenden Kunst*, Band 53, 2002, pp. 163–77; Lorenz Seelig, 'Christoph Jamnitzer's "Moor's Head": a late Renaissance drinking vessel' in Earle and Lowe 2005, op. cit. in n. 16 above, pp. 181–209, for an earlier reading of the cup, its dating and heraldic interpretation.

63   For the heraldry of the Pucci of Florence see Dora Thornton and Timothy Wilson, *Italian Renaissance Ceramics: A Catalogue of the British Museum Collection*, 2 vols, London 2009, vol. 1, cat. 161.

64   Hugh Tait, *Catalogue of The Waddesdon Bequest, The Jewels*, London 1986, cat. 9; see Eikelmann 2002, op. cit. in n. 58 above, cat. 74, for a splendid example set with rubies.

65   For Indian and Turkish associations see Tait 1986, op. cit. in n. 64 above, p. 93; for African associations see Hein 2002, op. cit. in n. 62 above, p. 171, fig. 9; Seelig 2005, op. cit. in n. 62 above, p. 208, esp. n. 71.

66   Hein 2002, op. cit. in n. 62 above, pp. 171–2.

67   Nabil Matar, *Turks, Moors and Englishmen in the Age of Discovery*, New York 1999, pp. 5–6, referring to the English experience of Muslim Africans.

68   A point made in Loomba 2002, p. 137; and in Vaughan and Mason Vaughan 1997, op. cit. in n. 1 above, p. 44. Published by: Omohundro Institute of Early American History and Culture.

Chapter 7

1   Thomas Pelletier, quoted in Stephen Porter, *Shakespeare's London: Everyday Life in London 1580–1616*, Stroud 2009, p. 82.

2   Kevin Sharpe, *Image Wars: Promoting Kings and Commonwealth in England 1603–60*, New Haven and London 2010, pp. 11–17.

3   J. Fenton, *King Iames His Welcome to London With Elizae's Tombe and Epitaph and our King's Triumph and Epitimie*, London 1603. Quoted in Sharpe 2010, op. cit. in n. 2 above, pp. 15–16.

4   For the patent see Samuel Schoenbaum, *William Shakespeare: A Documentary Life*, Oxford 1975, doc. 157, quoted by Charles Nicholl, *The Lodger: Shakespeare on Silver Street*, London 2007, p. 20.

5   Ernest Law, *Shakespeare as Groom of the Chamber*, London 1910.

6   Jonathan Bate, *Soul of the Age*, London 2008, p. 344.

7   Antonia Fraser, *The Gunpowder Plot*, London 1996, p. 81.

8   See S. Doran (ed.), *Elizabeth I*, London 2003, cat. 223, for a contemporary drawing of the Darnley murder and its significance.

9   Bate 2008, op. cit. in n. 6 above, p. 344; Roy Booth, 'Standing within the prospect of belief: *Macbeth*, King James and witchcraft' in John Newton and Jo Bath (eds), *Witchcraft and the Act of 1604*, Leiden 2008, pp. 47–68, esp. pp. 50–51.

10 Garry Wills, *Witches and Jesuits*, New York and Oxford 1995.

11 Bate 2008, op. cit. in n. 6 above, p. 342; James Shapiro, *1599: A Year in the Life of William Shakespeare*, London 2005, p. 160. The *Oxford English Dictionary* gives *Macbeth* as the earliest occurrence of the word 'assassination', but it was used in various pamphlets in the 1590s, reporting on assassination attempts upon Queen Elizabeth I and on the actual assassination of King Henri III of France. See, for example, *A True report of sundry horrible conspiracies of late time detected to haue (by barbarous murders) taken away the life of the Queenes Most Excellent Maiestie whom Almighty God hath miraculously conserued against the treacheries of her rebelles, and the violences of her most puissant enemies* (1594). But *Macbeth* stands as the first usage of the word in a work of literary/dramatic imagination.

12 For a historiographical account see Thomas McCoog, 'Remembering Henry Garnet, S.J.' in *Archivum Historicum Societatis Iesu*, vol. 75, 2006, fasc. 149, pp. 159–87. See also Michael Wood, *In Search of Shakespeare*, London 2003, pp. 283–90.

13 Lancelot Andrewes, 'A sermon preached before the king's majesty at Whitehall on the fifth of November 1606' in *Ninety-Six Sermons by the Right Honourable and Reverend Father in God Lancelot Andrewes*, 5 vols, Oxford 1841, vol. 4, p. 204. On Andrewes' 'royal interpretative program' of the Plot see Wills 1995, op. cit. in n. 10 above, pp. 23–4.

14 See M.J. Rodriguez-Salgado (ed.), *Armada 1588–1988*, London 1988, cat. 16.31, for a panel painting of the Armada in St Faith's Gaywood, King's Lynn, and its companion painting of James I and the Gunpowder Plot. Both paintings can be attributed to John Gipkyn: see Pamela Tudor-Craig, 'Old St Paul's': The Society of Antiquaries' Diptych*, London Topographical Society and Society of Antiquaries, London 2004, p. 31. For Gunpowder plays see Wills 1995, op. cit. in n. 10 above, p. 9.

15 See Fraser 1996, op. cit. in n. 7 above, pp. 110–13, on Catesby; Wood 2003, op. cit. in n. 12 above, pp. 283–4.

16 *Calendar of State Papers relating to English affairs in the Archives of Venice*, vol. 10, p. 333, quoted in Porter 2009, op. cit. in n. 1 above, p. 84.

17 Epigram LI: 'TO KING JAMES. Upon the happy false rumour of his death, the two and twentieth day of March, 1607' in C.H. Herford Percy and Evelyn Simpson (eds), *Ben Jonson*, 11 vols, *Volume VIII: The Poems; The Prose Works*, Oxford 1954, p. 43. We are grateful to James Shapiro and Peter Kirwan for this reference.

18 The same could be said of the medal struck in 1605 by the Dutch to commemorate the discovery of the Plot, which features a Jesuit snake slithering away between lilies and roses: see British Museum, M7013, Hawkins, eds. Franks and Grueber, see Chap. 8, n. 8, *Medallic Illustrations*, vol. 1, London 1885, no. 19.

19 See Philip Caraman, *Henry Garnet and the Gunpowder Plot*, London 1964, for Garnet's life; also Fraser

20 Alison Shell, *Oral Catholicism and Culture in Early Modern England*, Cambridge 2007, pp. 178 and 225; Wills 1995, op. cit. in n. 10 above, chapter 5; Peter Levi, *The Life and Times of William Shakespeare*, London 1988, p. 256; Wood 2003, op. cit. in n. 12 above, pp. 287–8; Bate 2008, op. cit. in n. 6 above, p. 345.

21 Malcolm Jones, *The Print in Early Modern England*, New Haven and London 2010, p. 64, fig. 65.

22 Ibid., p. 65.

23 Bate 2008, op. cit. in n. 6 above, p. 345. For Gerard's comments on the crowd's unusual compassion, see Caraman 1964, op. cit. in n. 19 above, pp. 438–9.

24 T. Cooper, revised Thomas McCoog, 'Oldcorne, Edward', *Oxford Dictionary of National Biography*, Oxford 2004. Father Oldcorne had a devout local following in Worcester and was arrested at Hindlip House, Worcestershire, on 23 January 1606. A tuft of grass in the form of a diadem or crown was said to have grown on the spot where his bowels were thrown into a fire which burnt for two weeks: see Philip Caraman (ed. and trans.), *John Gerard: The Autobiography of an Elizabethan*, London and New York 1951, pp. 202–3,276; Alexandra Walsham, *The Reformation of the Landscape*, Oxford 2011, p. 227.

25 Maurice Whitehead (ed.), *Held in Trust: 2000 Years of Sacred Culture*, Stonyhurst 2008, cat. 3.4. For attitudes to relics in the post-Reformation period in England see Alexandra Walsham, 'Skeletons in the cupboard: relics after the English Reformation' in Alexandra Walsham (ed.), *Relics and Remains*, Past and Present Supplement 5, 2010, vol. 206, pp. 121–43.

26 Peter Lake with Michael Questier, *The Antichrist's Lewd Hat: Protestants, Papists and Players in Post-Reformation England*, New Haven and London 2002, pp. 269–72.

27 Andrew Gurr and Mariko Ichikawa, *Staging in Shakespeare's Theatres*, Oxford 2000, p. 61.

28 P. Milward, 'Shakespeare's Jesuit schoolmasters' in Richard Dutton, Alison Findlay and Richard Wilson (eds), *Theatre and Religion: Lancastrian Shakespeare*, Manchester 2003, pp. 68–70, esp. p. 69 for this and other references in the plays.

29 Wills 1995, op. cit. in n. 10 above,

p. 100.

30 Shell 2007, op. cit. in n. 20 above, p. 21.

31 Caraman 1951, op. cit. in n. 24 above, p. 202.

32 Ibid., p. 201.

33 Lake and Questier 2002, op. cit. in n. 26 above, p. 307.

34 Jones 2010, op. cit. in n. 21 above, p. 66, fig. 68.

35 See Caraman 1964, op. cit. in n. 19 above, p. 446, for the Straw; H.L. Rogers, 'An English tailor and Father Garnet's Straw', *Review of English Studies*, vol. 16, 1965, pp. 44–9; Wills 1995, op. cit. in n. 10 above, p. 103.

36 Fraser 1996, op. cit. in n. 7 above, pp. 326–7.

37 Shell 2007, op. cit. in n. 20 above, pp. 134 and 225. We are grateful to Alison Shell, Thomas McCoog and Sheila O'Connell for discussing Garnet's Straw and its iconography with us.

38 Henry Foley, *Records of the English Province of the Society of Jesus*, 7 vols, London 1875–83, vol. 4, p. 38.

39 P. MacGrath and J. Rowe, 'Anstruther analysed: the Elizabethan seminary priests', *Recusant History*, vol. 18, no. 1, May 1986, pp. 1–13; discussed in F. Brownlow, 'Richard Topcliffe: Elizabeth's enforcer and the representation of power in *King Lear*' in Dutton *et al.* 2003, op. cit. in n. 28 above, pp. 161–78, esp. p. 167.

40 Margaret Spufford, *Small Books and Pleasant Histories*, London 1981, esp. chapter 5 on chapmen and their wares in the seventeenth century.

41 Clive Holmes, 'Witchcraft and possession at the accession of James I' in Newton and Bath 2008, op. cit. in n. 9 above, pp. 69–90, esp. p. 74.

42 See Spufford 1981, op. cit. in n. 40 above, pp. 116–17, on Autolycus and his wares.

43 Jones 2010, op. cit. in n. 21 above, pp. 262 and 263, fig. 252.

44 Whitehead 2008, op. cit. in n. 25 above, cat. 3.2. See Caraman 1951, op. cit. in n. 24 above, p. 184, for Gerard's account of how a convert left his robes as a member of the Order of the Bath to be cut up and used for vestments by the Jesuits, which Gerard duly did.

45 The list itself is preserved in the Archive of the Shakespeare Birthplace Trust, ER 27/14. See also Wood 2003, op. cit. in n. 12 above, pp. 283–4.

46 For Arrowsmith see Thomas

McCoog, 'Arrowsmith, Edmund', *Oxford Dictionary of National Biography*, Oxford 2004. The story of the discovery of the chest, its auction in the 1880s and its presentation to Stonyhurst College around 1916 is told in a series of letters from John A. Myerscough, SJ, to Father Chadwick: the letters are in the College Archive. We are grateful to Jan Graffius for making them available to us.

47 Wills 1995, op. cit. in n. 10 above, p. 37.

48 Holmes 2008, op. cit. in n. 41 above, esp. p. 84.

49 Sharpe 2010, op. cit. in n. 2 above, pp. 5–6.

50 Holmes 2008, op. cit. in n. 41 above.

51 Richard Wilson, *Secret Shakespeare*, Manchester 2004; Stephen Greenblatt, 'Shakespeare and the exorcists', *Shakespearean Negotiations*, Berkeley and Los Angeles 1988, pp. 94–128; F. Brownlow, *Shakespeare, Harsnett and the Devils of Denham*, Newark 1993.

52 Brownlow 2003, op. cit. in n. 39 above, p. 177, n. 29.

53 *The King's Book, His Majesties Speech in this Last Session of Parliament … Together with a discourse of the manner of the discovery of the late intended Treason, joined with an Examination of some of the prisoners*, London 1605. We are grateful to Frank Field for discussing James's response with us.

54 P.G. Maxwell-Stuart, 'King James's experience of witches, and the 1604 English Witchcraft Act' in Newton and Bath 2008, op. cit. in n. 9 above, pp. 31–46.

55 Sharpe 2010, op. cit. in n. 2 above, pp. 25 and 247, n. 107.

56 Julian Goodare, 'Scottish witchcraft in its European context' in Julian Goodare, Lauren Martin and Joyce Miller (eds), *Witchcraft and Belief in Early Modern Scotland*, Basingstoke 2008, pp. 26–50, esp. p. 41.

57 Booth 2008, op. cit. in n. 9 above, esp. p. 51

58 For votive ships, or church ships, in general see Basil Harley, *Church Ships*, Canterbury 1994, and Simon Stephens, *Ship Models*, London 1995. Although particularly associated with Denmark, which has around 1300 examples, they are a European-wide phenomenon. For a fascinating late fifteenth-century representation of votive ships hanging in the Church of Sant'Antonio in Venice see Agostino Carpaccio's painting of the interior, which is now in the Accademia in

Venice: see Alvise Zorzi, *Venezia scomparsa*, Milan 1984, pp. 208–12. The model of a merchant ship of about 1605–30 in the Tradescant Collection in the Ashmolean Museum (1685 B no. 758) has been interpreted as a church model: see Harley 1994, op. cit. above, p. 18.

59 The same cipher featured on a diamond brooch described by the Venetian envoy as a gift from Christian IV to his sister before he went into battle against Sweden: 'the splendid diamonds forming the letter C and 4, for the first letter of his name and because he is the fourth of that name'. She is portrayed wearing it in her collar in the portrait of about 1617 by Paul van Somer in the National Portrait Gallery. See D. Scarisbrick, 'Anne of Denmark's jewellery: the old and the new', *Apollo*, April 1986, pp. 228–36, esp. p. 231, pl. 1 and p. 234.

60 P.G. Maxwell-Stuart, 'The fear of the king is death: James VI and the witches of East Lothian' in William G. Naphy and Penny Roberts (eds), *Fear in Early Modern Society*, Manchester 1997, pp. 209–25. B. Liisberg tells the story from the Danish perspective in *Vesten for so og Østen for Hav*, Copenhagen 1909, pp. 9–15.

61 This chronology of events is taken from Lawrence Normand and Gareth Roberts (eds), *Witchcraft in Early Modern Scotland*, Exeter 2000, pp. 19–21.

62 Ibid., doc. 2, pp. 147–8.

63 *Warrender Papers*, edited by A. Cameron, 2 vols, *Scottish History Society*, Edinburgh 1931–2, vol. 2, p. 168.

64 *King James the First Daemonologie and Newes from Scotland*, Elizabethan and Jacobean Quartos, edited by G.B. Harrison, Edinburgh 1966, pp. 16–17.

65 Normand and Roberts 2000, op. cit. in n. 61 above, doc. 23, p. 267.

66 Goodare 2008, op. cit. in n. 56 above, p. 40; Normand and Roberts 2000, op. cit. in n. 61 above, doc. 20, p. 235.

67 http://www.shc.ed.ac.uk/Research/ witches has thrown up very few instances of the jougs or branks (bridle) being used in relation to witchcraft, a rare example being the trial of Agnes Hutcheon in Ayr in 1595. The tradition that they were so used explains their survival in public collections, as collected from the

late nineteenth and early twentieth centuries. We are grateful to George Dalgleish of the National Museums of Scotland for his comments.

68 When acquired by the National Museums of Scotland in November 1909, it was recorded that 'the use of the collar is alluded to in a seventeenth-century letter addressed to the session-clerk of the time, in which the correspondent enquires, among other matters, whether they have again had the occasion to use their collar among their sorcerous people'. See *Proceedings of the Society of Antiquaries of Scotland*, vol. 44, 1909–10, pp. 9–10. However, the letter was never given to the museum and has not been traced. Our thanks to George Dalgleish for this reference.

69 Normand and Roberts 2000, op. cit. in n. 61 above, p. 96; see Christina Larner, *Enemies of God: The Witch-hunt in Scotland*, London 1981, pp. 103–19 on the process from accusation to execution.

70 Russ McDonald, *Shakespeare and the Arts of Language*, Oxford 2001, chapter 7.

71 He saw the play on Saturday 20 April 1611. The reference is to his manuscript diary, Simon Forman, *The Book of Plaies and Notes therof by Forman for Common Policie*, 1611, Bodleian Library, ms Ashmole 08, f. 207r–v. Transcript: J.M. Nosworthy, *Shakespeare's Occasional Plays: Their Origin and Transmission*, London 1965, pp. 14–15. Samuel Schoenbaum, *Shakespeare: Records and Images*, Oxford 1981, pp. 7–20. We are grateful to Peter Kirwan for these references.

72 Normand and Roberts 2000, op. cit. in n. 61 above, doc. 20, p. 241, quoted by Booth 2008, op. cit. in n. 9 above, p. 56.

73 H. Cheape, '"Charms against witchcraft": magic and mischief in museum collections' in Goodare *et al.* 2008, op. cit. in n. 56 above, pp. 233 and 235–6, fig. 10.3.

74 R. Scot, *The Discoverie of Witchcraft*, facsimile of edition of 1584, Mineola 1989, chapter 4, p. 5.

75 E.H. Thompson, 'Macbeth, King James and the witches', http:// homepages.tesco.net/~eandcthomp/ macbeth.htm.

76 Cheape 2008, op. cit. in n. 73 above, p. 241, fig. 10.6.

77 Compare the rock crystal on the frame of the Mosan gable reliquary of 1165–70 in the British Museum,

PE 1978,0502.7. The rock crystal cabochon in the twelfth-century Ninian reliquary in the British Museum, PE 1946,0407.1a, resembles that on the clan brooches discussed here. For a ridge-backed crystal see St Fillan's Crozier (National Museums of Scotland) and the Ugadale Brooch in private hands. See also H. Cheape, 'Touchstones of belief', *Review of Scottish Culture*, no. 20, 2008, pp. 104–18, esp. p. 112, fig. 5.

78 It may be the charmstone referred to in the Black Book of Taymouth in 1640 as something which the first Laird of Glenurchy had worn at the Siege of Rhodes against the Turks. Owning a healing crystal as a family possession was a mark of status, and stories of Eastern crusading origin were part of their power. See H. Cheape, 'From natural to supernatural: the material culture of charms and amulets' in Lizanne Henderson (ed.), *Fantastical Imaginations: The Supernatural in Scottish History and Culture*, Edinburgh 2009, pp. 70–90, esp. p. 76 for the Clach Dearg or Red Stone of the Stewarts of Ardvorlich, which was reputedly brought back from the Holy Land by Seumas Beag Stewart, and p. 78 for reference to the Black Book of Taymouth and the Glenorchy Charmstone.

79 A. Stewart, 'Notice of a Highland charm-stone', *Proceedings of the Society of Antiquaries of Scotland*, vol. 24, 1889–90, pp. 157–60, esp. pp. 157–8 for the charm associated with the Keppoch Charmstone taken by a Scottish emigrant to Australia in 1854; see also Cheape 2008, op. cit. in n. 73 above, p. 237.

80 The Ugadale Brooch in this group is in private hands: a replica is in the National Museums of Scotland, NMS.H.NGD 11. The Glenlyon Brooch is in the British Museum, PE 1897,0526.1: neither is discussed here.

81 The Brooch of Lorn has a traditional association with Robert the Bruce, and is said to have been relinquished by the king, with the cloak it fastened, in order to escape John of Lorn following the Battle of Dalrigh in 1306. It became a talisman of the MacDougalls of Lorn. As we now see it, the brooch is currently dated to around 1600. This brooch was rediscovered in 1824; the Lochbuie Brooch, which had belonged to

the Macleans of Lochbuie in Mull, entered the British Museum in 1855 from the Bernal Collection. Both inspired countless copies and became part of Highland costume. See Charlotte Gere and Judy Rudoe, *Jewellery in the Age of Queen Victoria*, London 2010, pp. 455–6. For the Lochbuie Brooch see also D.H. Caldwell (ed.), *Angels, Nobles and Unicorns: Art and Patronage in Medieval Scotland*, Edinburgh 1982, cat. D15, p. 50.

82 The quotation is from James's *Basilikon Doron* of 1598: see David Armitage, *The Ideological Origins of the British Empire*, Cambridge 2000, p. 56. On the Ballochyle Brooch see George Dalgleish and Henry Steuart Fotheringham, *Silver: Made in Scotland*, Edinburgh 2008, p. 39, no. 3.13; and Rosalind K. Marshall and George Dalgleish, *The Art of Jewellery in Scotland*, Edinburgh 1991, p. 59. On this, the Lochbuie Brooch and the Brooch of Lorne see Cheape 2008, op. cit. in n. 77 above, pp. 112–13. On the Brooch of Lorne see *Archaeologia Scotica, Transactions of the Society of Antiquaries of Scotland*, vol. 4, part 3, 1857, p. 419 and pl. XXX. The brooch is still in private hands in Scotland.

83 Stephen Brogan, 'The Royal Touch in early modern England: its changing rationale and practice', PhD thesis, Birkbeck, University of London, January 2011. Clive Cheesman and Jonathan Williams, *Rebels, Pretenders and Imposters*, London 2000, p. 67. The British Museum also holds a similar token given to Dr Johnson as a sickly two-year-old in 1702.

84 Peter E. McCullough, *Sermons at Court*, Cambridge 1998, p. 193. We are grateful to James Shapiro for this reference.

85 Nick Aitchison, *Macbeth: Man and Myth*, Thrupp 1999, pp. 117–22.

86 For the portrait of Macbeth by Jacob de Wet the Younger see Steve Bruce and Steven Yearley, 'The De Wet portraits of the Scottish kings', *Review of Scottish Culture*, vol. 6, 1990, pp. 11–19. We are grateful to Deborah Clarke and Desmond Shawe-Taylor for this reference.

87 Hugh Tait, *Catalogue of the Waddesdon Bequest, The Jewels*, London 1986, cat. 33.

88 The presentation copy of the genealogy was handed over at the Palace of Whitehall on 12 August 1610 in the presence of Henry, Prince of Wales, the Archbishop of Canterbury, Robert Cecil and others as recorded by Thomas Lyte in *Britaine's Monarchy*, unpublished ms, British Library, Add MS 59741. For Lyte and his formation see Sir Henry Maxwell Lyte, *The Lytes of Lytescary*, Taunton 1895, pp. 62–3.

89 See Tait 1986, op. cit. in n. 87 above, p. 165, for Camden's Latin verse.

Chapter 8

1 See Kevin Sharpe, *Image Wars: Promoting Kings and Commonwealth in England 1603–60*, New Haven and London 2010, pp. 83–4, on the change to the royal arms and unionist iconographies on coins and medals. Andrew Hadfield, *Shakespeare, Spenser and the Matter of Britain*, Basingstoke 2004, pp. 1–11.

2 Neil Rhodes, 'Wrapped in the strong arms of the Union' in Willy Maley and Andrew Murphy (eds), *Shakespeare and Scotland*, Manchester 2004, pp. 37–52.

3 We are grateful to James Shapiro for this reference.

4 Proclamation of 20 October 1604.

5 John Russell, *A Treatise of the Happie and Blessed Union*, c. 1604–5, quoted in Mary Floyd-Wilson, *English Ethnicity and Race in Early Modern Drama*, Cambridge 2003, p. 171.

6 See Johann P. Sommerville (ed.), *James VI and I, Political Writings*, Cambridge 1994, p. 163, for a speech of 1605 describing the new union as a marriage.

7 Pamela Tudor-Craig, 'Old St Paul's', the Society of Antiquaries' Diptych, London Topographical Society and Society of Antiquaries, London 2004, col. pl. 6A.

8 See Edward Hawkins, eds A.W. Franks and H.A. Grueber, *Medallic Illustrations of the History of Great Britain and Ireland to the Death of George II*, London 1885, vol. 1, p. 191, no. 11. see Chapter 7, n. 18.

9 J.F. Larkin and P.L. Hughes (eds), *Stuart Royal Proclamations*, 3 vols, Oxford 1973, p. 346.

10 See Sharpe 2010, op. cit. in n. 1 above, p. 60.

11 J.J. North, *English Hammered Coinage*, 3 vols, London 1991, vol. 2, pp. 145–7. James's proclamation of 16 November 1604 describes the unite and other coins in detail with their legends as 'currant within this Our Kingdome of Great Britaine'.

12 See Tristan Marshall, *Theatre and Empire: Great Britain on the London Stage under James VI and I*, Manchester 2000, p. 1, for the 1620 proclamation, and pp. 52–79 for the role of the playhouse in imperial thinking in the first years of James's reign.

13 Jonathan Bate, *Soul of the Age*, London 2008, pp. 340–1.

14 See T.D. Kendrick, *British Antiquity*, London 1950, pp. 65–125, for late Tudor historiography and the end of the Brutus myth.

15 Hadfield 2004, op. cit. in n. 1 above, pp. 152–6.

16 Graham Parry, 'Earliest antiquaries' in David Gaimster, Bernard Nurse and Julia Steele (eds), *Making History: Antiquaries in Britain,* London 2007, pp. 37–8 and cat. 17; Floyd-Wilson 2003, op. cit. in n. 5 above, p. 172.

17 William Camden, *Britannia*, London 1610, p. 119, quoted in Floyd-Wilson 2003, op. cit. in n. 5 above, p. 173.

18 For the latest research on John White's voyages and drawings see Kim Sloan, *A New World: England's First View of America*, London 2007; and Kim Sloan (ed.), *European Visions: American Voices*, London 2009, p. 8.

19 Stuart Piggott, *Ancient Britons and the Antiquarian Imagination*, London 1989, p. 76.

20 A point first made by Kendrick 1950, op. cit. in n. 14 above, p. 123, showing how four of the White drawings engraved by de Bry were reproduced in Speed's 'the Portraiture of Ancient Britaines' in *The Theatre and Empire of Great Britain* in 1611.

21 Piggott 1989, op. cit. in n. 19 above, p. 82.

22 Camden 1610, op. cit. in n. 17 above, pp. 23–8; Kendrick 1950, op. cit. in n. 14 above, p. 108; Floyd-Wilson 2003, op. cit. in n. 5 above, p. 83.

23 Camden 1610, op. cit. in n. 17 above, p. 31.

24 Floyd-Wilson 2003, op. cit. in n. 5 above, pp. 111–31; Eldred Jones, *Othello's Countrymen: The African in English Renaissance Drama*, Oxford 1965, pp. 31–6.

25 Anu Korhonen, 'Washing the Ethiopian white: conceptualising black skin in Renaissance England' in T.F. Earle and K.J.P. Lowe (eds), *Black Africans in Renaissance Europe*, Cambridge 2005, pp. 94–112, esp. p. 101.

26 Quoted in Jones 1965, op. cit. in n. 24 above, p. 32.

27 Kate Lowe, 'The stereotyping of black Africans in Renaissance Europe' in Earle and Lowe 2005, op. cit. in n. 25 above, pp. 17–47, esp. p. 47.

28 Michael Gaudio, 'The truth in clothing: the costume studies of John White and Lucas de Heere' in Sloan 2009, op. cit. in n. 18 above, pp. 24–32, esp. p. 31; Ania Loomba, *Shakespeare, Race and Colonialism*, Oxford 2002, p. 8.

29 Gaudio 2009, op. cit. in n. 28 above, p. 30, fig. 17.

30 Sloan 2007, op. cit. in n. 18 above, cat. 33; Sam Smiles, 'John White and British antiquity: savage origins in the context of Tudor historiography' in Sloan 2009, op. cit. in n. 18 above, pp. 106–12, esp. p. 107. Giulio Bonasone's print of Diana, dating from between 1531 and 1576, is the kind of Italian source that lies behind White's image.

31 A point made by Sloan 2007, op. cit. in n. 18 above, p. 160.

32 Ibid., cat. 30; Piggott 1989, op. cit. in n. 19 above, p. 82.

33 The earliest complete set of such classically inspired armour is that made for Guidobaldo della Rovere, Duke of Urbino, by Bartolomeo Campi in 1546. See Stuart Pyhrr, *Heroic Armor of the Italian Renaissance: Filippo Negroli and his Contemporaries*, New York 1998, cat. 54.

34 Ibid., pp. 209–12.

35 Giorgio Vasari's costume design for Castor in his 1566 masque *The Genealogy of the Gods*, performed for the Medici, is a good example of the kind of fanciful classical armour seen in these elaborate court entertainments: see A.M. Nagler, *Theatre Festivals of the Medici 1539–1637*, New Haven and London 1964, p. 30 and fig. 13. Inigo Jones's costume for Oberon in Ben Jonson's 1611 *Masque of Oberon, the Faery Prince* shows how close the body-painting of White's Pictish warrior is to near-contemporary masquing costume in its proportions and details. Jones's figure shares the same classical, graceful stance. See John Harris, Stephen Orgel and Roy Strong, *The King's Arcadia: Inigo Jones and the Stuart Court*, London 1973, cat. 65.

36 Quoted in Floyd-Wilson 2003, op. cit. in n. 5 above, p. 122.

37 Andrew Hadfield and John McVeagh (eds), *Strangers to that Land: British*

Perceptions of Ireland from the Reformation to the Famine, Gerrards Cross 1994, p. 175. See also Tristan Marshall, '*The Tempest* and the British Imperium in 1611', *Historical Journal*, vol. 41, 1998, pp. 375–400; and Marshall 2000, op. cit. in n. 12 above, pp. 79 and 86, n. 107.

38 David Armitage, *The Ideological Origins of the British Empire*, Cambridge 2000, p. 57.

39 Hadfield 2004, op. cit. in n. 1 above, p. 166.

40 Marshall 2000, op. cit. in n. 12 above, p. 68.

41 Macolm Todd, 'Cunobelinus', *Oxford Dictionary of National Biography*, Oxford 2004. We are grateful to Richard Hobbs and Jody Joy for discussing the coinage of Cunobelin with us.

42 Parry 2007, op. cit. in n. 16 above, pp. 37–8 and cat. 17.

43 Richard Hobbs, *British Iron Age Coins in the British Museum*, London 1996, p. 125, no. 1,801.

44 See Hadfield 2004, op. cit. in n. 1 above, pp. 160–8, for Cymbeline's intellectual context.

45 Samuel Schoenbaum, *William Shakespeare: A Documentary Life*, Oxford 1975, p. 196; Ernest Law, *Shakespeare as Groom of the Chamber*, London 1910.

46 Michael Wood, *In Search of Shakespeare*, London 2003, p. 256.

47 C.H. Read, *Vetusta Monumenta: The Royal Gold Cup*, London 1904; Jenny Stratford, *The Bedford Inventories: The Worldly Goods of John, Duke of Bedford, Regent of France (1389–1435)*, London 1993, pp. 319–25; John Cherry, *The Holy Thorn Reliquary*, London 2010, p. 25.

48 Quoted in Floyd-Wilson 2003, op. cit. in n. 5 above, p. 129.

Chapter 9

1 Caliban's Setebos was a Patagonian deity mentioned by Magellan: see Antonio Pigafetta, *Magellan's Voyage: A Narrative Account of the First Circumnavigation*, translated and edited by R.A. Skelton, New York 1994, pp. 48–9, cited in Marina Warner, 'The "foul witch" and her "freckled whelp": Circean mutations in the New World' in Peter Hulme and William H. Sherman (eds), '*The Tempest' and Its Travels*, London 2000, pp. 97–113, esp. p. 99. Jonathan

Bate, *Shakespeare and Ovid*, Oxford 1993, p. 242. For the global presence of *The Tempest* see Hulme and Sherman 2000, p. 11.

2 Roberto Fernandez Retamar, *Caliban, apuntes sobre la cultura en nuestra America*, Mexico 1971, quoted and translated in Alden T. Vaughan and Virginia Mason Vaughan, *Shakespeare's Caliban: A Cultural History*, Cambridge 1996, p. 156.

3 Alden T. Vaughan, 'Shakespeare's Indian: the Americanization of Caliban', *Shakespeare Quarterly*, vol. 39, no. 2, Summer 1988, pp. 137–53; and Alden T. Vaughan, *Translatlantic Encounters: American Indians in Britain, 1500–1776*, Cambridge 2006.

4 Jonathan Bate, *Soul of the Age*, London 2008, p. 308. For Shakespeare's awareness of Irish issues and identities see Mark Thornton Burnett and Ramona Wray (eds), *Shakespeare and Ireland: History, Politics, Culture*, New York 1997, esp. the chapters by Andrew Hadfield and David J. Baker.

5 Michael MacCarthy-Morrough, *The Munster Plantation*, Oxford 1986.

6 For the significance of the Irish harp as a symbol of liberty see Dympna Callaghan, *Shakespeare Without Women: Representing Gender and Race on the Renaissance Stage*, London and New York 2000, p. 113.

7 Kim Sloan, *A New World: England's First View of America*, London 2007, fig. 52; Susan Doran (ed.), *Elizabeth I*, London 2003, cat. 17.

8 Virginia Mason Vaughan and Alden T. Vaughan (eds), *The Tempest*, Arden Shakespeare, London 1999, p. 193, n. 144.

9 David Armitage, 'The Elizabethan idea of empire', *Transactions of the Royal Historical Society* Sixth Series, vol. 14, 2004, pp. 269–77. Daniel Vitkus, *Turning Turk: English Theatre and the Multicultural Mediterranean*, New York and Basingstoke 2003, pp. 6–7. Jeffrey Knapp, *An Empire Nowhere*, Berkeley, Los Angeles and Oxford 1992, chapter 6.

10 Gary M. Walton and James F. Shepherd, *The Economic Rise of Early America*, Cambridge 1979, pp. 35–7.

11 Alec Bain Tonnochy, *Catalogue of Seal-Dies in the British Museum*, London 1952, no. 347; Sloan 2007, op. cit. in n. 7 above, pp. 40–1, fig. 26.

12 Vaughan 2006, op. cit. in n. 3 above,

pp. 21–41.

13 See Sloan 2007, op. cit. in n. 7 above, pp. 45–8, for the lost colony and p. 48 for the quotation from White.

14 Shannon Miller, *Invested with Meaning: The Raleigh Circle in the New World*, Philadelphia 1998, p. 51; Nicholas Canny, 'Raleigh's Ireland' in H.G. Jones (ed.), *Raleigh and Quinn: The Explorer and his Boswell*, Chapel Hill 1987, pp. 87–101.

15 William Strachey, *The Historie of Travell into Virginia Britania*, 1612, edited by Louis B. Wright and Virginia Freund, Hakluyt Society, London 1953, prefatory poem. For the Christianizing aspect of the colonization of Virginia see Achsah Guibbory, *Christian Identity, Jews and Israel in Seventeenth-century England*, Oxford 2010, pp. 50–1.

16 Joan Pong Linton, *The Romance of the New World*, Cambridge 1998, p. 158; Walton and Shepherd 1979, op. cit. in n. 10 above, pp. 35–7 and 41. See Vaughan 2006, op. cit. in n. 3 above, p. 41 and n. 65, for Thomas Harriot's and Raleigh's emphasis on language in intercultural exchange.

17 Pong Linton 1998, op. cit. in n. 16 above, p. 184.

18 Jerry Brotton, '"This Tunis, sir, was Carthage": contesting colonialism in *The Tempest*' in Ania Loomba and Martin Orkin (eds), *Post-colonial Shakespeares*, London and New York 1998, pp. 23–42, esp. p. 35.

19 Venetia Porter and Patricia Morison, 'The Salcombe Bay Treasure', *British Museum Magazine*, Spring 1998, pp. 16–17. We are grateful to Venetia Porter for information and references on this as yet unpublished find, of which this, and the article cited in n. 20 below, are the preliminary findings.

20 Venetia Porter, 'Coins of the Sa'dian Sharifs of Morocco off the coast of Devon, preliminary report', *XII Internationaler Numismatischer Kongress Berlin 1997, Akten*, edited by Bernd Kluge and Bernhard Weisser, Berlin 2000, pp. 1288–94, esp. p. 1291.

21 Todd Gray, 'Turkish piracy and early Stuart Devon', *Transactions of the Devon Association of the Advancement of Science*, vol. 121, 1989, pp. 159–71. For accounts by captives of Muslim culture, see Daniel Vitkus (ed.), *Piracy, Slavery and Redemption: Barbary Captivity Narratives from Early Modern England*, New York 2001.

22 Nabil Matar, *Turks, Moors and Englishmen in the Age of Discovery*, New York 1999, pp. 57–63.

23 Nabil Matar, 'Verney, Sir Francis (1584–1615)', *Oxford Dictionary of National Biography*, Oxford 2004.

24 William Lithgow, *The Totall Discourse, of the Rare Adventures, and Painfull Peregrinations of Long Nineteen Years Travayles, from Scotland, to the Most Famous Kingdomes in Europe, Asisa and Affrica*, Lyon 1632, pp. 197–8.

25 Frances Parthenope Verney, *Memoirs of the Verney Family during the Civil War*, London 1892, p. 68; Adrian Tinniswood, *The Verneys*, London 2007; Adrian Tinniswood, *Pirates of Barbary*, London 2010, pp. 47–9.

26 The surviving 'robe' at Claydon House is made of an Italian silk velvet, with silver braid and silk shag-pile lining and trimmings, cut in an English style of around 1610. The cap (not a turban) and slippers (pantofles) are also of an English style, and were made of the same velvet and braid as a group, though the slippers and the hat have a small and possibly feminine look to them. There is nothing Turkish about this ensemble, but it just might represent Sir Francis's investment of some of his ill-gotten pirate gains in a tangible expression of status as an English nobleman. If so, it is surprising – given the weight and value of the silk and trimings – that they would have survived his penury at the end of his life in Sicily. The only link to Sir Francis, however, is in the letter of John Machin of 1615 – now untraced – recording that he had sent back some of Sir Francis's things from Messina in 1615. The objects at Claydon do not appear to correspond to the Machin description of what were clearly seen as Turkish accessories, but they have until now been uncritically accepted and published as Sir Francis Verney's relics. It is to be hoped that new research at Claydon by Niki Miles will clarify their status and significance.

27 Daniel Vitkus (ed.), *Three Turk Plays from Early Modern England*, New York 2000, pp. 151–239.

28 See Lea Puljcan Jurk, 'Shakespeare's "Bargulus, the strong Illyrian pirate",' *Notes and Queries*, vol. 58, April 2011, pp. 233–6. The original source is Cicero's *De Officiis* (2.11): 'Bardulis Illyrius latro', translated as 'Bargulus' by Robert Whytington (1534) and

Nicholas Grimald (1533).

29 See Claire Jowitt, *The Culture of Piracy 1580–1630*, Farnham 2010, pp. 123–35, for Shakespeare's references to pirates generally from the 1590s.

30 Peter Earle, *The Pirate Wars*, London 2003, pp. 57–8. For the text of James's 1609 proclamation against pirates see Vitkus 2000, op. cit. in n. 27 above, appendix 2.

31 Nabil Matar, *Britain and Barbary, 1589–1689*, Gainsville 2005, p. 46.

32 Bate 2008, op. cit. in n. 4 above, p. 309.

33 David Armitage, *The Ideological Origins of the British Empire*, Cambridge 2000, p. 6.

34 Quoted in Jowitt 2010, op. cit. in n. 29 above, p. 3.

35 Hulme and Sherman 2000, op. cit. in n. 1 above, p. 8.

36 William H. Sherman, *John Dee: The Politics of Reading and Writing in the English Renaissance*, Massachusetts 1995, pp. 148–200, esp. p. 150. Professor Sherman has pointed out to us that Humphrey Llwyd beat Dee to it in inventing the phrase 'the British empire'. We are grateful to him for this reference.

37 For obsidian mirrors in Mehican culture see Colin McEwan and Leonardo López Luján (eds), *Moctezuma: Aztec Ruler*, London 2009, cat. 103 and p. 167. See Hugh Tait '"The Devil's looking glass": the magical speculum of Dr John Dee' in W. Hunting Smith (ed.) *Horace Walpole: Writer, Politician and Connoisseur*, New Haven and London 1967, pp. 195–212; and Michael Snodin (ed.), *Horace Walpole's Strawberry Hill*, New Haven and London 2009, cat. 108 and pp. 98–102 for Walpole's interpretation of the object and its link with Dee. See also Silke Ackermann and Louise Devoy, '"The Lord of the Smoking Mirror": objects associated with John Dee in the British Museum' in Jennifer M. Rampling (ed.), *Studies in History and Philosophy of Science Part A, John Dee and the Sciences: Early Modern Networks of Knowledge*, vol. 43, 2012, online 2011.

38 Robert Baldwin, 'John Dee's interest in the application of nautical science, mathematics and law to English naval affairs' in Stephen Clucas (ed.), *John Dee: Interdisciplinary Studies in English Renaissance Thought*, Dordrecht 2006, pp. 97–130.

39 Hulme and Sherman 2000, op. cit.

in n. 1 above, p. 5; Sherman 1995, op. cit. in n. 36 above, pp. 151 and 191. For an exceptional group of scientific instruments made for or owned by Robert Dudley (1573–1649), natural son of the Earl of Leicester and a friend of Essex, see Gerard L'E. Turner, *Elizabethan Instrument Makers: The Origins of the London Trade in Precision Instrument Making*, Oxford 2000, pp. 77–83.

40 See James McDermott, 'Humphrey Cole and the Frobisher voyages' in Silke Ackermann (ed.), *Humphrey Cole: Mint, Measurement and Maps in Elizabethan England*, London 1998, pp. 15–20, esp. p. 16, for a list of the instruments supplied.

41 Sloan 2007, op. cit. in n. 7 above, p. 18; Ackermann 1998, op. cit. in n. 40 above, pp. 29–89 for a catalogue of surviving Cole instruments. An inscription in a later hand on the mater suggests that the instrument once belonged to Henry, Prince of Wales, but the case bearing the monogram and the coat of arms of Henry is very likely to be a nineteenth-century addition.

42 Paul E.J. Hammer, 'Devereux, Robert, second earl of Essex (1565–1601)', *Oxford Dictionary of National Biography*, Oxford 2004.

43 See John Bruce, 'Description of a pocket dial made in 1593 for Robert Devereux Earl of Essex', *Archaeologia*, vol. 40, 1866, pp. 343–60, esp. pp. 354–5, for the inscription; Sloan 2007, op. cit. in n. 7 above, p. 18 and fig. 13. There is something biblical, reminiscent of the Book of Proverbs 11:28 and 13:7, in the contrast of outer and inner riches, but the quotation has not been placed. See also Turner 2000, op. cit. in n. 39 above, pp. 225–9, for this instrument.

44 Hulme and Sherman 2000, op. cit. in n. 1 above, p. 12. See John Gillies, *Shakespeare and the Geography of Difference*, Cambridge 1994, esp. pp. 92–8, for ways in which the Elizabethan playhouse functioned as a 'theatre of the world' and drew inspiration from maps and mapping.

45 W.B. Whall, *Shakespeare's Sea Terms Explained*, London 1910.

46 Richard Godfrey, *Wenceslaus Hollar: A Bohemian Artist in England*, New Haven and London 1994, p. 39, no. 2; Franz Sprinzels, *Hollar, Handzeichnungen, beschrieben und herausgegeben von Franz Sprinzels*, Leipzig, *c.* 1938, no. 83; Michael

Wood, *In Search of Shakespeare*, London 2003, p. 325; Vladimir Denkstein, *Hollar Drawings*, Prague 1979, p. 24, fig. 7.

47 Vaughan 1988, op. cit. in n. 3 above, pp. 137–53; Bate 2008, op. cit. in n. 4 above, p. 65.

48 Pong Linton 1998, op. cit. in n. 16 above, p. 7.

49 Sloan 2007, op. cit. in n. 7 above, cat. 14; for the role of women in mediating exchange between Old and New Worlds, see Pong Linton 1998, op. cit. in n. 16 above, p. 104. For the culture of the North Carolina Algonquians see Helen C. Rountree, *The Powhatan Indians of Virginia: Their Traditional Culture*, Norman 1989; and Christian F. Feest, *The Powhatan Tribes*, New York and Philadelphia 1990.

50 Sloan 2007, op. cit. in n. 7 above, p. 122, fig. 71.

51 Hazel Forsyth with Geoff Egan, *Toys and Trinkets*, London 2005, p. 153, fig. 38.

52 See Vaughan 2006, op. cit. in n. 3 above, pp. 55–6 and 77–96, fig. 5.1, for the engraved portrait illustrated here.

53 Michael Gaudio, 'The truth in clothing: the costume studies of John White and Lucas de Heere' in Kim Sloan (ed.), *European Visions: American Voices*, London 2009, pp. 24–32, esp. p. 29 and fig. 16.

54 Alden T. Vaughan, 'Trinculo's Indian: American natives in Shakespeare's England' in Hulme and Sherman 2000, op. cit. in n. 1 above, p. 56. See Arthur Mayger Hind, *Engraving in England in the Sixteenth and Seventeenth Centuries*, 3 vols, Cambridge 1952–64, vol. 2, 266.47, for the print.

55 Information provided by Jonathan King, who adds that the late Noah Piugaattuk, who contributed a bow to the British Museum's collections, Am 1994,06.20a–d, used to hunt narwhal across spring ice at a lead with a harpoon and inflated seal float.

56 Edward Webbe writes in 1590 of playing with young unicorns in the land of Prester John, 'as one would play with young Lambes', in his travel book, *The Rare and most wonderfull things which Edw. Webbe, an Englishman borne, hath seene and passed in his troublesome travailes*, London 1590, unpaginated and illustrated with a delightful woodcut of a unicorn. He also recounts having been saved by unicorn horn which

was used as an antidote to poison he had been given.

57 Richard Collinson (ed.), *Three Voyages of Martin Frobisher*, London 1867, p. 134; Doran 2003, op. cit. in n. 3 above, cat. 177.

58 Doran 2003, op. cit. in n. 7 above, cat. 177.

59 McDermott 1998, op. cit. in n. 40 above, pp. 15–20, esp. p. 18.

60 William C. Sturtevant and David Beers Quinn, 'This new prey: Eskimos in Europe in 1567, 1576 and 1577' in Christian Feest (ed.), *Indians and Europe: An Interdisciplinary Collection of Essays*, Aachen 1989, pp. 61–140, esp. p. 69 for the Best quotation.

61 See ibid., pp. 76–84, for the best account of these individuals and their fate.

62 Ibid., p. 81.

63 Vaughan 2000, op. cit. in n. 54 above, p. 51.

64 Ibid., pp. 55–6; Christian F. Feest, 'John White's New World' in Sloan 2007, op. cit. in n. 7 above, pp. 65–78, esp. pp. 73–4 and fig. 40; Christian F. Feest, 'The Virginian Indian in pictures, 1612–24', *Smithsonian Journal of History*, vol. 2, 1967, pp. 6–13.

65 Sloan 2007, op. cit. in n. 7 above, p. 59; see Sturtevant and Quinn 1989, op. cit in n. 60 above, p. 84, on burial and records.

66 William Brenchley Rye, *England as Seen by Foreigners in the Days of Elizabeth I and James the First*, London 1865, p. 18; quoted with a different translation in Ania Loomba, *Shakespeare, Race and Colonialism*, Oxford 2002, p. 15.

67 See British Museum CEM22239 for a duit struck in the province of Holland, 1590–9; and CEM22241 for one also from Holland, struck in 1605. Thanks to Barrie Cook for his comments on these coins.

68 For gaberdine see Chapter 3, p. 163.

69 Edward Webbe, 1590, quoted in Robert Hills Goldsmith, 'The wild man on the English stage', *Modern Language Review*, vol. 53, no. 4, 1958, pp. 481–91, esp. p. 488.

70 Timothy Husband, *The Wild Man: Medieval Myth and Symbolism*, New York 1980, cat. 25.

71 Claude Prieur, *Dialogue de la lycanthropie ou transformation d'hommes en loups, vulgairement dits loups-garous, et si telle se peut faire: auquel en discourant est traicté de la maniere de se contregarder des*

enchantemens et sorcelleries, ensemble de plusieurs abus et superstitions, lesquelles se commettent en ce temps, Louvain 1596.

72 Feest 2007, op. cit. in n. 64 above, p. 67.

73 Hills Goldsmith 1958, op. cit. in n. 69 above, pp. 481–91.

74 Susi Colin, 'The wild man and the Indian in early 16th century book illustration' in Feest 1989, op. cit. in n. 60 above, pp. 5–36; Roger Barta, *Wild Man in the Looking Glass: The Mythic Origins of European Otherness*, Ann Arbor 1994.

75 Husband 1980, op. cit. in n. 70 above, cat. 25.

76 Karen Ordahl Kupperman, *The Jamestown Project*, Harvard and London 2007, p. 249.

77 Sloan 2007, op. cit. in n. 7 above, cat. 7.

78 Ibid., cat. 74; Mason Vaughan and Vaughan 1991, op. cit. in n. 2 above, p. 13.

79 See also a portrait of Catalina Michaela of Portugal, Philip II's daughter, as a child with her pet marmoset on her arm, 1573: Annemarie Jordan, *The Story of Süleyman, Celebrity Elephants and Other Exotica in Renaissance Portugal*, Zurich 2010, p. 10, fig. 11.

80 Compare the Flemish drawing of a monkey, still at the Escorial in Madrid, PN 10034449, in ibid., fig. 29 and p. 57.

81 William C. Sturtevant, 'Le Tupinambiasion des Indiens de l'Amérique du Nord' in Gilles Thérien (ed.), *Les Figures de l'Indien, Les cahiers du Département d'Etudes Littéraires*, Montréal 1988, vol. 9, pp. 288–303; Warwick Bray (ed.), 'The meeting of two worlds: Europe and the Americas 1492–1650', *Proceedings of the British Academy*, vol. 81, 1993, pp. 289–321, esp. p. 310.

82 John Rowlands, *The Age of Dürer and Holbein: German Drawings 1400–1550*, London 1988, cats 158a–b; Jean Michel Massing, 'Hans Burgkmair's depiction of Native Africans', *RES, Anthropology and Aesthetics*, vol. 27, 1995, pp. 39–51, esp. p. 46, figs 6–7; Jean Michel Massing in Jay Levenson (ed.), *Circa 1492: Art in the Age of Exploration*, Washington 1992, no. 405; Feest 2007, op. cit. in n. 64 above, p. 66, fig. 35.

83 See Christian Feest, 'Mexican Turquoise Mosaics in Vienna', in J. King, C. McEwan, C. Cartwright,

M. Carocci and R. Stacey (eds), *Turquoise in Mexico and North America: Science, Collections, Art and Culture*, forthcoming, for the Burgkmair drawing and shield.

84 John Florio (trans.) and Henry Morley (ed.), *The Essayes of Michael Lord of Montaigne*, London 1894, book 1, chapter 30, pp. 92–9; Bray 1993, op. cit. in n. 81 above, p. 313.

85 Florio and Morley, op. cit. in n. 84 above, p. 96. Peter Burke, *Montaigne*, Oxford 1981, p. 47.

86 Mason Vaughan and Vaughan 1999, op. cit. in n. 8 above, p. 308.

87 Warner 2000, op. cit. in n. 1 above, pp. 97–104.

88 All quotations from Homer's *Odyssey* as translated by E.V. Rieu, revised by C.H. Rieu and Peter Jones, London 2003, pp. 130–2.

89 Warner 2000, op. cit. in n. 1 above, p. 103.

90 Barbara A. Mowat, 'Prospero's book', *Shakespeare Quarterly*, vol. 52, no. 1, Spring 2001, pp. 1–33.

91 Sherman 1995, op. cit. in n. 36 above, pp. 51–2.

92 Keith Thomas, *Religion and the Decline of Magic*, London 1971, pp. 228–9.

93 See British Library, MS Sloane 3188, fol. 30r, for the diagram of the vision. The inscription on the large wax seal (British Museum, PE 1838,1232.90a) is virtually identical to the diagram in Dee's manuscript. The only difference is the number of crosses inscribed in the arms of the two heptagons: on the wax disc the number has been increased. The inscriptions on the two small seals (1838,1232.90b–c) are also virtually identical to the diagram in Dee's manuscript. Here, the number of crosses has been reduced and faint concentric circles are visible towards the outer circle and around the inner pentagram. The AGLA cross inscription appears to be the same on the reverse of all three wax seals, with no significant differences to the one sketched by Dee on fol. 10r of the same manuscript. We are grateful to Louise Devoy and Silke Ackermann for checking these details on the wax discs against the manuscript for us: see also Ackermann and Devoy 2012, op. cit. in n. 37 above.

94 British Library, MS Sloane 3188, f. 10r.

95 Colin McEwan, *Ancient American Art in Detail*, London 2009, p. 27; see Neil MacGregor, *A History of the World in 100 Objects*, London 2010,

no. 65, for a Taíno ritual seat and its role in Taíno culture.

96 McEwan 2009, op. cit. in n. 95 above, p. 28.

97 See José R. Oliver, *Caciques and Cemí Idols*, Tuscaloosa 2009, chapter 6, for this process.

98 José R. Oliver, Colin McEwan and Anna Casas Gilberga (eds), *El Caribe precolombino, Fray Ramón Pané y el universo taíno*, Barcelona 2008, cat. 6.

99 Ovid, *Metamorphoses*, 7.263–89, for which see Bate 1993, op. cit. in n. 1 above, pp. 251–5.

100 Coleridge in Jonathan Bate (ed.), *The Romantics on Shakespeare*, London 1992, p. 530.

Chapter 10

1 See Eric Rasmussen and Anthony James West (eds), *The Shakespeare First Folios: A Descriptive Catalogue*, London 2012, pp. 144–8.

2 Michael Vickers, *The Arundel and Pomfret Marbles*, Oxford 2006, pp. 8–10.

3 John Johnstone, *Naturae constantia*, Amsterdam 1632, pp. 94–5; reprinted 1634, p. 80. Translated into English by John Rowland, *An History of the Constancy of Nature*, London 1657, pp. 100–1. Quoted in Robert Harding, '"The head of a certain Macedonian King": an old identity for the British Museum's "Arundel Homer"', *British Art Journal*, vol. 9, no. 2, Autumn 2008, pp. 11–16.

4 See http://www.westminster-abbey.org/our-history/people/william-shakespeare and Ingrid Roscoe, 'The monument to the memory of Shakespeare', *Journal of the Church Monuments Society*, vol. 9, 1994, pp. 72–82.

5 The following discussion is indebted to Martin White, 'Practising theatre history as performance', http://www.bristol.ac.uk/drama/jacobean/research2.html.

6 See Marion F. O'Connor, 'Theatre of the Empire: "Shakespeare's England" at Earl's Court, 1912' in Marion F. O'Connor and Jean Howard (eds), *Shakespeare Reproduced: The Text in Ideology and History*, London 1987, pp. 68–98.

7 *The Graphic*, 11 May 1912, pp. 674–5.

8 Anthony Sampson, 'O, what men dare do', *Observer*, 22 April 2001, http://observer.guardian.co.uk/print/0,,4173726-102273,00.html.

List of exhibits

The following objects illustrated in this book feature in the exhibition *Shakespeare: staging the world*. Details correct at the time of going to press. Further information about objects in the collection of the British Museum can be found on the Museum's website at britishmuseum.org.

Only select references are given: fuller references are provided in the notes. Where no literature is given, the object is believed to be previously unpublished.

Chapter 1

Fig. 3
Anthony Munday (1560–1633) (?) and Henry Chettle (d. 1603–7)
The Booke of Sir Thomas More, c. 1601–4
Manuscript, ink on paper; approx. 37 x 27 cm
British Library, London, Harley MS 7368, f. 9
Literature: J. Jowett (ed.), *Sir Thomas More*, London 2011; T. Cooper, *Searching for Shakespeare*, London 2006, cat. 66

Fig. 4
William Shakespeare (1564–1616), ed. John Heminge (c. 1556–1630) and H. Condell (d. 1627)
The 'First Folio': *Mr. Wiliam Shakespeares Comedies Histories, & Tragedies. Published according to the True Originall Copies*
'Printed by Isaac Jaggard, and Ed. Blount', London, 1623
Printed book; 31.9 x 20.7 cm (closed)
Six original preliminary leaves and all original text leaves present; the title page is a nineteenth-century facsimile with an original engraved portrait pasted onto it. It was common for First Folios to have their original title pages torn out and sold. For fuller bibliographical details on this copy, see Rasmussen and West 2011
Stonyhurst College, Clitheroe, Lancashire
Literature: E. Rasmussen and A.J. West (eds), *The Shakespeare First Folios: A Descriptive Catalogue*, Basingstoke 2011, pp. 144–8, no. 36

Fig. 5
Wenceslaus Hollar (1607–77)
London ('The Long View')
Published by Cornelis Danckerts, Amsterdam, 1647
Etching, comprising four sheets mounted together; 47.1 x 158.7 cm overall
Inscriptions: Dedication by the publisher to Queen Henrietta Maria; 'Wenceslaus Hollar delineavit, et fecit Londini et Antverpiae, 1647'; 'Prostant Amstelodami apud Cornelium Danckers via vitulina sub insigni Gratitudines ano. 1647'
British Museum, London, PD 1880,1113.1126.1–4
Literature: R. Pennington, *A Descriptive Catalogue of the Etched Work of Wenceslaus Hollar*, Cambridge 1982, no. 1014.I; F.W.H. Hollstein, *The New Hollstein: Dutch and Flemish Etchings, Engravings and Woodcuts 1450–1700*, Amsterdam 1993 continuing, no. 954.I; J. Bowsher and P. Miller, *The Rose and the Globe – Playhouses of Shakespeare's Bankside, Southwark: Excavations 1988–91*, London 2009, p. 91

Fig. 6
Unknown artist
Going to Bankside (London Bridge), c. 1619
From the *Album Amicorum* of Michael van Meer (d. 1653), f. 408v
Pen and ink with watercolour and gold highlighting on paper; 13 x 19 cm (sheet); 8 x 16.7 cm (image)
Edinburgh University Library, Edinburgh, Special Collections, La.III.283.
Bequeathed by David Laing 1878
Literature: J. Schlueter, 'Michael van Meer's Album Amicorum, with illustrations of London, 1614–15', *Huntington Library Quarterly*, vol. 69, no. 2, June 2006, pp. 301–14

Fig. 7
Wenceslaus Hollar (1607–77).
Sheet 2 from *London* ('The Long View')
Published by Cornelis Danckerts, Amsterdam, 1647
Etching; 46.6 x 39 cm
British Museum, London, PD 1864,0611.434.
Literature: See fig. 5 above

Fig. 9
John Gipkyn (*fl.* 1594–1629)
Diptych of Old Saint Paul's, London, 1616
Oil on two panels, one panel painted front and back; each panel 110.49 x 87.63 cm (excluding frame)
Inscription: (around the frame, part) 'So invented, and at my costs made, per me Hen: Farley.1616.Wrought by John Gipkyn ...'
Society of Antiquaries, London, LDSAL 304
Literature: P. Tudor-Craig, with C. Whittick, *'Old St Paul's': The Society of Antiquaries' Diptych, 1616*, London 2004; D. Gaimster, B. Nurse and J. Steele (eds), *Making History: Antiquaries in Britain 1707–2007*, London 2007, p. 42, cat. 1; J. Franklin, B. Nurse and P. Tudor-Craig, *Catalogue of Paintings in the Collection of the Society of Antiquaries of London*, forthcoming

Fig. 11
Attributed to Lucas de Heere (1534–84)
The family of Henry VIII: An allegory of the Tudor succession, c. 1572
Oil on panel; 131.2 x 184 cm
Inscriptions: (along the bottom) THE QVENE. TO. WALSINGHAM. THIS. TABLET. SENTE. MARKE. OF. HER. PEOPLES. AND. HER. OWNE. CONTENTE; (around the frame) A FACE OF MVCHE NOBILLITYE LOE IN A LITTLE ROOME. FOWR STATES WITH THEYR CONDITIONS HEARE SHADOWED IN | A SHOWE A FATHER MORE THEN VALYANT. A RARE AND VERTVOVS SOON. | A ZEALVS DAVGHTER IN HER KYND WHAT ELS THE WORLD DOTH KNOWE | AND LAST OF ALL A VYRGIN QVEEN TO ENGLANDS IOY WE SEE SVCESSYVELY TO HOLD THE RIGHT, AND VERTVES OF THE THREE
An engraving after the painting was made by William Rogers, c. 1595–1600, and was also in the collection of Horace Walpole (British Museum, PD 1842,0806.373)
National Museum of Wales, Cardiff, NMW A 564
Accepted by HM Government in lieu of inheritance tax, 1991
Literature: K. Hearn (ed.), *Dynasties: Painting in Tudor and Jacobean England 1530–1630*, London 1995, cat. 35; M. Snodin (ed.), *Horace Walpole's Strawberry Hill*, New Haven and London 2009, pp. 128–9, fig. 149

Fig. 12
The Bishops' Bible, London, 1569, open at frontispiece
Printed book; 21.5 x 16 cm (closed)
British Library, London, G.12188, f.1
Literature: J. King, *Tudor Royal Iconography: Literature and Art in an Age of Religious Crisis*, New Jersey 1989, pp. 233–4; S. Doran (ed.), *Elizabeth*, London 2003, cat. 56

Fig. 14
John Robinson (?) (d. 1591)
The Stonyhurst Salt, London, 1577–8
Silver-gilt, decorated with rock crystals, rubies and garnets salvaged from Catholic ecclesiastical plate or reliquaries of the 13th to 15th centuries destroyed at the Reformation; H. 26.2 cm
Maker's mark: IR, with flower between in shaped shield under junction of base and stem; hallmarked for London 1577–8 on centre of domed foot and centre of bowl
British Museum, London, PE 1958,1004.1 Acquired 1958 with a contribution from The Art Fund
Literature: H. Tait, 'The Stonyhurst Salt', *Apollo*, April 1964, pp. 270–8

Fig. 15
Robert Durrant (active 1560s–1591)
The Bishopton Cup, London, 1571–2
Silver; H. (cup) 12.7 cm, (lid) 3.3 cm

Maker's mark: three mullets (stars) over a crescent moon; hallmarked for London 1571–2; '1571' incised on lid. The lid doubles as a paten
Holy Trinity Church, Stratford-upon-Avon
Literature: V. Horsler, M. Gorick and P. Edmonson, *Shakespeare's Church: A Parish for the World*, London 2010, illus. p. 151

Fig. 16
Unknown maker
The Clifford Chambers chalice and paten, London, 1494–5
Silver-gilt; H. (chalice) 15.4 cm; diam. of paten 14.6 cm
Maker's mark (both items): a bird's head; hallmarked for London 1494–5
The letters IESUS on lozenges on stem of chalice, in relief on originally enamelled ground. Graffiti on lozenges: 'A pox on Y'
St Helen's Church, Clifford Chambers, Stratford-upon-Avon
Literature: E.A. Jones, 'Old plate at the Church Congress', *Burlington Magazine*, vol. 39, no. 225, Dec. 1921, pp. 254–67

Fig. 18
Unknown artist (Ottoman School)
Leaf from an album: *A briefe relation of the Turckes, their kings, Emperors, or Grandsigneurs, their conquests, religion, customes, habbits, etc.*, f. 46v
Istanbul, 1618
Opaque watercolour on paper and paper cut-outs; 19.9 x 13 cm
Inscriptions in English and Turkish
British Museum, London, ME 1974,0617.0.13.46.v
Literature: N.M. Titley, *Miniatures from Turkish Manuscripts*, London 1981, p. 22, no. 7 (48); D. Thornton, *The Scholar in his Study: Ownership and Experience in Renaissance Italy*, New Haven and London 1997, p. 82, fig. 80

Fig. 19
Ewer
Iznik, Ottoman Turkey, c. 1585; mounts added in London 1597–8
Iznik fritware (stonepaste) with spout, cover and foot of embossed, chased and gilt silver; H. 33.2 cm
On mounts: maker's mark HB; hallmarked for London 1597–8
British Museum, London, PE AF.3132
Bequeathed by Sir Augustus Wollaston Franks, 1897
Literature: C.H. Read and A.B. Tonnochy, *Catalogue of the Silver Plate, Medieval and Later, Bequeathed to the British Museum by Sir Augustus Wollaston Franks, K.C.B.*, London 1928, no. 23; N. Atasoy and J. Raby, ed. Y. Petsopoulos, *Iznik: The Pottery of Ottoman Turkey*, London and New York 1989, no. 775 and p. 269, as one of three with silver mounts which are date-marked

Fig. 20
Bowl and mount ('The Lennard Cup')
Ming dynasty, made in Jingdezhen, China, 1522–66; mount added in London 1569–70
Porcelain bowl with silver-gilt mount and cover; the exterior of the bowl incised with lotus scrolls and the interior decorated in underglaze blue with a hare against a landscape; H. (including mount) 16 cm, diam. 12 cm
Inscription: (in Chinese, on the base of the bowl) 'Long life riches and honours'
On mounts: maker's mark FR in monogram; hallmarked for London 1569–70
British Museum, London, Asia PDF.695
On loan from the Sir Percival David Foundation of Chinese Art
Literature: S. Pierson, *Illustrated Catalogue of Underglaze Blue and Copper Red Decorated Porcelains in the Percival David Foundation of Chinese Art*, London 2004, no. 695

Fig. 23
Bracelet
Sri Lanka (Kotte or Kandy), before 1587
Gold, rock crystal, rubies and sapphires; diam. 9 cm
Private collection, on loan to the Victoria and Albert Museum, London
Literature: Doran 2003, op. cit. fig 12, no. 104; A. Jordan-Gschwend and J. Beltz, *Elfenbeine aus Ceylon: Luxusgüter für Katharina von Habsburg (1507–1578)*, Zürich 2010, no. 35

Fig. 24
Unknown Mughal artist
A European, *c.* 1610–15
Opaque watercolour on paper; 32.9 x 18.8 (excluding borders)
Victoria and Albert Museum, London, IM.9-1913
Literature: S. Stronge, *Painting for the Mughal Emperor: The Art of the Book 1560–1650*, London 2002, p. 139, pl. 106

Fig. 25
Oil lamp
Originally made as a horn in Calabar (modern Nigeria) 1500s, recarved later that century, possibly in Europe, and turned into a drinking horn; and finally mounted as an oil lamp before 1753
Ivory and brass; L. 83 cm
Inscription: (on the central band) 'Drinke you this and think no scorne although the cup be much like a horne 1599 Finis'
British Museum, London, PE SLMisc.2012
Bequeathed by Sir Hans Sloane, 1753
Literature: E. Bassani, 'Additional notes on the Afro-Portuguese ivories', *African Arts*, vol. 27, no. 3, Memorial to William Fagg, July 1994, pp. 34–45; J. Warren, 'Sir Hans Sloane as a collector of small sculpture', *Apollo*, vol. 159, February 2004, pp. 31–8

Fig. 26
Unknown artist
Abd el-Ouahed ben Messaoud ben Mohammed Anoun, ambassador to England from the King of Barbary (Morocco), England, *c.* 1600
Oil on panel; 114.5 x 79 cm
Inscription: 100 ABDVLGVAHID, AETATIS: 42. LEGATUS REGIS BARBARIAE IN ANGLIAM
Shakespeare Institute, Stratford-upon-Avon (University of Birmingham), A0427
Literature: B. Harris, 'A portrait of a Moor', in C.M.S. Alexander and S. Wells (eds), *Shakespeare and Race*, Cambridge 2000, pp. 23–36 (first published in *Shakespeare Survey*, 1958)
We are grateful to Scotford Lawrence and James Hamilton for their help and for showing us the dendrochronological analysis for the painting.

Fig. 27
Attributed to Quentin Metsys the Younger (?1543–1589)
Queen Elizabeth I in the guise of the Vestal Virgin Tuccia ('The Sieve Portrait'), signed and dated 1583
Oil on canvas; 124.5 x 91.5 cm
Inscriptions: (below left) STA[N]CHO | RIPOSO | & RIPO | SATO | AFFA | NNO (Weary, I rest and, having rested, still am weary); (on the rim of the sieve) A TERRA ILBEN | AL DIMORA IN SELLA (The good falls to the ground while the bad remains in the saddle); (on the globe) TVTTO VEDO ET MO[LTO MANCHA] (I see all and much is lacking); signed and dated on base of globe: 1583. Q. MASSYS | ANT
Pinacoteca Nazionale, Siena, 454
Literature: Hearn 1995, op. cit. fig 11, cat. 40

Fig. 28a
Rapier, possibly England, late 1500s
Steel blade, iron guard and pommel, original wooden grip bound with copper alloy wire; L. 128 cm
Royal Armouries, Leeds, IX.1494 A
Literature: G.M. Wilson, 'Notes on some early basket-hilted swords', *Journal of the Arms and Armour Society*, vol. 12, no. 1, March 1986, pp. 1–19, esp. p. 13

Fig. 28b
Left-hand dagger, England, *c.* 1600
Steel blade, iron guard and pommel, original wooden grip bound with iron wire; L. 46.3 cm
Royal Armouries, Leeds, X.1764

Fig. 31
Unknown Anglo-Flemish artist
The Judgement of Solomon, *c.* 1586–*c.* 1602
Oil on panel; approx. 188.5 x 165 cm
Middle Temple, London
Literature: T. Cooper, 'Professional pride and personal agendas: portraits of judges, lawyers and members of the Inns of Court 1560–1630', in J.E. Archer, E. Goldring and S. Knight (eds),

The Intellectual and Cultural World of the Early Modern Inns of Court, Manchester and New York 2011, pp. 160–1

Fig. 32
Unknown Anglo-Netherlandish artist
Henry Carey, 1st Baron Hunsdon, dated 1591
Oil on panel; 90 x 75 cm
Inscriptions: (top right) ATATIS SVÆ 66 AN. 1591; (top left) 'Henry Carey / Lord Hunsdon / Mark Gerards' (later, probably 1700s)
Trustees of the Berkeley Will Trust
Literature: Cooper 2006, op. cit. fig. 3, cat. 45

Fig. 33
Baluster from the Rose Playhouse, 1587–1606
Oak; damaged L. 43.5 cm; max. diam. 6 cm
Museum of London, London, SBH88 <96>, [381]
Literature: Bowsher and Miller 2009, op. cit. fig. 5, fig. 62 and pp. 223–5, no. <ST7>

Fig. 34
Clay pipe from the Rose Playhouse, *c.* 1580–*c.* 1610
L. 6.2 cm; diam. of bowl opening 0.9 cm
Museum of London, London, SBH88,[79]
Literature: Bowsher and Miller 2009, op. cit. fig. 5, fig. 119 and pp. 175–80, no. <CP7>

Fig. 35
Ring from the Rose Playhouse, 1587–1606
Gold, H. 0.6 cm, diam. 2 cm
Inscription: PENCES POVR MOYE DV (Think of me God willing)
Museum of London, London, SBH88 <283>, [183]
Literature: Bowsher and Miller 2009, op. cit. fig. 5, fig. 114 and p. 203, no. <S79>

Fig. 36a
Fork from the Rose Playhouse, 1587–1606
Iron, with brass finial; L. 22.1 cm
Initials 'AN' engraved on finial
Museum of London, London, SBH88 <611>, [783]
Literature: J. Bowsher and P. Miller 2009, op. cit. fig. 5, fig. 115 and p. 212, no. <S160>

Fig. 36b
Dice from the Rose Playhouse, *c.* 1592
Bone; 0.7 x 0.7 cm and 0.4 x 0.4 cm
Museum of London, London, SBH88 <783>, [581] and SBH88 <875>, [730]
Literature: Bowsher and Miller 2009, op. cit. fig. 5, fig. 120 and p. 212, nos <S166> and <S167>

Fig. 36c
Manicure implement from the Rose Playhouse, 1587–1606
Bone; L. 8.8 cm
Museum of London, London, SBH88 <257>, [442]
Literature: Bowsher and Miller 2009, op. cit. fig. 5, fig. 120 and p. 208, no. <S138>

Fig. 37
Skull of a brown bear (*Ursus arctos*)
Probably a female; the skull lacks its lower jaw and some teeth, and shows that the bear had suffered a blow to the back of the head
H. 13.5 cm, W. 20 cm, L. 32 cm
Dulwich College, London, DC 760
Literature: Cooper 2006, op. cit. fig. 3, cat. 30
We are grateful to Calista Lucy at Dulwich College and to Daphne Hills and Richard Sabin of the Natural History Museum for the specimen identification.

Fig. 38
Advertisement for the Bear Garden, *c.* 1603–25
Manuscript, ink on paper, 25 x 19 cm
Dulwich College, London, MS II, f. 86r
Literature: G.F. Warner and F.B. Bickley, *Catalogue of the Manuscripts and Muniments of Alleyn's College of God's Gift at Dulwich*, 1881, repr. Delhi 2009, p. 83, no. 41

Fig. 40
Simon Forman (1552–1611)
Diary, open at a description of a performance of *The Winter's Tale*, 1611
Manuscript, ink on paper; approx. 30 x 20 cm (closed)
Bodleian Library, Oxford, MS Ashmole 208, f. 201
Literature: Cooper 2006, op. cit. fig. 3, cat. 61

Fig. 41
Anonymous author after Thomas Harman (active 1547–67)
The Groundworke of Conny-catching, open at title page, London, 1592.
Printed book; 18.5 x 14.5 cm (closed)
British Library, London, C.27.b.21
Literature: Cooper 2006, op. cit. fig. 3, cat. 34

Fig. 42
Money-box
Made *c.* 1550–1650 and found in the City of London
Lead-glazed earthenware; copper added to glaze to give green colour (Tudor Green ware); H. 9 cm
Pottery money-boxes of very similar form have been excavated on the site of the Rose Theatre in London
British Museum, London, PE 1895,0116.9
Given by Sir Augustus Wollaston Franks, 1895
Literature: R.L. Hobson, *Catalogue of the Collection of English Pottery in the Department of British and Medieval Antiquities and Ethnography of the British Museum*, London 1903, no. B181

Fig. 43
Unknown artist
Sir Henry Unton, *c.* 1596
Oil on panel, 74 x 16.3 cm
National Portrait Gallery, London, NPG 710
Literature: R. Strong, 'Sir Henry Unton and his portrait', *Archaeologia*, vol. 99, 1965, pp. 53–76; N. Llewellyn in *The Art of Death*, London 1992, pp. 13–15

Fig. 44
Michael Mercator (active 1589)
Medal commemorating Francis Drake's circumnavigation of the globe, London, 1589
Silver, cast in imitation of engraving; diam. 6.7 cm
Inscriptions: (on the side showing America) 'D.F. Dra. Exitus anno 1577 Id. Dece.' (The departure of Francis Drake, in the year 1577 on the ides of December [i.e.13 December]); 'Reditus anno 1580. 4 Cal. Oc.' (Return in the year 1580, on the 4th of the calends of October [i.e. 28 September])
British Museum, London, CM 1882,0507.1
Given by Sir Augustus Wollaston Franks, 1882
Literature: E. Hawkins, ed. A.W. Franks and H.A. Grueber, *Medallic Illustrations of the History of Great Britain and Ireland to the Death of George II*, London 1885, vol. I, p. 131, no. 83; R.M. Christy, *The Silver Map of the World: A contemporary Medallion Commemorative of Drake's Great Voyage, 1577–80*, London 1900; H. Wallis, 'Silver medal for the Golden Hind', *Geographical Magazine*, vol. 50, no. 2, Nov. 1977, pp. 112–17; H. Wallis, 'The cartography of Drake's voyage' in N.J.W. Thrower (ed.), *Sir Francis Drake and the Famous Voyage, 1577–1580: Essays Commemorating the Quadricentennial of Drake's Circumnavigation of the Earth*, Berkeley, Los Angeles and London 1984, pp. 121–63

Fig. 45
Unknown artist
Broadside: portrait of Sir Francis Drake, Germany, late 1580s
Hand-coloured etching and engraving; 29 x 54 cm
Inscriptions: 50 lines of verse in German, beginning 'Hier steh ich Drach in Engelandt'; also inscribed in Latin: FRANCISCVS DRAECK NOBILISSIMVS EQVES ANGLIAE . IS EST QVI TOTO T. TERRARVM ORBE CIRCVMDVCTO
British Library, London, HS.85/39
Literature: S. Reed, 'Notes: Sir Francis Drake', *Print Quarterly*, vol. 26, no. 3, Sept. 2009, pp. 274–5

Fig. 46
Emery Molyneux (d. 1598/9) and Jocodus Hondius
(1563–1612)
The Molyneux Globes, London (Amsterdam?), 1592; terrestrial
globe updated in 1603
Papier mâché, plaster and printed paper, with wooden stands
and brass surrounds; diam. of each 63.5 cm
Middle Temple Library, London
Literature: R.M. Fisher, 'William Crashawe and the Middle
Temple globes 1605–15', *Geographical Journal*, vol. 140, no. 1,
Feb. 1974, pp. 105–12; P. Barber and T. Harper, *Magnificent
Maps: Power, Propaganda and Art*, London 2010, pp. 60–1

Chapter 2

Fig. 1
Laurence Nowell (*c.* 1515–*c.* 1571)
'A general description of England & Ireland with the costes
adioyning', from the Nowell-Burghley Atlas, *c.* 1564
Ink and coloured wash on vellum; map 21.2 x 30.9 cm, on
sheet 23.3 x 33.9 cm, folded into a volume bound in limp
vellum in a half morocco case; 24 x 17.5 cm
Inscription: Initials 'L.N.' on base of pedestal
British Library, London, Add. MS 62540
Literature: P. Barber, 'A Tudor mystery. Laurence Nowell's map
of England and Ireland', *The Map Collector*, vol. 22, March
1983, pp. 16–21; P. Barber (ed.), *The Map Book*, London 2005,
p. 112; P. Barber, 'Mapmaking in England ca. 1470–1650' in
D. Woodward (ed.), *The History of Cartography*, III. *Cartography
in the European Renaissance*, Chicago 2007, pp. 1589–1669

Fig. 2
Christopher Saxton (1542/4–1610/11)
Map of Warwickshire and Leicestershire, 1576
Hand-coloured engraving, 49.7 x 37 cm
Shakespeare Birthplace Trust, Stratford-upon-Avon, 1933-31/444
Literature: P.D.A. Harvey and H. Thorpe, *The Printed Maps of
Warwickshire 1570–1900*, Warwick 1959, pp. 1–5 and 71–3;
T. Cooper, *Searching for Shakespeare*, London 2006, cat. 9

Fig. 4
Augustine Ryther (active *c.* 1579–93) after William Bowes
(active 1590–1605)
A pack of 52 playing cards depicting the counties of England
and Wales, with 8 introductory cards, dated 1590
Hand-coloured engravings; 9.5 x 5.7 cm
Inscription: The first of the introductory cards is lettered 'W.B.
inuen. 1590'
British Museum, London, PD 1938,0709.57.1–60
Literature: A.M. Hind, 'An Elizabethan pack of playing-cards',
British Museum Quarterly, vol. 13, 1938, pp. 2–4; G. L'E. Turner,
*Elizabethan Instrument Makers: The Origins of the London Trade in
Precision Instrument Making*, Oxford 2000, cat. 36

Fig. 5
'The Sheldon Tapestry Map of Warwickshire'
Perhaps made at the Sheldon tapestry workshops, Barcheston,
Warwickshire, or in London, *c.* 1588 (the border dates from
the 1600s)
Wool and silk; 390 x 510 cm approx.
Warwickshire Museum Service, Warwickshire
Literature: Barber 2005, op. cit. fig. 1, pp. 128–9; H.L. Turner,
No Mean Prospect: Ralph Sheldon's Tapestry Maps, Tonypandy,
2010

Fig. 7
Fragment from the 'Sheldon Tapestry Map of Oxfordshire',
with the coat of arms of Ralph Sheldon (1537–1613)
Perhaps made at the Sheldon tapestry workshops, Barcheston,
Warwickshire, or in London, *c.* 1588
Wool and silk; 122 x 61.5 cm
Victoria and Albert Museum, London, T.61A-1954
Presented by Mrs H. McKnight, 1954
Literature: M. Snodin (ed.), *Horace Walpole's Strawberry Hill*,
New Haven and London 2009, cat. 64; Turner 2010, op. cit.
fig. 5, p. 56

Fig. 10
Bed valance
Perhaps made at the Sheldon tapestry workshops, Barcheston,
Warwickshire, or in London, 1600–10
Silk and wool with some silver thread; 25 x 534 cm
Victoria and Albert Museum, London, T.117-1934
Purchased with the assistance of The Art Fund, an Anonymous
Donor, Sir Frederick Richard and the Vallentin Bequest
Literature: G.F. Wingfield-Digby, *Victoria and Albert Museum:
The Tapestry Collection, Medieval and Renaissance*, London
1980, no. 73

Fig. 11
Fragment from a tapestry showing a man hawking
Perhaps made in the Sheldon tapestry workshops, Barcheston,
Warwickshire, or in London, *c.* 1600
Silk and wool; 21 x 23.2 cm
Victoria and Albert Museum, London, T.645-1993
Given by Miss Wendy Hefford

Fig. 14
William Shakespeare (1564–1616)
Venus and Adonis, open at f. Eiij*v*
First edition, printed by Richard Field, London, 1593
Printed book; 18 x 13 cm approx. (page)
Oxford, Bodleian Library, Arch. G e.31(2)
Literature: Cooper 2006, op. cit. fig. 2, cat. 48

Fig. 16
Drainage spade, 1700s
Ash, carved from a single piece of wood, with iron sheath;
D-handle carved and branded 'AH' and 'X'; L. 110 cm
Shakespeare Birthplace Trust, Stratford-upon-Avon, 1996-21

Fig. 17
Watering-pot, 1500s
Found when digging the foundations for the Great Eastern
Railway Terminus, Liverpool Street, London
Lead-glazed earthenware; H. 31.5 cm
British Museum, London, PE 1887,1017.2
Given by C.J. Lucas, 1887
Literature: J. Cherry, 'La chantepleure: a symbol of mourning',
in J. Cherry and A. Payne Donington (eds), *Signs and Symbols*,
Harlaxton Medieval Studies, no. 18, Donington 2009, pp. 143–50

Fig. 18
Jacques Le Moyne (*c.* 1533–1588)
Gilliflower and Privet Hawk Moth, *c.* 1585
Watercolour and bodycolour; 21.5 x 14 cm
Inscription: in graphite, '16'
British Museum, London, PD 1962,0714.1.18
Purchased 1962 with a contribution from The Art Fund
and private individuals
Literature: P. Hulton, *The Works of Jacques Le Moyne de Morgues,
a Huguenot Artist in France, Florida and England*, 2 vols,
London 1977, no. 53

Fig. 19
Jacques Le Moyne (*c.* 1533–1588)
Pot Marigold and Green-veined White Butterfly, *c.* 1585
Watercolour and bodycolour; 20.7 x 14.5 cm
Inscription: in graphite, '17'
British Museum, London, PD 1962,0714.1.19
Purchased 1962 with a contribution from The Art Fund
and private individuals
Literature: Hulton 1977, op. cit. fig. 18, no. 54

Fig. 20
Jacques Le Moyne (*c.* 1533–1588)
Daffodil, *c.* 1585
Watercolour and bodycolour; 21.7 x 14.8 cm
Inscription: in graphite, '3'
British Museum, London, PD 1962,0714.1.5
Purchased 1962 with a contribution from The Art Fund
and private individuals
Literature: Hulton 1977, op. cit. fig. 18, no. 40

Fig. 21
Jacques Le Moyne (*c.* 1533–1588)
Rosemary and Lackey Moth Caterpillar, *c.* 1585
Watercolour and bodycolour; 21.5 x 14.2 cm
Inscription: in graphite, '6'
British Museum, London, PD 1962,0714.1.8
Purchased 1962 with a contribution from The Art Fund
and private individuals
Literature: Hulton 1977, op. cit. fig. 18, no. 43

Fig. 22
Woman's jacket
Britain, *c.* 1600–25 (ribbon fastenings modern)
Linen, hand-sewn and embroidered with silk, silver and silver-
gilt thread; L. (neck to hem) 66.5 cm
Victoria and Albert Museum, London, 919-1873
Given by A. Soloman
Literature: J.L. Nevinson, *Catalogue of English Domestic
Embroidery of the Sixteenth and Seventeenth Centuries*, London
1938, p. 70, pl. LIV; D. King and S. Levey, *The Victoria and
Albert Museum's Textile Collections: Embroidery in Britain from
1200 to 1750*, London 1993, fig. 52; A. Hart and S. North,
Historical Fashion in Detail: The 17th and 18th centuries,
London 1998, pp. 24–5; K. Hearn, *Marcus Gheeraerts II,
Elizabethan Artist*, London 2002, p. 44

Fig. 26
Unknown English artist
John Donne, *c.* 1595
Oil on panel; 72.4 x 60 cm
Inscription: (around the edge of the oval) ILLUMINA TENEBR
/NOSTRAS DOMINA (O Lady, lighten our darkness)
National Portrait Gallery, London, NPG 6790
Purchased with help from the National Heritage Memorial Fund,
The Art Fund, Lord Harris of Peckham, L.L. Brownrigg, the
Portrait Fund, Sir Harry Djanogly, the Headley Trust, the Eva
& Hans K. Rausing Trust, The Pidem Fund, Mr O. Damgaard-
Nielsen, Sir David and Lady Scholey and numerous Gallery
visitors and supporters, 2006
Literature: R. Strong, *Tudor and Jacobean Portraits*, 2 vols,
London 1969, vol. 1, p. 66; Cooper 2006, op. cit, fig. 2,
cat. 80; T. Cooper, *A Guide to Tudor and Jacobean Portraits*,
London 2008, p. 25

Fig. 27
Isaac Oliver (*c.* 1565–1617)
*Portrait miniature of Edward Herbert, 1st Baron Herbert of
Cherbury*, *c.* 1613–14
Vellum on card; 18.1 x 22.7 cm
Powis Castle, Powys, The Rt Hon. The Earl of Powis
Literature: R. Strong, *The English Renaissance Miniature*, London
1983, pp. 180–4; K. Hearn (ed.), *Dynasties: Painting in Tudor
and Jacobean England 1530–1630*, London 1995, cat. 86

Fig. 28
Jug
Probably Southwark, *c.* 1620
Tin-glazed earthenware, painted; H. 32.2 cm
Inscriptions: I. AM. NO. BEGGAR. I. CAN. NOT. CRAVE.
BUT. YU. KNOW. THE. THING. THAT. I. WOULD.
HAVE; (on neck) C/R E
Victoria and Albert Museum, London, C.5-1974
Literature: M. Archer, *Delftware: The Tin-glazed Earthenware of
the British Isles. A Catalogue of the Collection in the Victoria and
Albert Museum*, London 1997, pp. 241–2, no. C.1; R. Hildyard,
European Ceramics, London 1999, p. 40, fig. 43

Fig. 31
Antler headdress
Excavated at Star Carr, Vale of Pickering, Yorkshire
Early Mesolithic, *c.* 8000 BC
Red deer antler; H. 15 cm, L. 18 cm
British Museum, London, PE 1953,0208.1
Given by Sir Grahame Douglas Clark
Literature: J.G.D. Clark, *Star Carr*, Cambridge 1954; M. Street,
Jäger und Schamanen, Mainz 1989

Fig. 33
Block from 'Herne's Oak'. Windsor Great Park, Berkshire
H. 51.5 cm, W. 45 cm
One portion polished to show grain; carved with initials, now faint
British Museum, London, PE 1863,1207.1
Given by Queen Victoria after the tree blew down in 1863
Literature: E. Harris, J. Harris and N.D.G. James, *Oak: A British History*, Oxford 2003, p. 183, no. 299

Fig. 34
William Dethick, Garter King-of-Arms (1543–1612)
Draft grants of arms to John Shakespeare, dated 20 October 1596
Manuscript, ink on paper; 29.2 x 29.3 cm on backing (no.1) and 41 x 29.4 cm (no. 2)
London, College of Arms, Shakespeare Grants 1 and 2
Literature: *Heralds' Commemorative Exhibition 1484–1934*, London 1936, repr. 1970, no. 18; C.W. Scott-Giles, *Shakespeare's Heraldry*, London 1950; S. Schoenbaum, *William Shakespeare: A Documentary Life*, Oxford 1975, pp. 167–71

Fig. 35
William Dethick, Garter King-of-Arms (1543–1612)
Draft document confirming John Shakspeare's right to display the arms of Arden together with his own, dated 1599
Manuscript, ink on paper; 20.5 x 31.5 cm on backing
College of Arms, London, Shakespeare Grant 3
Literature: Scott-Giles 1950, op. cit. fig. 34; Schoenbaum 1975, op. cit. fig. 34, pp. 167–71

Chapter 3

Fig. 1
Unknown artist
Richard II, painted between 7 June 1394 and 15 December 1395
Oil on panel; 213.5 x 110 cm
Extensively restored in 1733, 1866 and 2011
Westminster Abbey, London
Literature: J. Alexander and P. Binski (eds), *The Age of Chivalry*, London 1987, cat. 713; J. Cherry and N. Stratford, 'Westminster kings and the medieval Palace of Westminster', British Museum Occasional Paper 115, London 1995, p. 91; J.J.G. Alexander, 'The Portrait of Richard II in Westminster Abbey' in D. Gordon, L. Monnas and C. Elam (eds), *The Regal Image of Richard II and the Wilton Diptych*, London 1997, pp. 197–206

Fig. 4
The Dunstable Swan Jewel (livery badge)
Made in England or France, *c.* 1400, and found at Dunstable Priory in 1965
Gold with white and black enamel; H. 3.4 cm
British Museum, London, PE 1966,0703.1
Purchased 1966 with contributions from The Art Fund, the Pilgrim Trust and the Worshipful Company of Goldsmiths
Literature: J. Cherry, 'The Dunstable Swan Jewel', *Journal of the British Archaeological Association*, vol. 32, 1969, pp. 38–53; Alexander and Binski 1987, op. cit. fig. 1, cat. 659; R. Marks and P. Williamson (eds), *Gothic: Art for England 1400–1547*, London 2003, cat. 70; J. Robinson, *Masterpieces of Medieval Art*, London 2008, pp. 172–3

Fig. 5
Badge in the shape of a seated hart, England, 1390–9
Lead alloy, mould-made; L. 3.91 cm
British Museum, London, PE 1856,0627.117
Literature: Cherry and Stratford 1995, op. cit. fig. 1, p. 94

Fig. 6
Horary quadrant engraved with the white hart emblem of Richard II
England, dated 1399, with some later additions attributed to Charles Whitwell, *c.* 1595
Brass, engraved and originally gilded; H. 9.2 cm, L. of straight sides 9 cm. Plumb line missing

British Museum, London, PE 1860,0519.1
Literature: Alexander and Binski 1987, op. cit. fig. 1, cat. 724; S. Ackermann and J. Cherry, 'Richard II, John Holland and three medieval quadrants', *Annals of Science*, vol. 56, 1999, pp. 3–23, esp. p. 20; G. L'E. Turner, *Elizabethan Instrument Makers: The Origins of the London Trade in Precision Instrument Making*, Oxford 2000, no. 44

Fig. 12
Unknown artist
Richard III with a broken sword, mid-1500s
Oil on oak panel; 48.5 x 35.5 cm
Society of Antiquaries, London, LDSAL 331
Bequeathed by Thomas Kerrich, 1828
Literature: *Thomas Kerrich Manuscript Catalogue of Drawings and Pictures*, 1805, transcribed by F. O'Donoghue, 1828, Society of Antiquaries of London, MS 1022; H. Scharf, *Catalogue of Pictures Belonging to the Society of Antiquaries*, London 1865, no. XXI; P. Tudor-Craig, *Richard III*, London 1973, cat. P40; D. Gaimster, B. Nurse and J. Steele (eds), *Making History: Antiquaries in Britain*, London 2007, cat. 50; J. Franklin, B. Nurse and P. Tudor-Craig, *Catalogue of Paintings in the Collection of the Society of Antiquaries of London*, forthcoming

Fig. 16
Livery badge in the shape of a boar
England (?), late 1400s. Found at Chiddingly, East Sussex
Silver-gilt; L. 3.2 cm
British Museum, London, PE 2003,0505.1
Purchased 2003 through the Treasure Act 1996
Literature: Marks and Williamson 2003, op. cit. fig. 4, cat. 69

Fig. 18
Processional cross with Yorkist emblems
1400s (before 1485)
Found *c.* 1788 in Leicestershire at what was then thought to be the site of the Battle of Bosworth, 1485
Bronze gilt; H. 58.4 cm, W. 27.9 cm
Society of Antiquaries, London, LDSAL 446
Literature: Gaimster *et al.* 2007, op. cit. fig. 12, p. 119, no. 83

Fig. 20
Helm associated with the funeral of Henry V in 1422
England, early 1400s
Iron or steel and copper alloy; H. 42.5 cm, W. 25.4 cm, depth 32.4 cm. The helm would once have had a crest
Westminster Abbey Museum, London, inv. no. 839
Literature: Marks and Williamson 2003, op. cit. fig. 4, cat. 54a; L. Monnas, 'Textiles from the funerary achievements of Henry V' in J. Stratford (ed.), *The Lancastrian Court. Proceedings of the 2001 Harlaxton Symposium*, Donington 2003, pp. 125–46 and pls 26–32

Fig. 21
Shield associated with the funeral of Henry V in 1422
England, probably late 1300s
Lime wood and textile; H. 61 cm, W. 39.4 cm
Westminster Abbey Museum, London, inv. no. 838
Literature: Marks and Williamson 2003, op. cit. fig. 4, cat. 54b; Monnas 2003, op. cit. fig 20, pp. 125–46 and pls 26–32

Fig. 22
Saddle perhaps associated with the funeral of Henry V in 1422
Early 1400s
Wood, hessian and leather; H. 39.3 cm (front), 33 cm (back), L. 67.3 cm, W. 54.6 cm
Westminster Abbey Museum, London, inv. no. 837
Literature: Monnas 2003, op. cit. fig. 20, pp. 125–46 and pls 26–32

Fig. 23
Sword perhaps associated with the funeral of Henry V in 1422
Probably England, 1400s or early 1500s
Steel, iron and wood; L. 89.5 cm (blade 73 cm)
Westminster Abbey Museum, London, inv. no. 840
Literature: Marks and Williamson 2003, op. cit. fig. 4, cat. 54c

Fig. 24
Seal-die of Henry, Prince of Wales (later Henry V) for the Lordship of Carmarthen
England, 1408–13
Bronze; diam. 7.1 cm (excl. lugs)
Inscription: (in reverse) 'S'. Henr' principis Wall' duc' acquit' lancastr' et cornub' comes cestr' de d'mio de kermerdyne' (Seal of Henry, Prince of Wales, Duke of Aquitaine, Lancaster and Cornwall and Earl of Chester for the Lordship of Carmarthen)
British Museum, London, PE 1987, 0404.1
Literature: J. Cherry, 'The seal matrix of Henry, Prince of Wales later Henry V for the lordship of Carmarthen', *Antiquaries Journal*, vol. 70, 1990, pp. 461–2; Marks and Williamson 2003, op. cit. fig. 4, cat. 34

Fig. 25
John Derricke (active 1578–81)
Rorie Ogie in the forest, from *The Image of Irelande, with a discoverie of Woodkarne*, pl. 11
Published by John Daie, London, 1581
Woodcut; (sheet) 20.5 x 32 cm; (image) 17.9 x 31 cm
Edinburgh University Library, Edinburgh, De.3.76
Given to Tounis College, Edinburgh, by William Drummond of Hawthornden, 1626
Literature: J. Small (ed.), *John Derrick, Image of Irelande with a discoverie of woodkarne* (London 1581) edited by Walter Scott in Lord Somer's tracts (I, London 1809), facsimile, Edinburgh 1883; R.H. Macdonald, *The Library of Drummond of Hawthornden*, Edinburgh 1971, p. 48 and no. 749; D.B. Quinn (ed.), *The Image of Irelande with a discoverie of woodkarne by John Derricke*, Belfast 1985

Fig. 26
Marcus Gheeraerts the Younger (1561/2–1636)
Captain Thomas Lee, dated 1594
Oil on canvas; 230.5 x 150.8 cm
Inscriptions: (upper right centre) 'Ætatis suæ 43 | An° D° 1594'; (in tree upper left) 'Facere et pati Fortia'; (bottom left in later script) 'S: Henry Lee of Ireland'
Tate Britain, London, T03028
Purchased 1980 with assistance from the Friends of the Tate Gallery, The Art Fund and the Pilgrim Trust
Literature: K. Hearn (ed.), *Dynasties: Painting in Tudor and Jacobean England 1530–1630*, London 1995, pp. 176–7, cat. 120; A.R. Jones and P. Stallybrass, *Renaissance Clothing and the Materials of Memory*, Cambridge 2000, pp. 50–2; K. Hearn, *Marcus Gheeraerts II: Elizabethan Artist in Focus*, London 2002, fig. 6 and pp. 18–21

Fig. 27
Lucas de Heere (1534–1584)
Wilde Iresche from *A short description of England, Scotland and Ireland*, 1573–5
Pen and ink and watercolour with bodycolour; 31.7 x 20.4 cm
British Library, London, Add. MS 28330, f. 34
Literature: K. Sloan, *A New World: England's First View of America*, London 2007, p. 153, fig. 95

Fig. 28
Thomas Cockson (active 1591–1636)
Robert Devereux, 2nd Earl of Essex, mounted on a horse, with a plan of Cadiz, the Azores and Ireland in the background, *c.* 1599–1600
Engraving; 33.2 x 26.3 cm
Signed at end of inscription in bottom margin: 'TCockson fecit'
British Museum, London, PD O,7.283
Probably from the bequest of the Revd Clayton Mordaunt Cracherode, 1799
Literature: A.M. Hind, *Engraving in England in the Sixteenth and Seventeenth Centuries*, 3 vols, Cambridge 1952–64, vol. 1, p. 245, no. 12

Fig. 29
Marcus Gheeraerts the Younger (1561/2–1636)
Robert Devereux, 2nd Earl of Essex, *c.* 1596–9
Oil on panel; 110 x 80.5 cm
Inscriptions: (in a later hand) '1601 Ætat.34'; (on either side of

the coat or arms below) 'EARL OF ESSEX'; (bottom left) 'Ex dono Rob:Moxon Armig: 1756'
The Master, Fellows and Scholars of Trinity College, Cambridge
Presented by Robert Moxon, 1756
Literature: Hearn 1995, op. cit. fig. 26, pp. 178–9, cat. 121

Chapter 4

Fig. 2
Henry Peacham (1578–1644 or later)
Performance of Titus Andronicus, 1594?
Manuscript, pen and ink on paper; 29.6 x 40.3 cm
Inscription: (vertically at left between the folds) 'Henrye Peachams Hand/1595'
Longleat House, Warminster, Portland Papers, vol. 1, f. 159*v*
Literature: J. Bate (ed.), *Titus Andronicus,* London and New York 1995, pp. 38–44, esp. p. 39, fig. 5;
T. Cooper, *Searching for Shakespeare,* London 2006, cat. 60

Fig. 3
Joris Hoefnagel (1542–1601)
The progress of Queen Elizabeth I to Nonsuch Palace, signed and dated 1568
Pen and brown ink, with grey-brown, blue and red wash; 21.6 x 45.6 cm
Inscriptions: 'PALATIVM REGIVM IN ANGLIAE REGNO APPELLATVM NONCIVTZ / Hoc est nusquam simile' and 'Effigiavit Georgius Houfnaglius Anno 1568'
British Museum, London, PD 1943,1009.35
Bequeathed by P.P. Stevens, 1943
Literature: L. Stainton, *British Landscape Watercolours 1600–1860,* London 1985, no. 1; S. Doran (ed.), *Elizabeth,* London 2003, cat. 96 and illus. p. 77

Fig. 5
Horn-book
Late 1600s
Papered wood; the alphabet, the Lord's Prayer, etc. under a horn sheet fixed by bronze strips; stamped on back with initials and King Charles II on horseback; L. 10.3 cm
British Museum, London, PE OA.9184
Bequeathed by Sir Augustus Wollaston Franks, 1897

Fig. 6
William Lily (1468?–1522/3)
A Shorte Introduction of Grammar, open at sig. A2
Printed by Reyner Wolfe, London, 1567
Printed book; 19 x 14.3 cm (closed)
Bodleian Library, Oxford, 4° A 17 Art, BS.
Literature: Cooper 2006, op. cit. fig. 2, cat. 16

Fig. 8
Workshop of Titian (c. 1488–1576)
Venus and Adonis, c. 1554
Oil on canvas; 177.9 x 188.9 cm
National Gallery, London, NG34
Literature: The National Gallery Complete Illustrated Catalogue, London 1995, p. 671; N. Penny, *National Gallery Catalogues. The Sixteenth-century Italian Paintings,* vol. 2, *Venice 1540–1600,* London 2008, pp. 274–91

Fig. 11
Unknown artist
Henry Wriothesley, 3rd Earl of Southampton, c. 1600
Oil on canvas; 204.5 x 121.9 cm
National Portrait Gallery, London, NPG L114, on loan from a private collection
Literature: Richard W. Goulding, 'Wriothesley portraits authentic and reputed', *Walpole Society,* vol. 8, 1919–20, pp. 17–94; A. Cobbe, A. Laing and D. Scarisbrick, 'A portrait of Henry Wriothesley as a youth' in S. Wells (ed.), *Shakespeare Found!,* Stratford-upon-Avon 2011, p. 30, fig. 33, and p. 31, fig. 33c

Fig. 12
Three-quarter field armour of Henry Wriothesley, 3rd Earl of Southampton

Probably French, perhaps acquired by the Earl in 1598
Steel, gilded, with internal leathers, brass buckle on the waist strap, velvet linings and piccadills all restored in the late 1800s, modern leather straps covered with velvet. Etched with a design of entwined snakes and foliage with birds, insects, squirrels and hares; H. (top of helmet to bottom of knee defence) 136 cm
Royal Armouries, Leeds, II.360
Purchased with the assistance of The Art Fund, the National Heritage Memorial Fund, Sir Emmanuel Kaye and a public appeal, 1984
Literature: J.G. Mann, 'The Master of the Snails and Dragonflies', *Waffen und Kostumkund*e, NF vol. 2, 1961, pp. 14–27, pls 14–18; S.W. Pyhrr, 'The "Master of the Snails and Dragonflies" revisited', in H. Nickel and S.W. Pyhr (eds), *Arms, Armour, and Heraldry: Essays in Honour of Anita Reinhard,* New York 1981, pp. 95–114, esp. p. 96; Sotheby's, *The Hever Castle Collection 1: Arms and Armour,* 5 May 1984, lot 47

Fig. 16
Pierced *aureus* of Marcus Junius Brutus
Mint moving with Brutus (probably Greece), 43–42 BC
Gold; diam. 2.01 cm
On the obverse a head of Brutus; on the reverse the assassins' daggers and a *pileus,* or freedman's cap, symbolic of Rome's escape from tyranny
Inscriptions: (obverse) BRVT IMP (Brutus Imperator) L. PRAET. CEST (L. Plaetorius Cestianus, the 'moneyer' who issued the coin); (reverse) EID. MAR (Ides of March)
Michael L.J. Winckless, on loan to the British Museum
Literature: H.A. Cahn, 'L'aureus de Brutus avec EID.MAR', in J. Babelon and J. LaFaurie (eds), *Congrès International de numismatique, Paris 6–11 juillet 1953,* II. *Actes,* Paris 1957, pp. 213–17; M. Crawford, *Roman Republican Coinage,* Cambridge 1974, footnote p. 522 (where incorrectly described as a fake)

Fig. 17
Cap
England, mid-1500s; found at Moorfields, London
Wool, knitted and felted, and silk (with modern repairs); diam. 24 cm
British Museum, London, PE 1856,0701.1882

Fig. 19
John Dee (1527–1608/9)
Unpublished treatise on calendar reform, 1583, open at frontispiece (ff. xiiiv–lr)
Book: 31.9 x 22.9 cm (closed); page: ink and colours on paper, approx. 29.4 x 20.5 cm
Bodleian Library, Oxford, MS Ashmole 1789
Literature: R. Poole, 'John Dee and the English calendar: science, religion and empire', http://www.hermetic.ch/cal_stud/jdee.html, further developed in his *Time's Alteration: Calendar Reform in Early Modern England,* London 1998, ch. 5, pp. 57–67; B. Woolley, *The Queen's Conjuror: The Life and Magic of Dr Dee,* London 2002, pp. 193–5

Fig. 20
Stefano della Bella (1610–1664)
Queen Elizabeth I and *Cleopatra,* from a pack of 52 playing cards of famous queens, 1644
Etching; 8.9 x 5.5 cm and 8.7 x 5.5 cm
British Museum, London, PD 1871,0513.506 and 511
Literature: A. De Vesme, rev. P.D. Massar, *Stefano della Bella,* New York 1971, nos 605.III and 630.III

Fig. 21
Pendant medallion ('The Phoenix Jewel')
England, c. 1570–80
Gold; bust of Queen Elizabeth I cut out in silhouette; on reverse in relief the device of a phoenix in flames under the royal monogram; enclosed within an enamelled wreath of red and white Tudor roses with green leaves and intertwined stalks; H. (including suspension loop) 6.1 cm, W. 4.6 cm
British Museum, London, PE SLMisc.1778
Bequeathed by Sir Hans Sloane, 1753
Literature: H. Tait, *Jewellery through 7000 years,* London 1976, no. 294

Fig. 23
Head of a woman resembling Cleopatra
Roman (acquired in Italy), c. 50–40 BC
Limestone, the lobes pierced for earrings; H. 28 cm
British Museum, London, GR 1879,0712.15
Literature: F.N. Price and A.H. Smith, *Catalogue of Greek Sculpture in the British Museum,* 3 vols, London 1892–1928, no. 1873; S. Walker and P. Higgs (eds), *Cleopatra of Egypt: From History to Myth,* London 2001, cat. 210; P. Higgs, 'Resembling Cleopatra: Cleopatra VII's portraits in the context of Late Hellenistic female portraiture' in S. Walker and S.A. Ashton, *'Cleopatra Reassessed',* British Museum Occasional Paper 103, London 2003, pp. 57–70

Fig. 25
Bartolommeo Neroni (active c. 1500–c. 1571–3), called Riccio
The death of Cleopatra, c. 1500–73
Pen and brown ink, grey-brown wash, over black chalk; 40.4 x 26.8 cm
British Museum, London, PD 1943,1113.53
Given by Eric Rose, 1943
Literature: Walker and Higgs 2001, op. cit. fig. 23, cat. 370

Fig. 26a
Cameo: the suicide of Cleopatra
North Italian, from Lombardy or Emilia, late 1500s
Sardonyx; H. 3.5 cm, W. 2 cm
British Museum, London, PE SLBCameos.86
Bequeathed by Sir Hans Sloane, 1753
Literature: O. Dalton, *Catalogue of Gems in the British Museum,* London 1915, no. 472; Walker and Higgs 2001, op. cit. fig. 23, cat. 379

Fig. 26b
Cameo: the suicide of Cleopatra
North Italian, perhaps from Milan, late 1500s
Sardonyx; H. 4.3 cm, W. 3.3 cm
British Museum, London, PE 1772,0314.188
Litearature: Dalton 1915, op. cit. fig. 26a, no. 319; I. Jenkins and K. Sloan, *Vases and Volcanoes,* London 1996, cat. 66; Walker and Higgs 2001, op. cit. fig. 23, cat. 380

Fig. 27
Giovanni Francesco Barbieri (1591–1666), called Guercino
Cleopatra, late 1630s
Red chalk; 29.2 x 21.5 cm
British Museum, London, PD 1895,0915.709
Literature: N. Turner and C. Plazzotta, *Drawings by Guercino from British Collections,* London 1991, cat. 120 and Appendix, no. 36; Walker and Higgs 2001, op. cit. fig. 23, cat. 369

Chapter 5

Fig. 1
Jacopo de' Barbari (c. 1460–1516)
Bird's-eye view of Venice from the south, 1498–1500
Woodcut printed from six blocks on six sheets of joined paper; 134 x 280.8 cm
Inscription: Lettered VENETIE MD, and the names of the eight winds around the edges. Some names of places and buildings are also given
British Museum, London, PD 1895,0122.1192–7
Given by William Mitchell
Literature: J. Schulz, 'Jacopo de' Barabri's View of Venice: Map making, city views and moralized geography before the year 1500', *Art Bulletin,* vol. 60, 1978, pp. 425–74

Fig. 2
Ewer
Venice, 1550–1600
Glass, mould-blown with square projections and decorated with spiralling filigree design made of twisted white canes (*vetro a retorti*) and plain white bands; H. 27.5 cm
British Museum, London, PE 1869,0624.45
Given by the Executors of Felix Slade, 1869
Literature: H. Tait, *The Golden Age of Venetian Glass,* London 1979, no. 158

Fig. 3
Odoardo Fialetti (1573–c. 1638)
Bird's-eye View of Venice, signed and dated 1611
Oil on canvas, executed on five pieces of linen stitched together
and lined to a second layer of canvas; 215.9 x 424.2 cm
Eton College, Berkshire
Bequeathed by Sir Henry Wotton, former ambassador to Venice
and Provost of Eton, 1639. Restored with the help of the
Friends of Eton Collections
Literature: E. Chaney, *Evolution of the Grand Tour*, London and
Portland, Oregon 1998, fig. 28, p. 165; L. Walters, 'Odoardo
Fialetti (1573– c. 1638): The interrelation of Venetian art
and anatomy, and his importance in England', PhD thesis,
University of St Andrews, 2009, I, pp. 169–70

Fig. 9
Goblet enamelled with a figure of a lady in a blue dress and with
a coat of arms
Façon de Venise, Venice or Northern Europe (Austria or South
Germany), 1590–1600
Blown glass, with enamelling and gilding; H. 21.5 cm, diam.
12.6 cm
British Museum, London, PE S.853
Bequeathed by Felix Slade, 1868
Literature: Tait 1979, op. cit. fig. 2, no. 40; D.P. Lanmon and
D. Whitehouse, *Glass in the Robert Lehman Collection*, New
York 1993, p. 66, fig. 21.2

Fig. 13
Chopines
Venice, c. 1600
Wood covered with kid leather with punched decoration and
figured silk underlay (the shoes are not identical in height or
decoration); L. 24 cm, max. H. of sole 19.5 cm (T.48-1914);
L. 23.5 cm, max. H. of sole 18 cm (T.48a-1914)
Victoria and Albert Museum, London, T.48&A-1914
Literature: W.B. Redfern, *Royal and Historic Gloves and Shoes*,
London 1904, p. 110, pl. XXXII; E. Semmelhack, *On a
Pedestal: From Renaissance Chopines to Baroque Heels*, Toronto
2009, fig. 34

Fig. 15
Sir Michael Balfour (d. 1619)
Album Amicorum (friendship album), 1596–9, open at f. 128r
Manuscript in a contemporary red morocco Venetian binding;
16 x 27 cm
National Library of Scotland, Edinburgh, MS 16000
Purchased with the aid of The Art Fund and the Friends of the
National Libraries
Literature: P. Humfrey, T. Clifford, A. Weston-Lewis and
M. Bury (eds), *The Age of Titian: Venetian Renaissance Art from
Scottish Collections*, Edinburgh 2004, cat. 169

Fig. 17
Marcus Gheeraerts the Younger (1561/2–1636)
Queen Anne of Denmark, c. 1611–14
Oil on canvas; 221 x 131 cm
Inscriptions: (upper right) 'La mia grandezza dal eccelso.'; (lower
right) 'fundamentum meum'; (on later cartellino) 'ANNE of
DENMARK | wife of K, James I'
Woburn Abbey, Bedfordshire
Literature: K. Hearn (ed.), *Dynasties: Painting in Tudor and
Jacobean England 1530–1630*, London 1995, pp. 192–3, cat. 130

Fig. 18
Handle for a feather fan, Venice, c. 1550
Gilt brass with openwork decoration and engraving;
H. 17.8 cm, W. 8.2 cm
Victoria and Albert Museum, London, 105-1882

Fig. 19
Dress fabric with a pattern of peacock feathers
Italy, 1600–20
Woven silk, brocaded with silver-gilt thread; L. 142.5 cm
(including fringe), W. 49 cm (assembled from a number of
pieces of varying size)
Victoria and Albert Museum, London, T.361-1970

Fig. 20
Medal of Elijah de Lattes (obverse) and his mother, Rica (reverse)
Veneto, 1552
Cast bronze; diam. 4 cm
Inscriptions: (obverse) ELIA. DE. LATAS. EBR EO. MD52
(Elijah de Lattes, the Jew, 1552); (reverse) RICA. SVA
GIENETRICE (Rica, his mother)
British Museum, London, CM 1912,1217.2
Given by Mr A. Rosenheim, 1912
Literature: D. Friedenburg, *Jewish Medals from the Renaissance
to the Fall of Napoleon*, New York 1970, p. 4; P. Attwood,
Italian Medals c. 1530–1600 in British Public Collections,
London 2003, p. 233, no. 420a

Fig. 21
Sabbath lamp, 1200s–1300s
Found at St Leonard's Hill, Windsor, in 1717
Bronze; H. 13 cm, W. 16.2 cm
The base is not original. Originally designed to be suspended,
the lamp would have had a drip-pan hanging below the burners
to collect leaking oil
Society of Antiquaries, London, LDSAL 56
Presented by Sir Hans Sloane, 1736
Literature: R.R. Emanuel, 'The Society of Antiquaries' Sabbath
lamp', *Antiquaries Journal*, vol. 80, 2000, pp. 308–15;
D. Gaimster, B. Nurse and J. Steele (eds), *Making History:
Antiquaries in Britain 1707–2007*, London 2007, p. 61, cat. 32

Fig. 22
Eisak Tyrnau, trans. Simeon (Levi) Ginzburg b. Judah
Sefer Minhagim (*Book of Customs*), open at f. 63v ('Sabbath
blessing')
Printed by Giovanni di Gara, Venice, 1600
Book: 19 x 14.5 cm; woodcut: 7 x 9.5 cm
Bodleian Library, Oxford, Opp.4° 1004
Literature: D. Wolfthal, *Picturing Yiddish: Gender, Identity and
Memory in the Illustrated Yiddish Books of Renaissance Italy*,
Leiden and Boston 2004, pp. 96–101, fig. 86b; figs 87–94a for
other woodcuts from this edition

Fig. 24
George Carleton (1559–1628), *A Thankfull Remembrance of
Gods Mercy*, London 1627, open at p. 164 showing an image
of *Lopez Compounding to Poyson the Queene* by Friedrich von
Hulsen (1580–1665)
Printed book; 20 x 14.5 cm (closed)
British Library, London, 807.C.22
Literature: D. Gaimster and R. Gilchrist, *The Archaeology of
Reformation 1480–1580*, Leeds 2003, pp. 206–7, fig. 1

Fig. 25
Supremacy Medal of Henry VIII
British Isles, 1545
Gold; diam. 5.4 cm
Inscriptions: (obverse) HENRICVS . OCTA . ANGLIÆ .
FRANCI . ET . HIB . REX . FIDEI . DEFENSOR . ET . IN
. TERR . ECCLE . ANGLI . ET . HIBE . SVB . CHRIST
. CAPVT . SVPREMVM (Henry VIII, King of England,
France and Ireland, defender of the faith, and under Christ the
supreme head on earth of the Church of England and Ireland);
(reverse) monogram H.R.; inscriptions in Hebrew and Greek
(content as on obverse); 'Londini . 1545'
British Museum, London, CM M.6802
Literature: E. Hawkins, ed. A.W. Franks and H.A. Grueber,
*Medallic Illustrations of the History of Great Britain and Ireland
to the Death of George II*, London 1885, vol. 1, p. 47, no. 44;
M. Jones, 'The medal in Britain', *Médailles*, 22nd Congress,
Helsinki 1990, p. 18; B. Cook in R. Marks and P. Williamson
(eds), *Gothic: Art for England 1400–1547*, London 2003,
cat. 353; R. Bishop, 'Hebraica Veritas' in *Auction Insider*, Spink,
London, Autumn 2009, p. 20

Fig. 27a
A group of Venetian ducats dating from 1500–1618, issued by
Doges from Leonardo Loredan (1501–21) to Giovanni Bembo
(1615–18)
Gold; diam. of each approx. 2 cm, weight of each approx 3.5 g

British Museum, London, CM 1993,0302.221,
1993,0302.245, 1993,0302.246, 1993,0302.908,
1993,0302.270, 1993,0302.272, 1993,0302.909,
1993,0302.283, 1993,0302.299, 1993,0302.910,
1993,0302.920 (The Greenall Gift); 1935,0401.9674,
1935,0401.9675, 1935,0401.9679 (T.B. Clarke-Thornhill
Bequest); 1859,1202.18 (given by Lord Boston); 1922,0522.58
(given by Miss Raper); 1849,1121.565, 1849,1121.568,
1849,1121.563, 1862,1001.179, 1860,1201.212,
1862,1001.232, 1862,1001.246, 1863,1001.378,
1862,1001.398, 1862,1001.49

Fig. 27b
Guillaum de Neve (alive or active 1600–54)
Coin weights, hand balance and box
Amsterdam, 1600–54
Weights: brass; approx. 1.5 cm along each edge
Balance: brass; H. 15 cm
Box: wood; L. 15 cm, W. 9 cm, H. 3 cm
British Museum, London, CM W.3132
Literature: V.B. Crowther-Benyon, 'Notes on coin weights
and coin weight boxes. Foreign', undated manuscript, British
Museum, Department of Coins and Medals, p. 300, no. B.28

Fig. 28
Scroll of the Book of Esther in Hebrew, with marginal
engravings designed by Andrea Marelli (active Rome c. 1567–72)
Italy, c. 1573
Engraving and watercolour on vellum; H. (including wooden
roller) 28 cm; L. of scroll 204 cm, W. 17 cm
British Library, London, MS Or. 13028
Given to the British Museum, Department of British and
Medieval Antiquities, 1983, by Hyman Montagu. Transferred
to the British Library, Department of Oriental Manuscripts,
1966
Literature: E. Frojmovic, 'The *Perfect Scribe* and an early
engraved Esther scroll', *British Library Journal*, vol. 23, no. 1,
Spring 1997, pp. 68–80

Fig. 29
The Bible, translated by William Whittingham, Anthony Gilby,
Thomas Sampson and perhaps others, open at Genesis 30
Geneva, 1560
Printed book; 26 x 19 cm (closed)
British Library, London, C.17.b.8

Fig. 30
Goblet enamelled with three figures from the *Commedia dell' Arte*
Façon de Venise, Venice or Northern Europe, c. 1600
Glass, enamelled and gilded; H. 19.2 cm, diam. 12.2 cm
British Museum, London, PE S.852
Bequeathed by Felix Slade, 1868
Literature: D.B. Harden, K.S. Painter, R.H. Pinder-Wilson and
H. Tait, *Masterpieces of Glass*, London 1968, no. 213; Tait 1979,
op. cit. fig. 2, no. 38; S. Ciappi, *Il vetro in Europa*, Milan 2006,
no. 27

Chapter 6

Fig. 1
Francisco Ruiz (recorded early 1600s) and possibly Claude
Savigny (recorded 1578–95 in Tours)
Rapier, blade made in Toledo, Spain; hilt made in France,
c. 1590
Steel, the hilt encrusted with silver and inlaid with silver chains;
L. 111 cm, W. 23.2 cm, depth 11.6 cm
Inscription: (on the blade) 'Francisco Ruiz en Toledo'
Victoria and Albert Museum, London, M.73-1953
Literature: J.F. Hayward, *Swords and Daggers*, London 1963, no.
15a; A.R.E. North, *An Introduction to European Swords*, London
1982, no. 16

Fig. 3
Unknown artist
True likeness of the beheaded Turkish officer Ali Bassa [Pasha]
Germany, c. 1571

Letterpress and woodcut with stencil and hand-colouring; 42.6 x 33 cm
Victoria and Albert Museum, London, E.912-2003
Purchased through the Julie and Robert Breckman Print Fund, and supported by the Friends of the V&A
Literature: W. Harms and M. Schilling (eds), *Die Sammlung der Zentralbibliothek Zürich, Kommentierte Ausgabe, Teil 2: Die Wickiana II (1570–1588)*, Tübingen 1997–2005

Fig. 4
Vincenzo Catena (active 1506–31)
A warrior adoring the Infant Christ and the Virgin, after 1520
Oil on canvas; 155.3 x 263.5 cm
National Gallery, London, NG234
Literature: G. Robertson, *Vincenzo Catena*, Edinburgh 1954, cat. 48

Fig. 8
Fire-blower (aeolipile) in the form of the bust of a black African
Venice, *c.* 1500
Embossed sheet copper with traces of patination and gilding; H. 25.4 cm
British Museum, London, PE SLMisc.1112
Bequeathed by Sir Hans Sloane, 1753
Literature: W. Hildburgh, 'Aeolipiles as fire blowers', *Archaeologia*, vol. 94, 1951, p. 48; J. Warren, 'Sir Hans Sloane as a collector of small sculpture', *Apollo*, vol. 159, February 2004, p. 36, fig. 11

Fig. 9
Jan Jansz. Mostaert (*c.* 1474–1552/3)
Portrait of an African man, *c.* 1525–30
Oil on panel; 30.8 x 21.2 cm
Rijksmuseum, Amsterdam, SK-A-4986
Purchased 2005 with support from the Vereniging Rembrandt, the Prins Bernhard Cultuurfonds, the Mondriaan Stichting, the VSBfonds, the Stichting Rijksmuseum and the BankGiro Loterij
Literature: Y. Hackenbroch, *Enseignes*, Florence 1996, fig. 237 and p. 239; J.P. Filedt Kok and M. de Winkel, 'A portrait of a black African man by Jan Mostaert', *Bulletin van Het Rijksmuseum*, vol. 53, no. 49, 2005, pp. 470–7; K. Lowe, 'The stereotyping of black Africans in Renaissance Europe' in K.J.P. Lowe and T.F. Earle (eds), *Black Africans in Renaissance Europe*, Cambridge 2005, pp. 44–7

Fig. 10
Pilgrim badge of the Madonna of Hal, Belgium
Made in Belgium or the Netherlands, probably early 1500s
Silver gilt, embossed and pierced; diam. 3.8 cm
Inscription: (on obverse) 'de hal'
British Museum, London, PE 1847,0829.1
Literature: H. Tait, *7000 Years of Jewellery*, London 1986, no. 520; A.M. Koldeweij, *Foi et bonne fortune: Parure et dévotion en Flandre médiévale*, Arnhem 2006, p. 47, figs 3.3 and 3.4, and pp. 55–7

Fig. 12
Attributed to the Huntington Master (active Venice *c.* 1580–*c.* 1600)
Leaf of a Doge's Commission from Pasquale Cicogna (r. 1585–95) to Tommaso Morosini dalla Sbarra (1546–1622) as podestà and capitano of Crema
Venice, 1587
Watercolour on vellum; 22 x 15 cm
British Library, London, Add. MS 20916, f. 22
Literature: P. Kaplan in D. Bindman and H.L. Gates, *The Image of the Black in Western Art, from the 'Age of Discovery' to the Age of Abolition*, Harvard 2010, p. 140 and p. 141, fig. 67; Anne-Marie Ezé, 'A Moor of Venice: Doge Pasquale Cicogna's Commission to Tommaso Morosini', *British Library Journal*, forthcoming

Fig. 14
Nicolas Cordier (1567–1612)
Bust of a black African
Rome, *c.* 1610
Black *bigio morato* marble and white marble; H. 34 cm
Dresden, Staatliche Kunstsammlungen, Skulpturensammlung,

Hm² 187a
Literature: S. Pressouyre, *Nicolas Cordier: recherches sur la sculpture à Rome autour de 1600*, Rome 1984, no. 21; R. Eikelmann (ed.), *Der Mohrenkopfpokal von Christoph Jamnitzer*, Munich 2002, no. 66

Fig. 15
Christoph Jamnitzer (1563–1618)
Moor's head cup
Nuremberg, *c.* 1602
Embossed silver, partially gilt, and rock crystal; H. 52.2 cm, diam. of foot 17 cm
Marks: N for Nuremberg and C over a lion's head for Christoph Jamnitzer
Munich, Bayerisches Nationalmuseum, 2000/81.1-2
Purchased 2000 with the support of the Bayerische Landesstiftung, Ernst von Siemens Kunstfonds, KulturStiftung der Länder and Beauftragten der Bundesregierung für Angelegenheiten der Kultur und der Medien
Literature: Eikelmann 2002, op. cit. fig. 14, no. 1; J. Hein, 'Der Mohrenkopfpokal von Christoph Jamnitzer: Provenienz, Deutung und Kontext', *Münchner Jahrbuch der Bildenden Kunst*, Dritte Folge, Band 53, Munich 2002, pp. 163–77; L. Seelig, 'Christoph Jamnitzer's "Moor's Head": a late Renaissance drinking vessel' in Earle and Lowe 2005, op. cit. fig. 9, pp. 181–209

Chapter 7

Fig. 1
Studio of John de Critz the Elder (1551/2–1642)
James I wearing the Feather Jewel in his hat, *c.* 1606
Oil on panel; 56 x 43 cm
Inscription: (upper left) 'King James'
Parham House, Sussex, Picture catalogue no. 220
Literature: R. Strong, 'Three royal jewels: the Three Brothers, the Mirror of Great Britain and the Feather', *Burlington Magazine*, vol. 108, no. 760, July 1966, pp. 350–3; K. Hearn (ed.), *Dynasties: Painting in Tudor and Jacobean England 1530–1630*, London 1995, cat. 125, for this portrait type

Fig. 3
'Guy Fawkes' lantern'
Sheet iron; H. 34.5 cm
The lamp originally had a horn window and could also be closed completely to hide the light
Ashmolean Museum, Oxford, AN 1887.2
Literature: W.D. Murray, *Annals of the Bodleian Library*, Oxford 1890, pp. 93–4

Fig. 4
Eigentliche Abbildung wie ettlich englische Edelleut einen Raht ...: a broadside on the Gunpowder Plot, depicting eight of the protagonists (named) and their execution
Germany, published by Abraham Hogenberg, 1606
Engraving; 25.5 x 30.6 cm
British Museum, London, PD 1868,0808.3207
Literature: F.G. Stephens and M.D. George, *Catalogue of Political and Personal Satires in the Department of Prints and Drawings in the British Museum*, vol. 1, London 1870, no. 71; J.R. Paas, *The German Political Broadsheet 1600–1700*, vol. 1, Wiesbaden 1995, nos P-75–P-78 and no. PA21

Fig. 5
Unknown artist
Princeps Proditorum (Leader of the Traitors): portrait of Henry Garnet with the Pope's pardon in his hands, *c.* 1606
Woodcut and letterpress; 29.5 x 16.5 cm
British Museum, London, PD 1886,0410.1
Literature: M. Jones, *The Print in Early Modern England*, New Haven and London 2010, p. 65

Fig. 7
Reliquary containing the right eye of the Blessed Edward Oldcorne SJ, *c.* 1606
Silver; diam. 4.6 cm, depth 1.7 cm

Inscription: (on back) OCVLVS DEXTER P ED: OLCORNI SOC . IESV
Stonyhurst College, Clitheroe, Lancashire
Literature: Dom Bede Camm, *Forgotten Shrines*, London 1910, p. 377; M. Whitehead (ed.), *Held in Trust: 2000 Years of Sacred Culture*, Stonyhurst 2008, no. 3.4

Fig. 8
Claes Jansz. Visscher (1587–1652)
Study for a print depicting the execution of the conspirators in the Gunpowder Plot, *c.* 1606
Pen and brown ink, brown wash, with lines indented for transfer; 23.9 x 34.2 cm
British Museum, London, PD 1919,0513.1
Literature: A.M. Hind, *Catalogue of Dutch and Flemish Drawings Preserved in the Department of Prints and Drawings in the British Museum*, IV: *Dutch Drawings of the XVII Century*, London 1931, no. 1 (under Visscher); L. Stainton and C. White, *Drawing in England from Hilliard to Hogarth*, London 1987, p. 72, cat. 32

Fig. 10
Pedlar's chest, *c.* 1600–30
Box: softwood covered with pony skin and lined with printed paper. Contents: 1 white linen alb; 1 green flowered damask chasuble; 1 green silk chasuble with stole, maniple, burse and pall; 1 altar stone; 1 altar cloth; 1 smaller altar cloth; 1 hanging, originally an embroidered bag; 1 embroidered corporal with lace edge; 2 plain corporals; 1 purificator (stained, perhaps with blood but more likely rust); 1 girdle; 1 green altar frontal; 1 white burse; 1 gold pall; 1 red burse; 1 brown veil with silver ornaments; 1 red maniple; 1 green maniple; 1 brown maniple; 1 rosary ring; 1 bracelet rosary; 1 pewter paten and chalice; 1 holland linen and pink silk lined bonnet
L. 85 cm, W. 37 cm, H. (closed) 34.5 cm
Stonyhurst College, Clitheroe, Lancashire
Found walled up in a compartment in Samlesbury Hall, near Preston, Lancashire, in the mid-1800s; bought at auction in the 1880s by the parents of Fr John Myerscough SJ, who donated it to Stonyhurst, *c.* 1916
Literature: Whitehead 2008, op. cit. fig. 7, no. 3.2

Fig. 13
King James VI and I (1566–1625)
Daemonologie, London 1603, open at title page
Printed book; 17.5 x 13.3 cm (closed)
Bodleian Library, Oxford, Douce I 210
Bequeathed by Francis Douce, 1834

Fig. 14
Church ship
Denmark, *c.* 1590
Wood; H. 65 cm, L. 64.5 cm, depth 29 cm
Inscription: (on taffrail) monogram of Christian IV of Denmark
Edinburgh, National Museums Scotland, H.1993.666
Literature: R. Morton Nance, *Sailing Ship Models*, London 1924, pl. 8; F.C. Bowen, *From Carrack to Clipper*, London 1927, pp. 15–16, pl. 6

Fig. 15
Newes from Scotland: declaring the damnable life and death of doctor Fian, a notable sorcerer, who was burned at Edenbrough in Ianuary last, 1591, London, 1591?, open at page preceding 'To the reader'
Printed book; 18.7 x 13.4 cm (closed)
Bodleian Library, Oxford, Douce F 210
Bequeathed by Francis Douce, 1834

Fig. 16a
Witch's collar (jougs)
Ladybank, Fife, 1600s
Iron; H. 9 cm; diam. 15.5 cm
Edinburgh, National Museums Scotland, H.MR 43
Literature: *Proceedings of the Society of Antiquaries of Scotland*, vol. 44, 1909–10, pp. 9–10

Fig. 16b
Witch's bridle (branks), 1600s
Iron; H. 19.2 cm
Edinburgh, National Museums Scotland, H.MR 24
Given to the Society of Antiquaries of Scotland by Adam Sim of Culter, 1882

Fig. 18
Calf's heart stuck with iron pins, mid-1700s
Found in 1812 under flagstones of a house in Dalkeith, Midlothian L. 8.5 cm, W. 7 cm, diam. 6 cm
National Museums Scotland, Edinburgh, H.NO 22
Literature: J. Skene, 'Letter addressed to Sir Walter Scott, Baronet, by Mr James Bowd, on a Popular Superstition formerly used to prevent Cattle from Witchcraft …', *Archaeologia Scotica: Transactions of the Society of Antiquaries of Scotland*, vol. 3, 1831, pp. 300–1; G.F. Black, 'Scottish charms and amulets', *Proceedings of the Society of Antiquaries of Scotland*, vol. 27 (1892–3), pp. 498–9; H. Cheape, T. Cowie and C. Wallace, 'Sir Walter Scott, the Abbotsford Collection and the National Museums of Scotland' in I. Gordon Brown (ed.), *Abbotsford and Sir Walter Scott*, Edinburgh 2003, pp. 71–2

Fig. 19
Witch's cursing bone
Glen Shira, Inveraray, Argyll, possibly 1800s
Deer or sheep's thigh bone and bog oak, 11 x 7 cm
National Museums Scotland, Edinburgh, H.NO 78
Given by Dr Arthur Mitchell and Captain F.S.L. Thomas
Literature: 'Donations to and purchases for the Museum', *Proceedings of the Society of Antiquaries of Scotland*, vol. 78, 1943–4, p. 141; H. Cheape, 'Charms against witchcraft', in J. Goodare, L. Martin and J. Miller (eds), *Witchcraft and Belief in Early Modern Scotland*, Basingstoke 2008, p. 241, fig. 10.6

Fig. 20
The Glenorchy Charmstone, 7th or 8th century (mount 1600s)
Crystal; mount silver and red coral, with suspension loop; H. 7 cm, W. 4.5 cm
National Museums Scotland, Edinburgh, H.NO 118
Literature: C. Innes, *The Black Book of Taymouth*, Edinburgh 1855, pp. ii–iii; R.K. Marshall and G.R. Dalgleish (eds), *The Art of Jewellery in Scotland*, Edinburgh 1991, cat. 20; H. Cheape, 'Touchstones of belief', *Review of Scottish Culture*, vol. 28, Edinburgh 2008, p. 112

Fig. 21
William Stalker (active 1590–1644)
The Ballochyle Brooch
Glasgow, *c.* 1610
Silver; diam. 13.8 cm
Marks: (on upper edge) VS in monogram twice; on underside as above
Inscription: 'De Serve and Haif the Hevin Bebeif' (Deserve and have the Heaven above); panels engraved with MacIver/Campbell arms, initials MC and strapwork
Edinburgh, National Museums Scotland, H.NGB 177
Literature: Marshall and Dalgleish 1991, op. cit. fig. 20, p. 59; G. Dalgleish and H. Steuart Fotheringham, *Silver Made in Scotland*, Edinburgh 2008, p. 39, no. 3.13; H. Cheape, 'The material culture of charms and amulets' in L. Henderson (ed.), *Fantastical Imaginations: The supernatural in Scottish history and culture*, Edinburgh 2009, p. 78

Fig. 22
The Lochbuie Brooch, *c.* 1600
Silver, set with crystals and pearls; diam. 12.2 cm
Inscription: (on the reverse) 'The Silver Oar of this Broch was found on the Estate of Lochbuy in Mull and made by a Tinker on that Estate about the year 1500. It was handed down by the Ladies of that family to one another untill Anna Campbell lady to Murdock McLean who had no Male Issue, gave it to Isabella McLean, their daughter, spouse to John Scrogie, Esq, to whom she presented it the day after their Marriage'
British Museum, London, PE 1855,1201.220

Fig. 23
The Brooch of Lorn, *c.* 1600
Crystal, set in a silver mount decorated with pearls; H. 40 cm, W. 10 cm (approx.)
MacDougall of Dunollie Preservation Trust
Literature: 'Notice and engraving of the Brooch of Lorn, exhibited to the Society in 1828', *Archaeologica Scotica: Transactions of the Society of Antiquaries of Scotland*, vol. 4, 1857, p. 419 and pl. XXX

Fig. 24
Gold coin ('angel')
Minted in England, 1605–6 (rose initial mark)
Weight 4.445 g
Inscriptions: (obverse) IACOBVS D G MAG BRIT FR ET HIB REX (James by the Grace of God King of Great Britain, France and Ireland); (reverse) A DNO FACTVM EST ISTVD (abbreviated version of *A domino factum est istud et est mirabile in oculis nostri* [Psalm 118: 23]: This is the Lord's doing and it is wonderful in our eyes)
British Museum, London, CM 1866,1001.12
Literature: J.J. North, *English Hammered Coinage*, London 1991, vol. 2, no. 2081

Fig. 25
Jacob de Wet the Younger (1640–1697)
Macbeth
From a series of portraits of real and legendary Scottish kings painted for the Great Gallery, Palace of Holyroodhouse, 1684–6
Oil on canvas; 79 x 81 cm
Inscription: 85. MACBETHUS. 1040
Royal Collection, Edinburgh, Palace of Holyroodhouse, RCIN 403309
Literature: S. Bruce and S. Yearley, 'The De Wet portraits of the Scottish kings', *Review of Scottish Culture*, vol. 6, 1990, pp. 11–19

Fig. 26
The Lyte Jewel: pendant containing a portrait miniature of James I by Nicholas Hilliard (*c.* 1547–1619)
England, between 12 July 1610 and 14 April 1611
Pendant: gold, set with diamonds, with coloured enamels; H. 6.5 cm, W. 4.8 cm. Miniature: on vellum on card; H. 3.9 cm, W. 3.2 cm
The diamond-set pendant drop is lost
British Museum, London, PE WB.167
Bequeathed by Baron Ferdinand Anselm de Rothschild 1898 (Waddesdon Bequest)
Literature: H. Tait, *Catalogue of the Waddesdon Bequest, I. The Jewels*, London 1986, pp. 174–88, no. 33; H. Tait (ed.), *7000 Years of Jewellery*, London 1986, pp. 182–4, no. 298

Fig. 28
Thomas Lyte (1568–1638)
'Brittans Monarchie': genealogy tracing the descent of James VI and I from Brutus, *c.* 1605
Pen and ink on vellum; five membranes (originally a rectangle of nine, but four corner membranes now missing), 189 x 212 cm
British Library, London, Add. MS 48343
Literature: Tait 1986, op. cit. fig. 26, pp. 179–84; British Library online Manuscripts Catalogue, Add. 48343

Chapter 8

Fig. 2
Designs for the Union Flag of Great Britain, *c.* 1604
Watercolour, pen and ink on paper; 29 x 43 cm
National Library of Scotland, MS 2517, f.67
Literature: National Library of Scotland, *Catalogue of Manuscripts Acquired Since 1925*, Edinburgh 1966, vol. 2, pp. 81–2; I. Gordon-Brown, *Rax me that Buik. Highlights from the Collections of the National Library of Scotland*, London 2010, p. 14, no. 2.1

Fig. 4
Medal struck for distribution at the coronation of James I on 25 July 1603
Silver; diam. 2.85 cm, weight 5.7 g
Inscriptions: (obverse) IAC : I : BRIT : CÆ : AVG : HÆ CÆSARUM CÆ. D. D. (James I, Caesar Augustus of Britain, Caesar the heir of the Caesars, presents this medal); (reverse) ECCE . PHAOS; POPVLIQ' . SALVS (Behold the beacon and safety of the people)
British Museum, London, CM G3,EM.316
Given by King George IV, 1825
Literature: E. Hawkins, ed. A.W. Franks and H.A. Grueber, *Medallic Illustrations of the History of Great Britain and Ireland to the Death of George II*, vol. 1, London 1885, p. 191, no. 11

Fig. 6
Unite of James I
Minted in England, 1612–13 (tower initial mark)
Gold; diam. 3.7 cm, weight 9.86 g
Inscriptions: (obverse) IACOBVS.D.G.MAG.BRI'.FRA'.ET.HI'. REX (James by the Grace of God King of Great Britain, France and Ireland); (reverse) FACIAM.EOS.IN.GENTEM.VNAM (I will make them one nation). The legend on the reverse is from Ezekiel 37:22
British Museum, London, CM, E.666
Literature: J.J. North, *English Hammered Coinage*, vol. 2, London 1991, pp. 145–7, no. 2084

Fig. 10
John White (*c.* 1540s–*c.* 1593)
A Pictish Woman, 1585–93
Watercolour over graphite, touched with bodycolour and white (altered) and pen and ink; 23 x 17.9 cm
British Museum, London, PD 1906,0509.1.27
Literature: K. Sloan, *A New World: England's First View of America*, London 2007, pp. 160–1, no. 33; S. Smiles, 'John White and British antiquity: savage origins in the context of Tudor historiography' in K. Sloan (ed.), *European Visions: American Voices*, London 2009, pp. 106–12

Fig. 11
Inigo Jones (1573–1652)
Masquer, A Daughter of Niger: design for a costume for Ben Jonson's *Masque of Blacknesse*, given at the Old Banqueting House, Whitehall, on 6 January 1605
Watercolour with gold and silver; 29 x 15.5 cm
Chatsworth House, Derbyshire, Devonshire Collection
Literature: National Gallery of Art, Washington, *Festival Designs by Inigo Jones: Drawings for Scenery and Costume*, 1967, cat. 4; S. Orgel and R. Strong, *Inigo Jones: The Theatre of the Stuart Court*, London 1973, vol. 1, p. 96, no. 1; *Treasures from Chatsworth: The Devonshire Inheritance*, International Exhibitions Foundation, 1979, pp. 55–6, cat. 108; Council of Europe, *Christian IV and Europe*, Copenhagen 1988, cat. 521

Fig. 12
John White (*c.* 1540s–*c.* 1593)
A Pictish Warrior Holding a Human Head, 1585–93
Watercolour and bodycolour over graphite, touched with pen and ink; 24.3 x 16.9 cm
British Museum, London, PD 1906,0509.1.24
Literature: Sloan 2007, op. cit. fig. 10, pp. 154–5, no. 30; Smiles 2009, op. cit. fig. 10, pp. 106–12

Fig. 16
Cameo engraved with a portrait of the emperor Augustus (27 BC–AD 14)
Roman, *c.* AD 14–20; the jewelled headband added later
Sardonyx; L. 9.3 cm, H. 12.8 cm
British Museum, London, GR 1867,0507.484
Literature: H.B. Walters, *Catalogue of the Engraved Gems in the British Museum*, London 1926, no. 3577; S. Walker, *Greek and Roman Portraits*, London 1995

Fig. 17
William Camden (1551–1623)
Britain, or a Chorographicall Description of the most flourishing

Kingdomes, England, Scotland, and Ireland, trans. Philemon Holland, London 1610, open at p. 89 ('Coines of the Britans') Printed book; 34 x 24 cm (closed) British Library, London, 456.e.16

Fig. 18

Gold stater of Cunobelin, *c.* AD 10–40
Minted in the North Thames area/Kent and found at Weston, Northants
Diam. 1.8 cm, weight 5.43 g
Inscriptions: (obverse) CAMV (Camulodunum = Colchester); (reverse) CVNO (Cunobelin)
British Museum, London, CM 1919,0213.339
Given by Sir Arthur John Evans, 1919
Literature: D.F. Allen, 'Cunobelin's gold', *Britannia*, vol. 6, 1975, pp. 1–19; R. Hobbs, *British Iron Age Coins in the British Museum*, London 1996, pp. 19–20 and p. 126, no. 1827

Fig. 19

Johann Sadeler I (1550–1600) after Dirck Barendsz. (1534–92)
Ignis (Fire), from a series of four entitled *The Four Elements*
Published Frankfurt, 1587
Engraving; 17.5 x 22.8 cm
Inscriptions: Lettered in lower corners: 'T.B.A. [Theodorus Bernardus Amsterodamus] in.' and 'I. Sadl. Scalps.'; lettering in Latin in the lower margin
British Museum, London, PD D,5.63
Literature: J.R. Judson, *Dirck Barendsz.*, Amsterdam 1970, nos 90–3

Fig. 20

Unknown artist
The Somerset House Peace Conference, c. 1604
Oil on canvas; 205.7 x 268 cm
National Portrait Gallery, London, NPG 665
Literature: Roy Strong, *Tudor and Jacobean Portraits*, 2 vols, London 1969, vol. 1, pp. 351–3; K. Hearn, *Talking Peace: 1604. The Somerset House Conference Paintings*, exh. leaflet, National Portrait Gallery, 2004

Fig. 21

The Royal Gold Cup, enamelled with scenes from the life and martyrdom of St Agnes
Paris, *c.* 1370–80, with later alterations
Gold with enamel and pearls; finial missing. The stem extended twice, once with a band of Tudor roses in opaque enamel and further with an inscribed band
Inscription: (translated from the Latin) 'This cup of solid gold, a relic of the sacred treasure of England and a memorial to the peace made between the kings, the Constable Juan de Velasco, returning thence after successfully accomplishing his mission, presented as an offering to Christ the Peacemaker'
H. (with cover) 23.6 cm; diam. of cup 17.8 cm
British Museum, London, PE 1892,0501.1
Acquired with contributions from HM Treasury, the Worshipful Company of Goldsmiths, Sir Augustus Wollaston Franks and others, 1892
Literature: O.M. Dalton, *The Royal Gold Cup in the British Museum*, London 1924; J. Stratford, *The Bedford Inventories: The Worldly Goods of John, Duke of Bedford, Regent of France (1389–1435)*, London 1993, pp. 319–25; J. Cherry, *The Holy Thorn Reliquary*, London 2010, pp. 24–6 (on the cup) and 39–48 (on Jean, duc de Berry)

Chapter 9

Fig. 1

Nicholas Hilliard (1547–1619)
Design for the obverse of Queen Elizabeth's Great Seal of Ireland, *c.* 1584–5
Pen and black ink, with grey wash, over graphite on vellum; diam. approx. 12.4 cm
Inscription: in graphite, ELISABET D.G. ANGLIE FRAN. ET HIBERNIE REGINA
British Museum, London, PD 1912,0717.1
Given by Peter Gellatly, 1912

Literature: W. de G. Birch, *Catalogue of Seals in the Department of Manuscripts in the British Museum*, London 1887, vol. 1, pp. 272–3; E. Croft-Murray and P. Hulton, *Catalogue of British Drawings*, London 1960, vol. 1, pp. 16–17, no. 1; S. Doran (ed.), *Elizabeth*, London 2003, no. 37; K. Sloan, *A New World: England's First View of America*, London 2007, p. 92, fig. 52

Fig. 2

Crispijn de Passe the Elder (*c.* 1564–1637)
Queen Elizabeth I
Published by Hans Woutneel, London, 1596
Engraving; 35 cm x 25.8 cm
Inscriptions: Lettered 'Elizabeta D.G. Angliae Franciae Hiberniae et Verginiae Regina' and 'In honorem serenissimae Suae Majestatis hanc effigiem fieri curabat Ioannes Woutnelius belga Anno 1596'
British Museum, London, PD 1868,0822.853
Bequeathed by Felix Slade, 1868
Literature: F.W.H. Hollstein, *Dutch and Flemish Etchings, Engravings and Woodcuts c. 1450–1700*, Amsterdam 1949, no. 714 (Passe); A.M. Hind, *Engraving in England in the Sixteenth and Seventeenth Centuries*, 3 vols, Cambridge 1952–64, vol. 1, p. 258, no. 2; Doran 2003, op. cit. fig. 1, cat. 260; Sloan 2007, op. cit. fig. 1, p.38, fig. 24

Fig. 3

Seal-die of Sir Walter Ralegh as Governor of Virginia, 1564
Silver; diam. 5.7 cm
Inscriptions: (in reverse, around the edge) * PROPRIA + TNSIHNIA + WALTERI + RALEGH + MILITIS + DOMINI + & GVBERNATORIS + VIRGINIÆ &; (on scroll) AMORE . ET . VIRTVTE
British Museum, London, PE 1904,0113.2
Given through Crichton Bros, 1904
Literature: A.B. Tonnochy, *Catalogue of Seal-Dies in the British Museum*, London 1952, no. 347; Sloan 2007, op. cit. fig. 1, p. 41, fig. 26

Fig. 4

Gold jewellery, ingots and coins
Morocco; from the site of a ship wrecked in the 1630s–1640s in Salcombe Bay, Devon
Double-sided pendant, H. 4.5 cm. Pendant, H. 2.7 cm. Part of a belt or buckle plate, H. 3.5 cm. Pendant, H. 2.8 cm. Pin of a pennanular brooch threaded onto part of an earring, L. 6 cm. Pendant fitting, H. 22 cm. Wristlet, W. 3.9 cm. Ornament, H. 3 cm. Ornament, H. 2.8 cm. Ingot, L. 3.3 cm. Ingot, L. 7.5 cm. Coins of Ahman al-Mansur (r. 1578–1603), minted in Marrakesh
British Museum, London, ME 1999,1207.16; ME 1999,1207.464; ME 1999,1207.466; ME 1999,1207.469; ME 1999,1207.470; ME 1999,1207.471; ME 1999,1207.473; 1999,1207.488; ME 1999,1207.490; ME 1999,1207.457; ME 1999,1207.462; CM 1999,1207.16–28; CM 1999,1207.30–1; CM 1999,1207.33; CM 1999,1207.40–3
Recovered in 1995 from the Salcombe Cannon Site, Devon; purchased 1999 with the assistance of The Art Fund, the British Museum Friends and the Brooke Sewell Fund
Literature: V. Porter and P. Morison, 'The Salcombe Bay Treasure', *British Museum Magazine*, vol. 30, Spring 1998, pp. 16–17; V. Porter, 'Coins of the Sa'dian Sharifs of Morocco off the coast of Devon, Preliminary report' in B. Kluge and B. Weisser, *XII Internationaler Numismatischer Kongress Berlin 1997*, Akten, Berlin 2000, pp. 1288–94, esp. p. 1291

Fig. 6

'Dr Dee's magic mirror' and case
Mexica, *c.* 1325–1521
Obsidian; wooden case covered in tooled leather; (mirror) L. 22.0 cm, diam. 18.4 cm
Two labels on case with inscriptions in the hand of Horace Walpole; another label on the case in a different hand with a quotation from Samuel Butler's *Hudibras*
British Museum, London, PE 1966,1001.1
Literature: H. Tait, '"The Devil's looking glass": the magical speculum of Dr John Dee' in W. Hunting Smith (ed.), *Horace Walpole: Writer, Politician, and Connoisseur*, New Haven and

London 1967, pp. 195–212; M. Snodin (ed.), *Horace Walpole's Strawberry Hill*, New Haven and London 2009, pp. 96–100, cat. 108; C. McEwan and L. López Luján (ed.), *Moctezuma: Aztec Ruler*, London 2009, cat. 103 (a similar mirror) and p. 167; S. Ackermann and L. Devoy, '"The Lord of the Smoking Mirror": objects associated with John Dee in the British Museum', *Studies in History and Philosophy of Science, Part A, John Dee and the Sciences: Early Modern Networks of Knowledge* (ed. Jennifer M. Rampling) vol. 43, 2012 (online 2011)

Fig. 8

James Kynvyn (*c.* 1550–1615)
Astronomical compendium: nocturnal; latitude-table for 39 world locations; magnetic compass; list of ports and harbours; perpetual calendar and table of fixed feast days; high tide computer for several European ports; lunar phase and age indicator volvelles; planetary aspectarium; remains of an equinoctial sundial. Made for Robert Devereux, 2nd Earl of Essex and engraved with his arms on the inner surface of the nocturnal disc
London, 1593
Gilt copper alloy; diam. 6 cm; depth 2.7 cm
Inscriptions: (on smaller volvelle) 'Iames Kynuyn fecit 1593'; (around rim) HE THAT TO HIS NOBLE LINNAGE ADDETH VERTV AND GOOD CONDISIONS IS TO BE PRAISED / THEY THAT BE PERFECTLI WISE DESPISE WORLDLI HONOR WHER RICHES ARE HONORED GOOD MEN ARE DESPISED
British Museum, London, PE 1866,0221.1
Given by Edward Dalton, 1866
Literature: G. L'E. Turner, *Elizabethan Instrument Makers: The Origins of the London Trade in Precision Instrument Making*, Oxford 2000, no. 66

Fig. 9

Wenceslaus Hollar (1607–77)
Fortune; Sea Goddess
Probably Prague, *c.* 1625
Pen and black ink on paper; 13.4 x 15.7 cm
Inscription: 'Vencelaus Hollar in:'
Victoria and Albert Museum, London, DYCE.371
Bequeathed by Revd. Alexander Dyce
Ltterature: South Kensington Museum, *A Catalogue of the Paintings, Miniatures, Drawings, Engravings, Rings and Miscellaneous Objects Bequeathed by the Reverend Alexander Dyce*, London 1874, no. 371; Franz Sprinzels, *Hollar, Handzeichnungen, beschrieben und herausgegeben von Franz Sprinzels*, Leipzig, *c.* 1938, no. 83; R. Godfrey, *Wenceslaus Hollar, A Bohemian Artist in England*, New Haven and London 1994, p. 39, no. 2

Fig. 12

Simon van de Passe (1595–1647)
Portrait of Pocahontas (also known as Matoaka and Rebecca Rolfe), aged 21, 1616
Engraving; 17 x 11.7 cm
Inscriptions: (around oval) MATOAKA ALS REBECCA FILIA POTENTISS: PRINC: POWHATANI IMP: VIRGINIAE; (below oval) 'Aetatis suae 21. Ao / 1616'; four lines in the margin: 'Matoaks … wife to the wor.th Mr Joh Rolff'; (below left) 'S. Pass: sculp'; (below right) 'Compton Holland exc'
British Museum, London, PD 1863,0509.625
Literature: D. Franken, *L'oeuvre gravé des van de Passe*, Paris 1881, no. 830; Hollstein 1949, op. cit. fig. 2, no. 106; Hind 1952–64, op. cit. fig. 2, vol. 2, p. 266, no. 47

Fig. 13

Narwhal tusk in a wooden case, 1500s
L. 224 cm (tusk); H. 272 cm (case)
Parham House, Sussex
Literature: Doran 2003, op. cit. fig. 1, cat. 177

Fig. 14

After John White (*c.* 1540s–*c.* 1593)
Kalicho, an Inuk from Frobisher Bay, 1585–93
Watercolour, with pen and grey ink on paper; 39 x 26 cm
British Museum, London, SL,5270.11
Bequeathed by Sir Hans Sloane, 1753

Literature: P. Hulton, *'America 1585', The Complete Drawings of John White*, Chapel Hill and London 1985, figs 40–1; W.C. Sturtevant and D.B. Quinn, 'This new prey: Eskimos in Europe in 1567, 1576, and 1577', in C.F. Feest (ed.), *Indians and Europe: An Interdisciplinary Collection of Essays*, Aachen 1989, pp. 76–112; Sloan 2007, op. cit. fig. 1, pp. 166, 224–5, figs 104–5

Fig. 16
Doit
Minted in the Netherlands, early 1600s
Alloy; diam. 2 cm, weight 4.07 g
British Museum, London, CM G3,FDSC.16
Given by King George IV, 1825

Fig. 17
Lucas Cranach the Younger (1515–1586)
Armoured Knight, Perhaps Hercules, Fighting Wild Men in a Wood, 1551
Pen and black ink with grey and pink wash; 18.1 x 21.8 cm
British Museum, London, PD 1997,0712.27
Bequeathed by Rosi Schilling through The Art Fund in memory of Edmund Schilling, 1997
Literature: J. Rowlands, *German Drawings from a Private Collection*, London and Nuremberg 1984, p. 51, cat. 47; H. Hoffmann, *Kunstsammlungen zu Weimar: die deutschen Gemälde des XVI Jahrhunderts*, Weimar 1990, p. 75, under no. 26

Fig. 23
Unknown German artist
Four Studies of a Marmoset (Hapale jachus), c. 1520–50
Pen and grey ink with watercolour and bodycolour, heightened with white; partly silhouetted; 39.6 x 28 cm
British Museum, London, PD SL,5219.35
Bequeathed by Sir Hans Sloane, 1753; transferred from the British Library in 1886

Fig. 24
Hans Burgkmair the Elder (1473–1531)
Standing Black Youth Dressed in a Feather Skirt, and Holding an Axe, 1520–30
Pen and black ink with grey, brown and green wash; 24 x 16.1 cm
British Museum, London, PE SL,5218.129
Bequeathed by Sir Hans Sloane, 1753
Literature: J.A. Levenson (ed.), *Circa 1492: Art in the Age of Exploration*, Washington 1992, cat. 405b; J. Rowlands, *Drawings by German Artists in the Department of Prints and Drawings at the British Museum*, London 1993, no. 100; C.F. Feest, 'John White's New World', in Sloan 2007, op. cit. fig. 1, p. 66

Fig. 27
Black-figured *skyphos* decorated with the loom of Circe
Boeotia, Greece; said to be from the Cabeirion Sanctuary, c. 450–420 BC
H. 19.05 cm, diam. 19.05 cm
Inscription: KIRKA
British Museum, London, GR 1893,0303.1
Literature: D. Walsh, *Distorted Ideals in Greek Vase-Painting: The World of Mythological Burlesque*, New York 2009, pp. 196–9, figs 76a–b, pp. 315–16, no. 94

Fig. 29
Melchior Lorck (c. 1526/7–after 1583)
A harpy or siren, 1582
Woodcut; 23.2 x 16.2 cm
Inscriptions: Signed with monogram and dated in upper left corner
British Museum, London, PD 1871,0812.4643
Literature: A. Bartsch, *Le peintre graveur*, vol. 9, Vienna 1808, p. 511, under no. 4; F.W.H. Hollstein, *German Engravings, Etchings and Woodcuts c. 1400–1700*, vol. 22, Amsterdam 1978, under no. 59; E. Fischer *et al.*, *Melchior Lorck*, vol. 3, *Catalogue raisonné. I. The Turkish Publication*, Copenhagen 2009, no. 124

Fig. 31
Wax disc associated with Dr John Dee
Late 1500s
Engraved wax; diam. 23 cm, depth 3 cm

British Museum, London, PE 1838,1232.90.a
Literature: Ackermann and Devoy 2012, op. cit. fig. 6

Fig. 32
Figure of a male spirit-being
Taíno, Jamaica, 1400s–1500s
Guayacan wood; H. 104 cm
British Museum, London, AOA, Am1977,Q.3
Literature: W. Fagg, *The Tribal Image: Wooden Figure Sculpture of the World*, London 1977, pl. 3; C. McEwan, *Ancient American Art in Detail*, London 2009, p. 27

Chapter 10

Fig. 1
See chapter 1, fig. 4

Fig. 2
Head from a statue, perhaps Sophocles (also known as 'the Arundel Homer'), Hellenistic Greece, c. 496–406 BC; probably found in Smyrna; acquired in Constantinople (modern Istanbul), Turkey
Bronze; H. 29.2 cm.
British Museum, London, GR 1760,0919.1
Given by Cecil Brownlow, 9th Earl of Exeter, 1760
Literature: H.B. Walters, *Catalogue of the Bronzes in the British Museum, Greek, Roman and Etruscan*, 2 vols, London 1899, no. 847; R.J.D. Harding, '"The head of a certain Macedonian King"; an old identity for the British Museum's "Arundel Homer"', *British Art Journal*, vol. 9, no. 2, Autumn 2008, pp. 11–16

Fig. 9
The Robben Island Bible
The Complete Works of William Shakespeare: The Alexander Text
First published 1951 by Collins, Glasgow and London; this edition 1970
Printed book, covered with images from Hindu greetings cards; 21.5 x 15 cm (closed)
This copy of the *Complete Works* belongs to Sonny Venkatrathnam, who was imprisoned on Robben Island in the 1970s with other political prisoners resisting apartheid in South Africa. Venkatrathnam smuggled his copy of the *Complete Works* inside the prison, after disguising it by covering it with images from Hindu greetings cards. Before he left the prison he passed the book round his fellow inmates. Each marked their favourite passage and signed it with the date. This unique document contains 32 signatures in all, including those of Nelson Mandela, Walter Sisulu and Govan Mbeki
Sonny Venkatrathnam, Durban

Objects not illustrated in the book

Nicholas Vallin (c.1565–1603)
Musical chamber clock
London, 1598
Weight-driven three-train clock with verge and balance; steel, brass and gold case with engraving and gilding; H. 59 cm, W. 26 cm, depth 23.3 cm
The clock strikes the hours and plays music on the quarters
Inscriptions: Dial signed and dated 'N. Vallin 1598'
British Museum, London, PE 1958,1006.2139
Given by Gilbert Edgar, 1958
Literature: D. Thompson, *Clocks*, London 2004, p. 56

Proclamation issued by James I for 'proroguing the Parliament' due to the plague of 1607
Printed by Robert Barker, London, 1607
Woodcut; 38 x 27.3 cm
British Museum, London, PD 1948,0315.9.111
Bequeathed by Hermann Marx, 1948

Citole
England, c. 1300–30
Wood gilded with silver and gold; H. 61 cm, W. 18.6 cm, depth 14.7 cm
Silver plate above pegbox engraved with the Garter, arms of Elizabeth I and arms of Robert Dudley, Earl of Leicester
British Museum, London, PE 1963,1002.1
Literature: M. Remnant and R. Marks, 'A medieval gittern', *British Museum Yearbook*, vol. I, no. 4: *Music and Civilisation*, 1980, pp. 83–134; J. Alexander and P. Binski (eds), *The Age of Chivalry*, London 1987, cat. 522

Unknown artist
Elizabeth I's Funeral Procession
England, c. 1603
Colour drawing in Indian ink; 61 x 191 cm
British Library, London, Add.MS 35324, ff. 37v – 38r
Literature: S. Doran (ed.), *Elizabeth*, London 2003, cat. 264

The Holy Bible, conteyning the Old Testament, and the New: Newly translated out of the Originall Tonges …
Printed for Robert Barker, London, 1613
Printed book; 38 x 25 cm (closed)
British Library, London, C.35.l.10 (1)

Michel de Montaigne (1533–92), trans. John Florio (1553–1625)
The Essayes, or Morall, Politike, and Militarie Discourses of Lo: Michaell de Montaigne…Now done into English by…John Florio, open at p. 102 (Book 1, Chapter 30)
Printed by Val Sims for Edward Blount, London, 1603
Printed book; 28.5 x 20 cm (closed)
British Library, London, C.28.m.8

John Speed (1552–1629)
Map of England, Wales and Ireland
London, 1603–4
Copperplate engraving on four sheets; 83 x 110 cm
British Library, London, Maps 118.t.1.(1.)
Literature: G. Schilder and H. Wallis, 'Speed military maps discovered', *The Map Collector*, vol. 48,1989, pp. 22–6; R. W. Shirley, *Early Printed Maps of the British Isles, 1477–1650*, Castle Cary 1991, pp. 106–7, no. 261; P.M. Barber, 'Mapmaking in England, c. 1470–1650' in D. Woodward (ed.), *The History of Cartography*, III. *Cartography in the European Renaissance*, Part 2, London and Chicago 2007, pp. 1589–1669; P. Barber and T. Harper, *Magnificent Maps: Power, Propaganda and Art*, London 2010, pp. 62–3

William Shakespeare (1564–1616), ed. John Heminge (c. 1556–1630) and H. Condell (d. 1627)
'The First Folio': *Mr. William Shakespeares Comedies, Histories, & Tragedies. Published according to the True Originall Copies*
'Printed by Isaac Jaggard, and Ed. Blount', London, 1623
Printed book; 34 x 21.9 cm (closed).The title page is an insert. For full bibliographical details on this copy, see Rasmussen and West 2011
Shakespeare Birthplace Trust, Stratford-upon-Avon, SR/0537-1623
Literature: C. Hinman, *The Printing and Proof-reading of the First Folio of Shake*speare, Oxford 1963; E. Rasmussen and A.J. West (eds), *The Shakespeare First Folios: A Descriptive Catalogue*, Basingstoke 2011, pp. 149–52, no. 37

Illustration acknowledgements

The publisher would like to thank the copyright holders for granting permission to reproduce the images illustrated. Every attempt has been made to trace accurate ownership of copyrighted images in this book. Errors and omissions will be corrected in subsequent editions provided notification is sent to the publisher.

All photographs of British Museum objects are © The Trustees of the British Museum, courtesy of the Department of Photography and Imaging. Registration numbers and provenance information for British Museum objects included in the exhibition *Shakespeare: staging the world* can be found in the list of exhibits on page 286. Details for British Museum objects not included in the exhibition can be found below.

Chapter 1

Fig. 1:   The National Archives
Fig. 2:   © Museum of London
Fig. 3:   © British Library Board
Fig. 4:   By permission of the Governors of Stonyhurst College
Fig. 6:   By courtesy of Edinburgh University Library, Special Collections Department
Fig. 8:   © Angelo Hornak/Alamy
Fig. 9:   © The Society of Antiquaries of London, 2012
Fig. 10: The Provost and Fellows of Worcester College Oxford
Fig. 11: © National Museum of Wales
Fig. 12: © British Library Board
Fig. 13: British Museum PE 1887,0729.2 and PE 1887,0729.3
Fig. 15: © John Cheal, Inspired Images 2010. By kind permission of Holy Trinity Church, Stratford-upon-Avon
Fig. 16: © John Cheal, Inspired Images 2010. By kind permission of Holy Trinity Church, Stratford-upon-Avon and St Helen's Church, Clifford Chambers
Fig. 17: © National Portrait Gallery, London
Fig. 21: Tokyo National Museum
Fig. 22: © Board of Trustees of the Armouries
Fig. 23: Private collection
Fig. 24: © Victoria and Albert Museum, London
Fig. 26: University of Birmingham Research and Cultural Collections
Fig. 27: Su concessione del Ministero per i Beni e le attività culturali. Foto Soprintendenza B.S.A.E di SIENA & GROSSETO
Fig. 28: © Board of Trustees of the Armouries
Fig. 29: British Museum PD 1880,1113.3672
Fig. 30: British Museum PE 1928,0315.1
Fig. 31: By kind permission of the Masters of the Bench of the Honourable Society of the Middle Temple © The Honourable Society of the Middle Temple 2012. Photograph © Prudence Cuming
Fig. 32: Berkeley Will Trust 2012
Fig. 33: © Museum of London
Fig. 34: © Museum of London
Fig. 35: © Museum of London
Fig. 36: © Museum of London
Fig. 37: © Dulwich College
Fig. 38: © Dulwich College
Fig. 39: SMK Photo
Fig. 40: © Bodleian Libraries 2012
Fig. 41: © British Library Board
Fig. 43: © National Portrait Gallery, London
Fig. 45: © British Library Board
Fig. 46: By kind permission of the Masters of the Bench of the Honourable Society of the Middle Temple © The Honourable Society of the Middle Temple 2012
Fig. 47: Photograph © 2012 Museum of Fine Arts, Boston

Chapter 2

Fig. 1:   © British Library Board
Fig. 2:   © Courtesy of the Shakespeare Birthplace Trust
Fig. 3:   © National Portrait Gallery, London
Fig. 5:   By kind permission of Warwickshire Museum Service
Fig. 6:   By kind permission of Warwickshire Museum Service
Fig. 7:   © Victoria and Albert Museum, London
Fig. 10: © Victoria and Albert Museum, London
Fig. 11: © Victoria and Albert Museum, London
Fig. 12: By Permission of the Folger Shakespeare Library
Fig. 13: By kind permission of Warwickshire Museum Service
Fig. 14: © Bodleian Libraries 2012
Fig. 15: © British Library Board
Fig. 16: © Courtesy of the Shakespeare Birthplace Trust
Fig. 22: © Victoria and Albert Museum, London
Fig. 23: © Victoria and Albert Museum, London
Fig. 24: © Tate, London, 2012
Fig. 25: Photograph provided by the Denver Art Museum
Fig. 26: © National Portrait Gallery, London
Fig. 27: ©NTPL/John Hammond/Powis Estate
Fig. 28: © Victoria and Albert Museum, London
Fig. 29: © John Cheal, Inspired Images 2010. By kind permission of Holy Trinity Church, Stratford-upon-Avon
Fig. 30: By Permission of the Folger Shakespeare Library
Fig. 32: © Simon Brighton
Fig. 34: © College of Arms
Fig. 35: © College of Arms

Chapter 3

Fig. 1:   © The Dean and Chapter of Westminster 2012
Fig. 2:   British Museum PD 1848,0911.748
Fig. 3:   © The National Gallery, London
Fig. 8:   Werner Foreman Archive
Fig. 9:   © British Library Board
Fig. 10: © National Portrait Gallery, London
Fig. 11: By Permission of Scarbrough Trustees
Fig. 12: © The Society of Antiquaries of London, 2012
Fig. 13: British Museum PE SLAntiq.364 Bequeathed by Sir Hans Sloane
Fig. 15: © The Society of Antiquaries of London, 2012
Fig. 17: Wendy Scott/Portable Antiquities scheme
Fig. 18: © The Society of Antiquaries of London, 2012
Fig. 19: © The Dean and Chapter of Westminster 2012
Fig. 20: © The Dean and Chapter of Westminster 2012
Fig. 21: © The Dean and Chapter of Westminster 2012
Fig. 22: © The Dean and Chapter of Westminster 2012
Fig. 23: © The Dean and Chapter of Westminster 2012
Fig. 25: By courtesy of Edinburgh University Library, Special Collections Department
Fig. 26: © Tate, London, 2012
Fig. 27: © British Library Board
Fig. 29: © Douglas Atfield 2012. By kind permission of Trinity College, Cambridge

Chapter 4

Fig. 1:   British Museum PD 1880,1113.5777
Fig. 2:   © Marquess of Bath
Fig. 4:   Drawn by David Honour for Martin Biddle
Fig. 6:   © Bodleian Libraries 2012
Fig. 7:   Reproduced by permission of the Provost and Fellows of Eton College
Fig. 8:   © The National Gallery, London
Fig. 9:   British Museum PD X,1.93
Fig. 11: © Private collection, on loan to the National Portrait Gallery, London
Fig. 12: © Board of Trustees of the Armouries

Fig. 14: © British Library Board
Fig. 15: © British Library Board
Fig. 18: British Museum PD 1877,0512.872
Fig. 19: © Bodleian Libraries 2012
Fig. 22: British Museum GR 1884,0614.12
Fig. 24: © The Walters Art Museum, Baltimore

Chapter 5

Fig. 3:   Reproduced by permission of the Provost and Fellows of Eton College
Fig. 5:   © RMN/Jean-Gilles Berizzi
Fig. 6:   The New York Public Library, Astor, Lenox and Tilden Foundations
Fig. 7:   © British Library Board
Fig. 8:   © British Library Board
Fig. 10: © Victoria and Albert Museum, London
Fig. 11: Private collection
Fig. 12: © British Library Board
Fig. 13: © Victoria and Albert Museum, London
Fig. 14: The Metropolitan Museum of Art/Art Resource/Scala, Florence
Fig. 15: © National Library of Scotland
Fig. 16: © Victoria and Albert Museum, London
Fig. 17: By kind permission of His Grace the Duke of Bedford and the Trustees of the Bedford Estates © His Grace the Duke of Bedford and the Trustees of the Bedford Estates
Fig. 18: © Victoria and Albert Museum, London
Fig. 19: © Victoria and Albert Museum, London
Fig. 21: © The Society of Antiquaries of London, 2012
Fig. 22: © Bodleian Libraries 2012
Fig. 23: British Museum CM 1923,0611.23
Fig. 24: © British Library Board
Fig. 26: Loddon Church, Norfolk, photo courtesy of the Hamilton Kerr Institute, Fitzwilliam Museum, Cambridge
Fig. 28: British Library Board
Fig. 29: British Library Board
Fig. 31: British Museum PD SL,5217.415 Bequeathed by Sir Hans Sloane
Fig. 32: Collection Rijksmuseum, Amsterdam

Chapter 6

Fig. 1:   © Victoria and Albert Museum, London
Fig. 2:   © Patrimonio Nacional
Fig. 3:   © Victoria and Albert Museum, London
Fig. 4:   © The National Gallery, London
Fig. 5:   © College of Arms
Fig. 6:   British Museum PE 1890,1004.1 Donated by Sir Augustus Wollaston Franks
Fig. 7:   Gabinetto dei Disegni e Stampe, Uffizi, Florence, Italy/The Bridgeman Art Library
Fig. 9:   Collection Rijksmuseum, Amsterdam
Fig. 11: British Museum PD 1870,0504.1463
Fig. 12: © British Library Board
Fig. 13: British Museum PE 1867,0507.746
Fig. 14: Skulpturensammlung, Staatliche Kunstsammlungen Dresden, © Jürgen Karpinski, Dresden
Fig. 15: Bayerisches Nationalmuseum München © Foto: Bayerisches Nationalmuseum, Walter Haberland
Fig. 16: British Museum PE WB.193 Bequeathed by Baron Ferdinand Anselm de Rothschild

Chapter 7

Fig. 1:   From the collection at Parham House in Sussex
Fig. 2:   The National Archives
Fig. 3:   Ashmolean Museum, University of Oxford
Fig. 6:   Photo: © The Trustees of the British Museum/The Roxburghe club. With kind permission of the Wormsley Library, Buckinhamshire
Fig. 7:   By permission of the Governors of Stonyhurst College

Fig. 9:   British Museum PD 1861,0518.1314
Fig. 10: By permission of the Governors of Stonyhurst College
Fig. 11: By permission of Llyfrgell Genedlaethol Cymru/the National Library of Wales
Fig. 12: The Trustees of Lambeth Palace Library (1597.15)
Fig. 13: © Bodleian Libraries 2012
Fig. 14: © National Museums Scotland
Fig. 15: © Bodleian Libraries 2012
Fig. 16: © National Museums Scotland
Fig. 17: By Permission of the Folger Shakespeare Library
Fig. 18: © National Museums Scotland
Fig. 19: © National Museums Scotland
Fig. 20: © National Museums Scotland
Fig. 21: © National Museums Scotland
Fig. 23: The MacDougall of Dunollie Preservation Trust
Fig. 25: The Royal Collection © 2012 Her Majesty Queen Elizabeth II. Photo: Sandy Young
Fig. 27: Somerset County Council Heritage Service
Fig. 28: © British Library Board

Chapter 8

Fig. 1:   Reproduced by kind permission of the President and Fellows of Queens' College, Cambridge
Fig. 2:   © National Library of Scotland
Fig. 5:   British Museum CM 1844,0425.24
Fig. 7:   © Bodleian Libraries 2012
Fig. 8:   British Museum PD 1906,0509.1.12
Fig. 9:   British Museum PD 1862,0208.94
Fig. 11: © Devonshire Collection, Chatsworth. Reproduced by permission of Chatsworth Settlement Trustees
Fig. 13: © Fitzwilliam Museum, Cambridge
Fig. 14: © British Library Board
Fig. 15: © The Society of Antiquaries of London, 2012
Fig. 17: © British Library Board
Fig. 20: © National Portrait Gallery, London

Chapter 9

Fig. 5:   © National Trust/Niki Miles
Fig. 7:   British Museum PE 1855,1201.223
Fig. 9:   © Victoria and Albert Museum, London
Fig. 10: British Museum PD 1906,0509.1.13
Fig. 11: British Museum PD 1952,0117.14.13
Fig. 13: From the collection at Parham House in Sussex
Fig. 15: With kind permission of the University of Edinburgh/The Bridgeman Art Library
Fig. 18: British Museum PD N,5.259 Bequeathed by Sir Hans Sloane
Fig. 19: British Museum PD 1854,1113.160
Fig. 20: British Museum PD 1910,0611.1
Fig. 21: British Museum PD 1906,0509.1.6
Fig. 22: British Museum PD 1906,0509.1.68
Fig. 25: British Museum PD SL,5218.128 Bequeathed by Sir Hans Sloane
Fig. 26: British Museum AOA Am,St.397.a
Fig. 28: British Museum PD 1918,1030.1 Donated by Sir Edward Priaulx Tennant, 1st Baron Glenconner
Fig. 30: © British Library Board

Chapter 10

Fig. 1:   By permission of the Governors of Stonyhurst College
Fig. 3:   © The Dean and Chapter of Westminster
Fig. 4:   Private collection
Fig. 5:   © Victoria and Albert Museum, London
Fig. 6:   Courtesy of University of Arizona Libraries, Special collections
Fig. 7:   Photo: The advertising archives © Reserved
Fig. 8:   Source BFI Stills, © British Film Institute
Fig. 9:   © Courtesy of the Shakespeare Birthplace Trust

List of lenders

The British Museum would like to thank all the lenders to
the exhibition *Shakespeare: staging the world* for their generosity.

Ashmolean Museum of Art and Archaeology, Oxford
Bayerisches Nationalmuseum, Munich
Berkeley Castle, Berkeley
Bodleian Library, Oxford
British Library, London
Chatsworth House, Chatsworth
College of Arms, London
Collegiate Church of Holy Trinity, Stratford-upon-Avon
Dulwich College, London
Edinburgh University Library, Edinburgh
Eton College, Windsor
Longleat House, Warminster
MacDougall of Dunollie Preservation Trust
Middle Temple, London
Museum of London, London
National Gallery, London
National Library of Scotland, Edinburgh
National Museum of Wales, Cardiff
National Museums Scotland, Edinburgh
National Portrait Gallery, London
Palace of Holyroodhouse, Edinburgh
Parham House, Storrington
Pinacoteca Nazionale, Siena
Powis Castle, Powys
Rijksmuseum, Amsterdam
Royal Armouries, Leeds
Shakespeare Birthplace Trust, Stratford-upon-Avon
Society of Antiquaries of London, London
Staatliche Kunstsammlungen, Dresden
Stonyhurst College, Clitheroe
Tate Britain, London
Trinity College, Cambridge
University of Birmingham Research and Cultural Collections,
    Stratford-upon-Avon
Sonny Venkatrathnam, Durban
Victoria and Albert Museum, London
Warwickshire Museum Service, Warwick
Westminster Abbey, London
Woburn Abbey, Woburn

Acknowledgements

Our thanks are also due to the following for assistance of various kinds:

Richard Abdy, Ian Adam, Philip Attwood, Susanna Avery-Quash, Natasha
Awais-Dean, Sir Nicholas Bacon, Leonora Baird, Peter Barber, Bruce
Barker-Benfield, Emma Barnard, Giulia Bartrum, Andrew Bashsam, John
Battersby, Andrea Bayer, Giulio Beltramini, Charles Berkeley, John Berkeley,
David Bindman, Paul Binski, Richard Blurton, Charlotte Boland, Anthony
Boswood, Julian Bowsher, Piet van Boxell, Tricia Boyd, Christopher Brown,
Clare Browne, Nicky Burman, Simon Callow, Tobias Capwell, Hugo
Chapman, Clive Cheesman (Richmond Herald), Tim Clark, Deborah Clarke,
Stephanie Coane, Alec Cobbe, Tarnya Cooper, Hannah Crawforth, John
Curtis, Vesta Curtis, Hilary Davidson, Vivian Davies, Aileen Dawson,
Stephen Deuchar, Louise Devoy, Nicholas Donaldson, Ann Donnelly,
Gregory Doran, Helen Dorey, Martin Drury, Julia Dudkiewicz, Richard
Edgecumbe, the late Geoff Egan, Renate Eikelmann, Mark Evans, Oliver
Fairclough, Frank Field, Laura Fielder, Lesley Fitton, Hazel Forsyth, David
Gaimster, Ciara Gallagher, Catherine Gillies, Daniel Godfrey, Moira Goff,
Iain Gordon-Brown, Martin Gorick, Janet Gough, Jan Graffius, Andrew
Graham-Dixon, Chris Gravett, Antony Griffiths, the late John Gross, Andrew
Grout, Matthew Hahn, John Hall, James Hamilton, Anna Harnden, Kate
Harris, Matthew Harvey, Karen Hearn, Peter Higgs, Matthew Hirst,
Francesca Hillier, Richard Hobbs, Eric Hobsbawm, Maurice Howard, David
Howell, Arnold Hunt, Clive Hurst, Mark Jones, Matthew Jones, Annemarie
Jordan, Jody Joy, Tim Knox, Paul Kobrak, Scottford Lawrence, Martin Levy,
Jack Loman, Christina Acidini Luchinat, Calista Lucy, Mari MacDonald,
Mark MacDonald, Madam MacDougall of MacDougall (Morag MacDougall
Morley), Arthur MacGregor, Catherine Macleod, Jonathan Marsden, Joseph
Marshall, Ellen McAdam, Elaine McChesney, Thomas McCoog, Colin
McEwan, Lyndsay McGill, Andrea de Meo, Nikki Miles, Ralph Moffat, Luca
Mola, Andrew Moore, Silvia Morris, Tessa Murdoch, Jacki Musacchio, Sandy
Nairne, Beverley Nenk, Henry Noltie, Susan North, Sheila O'Connell,
Barbara O'Connor, Roighnall O'Floinn, Mark O'Neill, Richard Ovenden,
Diana Owen, Kate Owen, Susan Owens, Richard Pailthorpe, David Paisey,
Nicholas Penny, Grayson Perry, Wim Pijbes, Venetia Porter, the Earl of Powis,
Paul Quarrie, Susan Reed, the Lord Rees of Ludlow, Christine Reynolds,
Thom Richardson, Ben Roberts, Paul Roberts, Mike Robertson, Christopher
Rowell, Heather Rowlands, Judy Rudoe, Henrietta Ryan, Nicholas Sagovsky,
Mario Scalini, John Scally, Richard Scarbrough, Diana Scarisbrick, Astrid
Scherp, Timothy Schroder, Timon Screech, Lorenz Seelig, James Shapiro,
Desmond Shawe-Taylor, Alison Shell, Robin Smith, Rosalyn Smith, Nick de
Somogyi, Joseph Spence, Simon Stephens, Gary Stevens, Simon Swynfen
Jervis, Dirk Syndram, Luke Syson, Ilana Tahan, David Taylor, Ian Taylor,
Lluis Tembleque, Sarah Thomas, David Thompson, Tony Trowles, Pamela
Tudor-Craig (Lady Wedgwood), Hilary Turner, An van Camp, Gillian
Varndell, Sonny and Theresa Venkatrathnam, Des Violaris, William
Waldegrave, Victoria Wallace, Alison Watson, Bruce Watson, Rowan Watson,
Sara Wear, Julia Webb, Evelyn Welch, Martin White, Lesley Whitelaw,
Arnott Wilson, Michael Winckless, Maurice Woelk, Linda Wolk-Simon,
Derek Wood, Maggie Woods, Bob Woosnam-Savage, Lucy Wrapson, Sue
Younge, Robert Yorke.

Index

SCIENCE AND ARTS ACADEMY
1825 MINER STREET
DES PLAINES, IL 60016